THE GURKHA WAY

THE GURKHA WAY

NEW HISTORY OF THE GURKHAS

JOHN SADLER

Pen & Sword
MILITARY
AN IMPRINT OF PEN & SWORD BOOKS LTD.
YORKSHIRE - PHILADELPHIA

First published in Great Britain in 2023 by
PEN AND SWORD MILITARY
An imprint of
Pen & Sword Books Limited
Yorkshire – Philadelphia

Copyright © John Sadler, 2023

ISBN 978 1 39906 823 9

The right of John Sadler to be identified as Author of this work has been asserted by him in accordance with the Copyright, Designs and Patents Act 1988.

A CIP catalogue record for this book is available from the British Library.

All rights reserved. No part of this book may be reproduced or transmitted in any form or by any means, electronic or mechanical including photocopying, recording or by any information storage and retrieval system, without permission from the Publisher in writing.

Typeset in Times New Roman 10.5/13.5 by
SJmagic DESIGN SERVICES, India.
Printed and bound in the UK by CPI Group (UK) Ltd.

Pen & Sword Books Limited incorporates the imprints of Atlas, Archaeology, Aviation, Discovery, Family History, Fiction, History, Maritime, Military, Military Classics, Politics, Select, Transport, True Crime, Air World, Frontline Publishing, Leo Cooper, Remember When, Seaforth Publishing, The Praetorian Press, Wharncliffe Local History, Wharncliffe Transport, Wharncliffe True Crime and White Owl.

For a complete list of Pen & Sword titles please contact
PEN & SWORD BOOKS LIMITED
George House, Units 12 & 13, Beevor Street, Off Pontefract Road,
Barnsley, South Yorkshire, S71 1HN, England
E-mail: enquiries@pen-and-sword.co.uk
Website: www.pen-and-sword.co.uk

or

PEN AND SWORD BOOKS
1950 Lawrence Rd, Havertown, PA 19083, USA
E-mail: uspen-and-sword@casematepublishers.com
Website: www.penandswordbooks.com

Contents

Acknowledgements	vii
Glossary	ix
Timeline	xii
Foreword	xiv
List of Maps	xvi
List of Plates	xvii

Introduction		1
Chapter 1	Hindu Rao's House	10
Chapter 2	Nepal: Home of the Gurkhas	28
Chapter 3	'Hillbilly Napoleons'	43
Chapter 4	Kipling's Wars	49
Chapter 5	Over the Black Water	69
Chapter 6	'Ragged-Arsed Barn-shoots' – Back to the Old Frontier	101
Chapter 7	The Great Crusade – The Beginning	115
Chapter 8	The Great Crusade (2) – The Beginning of the End	135
Chapter 9	The Great Crusade (3) – A Forgotten Army	150
Chapter 10	End of Empire	191
Chapter 11	On Infidel Hill	226
Chapter 12	'I Must Not Cry Out – I am a Gurkha'	256

Appendix 1	The Gurkha Battalions	274
Appendix 2	Ranks in the Gurkha Battalions	279
Appendix 3	Castes	280
Appendix 4	Badges of Courage	281
Appendix 5	Indian Army Gurkhas	284
Appendix 6	Gurkha Weaponry and Equipment	286

Notes   *291*
Bibliography   *324*
Index   *335*

Acknowledgements

This book could not have been completed without the generous assistance of the following: Gavin Edgerley Harris of the Gurkha Museum; The Gurkha Stories Oral History Project; Stephen Foggden; Major Aloysius Connolly RGR; Major S.T. Meadows RGR; Kit Pumphrey; Neville Jackson; the late Ben Smith; Patrick Mercer; Quentin Matthias; Sir David Kelly; and also Res Burman for permission to quote verse extracts. Thanks also to past and serving Gurkha soldiers and NCOs.

Thanks must also be given to the staffs of various war museums and memorials in the UK and abroad who have provided willing and friendly assistance over the years – 'In Flanders Fields', Ypres; the Memorial Museum Passchendaele at Zonnebeke; Tyne Cot Cemetery Visitor Centre; Hooge Crater Museum; the Trench of Death, Diksmuide; Newfoundland Park Visitor Centre; 'Ocean Villas' World War I and World War II Museum; Ulster Tower; Thiepval Visitor Centre; Museum of the South African Forces, Delville Wood; Historial de la Grande Guerre, Peronne; Somme 1916 Trench Museum, Albert; Vimy Memorial Park; Notre Dame de Lorette and the Wellington Tunnels, Arras. Other museums which have assisted include Cumbria's Museum of Military Life; the Museum of the Fusiliers Regiment of Northumberland; the Museum of the Green Howards; Roberta Goldwater from 'Charge! The Story of England's Northern Cavalry' at the Discovery Museum; the Durham Light Infantry Museum; the Museum of the King's Own Scottish Borderers; Richard Groocock at The National Archive; Tristan Langlois of the National Army Museum; the archive staff of the Defence Academy of the United Kingdom at Shrivenham; Steve Shannon from the DLI Museum; David Fletcher of the Tank Museum, Bovington; Rod Mackenzie of the Argyll and Sutherland Highlanders Museum; Thomas B. Smyth of the Black Watch Museum; Paul Evans of the Royal Artillery Museum; Ana Tiaki of the Alexander Turnbull Library, New Zealand; Christopher Dorman O'Gowan for information concerning his late father Brigadier E. Dorman-Smith; John Stelling and Henry Ross of North Land, Sea and Air Museum; Dr Martin Farr of Newcastle University;

Barry Matthews of Galina Battlefield Tours; Alan, Julia and Claire Grint of Cogito Books; Trevor Sheehan formerly of BAE Systems Plc; John Rothwell; James Goulty; Sir Paul Nicholson; Major (Retd) Chris Lawton MBE; Arthur W. Charlton; Colonel Anthony George; John Fisher; John Shepherd; Mary Pinkney; Brian Ward; Jennifer Harrison; Neville Jackson; the late Nigel Porter; Timothy Norton; Kit Pumphrey and the late Sir Lawrence Pumphrey.

Further thanks are due to Liz Bregazzi and colleagues at Durham County Record Office and the DLI Sound Recording Project; Newcastle upon Tyne Literary and Philosophical Society; Graham Trueman, Quentin Matthias, Ben Norfield and to Beverley Palin for compiling the index. I owe especial thanks to my agent Tom Cull and the editorial and production team at Pen & Sword for another successful collaboration and, as ever, to Chloe Rodham for the maps.

The Worthington quote is kindly supplied by Major S.T. Meadows of RGR. The Kipling quote at the start of Chapter 1 is from https://www.goodreads.com/author/quotes/6989.Rudyard_Kipling (accessed 12 June 2019). Throughout I have relied heavily on Major Reid's memoirs which are a superb primary resource for the defence of Hindu Rao's house. In Chapter 3 'A Snider squibbed in the Jungle ...' is from Kipling's 'The Graves of the Hundred Dead'.

For detail of the actions fought by Gurkhas on the Western Front, 1914–18 I have relied heavily on the superb *The Indian Corps on the Western Front* by Simon Doherty and Tom Donovan, a great achievement of both scholarship and battlefield detection, and a must for any visitor who wants to understand these various actions on the ground. I am further indebted to Major Aloysius Connelly for permission to use his excellent, unpublished essay on the Borneo conflict. Especial thanks to Major Gordon Corrigan for writing the Foreword and his invaluable help in editing and fine-tuning the text.

As ever, any errors or omissions are of course my responsibility and if any misquotes or failure to correctly acknowledge quotes or references are noticed, I will use best endeavours to see these are corrected.

Glossary

AFV	Armoured Fighting Vehicle
ANA	Afghan National Army
ANP	Afghan National Police
ANSF	Afghan National Security Forces
ANZAC	Australia and New Zealand Army Corps
ARRC	Allied Rapid Reaction Corps
BEF	British Expeditionary Force
Bivvy	Bivouac
Bn	Battalion
Brigade of Gurkhas	The current UK establishment, comprising 1st and 2nd Royal Gurkha Rifles, the infantry element, the Queen's Gurkha Engineers, the Queen's Gurkha Signals and the Queen's Own Gurkha Logistic Regiment
C in C	Commander in Chief
Casevac	Casualty evacuation
CGS	Chief of the General Staff
CO	Commanding Officer
COIN	Counter Insurgency
Coy	Company
CP	Command Post
DCM	Distinguished Conduct Medal
De-lousing	Minefield clearance
Div	Division
DLI	Durham Light Infantry
DSO	Distinguished Service Order

GCO	Gurkha Commissioned Officer (1957–2007). A Gurkha who held a Queen's Commission in exactly the same way as any other British officer; there were not a great number of such officers
GOC	General Officer Commanding
Governor General	East India Company's senior Indian official prior to the Mutiny
GPMG	General Purpose Machine Gun GSO1 General Staff Officer 1st Class Gurkhas Brigade of Gurkhas plus Staff and Personnel Support and Band Brigade of Gurkhas
Havildar	Indian Army rank equal to sergeant
Havildar Major	Sergeant major (Indian Army rank)
HE	High Explosive
HMG	Heavy Machine Gun
IOM	Indian Order of Merit
ISAF	International Security Assistance Force
Jemadar	Indian Army rank equal to lieutenant
KRRC	King's Royal Rifle Corps
Lance naik	Lance corporal (Indian Army rank)
LMG	Light Machine Gun
MC	Military Cross
MG	Machine Gun
MO	Medical Officer
Naik	Corporal
NATO	North Atlantic Treaty Organisation
NCO	Non-Commissioned officer
NGO	Non-Government Organisation
OH	Official History
Picquet	To take possession temporarily of a high or commanding position; a frequent duty in mountainous terrain such as the North-West Frontier.
POW	Prisoner of War
RA	Royal Artillery
RAF	Royal Air Force

GLOSSARY

RE	Royal Engineers
RMP	Royal Military Police
RPG	Rocket-Propelled Grenade
RUSI	Royal United Services Institution
SAS	Special Air Service
Sepoy	A private in the Indian Army; initially Gurkhas were sepoys until they became riflemen, a hike in status
Subadar	Captain
Subadar Major	Major (Indian Army rank; senior Gurkha officer in a battalion)
TTPs	Tactics, Techniques and Procedures
VC	Victoria Cross
VCP	Vehicle Check Point
Viceroy	The senior British administrator and political head in India, 1858–1947; literally a vice-regal position. All viceroys were male and their wives were referred to as vicereines

Note on Army Structure

The core tactical unit is the battalion, comprising about 600 men divided into 3 rifle companies, with each of these divided into 3 platoons, which in turn are divided into sections. A brigade is formed from 3 battalions and commanded by a brigadier, and 3 or 4 brigades make up a division led by a major general. Several divisions (from 2 to 5) become an army corps under a lieutenant general. Several corps form an army, and several armies form an army group.

Timeline

Gurkha forces have served in all the campaigns listed below.

1814–16	Gurkha War, first Gurkha troops raised
1817–19	Campaign against the Mahrattas and Pindaris
1824	Storming the fort at Koonja
1845–6	First Sikh War (battles of Aliwal and Sobraon)
1857–8	Indian Mutiny (the Siege of Delhi and defence of Hindu Rao's House)
1860	Mahsud Waziri Campaign
1872	Looshai Expedition
1875	Perak War
1878–80	Second Afghan War
1885	Third Anglo-Burmese War
1890	Manipur Campaign
1891	Hunza–Naga Campaign
1897–8	Tirah Campaign
1904	Expedition to Lhasa
1914–18	The First World War
1914–15	Gurkhas on the Western Front
1915	Gallipoli
1915–16	Siege of Kut
1917–18	War in Palestine
1919	Third Afghan War

TIMELINE

1939–45	The Second World War
1940–3	War in the Western Desert
1942–5	War in Burma
1943–5	War in Sicily and Italy
1947	Indian Independence and Partition
1948–60	Malayan Emergency
1962	Brunei Revolt
1965	Indonesian–Malaysian Confrontation (Borneo)
1974	Cyprus
1971–97	Hong Kong
1982 (and ongoing)	Falklands War
September 2007–April 2008	Afghanistan; Operation Herrick 7
May–November 2010	Afghanistan; Operation Herrick 9
September 2012–April 2013	Afghanistan; Operation Herrick 17

Also, in the last twenty-five years, Gurkha units have been deployed in Sudan, Estonia, Kosovo, Bosnia, Macedonia, Ivory Coast, East Timor, Iraq and Sierra Leone.

Foreword

Much of my generation's service with Gurkhas was devoted to a constant struggle to survive. In many ways the nation's darlings, we were mainly out of sight, stationed in the Far East and operating in remote parts of the world. We were always vulnerable when yet another round of defence cuts came along, particularly to the claim – untrue but widely canvassed – that the removal of a Gurkha unit meant the survival of a British one. Everything we did we did well, but the only Gurkhas that were in the public eye were those of the one battalion of Infantry and attached supporting arms that spent two years unaccompanied by their families in the UK. While in the UK we ran prisons, collected dustbins, put out fires and drove ambulances during the withdrawals of labour by those normally engaged in those activities, but there were always caveats hedged around operational deployment. Despite much havering on the part of the Foreign Office we went to Cyprus during the Turkish invasion of 1974 because there was no one else to send – and it was a great success; we were told that we could not send Gurkhas to Belize, but off they went and performed brilliantly; sending Gurkhas to the Falklands took much persuading but again they proved their worth. They never did get to Northern Ireland, although they would have been ideal in the bandit country of South Armagh. But, in the 1990s with the handover of Hong Kong to China looming the very existence of the Brigade was once again in doubt. Fortunately, thanks to a lot of hard work by a few people in the teeth of totally irrational opposition, the Brigade did survive, albeit in a much reduced form, with its focus in the UK rather than the Far East.

And then, everything changed. It began with the need to provide Gurkha companies to bolster up British infantry battalions that were under strength, which began to bring home to the rest of the army just how professional and adaptable Gurkhas were. Although the Gurkha involvement with the two Gulf campaigns was modest, the contribution to Afghanistan was not, and Gurkha units serving there performed magnificently, physically supremely fit, able to pick up the language quickly and understanding the local culture in a way that

FOREWORD

British units perhaps found more difficult. All this highlighted to those who mattered just how essential to the British military effort Gurkhas are – and not just the infantry, for all Gurkhas are trained as infantrymen first, and so parties from Gurkha engineer, signals and logistic regiments did not need an infantry escort – they could perfectly well protect themselves.

There have been many books written about Gurkhas, but this one comes when, for the first time since transfer to the British from the British Indian Army in 1947, the Brigade is expanding: more infantry, more squadrons for the engineer, signals and logistic regiments. Thankfully, the struggle for survival may be over and this book charts the progress to that happy state, from the very beginnings in the Anglo-Nepalese War of the early nineteenth century to Afghanistan in the early twenty-first.

Major J.G.H. Corrigan MBE FRHistS, late 6GR and RGR

List of Maps

1. Delhi, plan of the siege works, 1857
2. Nepal and the North-West/North-East Frontiers, 1839–1900
3. The Western Front, 1914–15
4. Second Battle of Ypres, 1915
5. Gallipoli Campaign, 1915
6. Palestine, 1917–18
7. Third Afghan War, 1919
8. Western Desert, 1940–3
9. Italian Campaign, 1943–5
10. Burma Campaign, 1942–5
11. Malayan Emergency, 1948–60
12. Borneo Confrontation, 1965
13. Helmand Province ISAF 1010

List of Plates

1. Forerunners of the 6th Gurkha Rifles, early nineteenth century
2. Gurkha rifleman armed with the Snider conversion of the Enfield percussion rifle, *c.* 1880
3. Gurkha and British soldiers on the North-West Frontier, 1880s
4. A native officer of the 48th Regiment of Bengal Light Infantry, 1880
5. Recruits for 44 Gurkha Rifles, also with Sniders, 1884
6. Another group of recruits for 44 Gurkha Rifles, 1886–93
7. A group of Gurkha officers, *c.* 1890
8. 2/2nd Gurkhas' action at Neuve Chapelle, 1–2 November 1914
9. Action at Neuve Chapelle, 2 November 1914
10. 2/2nd Gurkhas at the orchard and 1/1st Gurkhas in defence, Givenchy, 20 December 1914
11. Givenchy, 16–22 December 1914
12. Festubert and the Indian Village, 19–20 December 1914
13. The attack at Mauser Ridge, 26 April–1 May 1915
14. The actions at Festubert, 15–27 May 1915
15. The attack on the Ferme du Bois, 22–23 May 1915
16. A Gurkha VC, Gaje Ghale, havildar (later captain)
17. A Gurkha VC, Lachhiman Gurung, 4th Battalion 8th Gurkha Rifles
18. A Gurkha VC, Netra Bahadur Thapa, subedar, serving with 2/5th Gurkhas
19. Corporal Sachin with Rifleman Aita, Rifleman Chiran and Lance Corporal Arjun
20. Rifleman Aita and Captain Meadows

21. Group 2, Silicon 13, just prior to Operation Panther's Claw, June 2009
22. Nepalese Limbu woman, May 2009
23. Live mortars firing during Operation Herrick 14 pre-deployment training at Castlemartin, 2014
24. Corporal Pradeep sacrificing a goat during Dashain festival in Kabul, 2015
25. Colour Sergeant Yogendra Rai in the highlands of Sutherland during pre-deployment training for snipers for Operation Toral in Kabul, 2015
26. Mortar Platoon conducting training for Operation Herrick 14, Stonehenge, 2010
27. Operation Zafar, a view from Gurkha positions
28. Rifleman Chiran with the LMG
29. Rifleman Khagendra
30. Rifleman Prakash
31. Rifleman Pralon

Introduction

A Gurkha officer should be comely, sprightly and above all else, confident in his own dress and bearing. He should, where possible, eat a small piece of meat each morning with molasses and beans. He should air himself gracefully when under fire and never place himself in a position of difficulty when being shot at. He should eat his meals comfortably and ahead of his soldiers, for it is he whom is more important tactically on the battlefield and therefore he who should be well nourished. His hair should be well groomed and if possible he should adorn a moustache or similar facial adornment.

When speaking to his soldiers he should appear unnerved and aloof and give direction without in any way involving himself personally in the execution of arduous or un-officer like duties. He should smoke thin panatelas except when in the company of ladies where he should take only a small gin mixed with lemon tea. He should be an ardent and erudite gentleman and woo the ladies both in the formal environment and in the bedroom where he should excel himself beyond the ordinary soldier with his virulent lovemaking prowess. These I say to you are the qualities of an officer that set him apart from the lay person and the common soldier.[1]

Lieutenant General Hubert Worthington

On 8 June 2015 I attended a gala event to mark the 200th anniversary of the founding of the Regiment of Gurkhas, an original 'Band of Brothers'.[2] It was hosted by Joanna Lumley and Dan Snow in the presence of the Her Majesty the Queen, the Duke of Edinburgh, the Prince of Wales, Prince Harry, HM the Sultan of Brunei and the Chief of the General Staff (CGS), together with several previous chiefs, field marshals and the senior elements of the serving Brigade of Gurkhas. It was a glittering event, featuring lively re-enactments of several famed Gurkha actions, starting with the Siege of Hindu Rao's House during the Indian Mutiny (see Chapter 1). This wasn't just a celebration for the Gurkhas themselves and their families, but recognition of the vital role the brigade has played in UK defence for two centuries, through the rise and decline of empire and during two world wars, perhaps no more so than in 1940 when Britain was very short of allies indeed.

The event celebrated the role of Nepali Gurkhas in the service of the British Crown. This has been played out across the vast canvas of the Indian subcontinent, Afghanistan (three wars) and the North-West and North-East Frontiers, as well as over the bloody killing fields of Flanders, Gallipoli, the Western Desert, Italy and Burma, and out to the far distant Falkland Islands in the South Atlantic.

Few, if indeed any, of the world's elite armed forces have ever spanned so much of the globe. Current serving soldiers follow a path trodden by their fathers, grandfathers and even great-grandfathers. There is no other comparable unit in any of the world's armies (with the obvious exception of the Indian Army; see Appendix 5) or one more respected and loved by the British.

'Johnny Gurkha'

After the terrible ordeal of Kohima, the crux of the fight against the Japanese in 1944, returning British and Indian army troops, stumbling back from the killing ground, were still divided into two orderly queues lining up for the comforts of the NAAFI. The ladies of empire were serving hot tea to the Indian Army on one side, the British on the other. One of the starched helpers suggested Gurkhas should form up with the Indian soldiers. 'Oh no, miss,' retorted a British sergeant, 'Them's Gurkhas, they're *us*.'

In 2016 I took my son-in-law's Gurkha company on a battlefield tour of Flanders and Artois. These young soldiers – many of whom had seen action in Afghanistan – would learn about the terrible war their great-grandfathers had fought in just over a century earlier. Unlike many groups, they were very keen to understand and to show their respect and reverence for their ancestors who had fought so hard and bled so freely, so far from home. It was a profoundly moving experience for all of us.

Due to the continuing popularity of the Gurkhas (their profile much heightened by the stellar representations of Joanna Lumley) and their role in the UK's twenty-first-century campaigns, quite a lot has been written since John Parker's *The Gurkhas* in 1999 (Headline) and Chris Bellamy's

INTRODUCTION

The Gurkhas – Special Force in 2011 (John Murray), together with personalised accounts such as Colour Sergeant Kailash Limbu's *Gurkha – Better to Die than Live Like a Coward; My Life with the Gurkhas* in 2015 (Little, Brown), works by Major General Craig Lawrence and the 200th anniversary history.

Why is another book on the Gurkhas needed after the publication of so many others? There has not been much written about these extraordinary men since the theoretical end of the British Army's involvement in Afghanistan in 2014; thirteen years of conflict, one of the longest campaigns since 1945, as long as the earlier Malayan Emergency (1948–60) and second only to Operation Banner in Northern Ireland (1969–2007), which was a purely 'domestic' as opposed to overseas deployment.

Some would describe Gurkhas as mercenaries, a term heavy with disdain, but this is very unfair. Gurkhas are a recognised part of the UK and Indian army regular establishments and in the case of Britain, have been so for over two centuries. They are unique, steadfastly loyal, infinitely adaptable and hugely resilient. This thorny point is well covered in Tony Gould's penetrating study, from the late 1990s, *Imperial Warriors* (Granta, 1999). They have served in most of Britain's many conflicts since 1816 including both world wars and, at the time of writing, the brigade is being expanded. The new wars of the new millennium will be very different to old post-imperial and brush-fire strife: adaptability is the order of the day and the need for Gurkhas as a vital component of Britain's armed forces will not diminish – quite the reverse.

The MOD has a clear position on the term 'mercenary' in relation to the Brigade of Gurkhas. There are three drivers:

1. The UK government has promised the Nepalese government that this term won't be used due to the negative connotations associated with it.
2. MPs have said the same in the House of Commons; recorded in Hansard. The Army Secretariat in Andover has this as a clear policy position too.
3. UN Protocol 1 of 1977 – in addition to the 1949 Geneva Convention contains the only internationally agreed definition of 'mercenary'. This excludes anyone who 'is a member of the Armed Forces of a party to the conflict', thereby excluding Gurkhas in the British (and Indian) armies.

Primarily, this is a book about the Gurkhas themselves and their experiences of service life through both war and peace in the twenty-first century. There is particular focus on Operation Herrick, the UK's recent involvement in Afghanistan. There will be plenty of action, horror and pathos. Though, like the Gurkhas themselves, this will, at least in part, be viewed through the prism of their own inimitable brand of gallows humour.

'Johnny Gurkha' is a part of 'Empire' (even though the Kingdom of Nepal never was), however unfashionable that expression may now be. Since the time they first took the colours, the Gurkhas have been the stuff of *Boy's Own* stories and theirs is one of constant high adventure. I hope to do them full credit.

The Goorkhas

Roughly 90 miles north-west of Kathmandu stands the town of Gorkha, a high and imposing place with the backdrop of the sweeping, almost eerie immensity of the Annapurna Range. Crowning the settlement, nearly 1,500m above sea level, is the Gorkha Durbar, both palace and fortress: complex and mysterious. It resonates still with a level of cultural intensity which must appear alien to the West. Yet, this is where the Gurkha (originally 'Goorkha') story really begins. It is an ancient citadel, even though the most recent monarch added a very twenty-first-century helipad for his convenience.

It needs to be borne in mind that Nepal has changed a great deal in the last fifty or sixty years and, yet, in some ways, not at all. Even in the late twentieth century the remote shut-in kingdom had a sort of Shangri-La quality, as backward and squalid as it would ever be romantic, and young Gurkhas came down out of the hills from a tribal society largely unchanged for centuries. The West, since the advent of the Industrial Revolution, has conceived the notion of continual, never-ending material progress, fuelled by technological innovation – a new cultural paradigm our own rural ancestors could never have imagined. Nor could the Gurkhas: their society is more akin to Britain's eighteenth-century agrarian past. Their comprehension, world view and beliefs are formed from a very different mould.[3]

In the eighteenth century, a ruler, Prithvi Narayan, was born in Gorkha and would, through conquest, unite the many minor princedoms and tribal lands that made up the unfinished state of Nepal. He subdued the Kathmandu Valley, using modern weapons purchased from the Honourable East India Company. Once he had succeeded his father in 1742, he launched a series of campaigns to cow and coerce his neighbours. From the outset, his Goorkha warriors were renowned for courage, steadfastness and aggression. Further expansion was blocked to the north and east by the Chinese Empire, to the south and west by the Honourable East India ('John') Company. Conflict with both became inevitable.

INTRODUCTION

On 16 November 1814, Lord Moira, Governor General of Bengal, took the East India Company to war against Nepal. It was a very tough fight. Despite the overwhelming strength of British forces, the 'Goorkhas' resisted and made John Company fight for every pass and ragged mountain fort. Peace was agreed in March 1816. The House of Gorkha lost some ground but was amply compensated. Both sides developed a considerable respect for each other. Moreover, the British appreciated that these tough mountain fighters would make excellent soldiers.

A partnership was born. Goorkhas became enthusiastic recruits and, very soon, trusted allies. There is a parallel here with Scottish Highlanders. During the Jacobite Risings in Britain (1689–1746) the recusant or Tory clans were viewed with a mixture of contempt, fear and loathing. It was Pitt the Elder who, a decade after Culloden, had the idea of recruiting them into the British Army and using them as shock troops in emerging colonial wars – Gurkhas and Highlanders would find they had much in common.

Captain Hearsay, a nineteenth-century freelance, wrote of the Gurkhas: 'They are hardy, endure privations, and are very obedient, have not much of the distinction of caste, and are a neutral kind of Hindoo, eating in messes almost everything they meet with, except beef. Under our government they would make excellent soldiers.'[4]

The partnership between the British and Nepalese has been long, fruitful and, without exception, honourable. British officers and men who have served with Gurkha regiments have almost invariably come away with respect (the mercurial Orde Wingate being an exception; see Chapter 9). Even enemies as harsh as the Japanese learned to be wary: 'The very model of sturdy, honest and simple soldiers – and as front line troops during the war they had given the Japanese army a really rough time.'[5]

Field Marshal Lord Herbert Kitchener was normally an awfully difficult man to please. Having been warned when he came to India that the Gurkhas could stand anything but abuse, he was sufficiently impressed after the Tibet expedition to refer to the Nepalese as 'some of our bravest and most efficient soldiers'.[6] It is one of the more bizarre quirks of history that two groups from such wildly divergent backgrounds, 'Tommy Atkins' and 'Johnny Gurkha', get on so well. For two centuries these tough, hardy hill-men have fought in just about all of Britain's wars. The very thought that they would be unleashed against Argentinean forces occupying the Falklands was enough to send tremors of alarm through enemy ranks (see Chapter 10).

After Kitchener, a later but equally renowned Field Marshal, Lord Slim, who knew Gurkhas well, summed them up: 'The Almighty created in the Gurkha an ideal rifleman, brave, tough, patient, adaptable, skilled in field-craft, immensely proud of his military record and unswerving loyalty. Add to this his honesty in word and deed, his parade perfection, and his unquenchable cheerfulness, then service with Gurkhas is for any soldier an immense satisfaction.'[7]

When the Indian Mutiny erupted in 1857, John Company's hegemony began to come seriously unstuck, its inefficiencies and heavy-handed unfairness towards native troops (sepoys) producing a murderous backlash. Atrocities abounded on both sides. Nonetheless, 'Goorkha' (as they were then called) battalions and the King of Nepal remained loyal. Crucially, 2nd Goorkhas held Hindu Rao's House, the key bastion on Delhi Ridge, for three desperate months of bitter and close fighting. This action helped determine the final outcome and numerous gallantry awards were won.

As a component of empire, with the Company's influence removed, Gurkhas became indispensable, fighting continually on both the North-West and North-East frontiers and in the jungles of Burma. The Khyber Pass made famous by Rudyard Kipling – a narrow umbilical connection through harsh tribal territories, historically ungovernable – would keep the Gurkhas in constant action for ninety years.

This was asymmetric warfare (conflict in which the respective military capabilities of the combatants differ widely) of the most basic and brutal sort. The Pathans were not in the habit of taking prisoners and any who fell into their hands would wish they had saved that last bullet. If anything, it was even worse in Afghanistan, as Kipling so frequently described, perhaps nowhere better than in *The Man who Would be King*.[8]

Gurkhas would fight in the Second and Third Afghan Wars and in the Tirah Campaign of 1897. The ground over which the brigade would deploy during Operation Herrick would have been quite familiar to this generation of soldiers' great-great-grandfathers. The regiment still holds the venerable 'Kandahar Gun', captured during this campaign. They would be back for the Third Afghan War in 1919 and again during the 1930s, mastering the unforgiving art of frontier warfare against a very hardened indigenous opponent who relentlessly punished any mistake and exploited any and every chink of opportunity.

The Gurkha Way

When taking groups of serving Gurkhas on battlefield tours I am immediately struck by the differences between them and UK recruits. They are much more

INTRODUCTION

aware of their brigade history; many have relatives who served in one of the world wars and as a result some can trace their military family back to the days of the Raj. They show a willingness to listen and learn with an impressive grasp of tactics and an eye for ground.

These young men from the hills and mountains of Nepal are totally unlike most 'green army' recruits in the UK. They come from a tradition of service where the uniform is a badge of honour and respect and having worn it buys an individual a place in the complex social hierarchy of what is still, despite the impact of the hippie trail and mass tourism, an insular society. A Gurkha officer echoed Byron Farwell when he quoted from RGR fundamentals and the Support Company 2 RGR directive:

> To us Gurkhas, our history is especially important. It is how we keep our tradition alive. We remember and honour the great deeds of our ancestors, the men who have gone before us. When today a Gurkha does something heroic, he does not do it for himself, but for his comrades and in honour of those ancestors. For us, there is nothing greater a man can do than act courageously in battle, and we take enormous pride when one of our number is commended for bravery.[9]

This is the Gurkha way which goes to the soul of this book. He is part of the British Army, has a record within the British order of battle second to none, yet, culturally he is worlds apart. He comes from a background which could not be more different from that of most modern UK soldiers. His society is both remote and, by Western standards, under-developed, but one where tradition matters. He is physically tough and resourceful: for him to join the ranks is an honour, an achievement in itself. Receiving a military award is even more so. It is a matter of honour for the soldier's whole family: 'When Lachhiman Gurung was invested with the VC by the Viceroy of India in 1945, family members actually carried his disabled father for eleven whole days over the hills until he got to a road where he could take public transport down to Delhi.'[10]

For him the Brigade of Gurkhas is not just a job, it's a way of life. He is 'us' but also very much himself. His story is unique in the annals of warfare. He long since ceased to be a mercenary and became a patriot: to fight as a Gurkha is to fight as a Briton, yet, he never loses his cultural roots. Whether he returns home to become a valued civil servant or opens a restaurant in Camberley, he's still Gurkha. As the noted author Farwell confirms:

> Traditions matter. In themselves they count for little, but they combine to form part of the identity that makes our Regiment what it is. In our line of work, we have to do things that are far from normal – our Regiment provides us with some of the reference points that we need to bring sense into chaos. It is not easy to regain tradition once lost, so we must fight to keep it.
>
> It provides the framework for our relationships with one another which in turn serve us well in peace and on operations. We should also be extremely proud to be a part of the Royal Gurkha Rifles, and a way of showing that pride is to uphold the traditions that our forebears established. We call this *kaida*. Support Company *kaida* is about FAMILY (Fitness, Agility, Mutual Support, Initiative, Leadership and You) but it is underpinned by our *kaida*. History is like map reading – how do we know where we are, if we do not know where we came from, and how do we know where we are going if we do not know where we are?[11]

Gurkhas are lean and tough; their physical tests are exhaustive. In Afghanistan, the ability of Gurkhas to effectively live off the land meant soldiers were still far fitter than their contemporaries even after lengthy and exhausting marches. Officers, too, are different. The regiment has very exacting standards, and bonds between British and Gurkha officers and men are intense and tribal. Connections and networks are formed that extend into Civvy Street and are religiously maintained.

As Professor Sir Hew Francis Strachan commented in the Radio 4 Documentary *Ayo Gorkhali*:

> I'm a hard-bitten military historian who has learnt to be distrustful of the stories armies and their soldiers tell of themselves. The Brigade of Gurkhas has its fair share of legends. But do they and the undoubted pride that comes from them make the Brigade of Gurkhas any different from other tightly knit military communities? Despite my cynicism, I have to conclude that they do. The British officer serving with the Gurkhas has to work much harder to engage with the customs, language and religion of his men than do the British officers of other units. Similar cultural demands are made of the Gurkhas. That mutual effort creates a strength of relationship, a special and long-lasting bond, that I have not encountered in any other military community.[12]

INTRODUCTION

A Gurkha NCO I was chatting to in 2016 spoke of their heritage:

> According to history, the first time British soldiers came into contact with Gurkha warriors was during the siege of Kalunga in 1814. On that occasion, just 650 Gurkhas defended a hill-fort against a British force of 4,000. It is said that as the battle was raging, a single Gurkha soldier appeared behind British lines. He was holding his jaw, which had been shattered by a bullet, and indicated he wanted it bandaging up. No sooner had the bandage been tied in place than the soldier requested to be permitted to return to his own side to continue the fight. Not a lot has changed![13]

Gurkhas in the Twenty-First Century

In the modern world the Gurkha may seem like an anachronism to many, especially those who favour a passive defence policy, shrinking UK armed forces to some form of 'Dad's Army'. But the increasing trends for future conflict suggest that 'Johnny Gurkha' is more relevant now than ever (see Chapter 11). His genius for COIN operations, ably demonstrated in Afghanistan, shows he is in many ways the ideal soldier for twenty-first-century conflict and that his worth to Britain, and to any notions of a free world that might be held, is inestimable.

Since I began writing in 2018, the world has shifted with the eruption of a full-scale interstate war in Europe – the Russian invasion of Ukraine which opened on 24 February 2022. This has changed the entire dynamic of Western strategic thinking in ways that have yet to be appreciated and, at the time of writing, the war continues to rage with dire intensity. How this may yet impact the role of the Brigade of Gurkhas it cannot be determined. Ironically, despite Mark Lancaster's announcement, no 3rd Battalion has, as yet been formed.

Chapter 1

Hindu Rao's House

We have forty million reasons for failure, but not a single excuse.
Rudyard Kipling, *The Lesson* (1902)

India was the 'Jewel in the Crown' among Queen Victoria's vast and spreading domains. It was a cornerstone of the British Empire and to lose such a priceless gem would be unthinkable. In the mid-nineteenth century suspicions over Russian intentions towards India struck deep, but the spark that nearly burned down the whole edifice came from within and was accompanied by mutiny among the East India Company's native sepoys serving in the Bengal Presidency (the others were not affected), bursting into terrible flames in 1857. This would be the crucible in which Gurkha loyalties were fully tested. They passed with flying colours.

Delhi Ridge is the birthplace of a legend. A shallow slope, it rises a mere 60ft (18m) above the flat plain of the Jumna, the largest tributary of the Ganges. But it was here in the hot spring and arid summer of 1857 that a tiny, mainly British force, at any one time only 4,000 or so strong, laid siege to the vast city of Delhi, held by an army of rebels at least ten times more numerous. During this conflict, the defence of the position known as Hindu Rao's House by the Sirmoor Battalion of the Gurkhas would become one of the enduring epics of the Raj. It also marked the point when the Gurkhas came to be seen as fully part of the British Army: 'us' not 'them'.

The Quarrel

Although now sometimes referred to as a rebellion or even 'The Indian First War of Independence', the Mutiny was in fact exactly that: 'a rising by parts of the Native Army as opposed to a national movement'.[1] Sparked by the East India Company's abominable treatment of its native troops, it began on 10 May 1857 when rebellious sepoys attacked their European officers in the lines at Meerut. Women and children were hacked to death, an atrocity that began a war characterised by merciless savagery on both sides. Despite this, the flames did not spread beyond Bengal. Soon, the rebels had left the smouldering ruins and marched 40 miles south to Delhi[2] where they proclaimed the astonished, not to say alarmed, octogenarian Mogul survivor Bahadur Shah II as the new ruler of all India. The British, recovering from their initial shock, had different ideas. The good news for them was that the Gurkhas remained totally loyal and the King of Nepal promised support. This, even if it was initially declined, mattered: John Company would need all the help it could get.

At this time a typical company battalion of native infantry mustered in 8 companies, each of about 120 men with a British CO (Commanding Officer) and company officers.[3] Before the outbreak, Lieutenant Macintyre was in charge of a detachment of Gurkhas drawn from all three battalions then in service, attending a musketry course at Amballa. He received a request from the ranks: his men wanted to pitch their tents not with the native infantry but with the British. The Gurkhas did not care for the grousing of sepoys over the rumours about cartridges having been greased with pig or cow fat, offensive to both Muslims and Hindus; they 'emphasized their desire to be regarded as the equals of European soldiers by successfully asking permission to pitch their tents together with those of British troops'.[4] Moreover, they asked to be issued with these very same rounds, just to make the point that they would have no truck with ideas of mutiny. Both requests were immediately granted.[5] Despite being predominantly Hindu in terms of faith, and thus closer in religious and cultural affinity to the sepoys, the Gurkhas were making a plain statement that they were professional soldiers and not likely to be swayed by seditious agitators.

The Sirmoor Battalion

It was midday on a scorching May day when news reached the Sirmoor Battalion (later 2nd Gurkha Rifles) stationed at Dehra Dun that all hell had broken loose at Meerut. Major Charles Reid was in command and, obligingly for future historians, he kept a substantial body of papers from that time which provides great insight into the forthcoming campaign:

> About noon, on the 14th of May 1857, I received an express from Head-Quarters, directing me to march with my regiment, the Sirmoor Battalion, to Meerut, to aid the Europeans at that

station in suppressing the mutiny of the native troops. My orders were issued immediately, and four hours after the receipt of the Commander-in-Chief's order the regiment was on the move. Waiting for carriage for the conveyance of tents and baggage was out of the question, so we marched out of Deyrah [Dehra] with just what we carried on our backs; sixty rounds of ammunition in pouch, and two elephant loads of spare ammunition.[6]

The major commanded just short of 500 bayonets, mustered in 4 companies. The battalion marched by way of Roorkee, halting by the banks of the Ganges Canal to eat. A gang of mutinous sappers came out from the town, insisting that John Company had mixed in ground-up bones with their flour rations; as Reid noted, 'some of them passed close to me with an insolent look and an air of defiance'.[7] The Gurkhas laughed at them.[8] Reid got his men onto a flotilla of forty-five barges with flankers covering the banks. At Bhola they had their first brush with rebels. It was short and sharp: the attack was seen off, the settlement stormed, kit was recovered and prisoners were taken.

Reid ordered a trial: 'The prisoners will be tried this morning by a drumhead court martial, and if found guilty I shall shoot them.'[9] Thirteen unlucky prisoners were subsequently stood against a wall and although a handful were high caste, the Gurkhas didn't hesitate to shoot. The place was burned. When more Brahmans were sentenced to hang at the next village but two of the ropes snapped, they too were unhesitatingly finished off with gunfire. The Mutiny was nasty, on both sides, and this trail of burning houses and dead men was to be repeated many, many times.[10]

As the march resumed, Reid discovered that Major General Archdale Wilson was heading towards Delhi and he launched his slender column in pursuit, covering 27 miles in one night:

> Brigadier Wilson writes to me that he is hard up for troops on the Hindun. He has only one wing of a regiment of infantry. He tells me that the Commander-in-Chief had ordered that I should take up a position on the Hindun with my own regiment, 400 cavalry and four horse artillery guns. This order has not yet reached me; but as Brigadier Wilson appears most anxious that I should join him at once, I think I had better do so.[11]

It took three full days' hard marching to close the gap and the 60th Rifles, bringing up the rear of Wilson's force, thought the newcomers were mutineers and began shooting, happily to no effect. Once the Rifles realised these were Gurkhas, and on their side, they swapped bullets for cheers. Others higher up the command chain were not so sure and posted the battalion up with the guns, just in case.

Wilson needn't have worried about the reliability of the Sirmoor Battalion. Reid's Gurkhas, along with a Rifles detachment, beat up enemy quarters on 2 June. The raid was successful; an enemy-held village was destroyed even though the mutineers had already fled.[12] On 8 June the Gurkhas more than demonstrated their loyalty in a brisk scrap just 7 miles (11.2km) short of Delhi. The mutineers had dug in, up to 30,000 men backed by 30 guns. They were driven off and the bare escarpment known as the Badle-ki-Serai, roughly 5 miles (8km) north-west of the city, was secured. This was Delhi Ridge, which lay about a thousand yards west of the city walls and, uninviting as it was, it would form the key to unlocking the mighty walls of the old capital. Wilson was able to set up along a 2-mile (3km) front, running north–south.

Wilson's lines, such as they were, faced the western walls. The shallow escarpment was studded with various buildings, some of which – a former sepoy barracks – were demolished. This was unwise as the ridge otherwise had no shelter worth speaking of. All the wells were poisoned and water from the Jumna River undrinkable. One stroke of luck was the proximity of the Western Jumna Canal running behind the ridge, which provided water and a measure of rearward security. Wilson's force faced an enormous challenge.[13]

Delhi was extremely formidable, the great city fortified with a 7-mile (11km) circuit of old but intact walls, 24ft (7.3m) high and fronted on all but the river elevation by a deep, wide ditch 20ft (6m) deep and 27ft (7.6m) across. The enceinte was studded with stout bastions bristling with guns and boasted ten massive gateways. Three of these, the Kashmir, Kabul and Lahore, faced the shallow rise of the escarpment. The Delhi garrison consisted of at least 40,000 mutineers and at the outset the British, clinging to their toehold, could only muster 2,300 infantry, 600 cavalry and 22 field guns. This wasn't a lot and Wilson had absolutely no hope of taking the place by storm.[14] He didn't have the men, and, above all, he lacked heavy siege cannon; the far lighter guns he possessed had no chance of bringing down such strong defences.

Between ridge and walls, the plain was dotted with various buildings and vegetation, all offering excellent cover. The rebels knew they couldn't afford to be complacent and just sit behind their ramparts. The besiegers would be steadily reinforced, and at some point, a siege train proper would arrive. Old masonry, however massive, could never hope to resist the power of modern big guns. If they did nothing, the balance must tilt and the fight for Delhi was really the fight for India. Neither side could afford to lose.

Delhi Ridge

Probably none of the Sirmoor Battalion, now dug in on Delhi Ridge, had ever heard of the place; those who survived would never forget it. Each rifleman carried sixty rounds and the reserve ammunition was borne by those two handy elephants. The besiegers, isolated on the bare, desperate escarpment, were too few to assault or encircle the great sprawling heart of the old Mogul Empire. By 8 June they had reached the ridge: scorched, bone dry and barely defensible. This would be no Alesia[15] with vast ramparts of circumvallation. They weren't even enough to prevent supplies and reinforcements getting in. It wasn't really a siege; it was just stalemate.

One key feature on the right flank was an incongruous, rather grand villa in mock Palladian style, named after its most recent owner, Hindu Rao. The Gurkhas with two companies of the 60th Rifles were sent to hold it. As Reid described the place: 'Hindu Rao's House was the key to the position which the enemy was not long in discovering; they tried their utmost to drive me out of it on the first day and it became, ever after, the object of almost every attack, often by as many as 8,000 rebels at a time.'[16] It would in fact be the crucible.

Reid recorded their arrival:

> About 1 p.m. we reached the Ridge, when I was directed by General Barnard to occupy Hindoo Rao's House which is within twelve hundred yards of the Moree [Mori] Bastion; had just made ourselves comfortable when the alarm was sounded. In ten minutes, the mutineers were seen coming up towards Hindoo Rao's House in force. I went out with my own regiment, two companies of Rifles and two guns of Scott's battery, and drove them back into the city. This, however, was not accomplished till 5 p.m., so that we were under arms for sixteen hours ... heat fearful.[17]

It was now the anchor of a tenuous siege line, a fact clearly not lost on the mutineers, who were very keen to win it back. The house was about 12,000yd (1,100m) from the Mori Bastion, nearest in the mighty circuit of walls. It was an oven, with no shade from the demon sun and, on 9 June, the Sirmoor Battalion faced their first mass attack. It was seen off to the cheers of the British. Next day, the mutineers came back, trying to win over the Gurkhas. They failed and were scattered by a volley at close range. Reid was now holding the house as the anchor of his picquet line, together with three other posts – the Observatory,

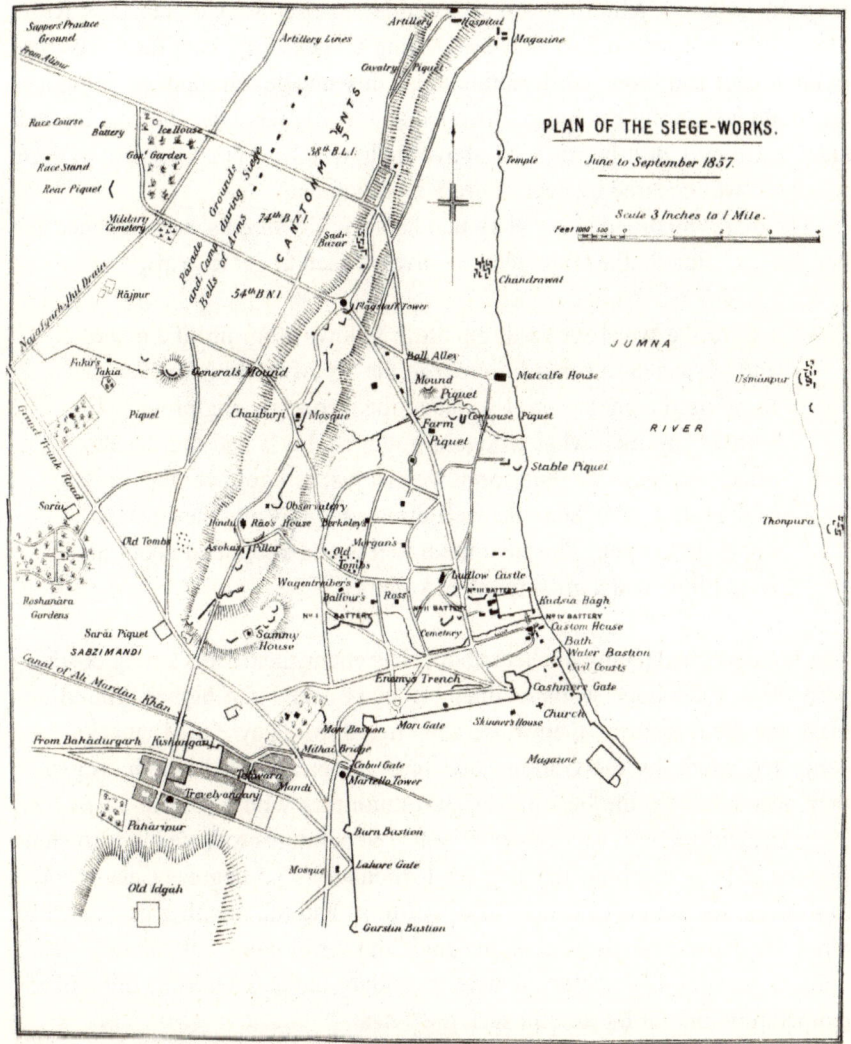

Map 1. Delhi, plan of the siege works, 1857.

Crow's Nest and Subzimandi. His battalion, with support from the Guides and 60th Rifles, would hold this desperately exposed line from 8 June until 14 September.

This set the pattern. Day after day, in seemingly inexhaustible numbers, the rebels swarmed up the shallow rise and, time after time, the Gurkhas beat them back. Many more mutineers were pouring into Delhi and fresh units were flung into the mincer. The Gurkhas' first fight for the ridge lasted, as Reid confirms, for a full 16 hours, a hurricane of shot with wave after wave of attackers. Rifles glowed red hot, men choked in the cloying clouds of reeking dust, bayonets blunted bent and bloodied. If nothing else this savage introduction convinced any doubters among European officers that not only were the Gurkhas on their side, but they could punch well above their weight. Their defence, as Reid recalled, 'was cheered by every European Regiment'.[18]

The major recorded in his diary that he never favoured a static defence and nor did his soldiers; the Gurkhas were always keen to get to grips:

> I gave the word forward; our little fellows were up like a shot and advanced in beautiful order to the top of the hill. By way of bringing the enemy on, I sounded the retreat having previously warned my men what we were going to do. It had the desired effect; on came the mutineers, we met just as I got over the brow of the hill. I gave them one well-directed volley and then ordered my guns to open. This sent them to a round-about and about 50 were killed and a great number wounded.[19]

The besiegers had plenty to cheer about. The enemy sent out a strong covering party from their huge walls to drag big guns nearer the higher ground and blast the British from their miserable trenches. They failed, thanks to a concerted attack by the Gurkhas and four companies of the 60th. Together, they accounted for the best part of 300 mutineers with a loss of 15 of their own. The summer sun was harder to beat. Temperatures rocketed to a crushing furnace of heat, reaching 131 degrees Fahrenheit (55.5 degrees Celsius). Add to that the discomfort of coarse wool uniforms and the ramping up caused by rapid fire, barrels hot as steel on the anvil and the cloying, dehydrating stench of black powder. Biting black powder cartridges induces a terrible thirst in any temperature, but far more so in such great heat.

From time to time the Gurkhas were joined in their tortured outpost by men from the 60th Rifles, Coke's Rifles (Indian Army, raised in 1849) and the Guides (Corps of Guides, raised in 1846 for service on the North-West Frontier). Charles Reid had plenty of time for the 60th as well: 'The feeling that existed between the 60th Rifles and my own men was admirable; they call one another brothers, share their grog with each other ... my men used to speak of them as "our Rifles" and the men of the 60th as "them Gurkhees [Gurkhas] of ours".'[20] A plan was hatched to seize Delhi by a *coup de main* on 13 June but like so many brave intentions, it failed to materialise.[21] The Gurkhas had many more weeks of their very personal Calvary to endure.

HINDU RAO'S HOUSE

Any Europeans who might have doubted the Gurkhas at the outset, who had felt that they were best kept under the watchful barrels of artillery, were soon cheering (as lustily as their parched throats would allow) each time the Sirmoor Battalion drew their bright-edged kukris (see Appendix 6) and charged. It is highly unlikely the original architect of Hindu Rao's ostentatious palazzo intended the place to function as a bunker, but its resilience was a tribute to the builder: 'We are under fire morning, noon and night ... We can hold our own, every attack having been at once repulsed ... Hindoo Rao's House is very strong but if they keep up the fire of their 32- and 24-pounders it cannot stand much longer.'[22]

By the end of that first month, the battalion had sustained 138 casualties. By the end of July, they could barely muster half their original strength.[23] British officers were seriously impressed not just with their hardiness and courage but by their unfailing humour and apparent indifference to the terrible hardships of the ridge: hunger, thirst, heat, disease and all-pervading squalor, not to mention constant enemy action. Among the many dead was the famous Tiger-slayer Taka Rama. Subadar Major Singbir Thapa, who had begun his military apprenticeship fighting the British forty years earlier, was seriously wounded.

The ground between city and ridge was strewn with hundreds of bloated corpses. Flies, in biblical numbers, tormented the besiegers. Short of food, of water, of ammunition and medical supplies, they clung on 'morning, noon and night'. Cholera and dysentery stalked the lines; ragged soldiers became increasingly emaciated. Hindu Rao's rather imposing house crumbled into a shell-torn ruin. For what would now be called rear echelon, the ration carriers, or *pipawallas*, also took huge risks; fifteen of them were sniped. Like Alec Guinness in *Bridge on the River Kwai*, when Reid combed the sickbay looking for anyone who could still heft a rifle, every patient volunteered.[24]

As if at some archaic medieval tournament, the King of Delhi erected tiers of lavishly decorated benches so that fashionable ladies might enjoy the sport of watching men die. The season finale would have been the planting of the royal standard above the shell of Hindu Rao's House. Reid rather hoped the king would come out on as large an elephant as possible, so as to make the biggest target for a 24-pounder. Both he and the glitterati of Delhi were disappointed.

In lulls between fighting, guns on both sides kept up their thunderous roaring. Without bigger, heavier artillery the besiegers couldn't hope to make a serious impression, but their strength was steadily increasing. By early July they had swelled to 6,600 and, on 14 August, the legendary frontiersman Brigadier John Nicholson, 'Lion of the Punjab', arrived with his crack Punjabi regiments, both infantry and cavalry. He was what was needed; his furious dynamism and grit contrasted with Wilson's caution though, to be fair, Wilson had much to be cautious about. To attack too soon and court defeat would have been disastrous; besides, the heavy siege train was still ponderously en route. Without those big guns the fight was going nowhere.

Time and again the mutineers attacked, sallying out from their huge walls to sweep these few besiegers clinging to their sketchy, scraped lines into total oblivion. The men of the Sirmoor Battalion doggedly held their battered redoubt. Hindu Rao wouldn't have recognised his house, once the pinnacle of *arriviste* chic. Its walls were scorched, denuded, peppered with round shot and bullet marks. It was a solid two-storey place, ponderously classical with a pillared mezzanine balcony at one end, somewhere between an overblown spa and the better class of bordello. It was rendered and would have originally blazed its whiteness through the dusty air. But it was solid and offered a good vantage. Behind its reassuringly thick walls there was good cover.

The Sirmoor men wore rifle green, commensurate with their status, and a cocked version of the Kilmarnock (Balmoral) bonnet, finished with red on black dicing and the famous bugle-horn badge. Their bayonets were hung from a waist belt and the kukri carried forward of the ammo pouch.[25] European officers dressed differently to other ranks, sporting their white cotton trousers, heroically oblivious to such an open invitation to any sniper. Both would be pretty shabby by now: attrition is as hard on cloth as it is on flesh and blood.

Gurkhas in this fight enjoyed the great advantage of being issued with rifles, a pattern of the Brunswick. Introduced in 1836, this was a percussion cap muzzle-loader .07in (17.99mm) calibre that fired a lead ball, though this was partially grooved to fit the rifling. A paper cartridge held powder and shot and was bitten off to pour; fulminate of mercury percussion caps, a big improvement on flint and invented by a Scottish clergyman, were kept in the separate pouch. The rifle kicked savagely with every round and that got progressively worse as the barrel fouled with powder residue. Men were grimed and parched by the harsh powder, each round blasting out a reeking cloud. It made up for its relatively short barrel length with a long sword bayonet, intended to give the same reach as a longer smooth-bored weapon. It was accurate to 300yd, six times the likely reach of the musket.

And on they came, time and again, banners fluttering, a great cloud of enemy, some in ragged John Company kit, many more in a mirage of native gear; a steel-tipped avalanche, rounds kicking and smacking off scarred walls, ricochets like deadly, singing fireflies. Volleys roared and their dense sulphurous clouds banged out yet more heat to add to nature's furnace; targets were obscured, then loomed nearer – the tidal wave that rushes, seemingly unstoppable, then wavers and sullenly falls back, buying another hour's deliverance. Day after day after day it continued, the ranks steadily thinning, familiar faces growing dim as time went on and the toll mounted.

Reid continued to be fearful of crashing roundshot from the enemy's big guns. 'At about 3 p.m. [on 17 June] a 32-pounder roundshot came smashing into the portico of the house which the officers occupy, killing Ensign Wheatley ... a havildar and four of my men ...'.[26] The major, with additional support, mounted an attack on the mutineers' outworks beyond those great walls. He led most of the Sirmoors and four companies from the 60th. He was attempting to outflank the face of the enemy battery by hacking a way through ancient dried-up waterways and various buildings. The enemy was fully alert and the rear entrance to their fort had to be bashed in by impromptu rams. A savage close-quarter fight ensued before the gunners were cut down and their guns spiked. Reid lost seven dead and more wounded in the raid. He estimated at least fifty mutineers killed and many more wounded.[27] It was a battle of attrition; each success, each repulse came at a price. The sapping, dangerous skirmishing, enlivened by snipers everywhere, took a steady toll.

The centenary of Plassey fell on 23 June[28] and the mutineers had clung to a prophecy that British rule would end that day. It didn't, but they certainly tried: according to Reid: 'I was attacked early this morning. The enemy turned out in greater force than I have ever yet seen them.' They had sworn before mustering that they would take Hindu Rao's House that day. This attack was no mad rush; it had been well planned with storming parties holed up in shot-up ruins dotting the plain. The roofs gave a good vantage for snipers, bringing Reid's guns on his right flank under intense fire. He had to counterattack. A detachment of Gurkhas, Rifles and Guides succeeded in driving the enemy back and taking the buildings, but they were soon forced out by a huge enemy reinforcement 'some ten times their number'.[29]

Reid beefed up his attacking formations and sent them back. Again, they drove out the enemy and this time kept their foothold. The pressure never slackened. Reid begged for reinforcements but everywhere was too hard pressed. About noon the mutineers threw in everything they had with a general assault on the whole of his position. They simply weren't giving up and just kept coming regardless of their dead piling in front, human wave attacks pressed home with an almost fanatical determination. It seemed the defenders' dreadfully thin lines must be swamped: 'They charged the Rifles, the Guides, and my own men time and again, and at one time I thought I must have lost the day.'[30]

Fighting raged until dusk when the mutineers finally conceded. Survivors pulled out, dragging their guns, which they had brought up, back with them. Reid estimated he had killed about 800 for the loss of three-dozen Gurkhas and about the same for the Guides.[31] The unrelenting attrition was truly dreadful; Reid himself was slightly injured by a ricochet. Suffocating, breathless heat was, as ever, as deadly as the enemy. Lieutenant Minto Elliot, commanding Reid's light guns, was recommended for a VC.

Havildar Badar Singh, who had previously earned an Indian Order of Merit 3rd Class[32] in the Sikh War at Aliwal where he'd taken a Khalsa standard, now, in true swashbuckling style, cleared a particularly annoying outpost. Reid had ordered him to take his company and eject mutineers from a fortified building, possession of which enabled them to enfilade the entire British position. They knew he would be coming and had barricaded their walled enclosure, lined with muskets. The havildar left half his men to keep the enemy pinned by the gateway and led the remainder around the back of the position. Using his men's shoulders as ad hoc human scaling ladders, he got onto the walls and blasted the incumbents who, attacked from front and back, swiftly vacated leaving dozens dead.[33] This earned Badar Singh an IOM 2nd class.

Overall, despite such stellar successes, the pressure never eased: 'June 27th – we were attacked again this morning in greater force than ever. I occupied all the buildings in the 'Subzee-mundee' [no man's land] consequently did not lose near so many men as on the 23rd. The enemy was somewhat astonished to find the place occupied.'[34] It never seemed to vary. Hindu Rao's House was tottering, and casualties continued to mount. 'July 10th – we had another grand scrimmage yesterday, the same old story, an attack on my position. The enemy was about 8,000 strong and I fought desperately …'.[35]

Despite the pressure and the unrelenting pounding by enemy guns, Reid was still begging to be allowed to leave off defending and show some real aggression. So, on 10 July, despite the unending pressure, he went over to a counterattack and drove the mutineers back over the plain, through the scrub and almost under their own walls. Despite fire from their massive bastions and lighter field pieces, he got some of his own guns up which sent the mutineers scurrying to safety, clearly thinking they were about to be stormed.

Nonetheless, the enemy forces soon recovered and by 15 July were attacking all-out once again (the twentieth major sortie). Reid had apparently earned the sobriquet 'Prince of Devils'.[36] Somehow, Hindu Rao's House stayed standing; patches of scrub and jungle were cleared in lulls and impromptu breastworks thrown up as an outpost line while mini-redoubts such as the 'Sammy-House' were improvised. Yet, men continued to drop, sniped or laid low with heatstroke or sickness. There were no desertions. Reid continues:

> An officer of the 60th called James Hare observed how they dealt with a sepoy sniper on the 23rd during an 11-hour attack. The marksman had holed up in one of the huts between the ridge and the walls. He was shooting out and making a nuisance of himself. Two Gurkhas resolved to bag him and worked their way forwards and crept up either side of the door. The next time the sepoy poked his head out of the doorway, one caught hold of his head by his hair, and the other promptly lopped it off with his kukri.[37]

Beyond the Ridge

Meanwhile, away from the cauldron of Delhi, in the Kumaon Hills the 66th Gurkhas along with British units were defending Haldwini, firmly sandwiched between two rebel detachments. A large raiding party of Gurkhas, most of the battalion in fact, backed by two field guns, undertook a night march through woodland (no easy matter even for a modern force with good communications) and 'brassed up' the enemy outpost at Charpura. Stealth, surprise and steadiness did the job, and a far bigger force of mutineers was routed. The whole march, there and back, covered a distance of 34 miles (54km) and including the fight was accomplished in under 13 hours.[38]

Back on Delhi Ridge, when the enemy wasn't attacking, they were bombarding: a constant 'hate' of shells battered the position. Despite their difficulties, weakened by hunger and sickness, the Gurkhas took the fight to the mutineers at every opportunity. Many attacks were delivered by fanatical berserkers, high on dope, but they were seen off just the same. By the end of the month the battalion had withstood a score of major sallies. Casualties were high at over 200 but any lingering suspicions had been blasted away and the 60th formed strong bonds with their Gurkha comrades. It was no more 'us and them', only 'us'.[39]

On 1 August, the enemy made yet another grand sally 'like so many bees'.[40] Ten-thousand of them, a seemingly unstoppable storm, came on with plenty of guns and kit for scaling ladders. Part of the plan was a grand enveloping and out-flanking move, though this meant bridging the canal; merciless heat had given way to monsoon rain, coming down in torrents. The plan was clearly to mount an all-out assault from all sides but despite the mutineers bringing up mortars, it just fizzled out, as Reid describes: 'Perfectly wonderful how I escape. Round shot, shell, and musket balls come phit, phit, phee, phish, past my old head, but still here it is all safe on my shoulders.'[41]

With the sacred festival of Eid approaching, the enemy braced himself for one great superhuman effort. Reid estimated that 20,000 mutineers attacked his mixed bag of 900 defenders. Again, the fight lasted all day; yet again, the defenders held their ground and saw off repeated charges, from dawn till dusk. Only evening produced any kind of respite.[42]

At the end of the fight Reid encountered a 'line boy', a lad of 13 who had been born in the regimental lines, rather than being from the mountains of Nepal. There were many line boys in the different regiments, and they were usually forbidden to join the action. This one, however, had gone out to join his father, and had loaded his musket for him until he had been shot down. With his father dead, the boy offered his services to a rifleman of the 60th, who was then wounded and sent him back to fetch a doolie to evacuate him.[43] When this job was done he joined the action himself and was wounded in the leg. Reid examined the wound, which the boy proudly presented to him, and he was enlisted on the spot. He later commented that twelve line boys received the Order of Merit for bravery at Delhi.[44]

Even in the furnace heat of August, baking on the exposed ridge, the fight went on. Reid's tattered, exhausted survivors were reinforced by the Kumaon Battalion on 1 August (they had been ordered up from Rawalpindi as far back as 23 June). This was just as well, since on 9 August a force of some 10,000 of the enemy came out to fight once again. Reid himself was one of the lucky ones that day. Stationed on the right flank, he was handing his telescope (now in the Gurkha Museum) to an orderly when a random cannonball neatly decapitated the man and injured a bearer delivering the major's tea (without which, of course, no British force can possibly fight).

Blowing the Kashmir Gate

When far-famed John Nicholson arrived on the ridge bringing both additional troops and his own brand of demonic dynamism, he was already a legend. Reid, however, was far from impressed: 'I had never seen a man I disliked so much at first sight. His haughty manner and particular sneer I could not stand. Happily, the first impression soon wore off and we became the best of friends.'[45]

A few days later, accompanied by Nicholson, Reid was observing from the exposed flat roof of the villa when a shrapnel round burst overhead, a trio

HINDU RAO'S HOUSE

of fragments rattling off the major's telescope. Two riflemen nearby were injured but both officers got off without a scratch.[46] Not everyone was that fortunate. When General Lyte was holding an 'orders' group on the bullet-riddled verandah, close to the colours, a roundshot cut the duty sentry in half. The corporal of the guard smartly stepped out and brought up another sentry and, calm as you like, gathered up the body parts. Lyte and his bevy of officers were duly impressed.

Nicholson with his customary disregard for danger was a frequent visitor, scrambling up to the exposed rooftop for a shufti. Despite his fame and popularity, he always had to give out the password; the Gurkha guards took sentry duties very seriously. The mutineers hadn't given up trying to win Gurkhas over, frequently shouting inducements. This sport ended when a detachment of soldiers went out seemingly to defect, got to point-blank range, blasted a volley and charged. That was rather the end of that and from then on, the mutineers offered 12 rupees for the head of every Gurkha[47] (the same rate as for an Englishman). This was, in a bizarre way, almost a compliment.

A nasty incident occurred during the morning 'hate' on 17 August, just as the *khits* (mess orderlies) were preparing breakfast. A 24-pound ball had passed clear through the galley, miraculously without causing injury, and the precious stove, while shaken, was undamaged. Catastrophically, as it blasted clear out of the back wall it smashed the hamper containing all the delicacies sent out by Messrs Peak, Allan & Co. from Umballah, a true tragedy![48] The cooks were devastated.

By early September, those ponderous siege guns were finally getting close. Sensing which way the wind was shifting the mutineers had, on 30 August, tentatively asked for terms. They were offered none and so attempted to ambush the column. This didn't work out either. Nicholson's finely nuanced spy network picked up on the enemy's plan and he blitzed them as they deployed to attack, killing some 800 in the rout. This was just the kind of morale boost the besiegers, perched on their threadbare ridge, really needed. Meanwhile, Reid was still under regular attack: 'The enemy thought we had sent the whole force out with Nicholson's column, so took the opportunity of once again attacking me. They found me at home and got a good thrashing.'[49] Though starvation had been averted and rations were getting through, cholera, that grim, rapacious reaper of nineteenth-century armies, was relentlessly stalking the lines.

If enough food, just enough, was coming in, replacement kit was not and, by the end of August, the men's gear was reduced to rags. No new uniform seemed to be in the offing until a surprise delivery arrived. Reid describes this sartorial deliverance:

> This morning five bales of flannel shirts, blouses, shoes etc arrived from Mussoorie for my Gurkhas; the good ladies at that place, on hearing that the little fellows were in rags, held a meeting, when it was decided that they should themselves provide for our wants, and a subscription should be got up among the ladies of Landour and Mussoorie, and that they should daily meet for the purpose of working, cutting out shirts, blouses, etc with their own hands.[50]

This gesture had the added benefit of convincing watching mutineers that the Sirmoor Battalion had been significantly reinforced.

As blistering August drew to a close, attacks on Reid's ravaged lines dwindled. The fire seemed to have gone out of the mutineers, as though they gauged the pendulum was swinging and the odds shifting. On the last day of the month, they had another go at Fort Sammy, the Gurkhas' forward redoubt, but were driven off. Reid was minded to attack, clearing the scrub and driving the enemy from their own outposts. On 1 September, he did just that: '"Pandy" [after Mangal Pande, an early Mutineer 'martyr'] got in an awful state of mind and we heard about a dozen bugles in the city sounding first the "turn out", then the "advance" … and then the "retreat" – the only one which was obeyed.'[51]

By 8 September the British guns were creeping steadily and inexorably closer, at great cost in blood and treasure, to only 700yd (640m) from the Mori Bastion which was steadily pounded into rubble: 'September 10th – we are hard at work with our heavy batteries on the left…. Whilst they are getting ready on the left, we are hard at work here on the right pounding the old Moree Bastion with six guns.'[52] By dusk on the 13th these widening breaches were deemed 'practicable' (i.e. infantry could assault). Wilson was still wary about committing his forces to an all-out attack, despite Nicholson's almost messianic bullishness. To be fair, the risks were enormous.

Still, on the 14th, five columns massed in the cool pre-dawn before the fiery sun erupted over the horizon. Reid was leading the fourth of these, and each was tasked to assault a particular feature. It was desperate and bloody work as the British clawed their way in. Even the far-famed blasting of the Kashmir Gate with all the fury and courage shown by both sides failed to achieve a result on the first day. Nicholson, leading the Kumaon Gurkhas, was among the hundreds mortally wounded. His Gurkhas, having cleared a main bastion, fought their way, yard by tortured yard, through the streets, down the great thoroughfare of the Chandni Chauk until brought up by the massive redoubt of the fortified Jamna Masjid Mosque. It required several days of nasty, vicious hand-to-hand street fighting, the sort any soldier dreads, to finally secure the whole sprawling metropolis.

Reid had his column ready by 4 a.m. but was delayed (to his fury, as one can well imagine) by the late arrival of his supporting horse artillery who, when they did appear at 5.30 a.m., were still short of a full complement of gunners. He was waiting for the bang as the Kashmir Gate went up, but no explosions came; only when troops on his right were clearly engaged did he give the order – still short of gunners. The enemy was directly in front, manning their surviving redoubts and controlling the approaches to the canal bridge. This first obstacle was cleared with the bayonet. The next barrier would be tricky: reinforcements were pouring in and Reid judged them to be 15,000 strong. Although this was probably an over-estimation, there were still an awful lot of them.[53]

Just at this point Reid's considerable store of luck finally ran out and he suffered a debilitating head wound, leaving his subordinate Captain Lawrence to press the attack. For whatever reason, after Reid was taken away for treatment, the attack stalled and was finally forced back with significant losses, about a third. Up to that point the Sirmoor Battalion had lost 327 out of its original muster of 490; 8 out of 9 officers had also become casualties.[54]

Overall, the fight for Hindu Rao's House lasted for three months and cost the Sirmoor Battalion 75 per cent casualties. Total British losses had amounted to about a thousand dead and three times as many wounded. Nobody now questioned the Gurkhas' loyalty or bravery, and the battalion were made full riflemen. Desperate, bloody and exhausting as the fight had been, the Gurkha legend was born. So was the lasting friendship with 60th Rifles (the Royal Green Jackets, now the Rifles) which led to the Gurkhas sharing many kit details: scarlet facings, red-and-black headgear dicing[55] and the *esprit* of the Rifles. The Gurkha force was well on the way to becoming a real elite.

Meanwhile in Nepal

There were plenty of Nepalese who would remember the war against the British and Nepal was never part of anybody's empire. Pre-Mutiny diplomacy had included a state visit to Britain by the ruler Jung Bahadur Rana and a charm offensive resulting in the establishment of closer relations. The British Empire's hour of trial created an opportunity for the king and his prime minister (also his maternal uncle) to stage a diplomatic coup by supporting Queen Victoria to the hilt.

At first offers of assistance were turned down, but in the early months of 1858 help was requested. Jung Bahadur sent a strong brigade to intervene and clear mutineers from Jaunpur and Azamgarh. The king himself led a division of about 6,000 troops[56] which did good service during the tortuous relief of Lucknow. Lord Canning, the Governor General, was extremely glad of such first-rate allies: a full fourteen battalions with two-dozen guns was a pretty significant gesture and the King of Nepal was active in retrieving much ground in Oudh that had been lost earlier to the mutineers.

All in all, Jung Bahadur Rana did quite well out of war. It earned him, if belatedly (he had to wait two years), a knighthood and, of more material value, the return to Nepal of a 200-mile (322km) contested frontier strip (the Terai). He benefited from accumulated loot as well; gossip claimed he had amassed a huge store of jewellery, formerly the property of the brothel-keepers of Lucknow.[57] Such steadfast support from the mountain kingdom not only significantly assisted Canning and a beleaguered administration, while boosting the Nepalese economy, it also persuaded John Company to hire in more Gurkhas.

Since the institution of the award in 1856, 1,356 Victoria Crosses have been awarded (as of April 2020). Of these, twenty-six have been awarded to Gurkhas. In February 1858 the 66th Gurkhas were back at Haldwini. On 9 February Lieutenant John Adam Tytler was part of a detachment, 500 strong and commanded by a Captain Ross. The force had a couple of hundred additional infantry and as many cavalry beefed up with two 6-pounders. They pushed up against a force of mutineers which easily outnumbered them by ten to one. Next day, undeterred, the Gurkhas attacked:

> … under a heavy fire of round-shot, grape and musketry, Lieutenant Tytler dashed up on horseback ahead of all, and alone, up to the enemy's guns, where he engaged hand to hand, until they were carried by us; and when he was shot through the left arm, had a spear wound in his chest and a ball through the right sleeve of his coat.[58]

Tytler became the first Gurkha officer to be awarded a Victoria Cross. At the time he was 33 and had joined the Bengal Infantry fourteen years before, being posted to the 66th Native Infantry (latterly the 66th Gurkhas). He rose to command the 4th Gurkhas (originally raised in 1857) and was twice Mentioned in Dispatches. He was appointed a Companion of the Most Honourable Order of the Bath (CB) and finally led a brigade on the North-West Frontier before succumbing to pneumonia at the early age of 54.

HINDU RAO'S HOUSE

As for Jung Bahadur, he lasted for nearly another twenty years, dying in 1877. His remains, according to custom, were cremated on the banks of the holy River Baghmati. Those close ties between the Raj and Nepal survived his death, however, and Britain would be a significant beneficiary. Reid himself should be allowed the last word: 'Let every recruit who is enlisted understand that he has joined a good fighting regiment and that if he does not possess sufficient pluck to keep up the name of the regiment, he had better walk off somewhere else.'[59]

Chapter 2

Nepal: Home of the Gurkhas

A traveller's first glimpse of the beautiful valley of Nepal where beats the real pulse of the Nepalese nation ... is gained from the top of Chandragiri, a hill that serves as the southern rampart. The beautiful panorama of golden pagodas, brown temples, white edifices and red hamlets seen in a romantic setting of hill and dale remains an ineffaceable memory. Far away on the northern horizon, dominating the whole scene, rise the snow clad peaks of Dhaulagiri and Gosainthan, and in front of them a majestic series of smaller mountains, tier upon tier, in bold relief against the clear blue sky, sloping down to the very edge of the valley. Kathmandu, the capital, lies in the heart of this valley.

Frank Smythies,
Big Game Shooting in Nepal (1933)

Nepal is a trapezoidal country about 500 miles (800km) by 120 miles (200km), a total expanse of nearly 57,000 square miles (147,000 square km) – a little larger than England. The country is divided, broadly, into three differing regions, running east–west and all bisected north–south by principal river systems. In the south the lowland Terai territory borders the Indian subcontinent, forming the northern flank of the vast Indo-Gangetic Plain. Lowlands they may be, but the area is not flat and is fed by the waters of three significant rivers, the Kosi, Narayani and Karnali, and a host of lesser waterways. The climate is lush, subtropical. The Sivalik Hills, rising to Scottish 'Munro' height at about 3,000ft (1,000m), mark the limit of the great river plain stretching south, with further fertile and very similar valleys spreading north.

Next lies the Pahar, a more mountainous region but rarely snowbound, with elevations ranging from a modest 3,000ft (1,000m) to 13,000ft (4,000m). At the lower levels it is subtropical but progresses to a more alpine feel as you ascend. Its southern border flanks the lower reaches of the mighty Himalayas and it is cut with teeming river valleys, settlements getting sparser the higher up you climb. To the north is the Himal region, epic home to Everest and a dazzling array of famous mountains. The varying altitudes create five distinct climatic zones: tropical, subtropical, temperate, a cold zone and a very chilly arctic zone. Correspondingly, the country has five seasons: summer, monsoon, autumn, winter and spring.

It is the sort of place that has always appealed to Western travellers because of its remoteness and grandeur, sealed in against history – a land of rushing icy streams, clear as diamonds, dizzying ascents on narrow tracks, twisting in seemingly interminable hairpins towards some mist-shrouded Olympus. The Nepalese people conformed to the semi-romantic notion of being very 'different'.

Nepal's past is as shrouded as its hills, almost as mysterious as that of Tibet which was only really 'opened up' by Younghusband's aggressive expedition in 1904 (see Chapter 4). The idea of 'Nepal' initially occurs in the ancient Vedic period of the Indian subcontinent when Hinduism was first being preached. Several centuries BC Gautama Buddha was born in the southern Nepalese region of Lumbini. More northerly districts developed culturally akin to Tibet.

The strategic and economically significant Kathmandu Valley, however, was more influenced by Indo-Europeans. This lay on the vital umbilical route of the legendary Silk Road which imported distinctly cosmopolitan ideas. Late Vedic texts speak of the region as being an exporter of blankets, but settlement seems to date back further, to the third or fourth millennium BC. A dynasty known as the Kiratas ruled Nepal for several centuries, with a line of perhaps thirty successive monarchs. Their territory was not well defined and various clanships and petty principalities jostled for both space and supremacy. It was one of these kinships that produced Gautama Buddha (563–483 BC).[1]

Two-hundred years after the death of Buddha, what is now southern Nepal was annexed by the Maurya Empire of North India.[2] A new ruling dynasty in Nepal, the Lichhavi, succeeded the Kiratas and was entrenched by about AD 250. By the late eighth century their line was faltering, and successor dynasties took over. By the time of the High Middle Ages in Europe the Nepalese polity had fractured into as many as two-dozen petty states. In 1482, after a limited period of re-unification, three clear mini-kingdoms, Kathmandu, Patan and Bhaktapur, had emerged. Modern day Nepal was largely the creation of Prithvi Narayan Shah, a Rajput, the first ruler from Ghorka, though this small city was always overshadowed by its larger and better sited rival Kathmandu, 60 miles east in the Nepal Valley which would finally gift the country its name.

Game of Thrones

Prithvi Narayan Shah (1723–75) was destined to be the pivotal figure in creating a cohesive state from a mesh of minor princedoms. Though this process had tentatively begun in his father's day, it was he who carefully refined a strategy of planned and ruthless expansion. He was thorough, visiting India to learn from John Company, buying and stockpiling weapons. He bided his time for over a quarter of a century until his predecessor finally obliged him by dying. By this point (1742) he had built up an efficient, well-trained and well-equipped army.[3]

At this time there were some fifty odd petty kingdoms and states in what would become Nepal. Prithvi Narayan's first target was Nuwakot, lost earlier in his father's reign. Despite his careful preparations he didn't have it all his own way and his initial attempt at re-conquest in the year of his accession was humiliatingly seen off.

The following year, 1744, he was ready: having isolated Nuwakot diplomatically, he attacked with an effective three-pronged pincer movement which was successful. This was the first of many such conquests. Gradually, he extended his rule towards the key Kathmandu Valley. Though often victorious, his armies were far from invincible. Kirtipur held out firmly. He was defeated again there and badly in 1757, losing heavily. He would be back, but temporarily focused on reducing Makwanpur, the gateway between Nepal and Bengal, to ruin. The local people begged aid from the Nawab of Bengal, but Prithvi beat him then turned his attention back to Kirtipur which was finally and mercilessly battered into submission.

Terror, however, regrettably, often pays dividends and the fate of Kritapuris convinced many to throw in the towel while they could. He had to fight hard for Chaukot, a grinding battle of attrition. By 1767, he was banging on the doors of Kathmandu. Frantic appeals brought the British in, but the attempted intermeddling was a disaster for John Company. When he died, Prithvi left his heirs a kingdom, the Kingdom of Nepal – born in bloodshed, slaughter and oppression, it still survives.

Prithvi Narayan was the last ruler of the petty Ghorka principality and first sovereign of what is now known as Nepal – a united polity, albeit united by force, terror and coercion. By 1790 his successors were heading east towards Tibet. This threat woke the Chinese dragon and the emperor retaliated by sending in a massive army, defeating the Gurkhas and imposing a humiliating settlement. One consequence of this was to force successive rulers to look more to the West, the way East now firmly blocked. Nibbling at the rim of India, Prithvi's descendants were bested by the Sikhs in 1809. This failed bid brought

Gurkha and Britisher into more direct contact and inevitable collision, leading finally to the Anglo-Nepalese War of 1814–16.

The Anglo-Nepalese War

On 29 May 1814, Nepalese warriors attacked three East India Company police outposts in the Butwal District, leaving twenty native police and at least one European dead. The East India Company's frontier militia had been extending into villages from which Nepal's influential prime minister, Bim Sen Thapa, derived a significant return – his personal fiefdoms. What one side saw as consolidation, the bureaucrat's desire for drawing clean lines on a map, the other took as aggression. This attack was the culmination of a series of border incidents along a very ill-defined frontier between John Company's lands and the territory of the Kingdom of Nepal.

This untidy boundary had been a source of friction for some time and the opportunistic aggression of the Nepalese was increasingly irksome to the British. Something had to be done. If you can't send a gunboat, fetch an army; in this case 30,000 soldiers, 12,000 native auxiliaries, 60 cannon, 1,113 elephants and 3,682 camels. Moreover, and to the joy of the directors, the Prince of Oudh had contributed to the Governor, Lord Moira's[4] (later Marquess of Hastings) war chest, as an investment in anticipated gains.[5]

This wasn't just a case of Nepal flexing its muscles: the dispute was long running, and tensions had been mounting since British expansion along Oudh's borders brought the two sides into closer proximity. Moira's predecessor Lord Minto had described the Nepalese as 'insolent' and 'aggressive'.[6] In November 1814, this proud imperial force set off, a glorious spectacle of the swelling Raj, lines of red and blue with pennons waving and drums beating; an Anglo-Indian force, guns drawn by elephants and mile after mile of lumbering bullock carts humping supplies. Officers didn't travel light; a fellow would take his dress uniforms, his table linen, silver and perhaps one or several campaign wives to ease the tedium of long evenings in the field. Copious quantities of wine and spirits would be carefully crated up with crystal to swig from. There would be clouds of servants, great acres of baggage.

Four marching columns would assault this natural fortress of hill and mountain. No easy matter: the geography was as hostile as its inhabitants and this first quartet of commanders were soon found wanting. General Gillespie, who had launched his thrust from Meerut (to become infamous during the Mutiny) with 4,000 soldiers, managed to take Dehra Dun but got bogged before the walls of Kalunga. Byron Farwell describes him as 'not entirely sane'.[7] He seems to have suffered an earlier head wound which had affected his judgment, not helped by alcohol addiction.

At Kalunga, the defenders' stockade was substantial, perched on a wooded knoll and held by 600 or so locals. This was the first real head-to-head encounter between Brits and Gurkhas, and from the outset these tough hill-men commanded respect. The redcoats took significant casualties including their splenetic commander, a kind of Ben Ritchie-Hook type[8] who died alone and without mourners in a sole, suicidal charge. What everyone could agree was that these Gurkhas were seriously impressive. One young ensign wrote: 'I never saw more steadfastness or bravery exhibited in my life. Run they would not, and of death they seemed to have no fear, though their comrades were falling thick around them, for we were so near that every shot told.'[9]

Even when the place was finally so pulverised it couldn't be defended, a company-sized group of unwounded survivors staged a breakout and got clear away. The fight had cost John Company and the empire nearly 800 dead, almost double the Gurkha losses. The desperate state of the many wounded was a fearful reminder of just how murderous the combat had been.[10] Following this pyrrhic victory the invaders withdrew, they had had few successes. After regrouping, Hastings tried again in 1815, the year of Waterloo, though there was no such triumph in Nepal. The following season General David Ochterlony[11] did better, winning a major fight at Malaun. The Gurkhas, led by Amar Sing, had fought so hard that they were accorded the full honours of war; few native opponents were accorded this level of courtesy.

Finally, on 4 March 1816, a peace treaty was signed at a place called Segauli. Nepal had to concede two provinces, Kumaon and Garwhal, together with the lowland strip known as the Terai (later returned after the end of the Mutiny). Neither British nor American soldiers could serve in the Nepalese forces (they were none too keen to do so anyhow). Kathmandu had to accept, with whatever bad grace, the imposition of a resident diplomat. Most tellingly, the Raj unofficially awarded itself the right to recruit Gurkhas, and it really couldn't wait.[12] These tough, stocky Gurkhas had seriously impressed their British enemies who were about to become their new employers. Even when still at war with them, Ochterlony had favoured recruiting among the hardy and resilient hill tribes (see Chapter 3).

After losing the fight against John Company, internecine strife, massacre and murder were the order of the day in Nepal. A feud between the regnant queen and her emerging star General Jung Bahadur Kunwar (latterly known as Jung Bahadur Rana, Britain's staunch ally during the crisis of the Mutiny) was resolved by a real Night of the Long Knives – the Kot Massacre,[13] a gore-fest that saw an awful lot of blue blood being spilled. The role of a hereditary monarch was sidelined in favour of an executive prime minister, effectively presidential.

Nepal's eventual, long amity with the Raj persisted well into the twentieth century.

Latterly, Rana's rule became synonymous with decadence and oppression, economic stagnation and religious intolerance. After the Second World War pro-democracy opposition groups began to appear and India, seeing China invade and conquer Tibet, attempted to assert more direct influence in Nepal, a new front line in the simmering war between Delhi and Communist China. A form of constitutional monarchy evolved during the early 1950s, but King Mahendra reverted to absolutism in 1959. It was not until thirty years later that the reigning ruler, King Birenda, was forced to accept new reforms.

Forty years on, in the 1990s, a new communist party emerged to challenge this form of democracy, aiming to install a people's republic. This attempt kicked off another round of bloodletting which festered for a dozen years and resulted in thousands of deaths, including yet another palace cull in June 2001 when King Birenda, his queen and a clutch of fellow royals were loudly assassinated by Prince Dipendra. Ostensibly this was domestic rather than political; a bullet-riddled soap opera of frustrated hopes and ambitions. Last man standing was the dead king's brother who sacked the whole administration and took dictatorial power in order to crush those irritating communists.[14]

This engendered yet another four years of civil war with neither the Maoists nor the king and army gaining an upper hand. In 2006, the Nepalese opted for another go at democracy. Consequently, the power of the king largely evaporated, the state became formally secularised and, by May 2008, emerged as a federal republic. Several millennia of royal rule were at an end.

Until relatively recently, with the great influx of tourists following the Kathmandu trail and turning Everest base camp into an eyesore, the country was generally regarded as under-developed. Aside from the regular vendettas and murderous internecine blood-spilling, there was very little distance of surfaced roads or infrastructure. Most of what is considered modernism is as yet relatively rare, back-packing often still the main mode of moving stuff. Infant mortality, until very recently, has remained high.

Dizzying climbs, perilous rope bridges over plunging gorges – the sort beloved of Hollywood and *Shangri-La* horizons – remain the norm.

If this astonishing landscape or series of landscapes, breathtaking, dark, primeval and utterly exotic, hadn't existed, then Kipling, Rider Haggard or James Hilton[15] would have had to have magicked the place into existence. Nineteenth-century Britain was fascinated by the remoter reaches of empire; a better educated public read newspapers, journals and adventure stories and always craved more. Nepal resonates as the very expression of Victorian high adventure.

In the words of Kipling:

> That was in a most mountainous country, and our camels couldn't go along anymore because of the mountains. They were tall and black, and coming home I saw them fight like wild goats – there are lots of goats in Kafiristan. And these mountains, they never keep still, no more than the goats. Always fighting they are, and you don't sleep at night.[16]

That sons reared in the shadow of these dark and distant peaks should become such trusted and devoted servants of the Raj is not so surprising; uniquely integrated and becoming 'us' as opposed to any version of 'them'. Sepoys were generally serfs in uniform, not much thought about, but Gurkhas, almost right from the start and certainly in the wake of the Mutiny, were something quite different, 'little Britishers'. They might fight for the British but respect had to be earned and maintained.

It had only been a century earlier that young men from the dark, savage and hitherto Jacobite glens of the Scottish Highlands – to the eighteenth-century mentality, an area as wild and remote as Nepal a hundred years later – had been assimilated into the British Army, becoming redcoats not rebels and, almost overnight, figures of romance. Tartan (insofar as it had existed before Scott had commercialised Scottish history into an industry) became fashionable, from the fat, silly posturing George IV to Victoria's Highland jaunts and her intimate friendship with John Brown. Wild became fashionable, no longer subversive. The Gurkhas fitted a similar bill. Kipling did the rest.

Maps are still poor, and the Nepalese government long remained fearful of foreigners in general. Sightseeing, before the current boom, certainly into the middle of the twentieth century, wasn't encouraged. Earthquakes are not uncommon; the most recent struck savagely in April 2015, killing at least 9,000 people and injuring over 20,000 more, leaving huge devastation centred on the Ghoorka district. British Gurkhas, many of whom, of course, had family in the wrecked zone, participated in the subsequent major relief effort.[17]

The Nepalese

Who are the Gurkhas exactly? Inevitably, no one can precisely agree. As a rule, most recruits into the Raj and after Independence have derived from four principal tribal groupings:

> ... which have markedly Mongolian features; a comparatively fair, clear skin; little, if any, hair on the face or body (young men usually pluck out any facial hairs); and the most characteristic feature of all, the epicanthic fold which creates the almond-shaped eyes. Magars (pronounced 'muggers') and Gurungs are 'parbatiya'; Limbus and Rais are 'kiranti' from eastern Nepal.[18]

Magars are the largest tribal grouping, making up about 30 per cent of the overall population, primarily from agrarian stock and inhabiting the temperate zone. Eden Vansittart, who was writing for the Raj in the final years of the nineteenth century, describes the Magars as 'the basic Mongolian peasant of Central Nepal'.[19] Their social structure is complex; it is not often British encounter a society as caste-ridden as their own. There are two major social classes: upper echelons, or gentry, are sub-divided into four basic kinships; the second, yeoman class, comprises sixteen such affinities. Then there are additional clan groupings, each with its defined characteristics.[20]

Gurungs, northerly neighbours of the Magars, have a similar social structure and their particular dialect, almost a separate language, has much in common with Tibetan, generally viewed as less 'Hindu-ised' than its southerly contemporaries. Vansittart, in 1894, described both clan groups as being:

> ... intensely fond of soldiering. They are very hardy and extremely simple minded. They are kind hearted and generous and as recruits, absolutely truthful. They are very proud and sensitive, and they deeply feel abuse and undeserved censure. They are very obstinate, very independent, very vain, and in their plain clothes inclined to be dirty. They are intensely loyal to each other and their officers in time of trouble or danger.[21]

Rais and Limbus are not dissimilar. These eastern Nepalese have, or are said to possess, a different temperament to those from the west. The easterners live in more scattered hamlets, less sociable. Of Rais and Limbus, the former appear more Mongolian in appearance, although they are split into many clan groups, with ten separate languages and over seventy dialects, to the extent that it is a standing joke that every Rais has his own tongue.[22] Between the bigger septs of Rais and Limbu live the Sunwar, smaller in numbers but equally split into micro-groupings. The Tamang are also easterners, more Buddhist than Hindu but ranked as inferiors in the tribal pecking order. There are other inhabitants, including Sherpas, but as a rule these are not part of the warrior elite.

Traditionally, only 9th Gurkha Rifles drew recruits from the high-caste Rajputs, Chhetris and Thakurs, socially elevated and very different from the other tribes and clans. Their origins are probably Indian and Nepalese, and they are reputed to be very smart in appearance and intelligent. The more eastern tribes are of Mongolian descent and thought of, certainly unfairly, as less intellectually capable.

Confusingly, a Gurkha will use his first or given name then append his tribal affinity. First names are relatively few: say Ganesh (Brave), then linked to a following name which might be anglicised as 'Spirit' or 'Heart' or 'Loyal'. Parents tend to adopt an efficient if perhaps rather impersonal system of naming their offspring according to their precedence: Jetho (Oldest), Mainlo (Second), Sainto (Third).[23] This tends to confuse regimental records where service numbers are added to names to inject clarity. Gurkha wives learn their husband's military number. Idiosyncratically, Limbus never refer to their spouses by name, so if a wife is asked, she'll just give out his number.

Given how important tribal names are, recruits without any of the magic appellations would often lie and blag themselves into the fold by simply adopting one. Gyamsu Lama, who wasn't Nepali but from Sikkim in India, signed on for the Second World War with a made-up ID; recruits were needed so nobody asked too many questions. His real identity only surfaced after he had won a VC.[24]

Britain, like Rome before it, has a long history of recruiting local forces. It is what empires do, and the queen empress's domains were flung across a wide spread of the globe – all those bits that used to be coloured light pink in old British school atlases. Even once the war with Nepal was over and the notion of recruiting Gurkhas had taken hold, the country itself remained shut off. Prior to the Mutiny of 1857, British recruiting parties couldn't cross the border to visit this remote, dazzling land from which their soldiers were emerging. Rather, they had to haunt the frontier seeking to hire from porters and others found on the marches. Country fairs and markets provided good opportunities where blandishments, laced with grog, might lure forth those fancying adventure.[25]

In the eighteenth century Narayan Shah had taken a pejorative view of foreign encroachment: 'First the bible, then the trading station, then the cannon.'[26] As a one-sentence exposition of colonialism, this was fairly accurate. Despite being denied access, John Company recruiters weren't generally short of trade. Word that men were being sorted travelled inland and each battalion would appoint its own Gurkha agents, latterly called '*galla wallahs*'.[27] Kathmandu mightn't want British interlopers, but they had no objection to the regular tide of recruits going out. And they were needed. Britain's piecemeal acquisition of Indian territories, imperialism fuelled by commercialism, produced a whole series of petty brush-fire wars and alarums as gradually the whole of the vast, infinitely faceted Indian subcontinent was brought under the banners of the Raj.

Religious Festivals

Religion is important to soldiers – 'no atheists in a foxhole'[28] and all that. Nepal has a range of faith cultures. While Hinduism is perhaps the primary belief, Buddhism and primitive animism are not uncommon. In broad terms Hinduism is more prevalent in the south and Buddhism in the north, though the various genius loci are still plentiful in the streams and high peaks. Nobody is intolerant and the main 'soldier's' festival is *Dashera*,[29] held in honour of Durga, goddess of destruction in the Hindu pantheon, a manifestation of fierce and bloody Kali, so beloved by the Stranglers.[30]

It is a lengthy business, running for ten days, though the army tend to set aside less than half that time. On day one the battalion's resident Hindu religious leader, the *pandit*, would begin the festival with prayers and sowing maize, barley and rice in an enclosed, darkened space. After a week he, the priest, led out a sacred procession of soldiers bearing an effigy of the goddess, built from coloured clay and ritually smashed at the end. The column wound a slow route over the country picking flowers while, from time to time, letting go a volley of blank rounds to ensure the goddess was paying attention.

There was entertainment as well and the subadar major was major-domo, a heavy responsibility and he'd be judged critically if things didn't go as they should. Dancing, singing and drinking were all involved. This took in the whole battalion, but the real stars were the young drag artists, the prettiest recruits who dressed as girls. European officers and local bigwigs were always invited; curry and strong drink were enthusiastically consumed. At midnight, after the dancing maidens had spun coyly off, a black goat was sacrificed.[31]

British officers were expected to join in, and drink was always good for overcoming inhibitions. Some, those younger and less experienced, found the dancing boys/girls a little too convincing for ease. Next day, *Mar*, witnessed the denouement of the festival where a male buffalo was beheaded. This was an important ritual, and the beast was led out, tied to a stake, anointed, decorated with garlands and made ready. The efficacy and style of the kill was crucial. The creature had to be decapitated by a single downward cut using a heavy pioneer kukri, even better if the carcass fell forward to its knees rather than keeling over. A botched slash was very bad karma and the executioner would have to run for it. Only if the kill was precise and balletic could the soldier expect the purse full of coins and the scarf of honour. Other, less significant sacrifices followed while the blood-garnished corpse of the headless buffalo was dragged around the arena for all to applaud.[32]

The Gurkhas

It should be remembered that in an age when many British recruits were dragged from the dregs of industrial slums or from agricultural recession, when going for a soldier was more last resort than vocational choice, the Gurkha was a different breed altogether, used to coping with disaster, landslides, floods, high mortality, teamwork and a hierarchical society. Sir Francis Tuker called him honest and incorruptible. Honesty wasn't a characteristic necessarily in evidence with the British 'Tommy'. A later British commentator, Patrick Davis, who served with the Gurkhas, wrote in 1970: 'In a world where grand and petty larceny are habitual, distortion of truth and self-deceit commonplace, the honesty of the Gurkha seemed unique.'[33]

Gurkhas also have a constant sense of humour, with less of Tommy's habitual grousing. This tends to be macabre but military humour often is. Byron Farwell recounts a tale from Burma during the Second World War, when high explosive blew Gurkha Bhimbahadur into fragments. One of his comrades immediately joshed that if the deceased was hopelessly turned out in life, what would the gods do with him in six bits?[34] Gallows humour is a soldier's solace. Farwell recounts the Gurkhas' introduction to airborne warfare, not by any means a preferred choice:

> As the use of paratroops was increasing during the Malaya confrontation in the 1950s, a British colonel asked the leader of

a platoon of Gurkha if they would be prepared to jump from a C130. Somewhat to the colonel's surprise, the Gurkha sergeant requested a day to talk it over with his men. The next day, the Gurkha duly reported that they would do it, but only over marshy ground with the aircraft flying at no more than 100ft. 'But at a hundred feet the parachutes wouldn't work,' the colonel explained. The Gurkha replied, 'Parachutes? No-one mentioned parachutes!'[35]

Humour is a function of discipline and Gurkhas understand discipline: not the old force of the lash but a ready willingness to obey orders and bear hardship, born not out of fear but out of pride and self-respect. War is horror and new recruits are never prepared; most find it deeply traumatic and some can't cope at all. But the Gurkhas do; they soak it up. Their toughness, sense of pride and fellowship gets them through, apparently unscathed.

The Gurkha's physical toughness and capacity to endure is legendary. He's said to have a very thick skull: Lieutenant Swinton of 8th Gurkhas was leading a patrol in hill country along the North-East Frontier in 1890. A stray round struck firstly his orderly Gorey Thapa, ricocheted and killed the luckless young officer. Thapa had a headache.[36] He is born in poverty, often the hope and prayer of his family. It's not just he doesn't nick kit: he guards it with his life. Brigadier Mark Taversham, commanding 62nd Brigade in 1943, threw himself unthinkingly into a river when he saw one of his Gurkha Bren-gunners from 4th Battalion 4th Gurkhas go in. He had sunk to the bottom and the brigadier swimming down found out why: he was still clinging to the great heavy Bren and nearly drowned before he let go. He wasn't charged.[37]

Becoming a Gurkha

Over half a century ago when Satya Bahadur Pun enlisted with the Gurkhas they were not permitted to join directly as officers (nor can they today). After promotion through the ranks, Satya was commissioned, eventually attaining the rank of major (Queen's Gurkha Officer), which is the highest rank a Gurkha soldier could, at that time, aspire to. The rank no longer exists, and Gurkhas are commissioned as Late Entry Officer (Gurkha). On retirement, Gurkha majors are often awarded an honorary rank of Gurkha Commissioned officer (GCO). He was made a Member of the British Empire (MBE) for services in the army and Nepal.

The mountain village where Satya was born had no school and at the age of 7 arrangements were made for him to live with his uncle in the lower lying Terai, hundreds of miles from his home village, where he could attend the middle school. From such a remote region, his chances of picking up a plum civil service job (an opportunity still denied to many retired Gurkhas) were non-existent. His opportunity came when Lieutenant Colonel Langland, a British recruiting officer, came to visit Satya's uncle: 'He saw me and then he said, "If you want to join the British Army, you are most welcome, and you can see me in Paklihawa in Bhairahawa."'

Satya thought, why not? He liked playing with guns and the army certainly provided ample scope. 'I didn't discuss it with my parents because they were up on the hill in the village; I was down in Terai area, plain area, living with my uncle. My uncle said, "Okay, if you have decided, go on."' And so he, like so many other would-be recruits, trekked to the muster. A couple of lads bottled it and ran off back home, but the rest stayed the course: 'So I was in, and then I was recruited for 2nd Gurkha Rifles.'

In order to be X-rayed they had to travel east; this involved a slow journey by train, a real novelty for these boys who had hardly ever left their mountain villages before. If you got through the medicals then it was back on a train to Calcutta then, even more novel, over the dark sea to Penang and back on a train to Sungai Petani, the Gurkha Brigade's training centre in Malaysia. Satya remembers that: 'We were so many at that time; we were five companies. So, I was in Number One Company, 2 Gurkha Rifles, three hundred and fifty of us. We were lucky because there we had quite a lot of periods for education, but not that much English, only mathematics, map reading and Roman Gurkhali.' His father, who had served previously in the Indian Army, had told him it was forbidden for the recruits to speak English but those days and the Raj itself were gone. After ten months of intensive training Satya passed out top of his class and joined C Company, 1/2nd Gurkhas, based, at that time, in Singapore. They were only there for a month or so then sent off for further training. It was December 1962 and just as they were loading up their 4-tonner, fresh orders came through and they were suddenly en route to Brunei and active service.[38]

Hardly any recruits, even today, have stepped outside their own tribal boundaries or high distant valleys before joining up, even to the extent they must learn how to walk on the flat. Yet, they are serenely untroubled by the change in environment. They accept white officers, the drill, graft and bureaucracy of military life with equanimity. Why not; for them this is a culmination not a burden.

NEPAL: HOME OF THE GURKHAS

The recruiting process still begins in early spring and is sophisticated. Selection criteria are circulated via MoD websites and social media. These requirements cover educational attainment, age, height, weight and a list of the physical tests which will apply at selection. Some while later, thousands of hopefuls will trek to one of the two current centres in Nepal, Dharan in the east or Pokhara in the west. Recruitment is a fiercely competitive business; to be chosen is a point of honour, no question of this being the career choice of base necessity. Straight off, these youths are competing for a right to belong; many will come from families with an established Gurkha connection. And it has an economic impact: the wages these boys will earn as soldiers will sustain their families back home in what is still an extremely poor country.

These lads don't turn up unprepared; most will already have spent months (and their family's hard-earned savings) working hard to be fit enough. Those with no cash may have to borrow; this is an investment as well as an opportunity. Failure can be costly. Recruitment begins early at 4 a.m.: their ID and school reports ready, they're checked out for doping then inscribed with an initial registration number, originally written onto bare flesh (bibs are used now). Then it begins: a comprehensive set of tests, mental and physical. Failure means expulsion, so it is as much a test of nerves and stamina. For those who get through this, the next phase is a personal interview with both British and Gurkha officers.[39]

Quirky as this may seem, it is by the Internet that the lucky 400 receive notification. However, this is not the end: all report to Pokhara where they are in for a gruelling second round, three weeks of more physical and mental exertion and the highly competitive Doko Race over 5.8km. This is a test of endurance and grit; the recruits, as they run, hump a pannier (the '*doko*') crammed with 15kg of sand and the track is not flat or level. A last grilling and you're in or out. If you're in, you're handed over to Gurkha drill sergeants and fitted out with kit, boots and personal gear. It's square bashing, preliminary lectures then a final swearing in, and the new recruit is on his way to the UK.[40]

My own experience with men of 2 RGR comes from leading battlefield tours. They are materially different, as might be expected, to 'green' army recruits. I have always found them to be polite and courteous, attentive and respectful, even when probably bored rigid. On a tour of the Ypres Salient, Armentières and Loos battlefields in 2016, what did strike me was their willingness to be aware of their own history, the reverence they have (rightly) for their great-grandfathers who fought there and a real pride in their astonishing endurance, resilience and achievement.

Like any elite force, they were self-contained and at ease with both themselves and their surroundings; being in civvies didn't make them look less like soldiers. Many had seen action in Afghanistan, had medals to prove it and knew people who hadn't come back. Locals in Belgium didn't quite know what to make of these smart, stocky strangers. Quite a few got it straightaway and I, as a white Englishman, was surprised at the levels of casual racism I encountered on their behalf. One fat, slobby hotel clerk referred to the group as 'my' Mongols. It wasn't intended as a compliment, though the guys found it funny; after all many of them are of Mongolian stock and such petty slights just glance off.

One who got it straightaway was a northern French farmer, his acres astride the old Loos battlefield of 1915, those deadly double *crassiers* clearly in view when I asked for permission to walk over one of his fields. He readily assented and recognised the Gurkhas straightaway; a veteran of the *Régiment Etranger de Parachutistes* (part of the Foreign Legion) and the old war in Algeria, he knew a fellow elite as soon as he saw them. The 'boys' were delighted with their finds, discarded .303 cartridge cases, lumps of gnarled rusted shrapnel, scraps of webbing and even an eminently collectible fuse cap from an 18-pounder. History does have this habit of coming around.

Chapter 3

'Hillbilly Napoleons'

> For the warrior there is nothing more
> Blessed than lawful strife
> Happy the warriors who find such a strife
> Coming unsought to them as an open
> Door to Paradise
>
> *Bhagavad-Gita II*, 31 and 32

First Recruits

Half a century before the epic events at Hindu Rao's House, such an impression had been made on the British by the Gurkhas in the Anglo-Nepalese War that recruitment started immediately. A first attempt, however, did not work out as well as anticipated. Lieutenants Ross (6th Native Infantry) and Young (13th Native Infantry)[1] raised a frontier force with soldiers from Garwhal[2] and Kumaon[3] who, while not entirely dissimilar, were not strictly Gurkhas. They fled at the first shot. Lieutenant Young, who was determined not to suffer the same shame, stood fast and was captured. It was his defiance that won the respect of the Gurkhas who affirmed they *would* fight under such brave officers.

During his time as a POW, Young came more and more to admire his enemy. The Governor General Lord Hastings, even before the war was over, on 24 April 1815, authorised the recruitment of a Gurkha battalion. Many were now to hand, banged up in the Company's POW compounds, and Young soon had his complement. The men were raised at Sirmoor, near Dehra Dun; thus they became the Sirmoor Battalion (latterly the 2nd King Edward's Own Gurkha Rifles). Young himself would be their first CO and would hold that position for no less than twenty-eight years.[4]

Another couple of ad hoc units also came into existence: the Kumaon Battalion, despite their unpromising start, and another friendly native unit recruited from the Simla Hills. Soon these two were amalgamated to form 1st Gurkha Rifles. A second Kumaon battalion began recruiting in 1815, the 3rd Gurkha Rifles. These newly raised units, as mentioned previously, were formed into 8 companies, each about 120 strong with a British commandant and adjutant. John Company, ever mindful of the burden on shareholders, reminded Hastings that they expected these new battalions to be disbanded as soon as might be expedient.[5] That never happened, nor has it yet. The 'Hillbilly Napoleons', as British Army slang affectionately termed its Nepalese fighters, are here to stay.

At first, aside from initial recruitment, the 'peace' dividend for John Company was muted. Kathmandu wasn't looking for any kind of relationship, smarting over the humiliation of their defeat, and the government there was thoroughly immersed in its habitual in-fighting. The ice began to thaw when Bhim Sen Thapa, who had been the instigator of the original border fracas, was finally ousted twenty years later,[6] but it wasn't until the rise of Jung Bahadur Rana that it finally melted. But 'Johnny Gurkha', as an individual, was enthusiastic in his service. He wore a pillbox hat with a uniform of rifle green, collared and cuffed in red. He enjoyed soldiering; it was a natural and easy transition. He fought, in the Sirmoor Battalion, against Mahrattas and Pindaris from 1817–19 but he was still seen as just another brand of sepoy, the hired help. He wasn't 'us' to the British, not yet.

In Bandit Country

The British in India were having bother with dacoits,[7] lots of it in fact.[8] On 2 October 1824, the resident magistrate at Saharanpur requested military assistance. In addition to robbing convoys, a large gang of outlaws had seized an old fort at Koonja in the south-eastern part of his district, at least 800 of them under 2 gang-leader brothers, Kulwa and Bhoora. They had instigated a reign of terror, and something had to be done. Frederick Young, with two companies drawn from the Sirmoor Battalion, was just the man to do that something.

When the detachment had marched as far as Saharanpur, they picked up a unit of police and another 150 Gurkhas with a couple of willing volunteers: Lieutenant Debude, a sapper and young botanist turned adventurer, and Dr John Forbes Royle.[9] After a forced march of 36 miles in only 12 hours they arrived in sight of the fort. The dacoits, aware of the intrusion, were waiting with an extended skirmish line deployed along the frontage of the village. The fort with its high walls of mud brick occupied the northern part of the settlement.

Greeted by a ragged volley, Young ordered his men to dump their packs and advance in battle order. The bandits got that message pretty quickly and scampered back into their redoubt. So far, so good; but the Gurkhas had no big guns or any manner of siege equipment. The parapets were manned by sharpshooters armed with long-barrelled matchlocks, old and slow but deadly enough in the right hands. Young ordered a handy tree cut down (kukris made good pioneer tools) and, slung on ropes, the timber beam made an effective ad hoc ram. Lieutenant Debude and Frederick Shore, the superintendent from Dehra Dun,[10] guided the battering with Gurkhas swinging the ropes.[11]

As their muskets gave covering fire the assault team went into action, hammering a wedge into the heavy iron-bound gates. Only two men could get in at once. Young was first through, next a brace of Gurkhas, then Shore with the rest of the attack group. Straight off it was hand to hand. Shore cut down one bandit about to slash Young's neck. An instant later the superintendent was facing a huge bandit, intent on carving him into very small pieces. Young opened fire with his double-barrelled Manton pistol. The first chamber misfired but – demonstrating the advantage of having two – the second one dropped the dacoit, though Shore still took a nasty cut.[12]

Piling in through the breach, Gurkhas were stabbing with their long triangular bayonets and hacking with kukris, spraying bright arterial blood from screaming bandits. The rest were, by now, seeking safer residence elsewhere, leaping from the high walls. One, it is said begged for his life, stuffing grass into his mouth, a gross humiliation for any Hindu, so profound was his fear. It didn't do him any good.[13] Leaving bayonet squads to flush out any survivors inside the fort, Young took more to beat the dense fields of waving sugarcane, killing another score of dacoits.

Over 150 were dead in the wreckage, 30 more in chains. Kulwa the bandit-king was dethroned; dead, though his brother got away, at least for long enough to die of his wounds. The Gurkhas lost five men killed and thirty-three injured. Soon Kulwa's head was swinging in the breeze in a cage above the gateway of the gaol at Dehra Dun as a warning to others. A pair of small cannon lifted from the fort at Koonja stayed as trophies of 2nd Gurkhas, last seen guarding the barracks in Hong Kong. Young included in his after-action report a comment that none of the many women inside the bandit fortress had been molested.[14]

Army of the Free – The Khalsa

It would be another twenty years before the Gurkhas were back in serious action, this time in the Punjab against the Sikhs, whose renowned 'Army of the

Free', the Khalsa, had launched a pre-emptive strike across the Sutlej River.[15] A wide triangular land, the Punjab extended in the north-east as far as the foothills of the Himalayas, and south and west to the confluence of two great river systems, the Sutlej and Indus. The flat, fertile land was watered by another four major streams. The Punjab was key to India's security but during the early decades of the nineteenth century was a free and independent state. Though dominant, the Sikhs made up only about a sixth of the population, the rest being Punjabi Muslims and Hindus.

Sikhism had begun as a Hindu sect in the fifteenth century, initially dedicated to peace. That didn't last within 200 years and, under relentless pressure from Islam, the Sikh people geared up for aggression and made a particularly good job of it. Soon they had thrown off any prior allegiance to Afghan warlords and by 1793 their territory had fully expanded. It was the great leader Ranjit Singh, a brilliant and dissolute maverick, who made them powerful. He became Maharajah of Lahore and built up a professional military elite trained by French and Italian Napoleonic veterans. He still found time to maintain a hedonist division of concubines and catamites. In spite of his achievement, when he died in 1839, there was no able successor, and the vacuum produced a slew of murderous internecine rivalries.

One of his many sons by many wives, a boy of 6, became nominal ruler whilst his mother Rani Jindan assumed the regency. But it was the army who called the shots and emptied the treasury. Jindan's equally greedy and degenerate brother Jawahir Singh made himself treasurer or vizier, but the Khalsa soon tired of his excesses and he was spectacularly and very publicly bayoneted in front of his screaming sister and her child. Overall, the civilian polity was not overly concerned about taking on the British, viewing the army as the greater threat.

It was the Sikhs who had, earlier in the century, blocked any further westward expansion by the Nepalese. Their army of over 50,000 included about 1,500 Gurkha mercenaries organised in 2 battalions. There is no evidence that these men ever fought against Anglo-Indians during either of the Sikh wars that followed. In March 1837, the Governor General Sir Henry Vane had attended a royal wedding, that of one of Ranjit Singh's grandsons, in Lahore. Despite the pomp and opulence, Vane could see that the Punjab could become a running sore, a back door into British India, though at that time the Raj had little or no appetite for more acquisitions; besides the Khalsa was formidable, well-armed, trained and equipped with plenty of guns.

Ranjit Singh's death and the instability that followed turned ripples of alarm into floods. Vane's successor Sir Henry Hardinge reluctantly geared up for war and Sikh aggression led the Khalsa, already stirring up discontent among John Company's sepoys, to get in the first punch, moving troops up to the demarcation line of the Sutlej. On 11 December 1845, their lead units splashed across and the First Sikh War was on. Both the Nasiri and Sirmoor battalions were rushed in to beef up Indian Army forces and soon thrown into the fight to retake the key supply base at Ludhiana.

Sir Hugh Gough, a peppery old soldier never given to subtlety, was put in command and, during the campaign, fought a quartet of slogging battles, all of which were narrow British victories won at considerable cost. No Gurkhas fought at Mudki or Ferozeshah.

In January 1846, Sir Harry Smith was leading a detached force, some 10,000, which clashed with a superior force of Sikh troops at the small village of Aliwal. During this battle, the Sirmoor Battalion, commanded by Lieutenant Colonel John Fisher, was first into the enemy trenches, spiking their artillery (Sikh artillerymen were as tough at their infantry and fought their guns to the death). The melee was intense and bloody; the battalion's colours were lost when the ensign went down but a section led by Havildar Badal Sing Thapa got them back, earning him an IOM. Lachhiman Sarki was made up to subadar for taking out one of the guns but died from wounds before he could enjoy his promotion.[16]

By 10 February, Gough, substantially reinforced, was ready to take on the strong Sikh defences at Sobraon. These were extraordinarily strong. Along a curving line of 3,000yd with their backs to the river, the Sikhs had dug in with three lines of trenches, studded with guns. Their reserves were mustered on the far bank, connected by a pontoon bridge. Some officers argued that Gough, with only half those numbers, should try to outflank the redoubt, but that wasn't his style: he preferred to kick in the front door.

What he had seen was that the right flank of the enemy line was weakest and, oddly, manned by largely second-rate units. He therefore proposed to mount his main thrust here and only feint at the centre and left. He had enough guns for a massive bombardment, which commenced at 8.30 a.m., but not sufficient ammunition. It ran out in just under 2 hours so both infantry and cavalry attacked without artillery support.[17]

On the right General Dick's division made progress but this soon stalled in the face of determined counterattacks and rapidly mounting losses. Gough pressed home the diversions in an attempt to ease the pressure on his left but these assaults also ground to a halt in the face of withering, well-directed fire. However, the all-out assault all along the line did force the Sikhs to divert men from their right to shore up the centre. The embattled wing gave way soon after in the face of a renewed British-Indian lunge and the whole line began to crumble and then dissolve. Hundreds were shot down as they broke, many more drowned as they swamped the pontoon. In all they lost perhaps 10,000 while British dead totalled just 320, though 2,000 at least were wounded.

During the deadly slogging match, a full quartet of Gurkhas won the IOM – though Colonel Fisher was killed in action, as were 144 of his men from the Sirmoor Battalion. The Nasiri lost only seven dead and seventy-seven wounded. It speaks volumes about the ferocity of the fight that ten IOMs were awarded. One of these was to Subadar Major Jase Rajput – he also became the first Gurkha soldier ever to be photographed.

General Gough, as hard-bitten a professional soldier as ever breathed, was impressed enough to write:

> I must now pause in this narrative especially to notice the determined hardihood and bravery with which our two battalions of Gurkhas, the Sirmoor and Nasiri, met the Sikh whenever they were opposed to them. Soldiers of small stature and indomitable spirit, they vied in ardent courage in the charge with the Grenadiers of our own nation and, armed with the short weapon of their mountain, were a terror to the Sikhs throughout the great combat.[18]

By now the Khalsa had had enough and the Treaty of Lahore was signed off in March. The Sikhs were hit by swingeing reparations, stripped of some borderlands with a deep pale or frontier zone being established. The Punjab was tamed and partly occupied but not annexed, more reduced to the status of a client state. Needless to say, this did not sit well with the army, simmering from its humiliation and degradation. In April 1848, tensions boiled over, and two political agents were hacked to death while their local escort stood idly by. It was war again and this time the Punjab finally fell to the Raj – no Gurkha units fought this time though.

Chapter 4

Kipling's Wars

> My thoughts return to you who were my comrades, the stubborn and indomitable peasants of Nepal. Once more I hear the laughter with which you greeted every hardship. Once more I see you in your bivouacs or about your camp fires, on forced march or in the trenches, now shivering with wet and cold, now scorched by a pitiless and burning sun. Uncomplaining you endure hunger and thirst and wounds; and at the last your unwavering lines disappear into the smoke and wrath of battle; bravest of the brave, most generous of the generous ...[1]
>
> R.L. Turner (1931)

Though Great Britain's global empire didn't reach its peak, in terms of territories, until the 1920s, its heyday was during the nineteenth century. India was the 'jewel in the crown', glowing with what seemed like timeless lustre when Disraeli cannily elevated Queen Victoria to empress. Serene as this imperial canvas appeared, there had always been cracks, fissures which would begin to spread in the unhappy, restless aftermath of the First World War. Victoria's wars were to keep the Gurkha forces remarkably busy.

A Very Rough Neighbourhood

The North-West Frontier, steeped in romance, particularly for those who have never been there, has consistently been a very rough neighbourhood. John Masters[2] was there as a very green subaltern in 1937:

> As the conquering British, more than a hundred years ago moved diagonally across India from their original trading posts in Surat, Calcutta and Madras, they eventually reached the mountains that

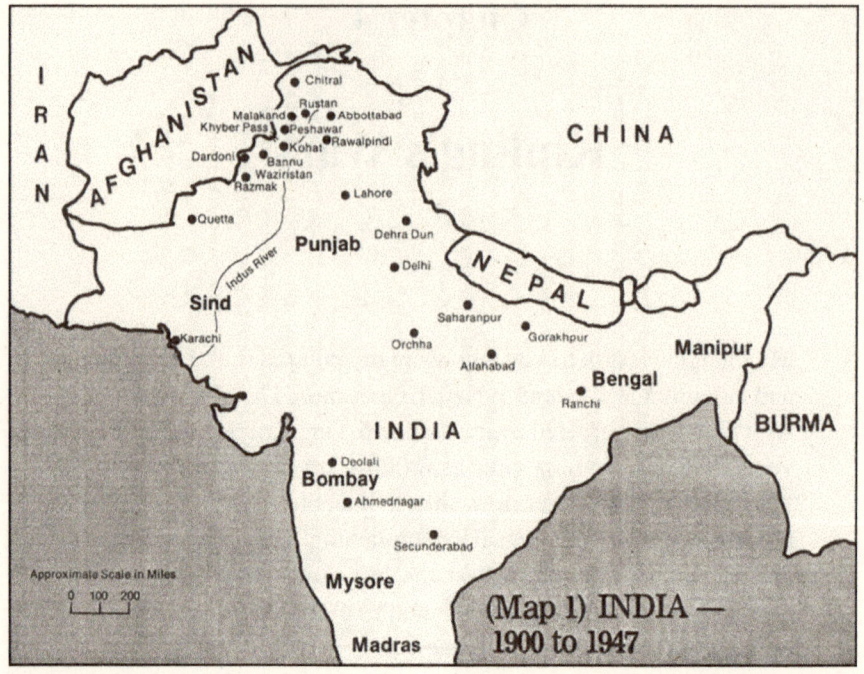

Map 2. Nepal and the North-West/North-East Frontiers, 1839–1900.

separate the sub-continent from Afghanistan. These mountains extend four hundred miles from the Khyber Pass in the north to the Bolan Pass in the desert of Baluchistan to the south. They are raw and bare and a proudly independent people live in them. These people, Semitic in origin, Moslem in religion Pushtu in speech, are the Pathans ...[3]

These tough and fractious hill-men lived along the broad spine of a border that runs like a surgical cut down the length of high ground. They were no respecters of formal frontiers, steeped in the savage realities of asymmetrical warfare centuries before the term was first coined. They were semi-nomadic, semi-pastoral and always contentious. Raiding the soft plains on either side of the line was a hallowed and profitable custom. Add into the mix a slew of deadly feuds and vendettas, regularly stirred, and the Pathans are a fastidious imperialist's nightmare, especially as the exact line of the border could never be precisely agreed. The tribesmen didn't really care anyway. All commercial traffic passing through the great mountain barrier, and there was a lot of it, via the high passes and river valleys, had to pay their tolls or suffer the consequences.

It was dangerous and forbidding country. Europeans would stick out a mile, as Kipling discovered: 'Carnehan leaned down and shook hands. Then the camels passed away along the dusty road, and I was left alone to wonder ... there was just the chance Carnehan and Dravot would be able to wander through Afghanistan without detection. But beyond they would find death – certain and awful death.'[4]

While the colonial administration could simply seek to occupy the whole contentious belt of hills and keep a lid on the locals, this was easier said than done, vastly expensive and most unlikely to succeed. Moreover, this could only work on the British-controlled side of the divide, never over the border in Afghanistan where whatever passed for central authority had no currency whatsoever among the Pathans. This was a Hadrian's Wall job, and it was estimated the campaigning would have cost 20,000 casualties and taken a decade to achieve – if it could ever be accomplished at all.[5]

The next alternative was to write the mountains off and fall back to the eminently defensible line of the Indus, but that meant leaving a wild marcher realm beyond and an equally large garrison would be needed. And – a very big 'and' too – there was always the Russian bear to worry about. He was long suspected of wanting to get his claws into India, and Afghanistan was his preferred axis of advance. The ambitious Romanovs had been steadily expanding their territories eastwards across the limitless horizons of steppe since the start of the century. With huge armies at their beck, the threat was tangible.[6]

A compromise, never ideal, was worked up: the British created an administrative border with tribal districts, varying in depth from 10 miles (16km) to 100 (161km): a pale or buffer zone run by the tribes but with a series of strategic outposts guarding key choke points. These were linked by a road network with a de-militarised strip 100yd (91m) wide on either side. Tribal leaders were buttered up with hefty bungs, dependent on toeing the line. Any pious hopes that the Pathans might be converted into model citizens along European lines soon disappeared. This would always be an armed frontier with the spectre of conflict bubbling away, regularly bursting into flames of varying intensity.[7]

Beyond the Khyber

Then there was Afghanistan itself. The British and their allies have an unfortunate relationship with that wild, ungovernable country. The first intervention from 1839–42, aimed at regime change, ended in catastrophe – Britain's worst defeat in the nineteenth century (Gurkhas weren't involved in this campaign). Elphinstone Bey's grandly named Army of the Indus endured a nightmare retreat from Kabul which cost the lives of 4,700 soldiers, mainly native troops, and uncounted thousands of camp followers. Dr William Brydon was the only man to make it out, reeling and frozen on a half-dead horse which stumbled into Jalalabad on 13 January 1842. It was a dire precedent and Afghanistan would be the graveyard for many of Kipling's 'Tommies':

> When you're wounded and left on Afghanistan's plains
> And the women come out to cut up what remains
> Jest roll to your rifle and blow out your brains
> An' go to your Gawd like a soldier.[8]

Once the embers of Mutiny had been stamped out in 1858 with serious vindictiveness – the war, as discussed, was characterised by terrible atrocities on both sides – John Company was shoved aside, and the Crown took over direct rule of India. This was a key moment, the real birth of the Raj as such rather than a fief of private enterprise. As for the Gurkhas, after their Homeric defence of Hindu Rao's House, their stock was running high:

> The loyalty and obedience of the Gurkhas became the subject of several studies and official reports after the collapse of the Indian Mutiny. It was noticed, for example, that although desertion was commonplace in the armies of Europe, and that mercenary forces like the French Foreign Legion suffered dramatically from it, it was virtually unknown in Gurkha regiments ... Theft and dishonesty were virtually unknown, and to be wrongly accused of them caused great consternation. The Gurkhas also showed none of the anguish usually evident among new recruits confronted for the first time with the blood and guts of battle, nor with the hardships of forced marches, rough terrain and the necessity to kill your own food if you wanted to eat.[9]

Mostly in Rifles' green, though the Malaun Battalion clung to their prized red coats (taken from disaffected Bengal Native Infantry) until as late as 1888, they were climbing towards elite status. Three years later all Gurkha regiments were designated as Rifles.[10] They wouldn't be under-employed. The nascent Gurkha Brigade of four battalions would soon be strengthened by a fifth, the

Hazara – an amalgamation of several ad hoc frontier outfits, formerly the 25th Punjab Infantry (raised in 1858). They would spend very nearly a century on the frontier and win seven VCs there.[11]

Their accumulated skills would be desperately needed; the Pathans were tremendous adversaries. Like cats, they could infiltrate as though invisible and lift a rifle or slit a throat unseen and unheard. After all, they had had plenty of practice. Life on the frontier was hard, mostly tedious but always dangerous. Caravans and columns had to be guarded. Gurkhas would be flung out on point along high ridges overshadowing dark passes. You were never safe, and the enemy was patient, infinitely, almost inhumanly so. He'd wait until the last moment when the picquets were withdrawing, poised like a cobra. So, forming up as the rear-guard was always very risky, the enemy waiting like vultures to swoop. It was handy if some mountain guns were deployed as they could plaster the last position, ideally just as the tribesmen slid forward.[12]

In 1860 one of those brush-fire wars, the Mahsud Waziri Campaign, flared up.[13] A Gurkha officer, Captain Charles Keys, duelled in the open with a Waziri champion and felled him, leading to the hasty withdrawal of a substantial enemy force.[14] This fight was straight from Dumas, heroes banging it out in front of the armies. Young English gentlemen were taught swordsmanship as a matter of course; the dominance of small arms and artillery on the battlefield did not remove the impetus for individual prowess and showing skill at arms. Aggressive as they were, the Pathans liked a good scrap and shows of manly skill at arms; so, by and large did the Raj. Myths are made this way.

Four years later the 3rd Gurkhas (originally the Kumaon Battalion) served in a punitive campaign in remote Bhutan,[15] skirmishing through virgin forest and infested marshland; in such places and remote, forgotten little wars were the prestige and security of the Raj preserved. Gurkhas, at least those in British service, had moved far beyond the closeted realm of their mountain home onto a very much broader canvas. They had become an organic part of the huge edifice of Britain's global empire, the grandest since Rome.

Meanwhile, in Nepal, Jung Bahadur Rana was still going almost strong. In 1875 he planned another state visit to England but was laid low by a riding accident. Queen Victoria sent out her son Bertie, the future King Edward VII, instead, who enjoyed tiger shooting in the Terai. This was the apogee of the imperial dream, a magnificent if in modern terms reprehensible spectacle, an almost medieval pageant of extreme blood sport with the hunter, if he wasn't careful, ending up as the hunted. Topi-wearing sportsmen swayed in elephant-borne howdahs with a small army of beaters driving the great predators onto heavy calibre express rifles. Two years later the queen herself was promoted to full empress, a cunning flattery from Disraeli. Jung Bahadur would have thoroughly approved, though he died before the fireworks were over.[16]

The Great Game

By now a series of recruiting stations had been set up in India to supply the four regular battalions: for the 1st at Dharmsala, the 2nd at Dehra Dun, 3rd at Almora and 4th at Bakloh. Service in the Gurkhas was popular as forces of the Raj they were fast becoming indispensable. Just as well, since serious trouble was brewing with the Russians. The Great Game, high-stakes poker across a huge swathe of central Asia, was a constant factor in British nineteenth-century imperial policy and fears over Russian intentions ran deep. This perceived menace had sparked the ill-judged intermeddling in Afghanistan in 1839; a generation on these fears, never really dormant, would once again re-awaken.

In 1878 at the Congress of Berlin, Britain and Russia had signed an accord which was intended to remove tensions between these two grand European superpowers. That just shunted the problem eastwards. In July, the Russians bullied their way into Kabul demanding that the emir, Sher Ali Khan, accept a permanent residency. Sher Ali was unable, or perhaps just unwilling, to resist. The British Governor of India Lord Lytton riposted by demanding he also accept a British residency, but the party only got as far as the Khyber Pass before being ignominiously turned back. This wouldn't do at all and on 21 November the Raj went to war in Afghanistan, again.[17]

Sir Frederick Roberts ('Bobs'),[18] who had won his VC during the Mutiny, would lead three marching columns, striking towards Kabul through the Khyber and Peiwar passes. The 3rd Gurkhas were ordered up from Almora as early as 10 October; a long slow trail by road, rail and steamer reaching the Indus south of Quetta five days after war had been declared. They trekked over 200 miles across the arid Dera Bugti Desert in Baluchistan, a long sinuous column of marching men with an endless tail of camels carrying kit and supplies, straining bullocks heaving cumbersome 40-pounders. These hefty Armstrong guns weighed in at 32 hundredweight (1,626kg) and were immensely difficult to move over such bad ground. The beasts foundered in that baking, furnace heat and the Gurkhas themselves had to manhandle the monsters; they didn't founder.[19]

Through the Bolan Pass lay the valley of Pishin and the Khoja Amran Range, opening up the southern route to mystical Kandahar, second city of the country, standing on the Arghandab River 3,000ft (1,000m) up. Initially, the terrain proved more trouble than the local inhabitants who were concentrating on blocking Roberts' own column. This apparent calm didn't last.

In concert with the 72nd Highlanders (the Seaforths), 5th Gurkhas stormed hostile heights, the Spingawai Kotal, in a daring night assault one dark and stormy evening. Confused fighting raged, kukris and broadswords together doing some serious killing. The enemy broke and the position was taken. There is a certain historical irony in that Gurkhas had initially fought so hard against the British Crown, as had many of the great-grandfathers of the Highlanders; those who had come out for Bonnie Prince Charlie in 1745–6 and suffered the price of treason. A decade later, as previously mentioned, Pitt the Elder had the clever notion of recruiting these difficult hill-men to fight for him and King George. It worked just as well as recruiting Gurkhas.[20]

* * *

'If it's a miracle, it's a Boxer Henry .577/.450 miracle!' Thus, the late Stanley Baker, playing Lieutenant John Rouse Chard in the 1964 blockbuster *Zulu* – a film that inspired me and a whole schoolboy generation – ascribes the epic win at Rorke's Drift in the 1879 Anglo-Zulu War to the proficiency and stopping power of the Martini–Henry Rifle.[21] This was a dropping block action, purpose-built breech-loader which entered service in 1871 and had a long career. This was the first true breech-loader the British and thus the Gurkhas ever used.

It replaced the earlier Snider Conversion which, though ingenious and effective, was essentially a War Department bodge. The Martini fired the Boxer Henry round which had a longer range than its predecessor and was far more accurate. Probably as many as a million were built and the clever gunsmiths along the North-West Frontier were soon turning out bespoke copies of variable quality.[22]

Firepower would be needed in Afghanistan. The next obstacle in the march to Kabul was the Reiwar Kotal Ridge, a natural defensive line and a tough proposition. Roberts found 18,000 enemy infantry backed by 11 guns lining the escarpment which stands at nearly 9,500ft (2,865m). Major John Cook staged several charges leading both 5th Gurkhas and Seaforths against ad hoc but effective Afghan abbatis (improvised timber defences with bristling sharpened points facing outwards). Next dawn the Afghans had pretty much cleared out but a determined party stayed, trying to recover one of their cannon. With a scratch force, Cook charged them and in the ensuing scrap, saved Major Galbraith, Assistant Adjutant General, from the attentions of a very determined enemy marksman. Cook was awarded the VC, and according to his citation:

> ... during very heavy fire, Captain Cook charged out of the entrenchments with such impetuosity that the enemy broke and fled, when perceiving at the close of the melee, the danger of Major Galbraith who was in personal conflict with an Afghan soldier, Captain Cook distracted his attention to himself and aiming a sword cut which the Douranee avoided, sprang upon him and grasping his throat, grappled with him. They both fell to the ground. The Douranee, a most powerful man, still endeavouring to use his rifle, seized Captain Cook's arm in his teeth until the struggle was ended by the man being shot through the head.[23]

Another five Gurkhas were also awarded IOMs in the fighting. Cook's luck ran out in December 1879. By then he was a major and led one charge too many, dying of his wounds.

Meanwhile things had changed in Kabul. The Russians had decamped and Sher Ali, obligingly, had died. His son and successor Yakub Khan appeared, outwardly anyway, more amenable and terms for a ceasefire were signed off at Kabul on 26 May. Sir Louis Cavagnari was duly installed as resident and lasted till September when he and his personal bodyguard of Guides were wiped out in a concerted attack on the residency[24] (rather poorly chosen as it turned out for defence, which should always be a prime consideration in Afghanistan).

Both 5th Gurkhas and Highlanders (Gordons this time) were soon back at the sharp end as part of a field force aiming to relieve Kandahar and re-take Kabul. On 6 October, the British fought and won a battle at Charasiab,[25] a small town only 7½ miles (12km) south of the capital, opening the road. Yakub Khan was more than implicated in the destruction of Cavagnari's diminutive force and Afghans had besieged a small British garrison in the Sherpur Cantonment, near the capital. Yakub was duly de-selected and his cousin Abdur Rahman set up in his place; musical regime change.

This proved seriously contentious. Yakub's brother Ayub, Governor of Herat, now threw his cap in the ring and rebelled. He succeeded in inflicting a sharp defeat on the British at Maiwand in July 1880, obliging Roberts to undertake his famed march from Kabul to Kandahar where his fast-moving column covered over 300 miles in a score of days – pretty good going over such difficult ground – and then trounced Ayub's forces in the battle for Kandahar.

Earlier in April 1880, at the Second Battle of Charasiab, 3rd Gurkhas had avoided another disaster when the column they were with, en route from Kandahar to Kabul, led by a Colonel Jenkins, was attacked by Afghan horsemen, Logaris from that easterly province, and mainly Pushtu. The Gurkha

Commandant, Colonel H.H. Lyster VC, ordered his men to form square and see off the insurgents. With customary elan and backed by artillery support, they did just that.[26] Five months later hostilities were finally ended by the Treaty of Gandamack. The Gurkhas had added lustre to their laurels during this difficult and deadly campaign; to the British they were now very much 'us'.

Captain Ernle Money of the 11th Bengal Lancers, the epitome of a stylish and dashing regiment, enthused in a letter home: 'You have no idea what fine little fellows the Gurkhas are, they actually do not know what fear is. They have throughout the campaign behaved gloriously. Everyone admits that they have, as a body, marched and fought better than anyone – no matter who …'[27] He clearly influenced his son who would, in due course, come to command 4th Gurkhas. Captain Money wasn't the only one to be impressed. Roberts, 'Bobs', was equally enamoured of his mountain men from opposing sides of the globe: 'You beat them at Kabul, and you have beaten them at Kandahar and now you are about to leave the country you may be assured that the very last troops the Afghans ever want to meet in the field are Scottish Highlanders and Gurkhas.'[28]

Barely were they clear of Afghanistan's plain when 3rd Gurkhas were back in action against fractious clans in Baluchistan. Five years after the end of the Second Afghan War there were still rumbling alarums over Russia's menacing attentions. Roberts, by now Commander in Chief India, proposed to recruit more Gurkha battalions, a second for each of the five Gurkha regiments then in service. In Nepal, Jung's nephew Bhir Shamsher was in charge. His preference was just to hire out his own forces as mercenaries, keeping a firm hand on the cashflow, but 'Bobs' bought him off with gold and supplies, setting up new recruiting centres at Ghoom near Darjeeling, west of Nepal and at Gorakhpur, south. There was no shortage of takers.

That Other Frontier

Trouble next arose on the North-East Frontier where King Thibaw Min of Burma,[29] last ruler of the Konbaung Dynasty (Myanmar) and last Burmese sovereign, was leaning rather too much towards the French – never acceptable in British eyes – and was oppressing British trading interests in-country. This led to a march upon Mandalay, the capture and deposing of Thibaw and north Burma being annexed directly by the British Crown. Counterinsurgency tied up both 3rd Gurkhas and the nascent 8th Battalion, formed of new drafts from a Bengal Native Infantry Regiment, for over a year. This was pretty grim sapping work: no glories to be harvested, just a steady attrition of outposts.

Such brush-fire conflicts on the fringes of empire were now the Gurkhas' stock-in trade. Imperial expansion brought the Raj on both North-West and North-East frontiers into potential conflict with independent tribes who weren't used to central authority being imposed on them and didn't care much for it. Ground was usually difficult: tall mountains with soaring peaks and narrow passes; high-up belts of dense woodland; fly-infested swamps; little or no infrastructure – pretty much what Gurkhas were used to.

One legacy of their service with Highlanders in Afghanistan was the Scottish pipes – Gurkhas took on both pipes and drums. By 1888 the 3rd Battalion was forming its own pipe band and would-be pipers were sent off for half a year to learn the art from Highland masters. Such legacies persist today; 7 GR wear Douglas tartan and 10 GR Hunting Stewart. Additional lingering relics feature on Gurkha hats and badges, RGR officer's tropical mess kit, pipes and drums. Regimental affiliations with the Gurkhas Highland brethren have also carried on.[30]

A year later Gurkhas were dispatched across the very heavens to the borders of Tibet, a far-flung, remote and largely unknown region. Their own pipers played them on the road, but this wasn't an invasion, just a recce in force. It was suspected that the Tibetans, none too keen on visitors at the best of times, were setting up defences at Niti on the British side. For three weeks the Gurkhas marched, up dizzying heights reaching up almost beyond the clouds to 18,000ft (5,486m). When they got there it was nothing, a false alarm – all the Tibetans were building were shelters for travellers. No need to fix bayonets. The Gurkhas felt cheated.[31]

The Gurkha forces at this point were far from finished with the North-West Frontier. In August 1895, the British lost their tenuous grip on the vital umbilical connection of the Khyber. Local tribes, Afridis and Orakzais, inhabited a wild district of the Tirah, a dark corner of a dim frontier, south-west of the Peshawar Valley. These were targeted for retribution after the Afridis, who had been paid by the administration to provide a frontier force guarding the pass, collectively went AWOL and seized control for themselves.[32]

A very substantial force, 35,000 soldiers, 20,000 and more assorted camp followers and a vast baggage train of biblical proportions, all under General Sir William Lockhart commanding the Punjab Army Corps, was assembled. It was a pretty big undertaking; the rebel tribes were numerous, perhaps collectively able to field over 40,000 warriors, and they knew every inch of the ground. Base camp was the fort and outpost at Kotal on the frontier rim where the army was concentrated, a hybrid of imperial scarlet, rifle green and all those riotous colours of the bazaar, about to fight over the inhospitable and intensely hostile roof of the world.[33]

It was a thoroughly nasty little war. The locals were too canny to take the British head-on but made full use of the ground for ambush, sniping and outpost-raiding. Unable to land a blow on their wily opponent who clung to every vantage point and narrow ascent, of which there were many, the army resorted to scorched earth, destroying hilltop villages, lifting livestock and waging a war of attrition. It was on 18 October 1897 that the huge lumbering column got started. First blocking positions were on the epic Dargai Heights. These were taken with ease but couldn't be held through lack of water. Next time, on 20 October, they would have to be recovered the hard way.

This unenviable task fell to the Gordon Highlanders ('Dargai Day') and 2nd Gurkhas. Together they stormed the heights. Subadar Kirparam Thapa of 2/2nd Gurkhas was first into the enemy's rifle pits and, overall, four VCs were won.[34] The enemy was well prepared and dug in, his rifles sighted on the belt of exposed ground the attackers must cross to gain the goat track leading to the heights proper. A forlorn hope drawn from 1/2nd and 1/3rd Gurkhas, commanded by Lieutenant A.B. Tillard, led the sprint. They got across but the Afridis laid down heavy fire which prevented reinforcements from getting up, a real no-man's-land situation. Nearly a hundred men were lost; Tillard's vanguard were pinned down short of the summit until the Gordons and 3rd Sikhs, the Highlanders' pipes skirling 'Cock of the North', rushed the gap and swarmed up the slope.[35]

The heights were taken but at a cost of nearly 200 casualties among the attacking units. Gurkhas had made more Highland friends and it was the Highlanders who helped carry their many wounded down the precipitous slopes to the forward aid stations. This blossoming friendship matured during the difficult campaign and has persisted ever since.

Every key feature was contested. On 29 October the expeditionary force had to claw its way through the Sampagla Pass, then two days later encountered another at Arhanga. Having finally broken into the Tirah Valley, brigade columns scoured the harsh land, demolishing forts and destroying settlements. It was very inglorious, and every move was tracked by marksmen, every rear-guard attacked. Casualties were never heavy but mounted rapidly in the steady, unrelenting attrition. Having wasted the territory and regained control of the Khyber forts the expedition withdrew, and hostilities wound down by the following April. And for a while – nearly fifteen years, something of a record – the Frontier was almost quiet.

Into the Jungles

> A Snider squibbed in the jungle,
> Somebody laughed and fled,
> And the men of the First Shikaris,
> Picked up their subaltern dead,
> With a big blue mark on his forehead
> And the back blown out of his head
>
> Rudyard Kipling,
> 'The Grave of the Hundred Dead'

Kipling can probably be blamed or credited for the enduring fame of the Khyber Pass and the North-West Frontier. The landscapes here are among the highest and most spectacular anywhere in the world and the locals the very image of the proud, independent and immensely cruel mountaineers of imperial legend. The Great Game was two great superpowers competing across the tilt of the globe. But Britannia's jewel in the crown had another frontier on the east, quite different but equally tricky. The rolling high hills of Assam (which Field Marshal Slim's 'Forgotten' Fourteenth Army would come to know so well in the campaigns of 1942–4 – see Chapter 9) were often deep jungle and home to tribes such as the Abors, Nagas and Lushais, who, while undeveloped and equipped with only bows and spears – low-tech weapons in modern terms but highly effective in the hands of those who knew how to use them – were masters of their own jungle turf.

Farwell quotes Captain Leslie W. Shakespear of 2nd Gurkhas:

> Throughout the entire region there is no level ground beyond the small stretches of a few hundred yards, the rivers are mountain torrents, the lower hills covered with the densest bamboo jungle, which in the higher ranges gives place to evergreen trees, oak and pine, and the only communications are along narrow goat trails leading from village to village.[36]

In 1871 a European child, Mary Winchester, was kidnapped by Lushais and when diplomacy and negotiation failed to recover her, a force was sent in by the Governor of Bengal. Both 2nd and 4th Gurkhas took part in this action which was successful in rescuing the little girl – who seemed to have become a figure of adoration to her captors. Her rescuers were now not quite sure what to do with their mini-heroine as both parents had died. She was eventually shipped back home to Elgin and the care of her grandparents (where she disappears from history) with quite a tale to tell her own children.[37]

Nineteen years later there was trouble in Manipur, a small state in southeast Assam where the Maharajah was dispossessed by his army commander the Senapti. The British resident was Frank St Clair Grimwood who had an under-strength company drawn from 43rd Gurkha Regiment of Bengal Light Infantry (latterly 2/8th Gurkhas). The Raj was none too keen on the usurper, but Grimwood wasn't strong enough to do anything about it, so requested aid from the Chief Commissioner who dispatched a weak battalion of Gurkhas commanded by Lieutenant Colonel Charles Skene. Badly underequipped, this miniscule task force sought to capture the Senapti in his lair at Imphal (of Second World War fame). The effort failed and, under a nominal flag of truce, Grimwood, Skene and two others accepted the Senapti's bland assurances. This was an even worse idea as all four were promptly slaughtered.

What remained of the force retreated to the residency where they came under fierce attack. The surviving officers[38] and the young widow Grimwood managed to get out and, after a long trek, reach safety. Ethel Grimwood knew the country and guided them through, dogged by hostile natives. Happily, the party ran into two more companies of Gurkhas headed for Imphal unaware of what had occurred. Meanwhile, those surviving Gurkha soldiers, abandoned in the wrecked residency, were left to their fate, all killed or captured.

One other tiny platoon-sized unit of Gurkhas, led by Jemadar Birbal Nagarkoti and based only 4 miles from the doomed residency, perceived what was going wrong but were too few to influence the outcome. Rightly, the Jemadar decided to make a break for another outpost at Tamu 60 miles off. Battering through the closing ring, they got clear and made it to safety.[39]

Lieutenant Charles Grant at Tamu now had thirty Gurkhas to bolster his very slim force of a platoon of Madras Native Infantry. Undeterred and with a trio of elephants loaded with gear and spare ammunition, he sallied out and attacked the far superior Manipuris, winning several skirmishes and inching ever closer to Imphal, till the Senapti threatened to execute his hostages who included fifty Gurkha POWs. Grant now set about negotiating, promoting himself to colonel to add more gravitas. Disdainfully, he returned a bribe of (much-needed) supplies and insisted on the release of the captive Gurkhas while demanding a high-ranking hostage for the treacherous Senapti's good behaviour. This was a bluff too far and the Manipuris attacked. Grant held on, his ammunition dwindling, till he was actually ordered to withdraw.[40]

The job wasn't left undone for long. A full brigade was sent in and took Imphal in April 1891. The royal dynasty was restored and the Senapti hanged.

Grant won himself a VC; Jemadar Nagarkoti was awarded an IOM, as were several other Gurkhas. The brave and resourceful Ethel Grimwood received the Royal Red Cross (instituted in 1883), normally awarded for nursing services.

Riflemen

Throughout these campaigns and even today Gurkha private soldiers are rightly referred to as riflemen. Until the mid-ninteenth century the general infantry firearm was the smooth-bore musket. Brown Bess, the British Army's standard issue, had been in service for well over a century. Muskets were inaccurate, lacking muzzle velocity, outclassed by the rifled gun which came into more widespread use during the frontier wars in America, the legendary Pennsylvania or Kentucky rifle of (fictional) Hawkeye and (real) Davy Crockett. The British came on the receiving end during the American Revolution. After such a rude awakening they countered by forming the Royal Americans who carried the *longue carabine*.

Troopers wore green, not scarlet, and skirmished rather than volleyed. This was the basis of the subsequent Rifle Regiments such as the green-clad 95th who fought so hard and so well in Wellington's Peninsular Campaigns, made popular by Bernard Cornwell's idealised Richard Sharpe. The rifleman's appearance became distinctive: 'They wore dark green uniforms and black buttons and boasted that they were always first into action and last out. They had to develop a special quick step of 140 paces a minute to enable them to get out ahead of the rest of the army in advance and catch up from rear-guard positions in retreat.'[41]

The Baker Rifle was the first British purpose-made weapon, succeeded by the Brunswick which the Gurkhas carried during the Mutiny, before the Minie Rifle became the standard infantry weapon throughout. Riflemen and Gurkhas as riflemen maintained their elite status, with rapid marching and referring to their bayonets as swords. Such proud traditions persist to this day.

A Forbidden Realm

When, half a century ago, I was just a lad, obsessed with wars and militaria, with beat of drum and swirl of silken colours, I chanced in a junk shop on a sword I couldn't identify (which didn't happen often). This was the sort of wonderfully eclectic scrambling kind of place where you could pick up SMLE bayonets for under a quid and the sword, filmed with surface rust and battered scabbard, reminded me a bit of a Roman *spatha*. The old soldier who ran the place told me it was Tibetan and had come back from a war there, fought long ago – 'Them Gurkhas were there an' all mind.' As it happened, I'd found a couple of kukris in his shop before and the sword duly went into the collection.

If Nepal was exotic and remote then Tibet was mythical, literally a kingdom in the clouds, unimaginably distant, secretive and in the early years of the twentieth century a province, nominally at least, of China. But it wasn't the Chinese who bothered the Raj. As ever it was the Russians and it was a Russian, Gombojab Tsybikov, who had been the first European explorer to visit and photograph distant Lhasa in 1901. It seemed the 13th Dalai Lama was none too keen on Calcutta, preferring overtures from Moscow. The Viceroy, Lord Curzon,[42] was more than a trifle vexed; the last thing he wanted to see was the Russian bear getting its greedy paws on Tibet which, however far off, was still close enough to India. He made representations to both Peking and Tibet but while the Chinese proved amenable, the Tibetans did not.

In charge of the non-existent frontier negotiations and heading the grandly badged Tibetan Frontier Commission was Colonel Francis Younghusband,[43] a seasoned performer in the theatre of the Great Game. Tibetan truculence and Younghusband's belligerence turned any potential for discourse into an actual stand-off and by December 1903, the colonel was leading a column over the high border. The pretext was an alleged incursion and a build-up of Russian influence, though Curzon, fearful of repercussions, downplayed these alleged alarums, preferring to rely on the unreasonable nature of Tibetan disdain towards his careful diplomatic overtures.

Younghusband had a full brigade under his command with twice as many porters and auxiliaries. His force included four companies from 8th Gurkhas with two more on outpost duty.[44] At first progress was peaceful; the Tibetans weren't looking for a fight and pledged not to attack if the British behaved the same way. Ostensibly, Younghusband was simply moving on Lhasa to establish a diplomatic presence; this wasn't a war of aggression. That didn't last. Brigadier James Macdonald was the more senior officer and he had acclimatised his troops in winter quarters just over the frontier. In March, the army set off toward the Pass of Guru where a large Tibetan force was barring the way.

This quickly developed into a stand-off. The locals didn't open fire but nor did they clear the pass – they had thrown up breastworks across the road and had musketeers crouched in *sangars*[45] on the slopes above. Younghusband's subsequent version was that he intended just to disarm this militia and carry on. Scuffles led to angry shots and then a full fight, with British breech-loaders and Maxims making pretty short work of the defenders. Gurkhas were very much up front during this short, very bloody and wholly one-sided fight. Hundreds of Tibetans were killed; the British suffered a dozen wounded. The Gurkhas did what they do so well, scrambling up the steep sides: 'Up on the escarpment the 8th Gurkhas and the 23rd Pioneers began to hustle the grey-clad musketeers out of their sangars; this was done in silence and with something of the good-humoured severity that London policemen display on boat race night.'[46]

So much for peaceful intentions; Younghusband led the column relentlessly over the roof of the world towards Lhasa. On 9 April, the next defensible obstacle, the wonderfully named Red Idol Gorge,[47] loomed up ahead. This had been thoroughly entrenched with crowded *sangars* dotting the high slopes. Macdonald again sent in the Gurkhas to scramble up the steep, scree-logged heights. At this point nature intervened with a screaming blizzard blotting out the battlefield and severing all contact with the Gurkhas.

When the storm finally lifted, around noon, 8th Gurkhas had completely outflanked the sharpshooters in their *sangars*, who promptly bolted. The attackers could now blast volleys down onto the exposed warriors crowding the pass. It was a turkey shoot and the Tibetans fled, leaving behind significant casualties. For the British, it was yet another almost bloodless victory.[48] Most of these militias were peasant conscripts, not overly imbued with martial vigour. Even if they had been, their matchlock *jingals* (muskets) would easily have been obsolete two centuries before.

These conquerors were an oddly polyglot army, not necessarily a shining representation of the glories of the Raj. The baggage train was a strange mixture of everything that moved on four legs; mules, ponies, donkeys, bullocks, yaks and even sheep, tended by a biblical sprawl of assorted herders including many Tibetans who simply saw a lucrative opportunity. Perhaps even odder was a troop of mounted Gurkhas, normally, as Peter Fleming rightly observes: 'the least equestrian race in Asia'.[49] Gurkhas are rightly noted for their adaptability, but this was a challenge indeed. Their steeds were scrappy ponies barely 13 hands high, dragged out of the supply column, bearing no suitable girths or bridles and with improvised saddles. While the ponies were hardly destriers, their riders' short stature at least meant that frequent fallings-off were less painful.[50]

Advancing towards the town of Gyantse, which fell without a shot on 11 April, Younghusband set up shop, establishing his mission post there. It was all rather agreeable. Officers hunted and acquired whatever was worth acquiring; medical services were extended to locals (cleft palates were a regular feature of the region). As all seemed so peaceful, Younghusband sent back a large part of his forces to secure lines of communication and supply. He proposed to press on to Lhasa but there was disquiet at home: gunning down masses of ill-armed peasants didn't smack too much of diplomacy and more Tibetan forces were concentrating at Karo La, 45 miles (72km) to the east.

Macdonald was absent from the mission back at base camp and would not have approved of a proposal put forward by his subordinate, Lieutenant Colonel Herbert Brander, that the British launch a pre-emptive strike and disperse these 'enemy' forces. This went rather beyond just clearing the route but Younghusband was typically bullish. By the time Macdonald got to hear of the plan, it was already unfolding. The fight at Karo La took place at an altitude of nearly 17,000ft (5,200m), probably the most elevated military action of all time. Again, it was Gurkhas who won the day. Brander had only 400 men, the enemy nearly 10 times that, and they had thrown up an immensely strong wall, pierced with hundreds of loopholes. The attackers could make no impression whatsoever; even their handy little mountain guns ('Bubble' and 'Squeak') couldn't dent the stones.[51]

This left the onus on 8th Gurkhas, mountaineering to the left while a Sikh battalion scrambled right. Both storming parties were now at 18,500ft (5,600m) and it was immensely cold. This was a battle in the permanent snow line, way above any altitude they had reached before. If such a fight was fictionalised it would be described as pure fantasy; not even Cornwell's Richard Sharpe ever ventured that high. Such Olympian heights could induce altitude sickness; conventionally equipped infantry would never be expected to fight in such conditions, as in extreme cases exposure can lead to life-threatening pulmonary oedema.

Doggedly, the Gurkhas kept going and soon their comrades in a stalemate in the high pass below heard the rattle of Lee–Metford Rifles banging away, sound bouncing off the cavern walls. Tibetan fighters tumbled out of their eyries, some shot, others toppling into the void. On the other flank, the Sikhs were equally successful and with their main defensive line outflanked, the Tibetans conceded defeat.[52]

Not a moment too soon, for another Tibetan force had now attacked Younghusband at his base of Changlo outside Gyantse. Attacks were seen off, but sniping took a steadily increasing toll: a seriously tricky moment but one which nonetheless gave Younghusband his pretext for pushing on to Lhasa. With the mission surrounded and under siege, Calcutta hurried in reinforcements. Tibetan marksmen were pressing close and casualties within the improvised compound were beginning to climb alarmingly.

Younghusband went over to the attack, re-taking a key position between 18 and 19 May – this was dubbed Gurkha House in tribute to the soldiers' actions. More and more troops were being pushed forward and, by the end of May, the siege was effectively lifted. Lord Kitchener, then in charge of the Indian Army and generally at odds with Curzon, the Viceroy, was still alarmed by Younghusband's gung-ho bullishness (the emissary was by now convinced it was the Russians he was fighting) and he, as Commander in Chief India, intended that the more cautious Macdonald should run the show from now on. Having regrouped at New Chumbi, the main British supply base, the army – as indeed it now was – marched forth again on 12 June.

Despite the relief of the mission compound, the next and very near block was the immensely strong obstacle of the Gyantse Jong (fortress), still held by Tibetan forces, a seriously tough proposition. On 26 June, the Gurkhas with Pathan irregulars seized a key Tibetan outpost, the monastery at Naini. Two days later the Gurkhas grabbed another fortified religious house, the Tsechen monastery. Later, a whole cache of important historical and cultural artefacts were 'recycled' and many subsequently featured in a Christie's auction late that summer.

Though the fortress hadn't yet fallen, exploratory talks were held at the mission on 3 July. Younghusband was unyielding and, at the same time, appears to have instigated a whispering campaign against the more pliant Macdonald. Taking the fortress would be the toughest task so far. It was huge, high up and studded with artillery, the only guns that the Tibetans actually possessed. The fort stands on a near vertical slab of rock, with just one narrow, fire-swept, stepped access, two lines of great thick, slab-sided walls and a massive squat citadel capping the summit. Macdonald might be naturally careful, but he had a tactical plan for taking the place. He intended to feint against one flank of the plateau to the west and draw out the enemy forces while his guns pounded a breach, and the main attack went in from the south. Meanwhile, the Teschen monastery, a medieval gem, was torched to prevent any Tibetan soldiers from filtering back in.[53] The Raj wasn't there for the culture.

Macdonald sent in three columns, approaching from the south-west, south and south-east, stepping out in the pre-dawn. The plan started to unravel almost straightaway when two of the attacking formations bumped into each other. This wasn't an auspicious start and even when battle was joined, the fighting was long and hard. It took nearly 12 hours to punch through the outer curtain and darkness was threatening when 8th Gurkhas and the Royal Fusiliers charged into the breach. To reach the next, upper level they had to scale a near-vertical cliff with rocks and random musketry raining down, ricocheting and pinging off masonry. Deadly enough: but even worse was the 'friendly fire' from British Maxims which killed and wounded more Gurkhas than the enemy's best efforts.

Above them was a narrow breach in the walls blasted through by hefty 10-pounders. Lieutenant John Duncan Grant with Havildar Karbir Pun managed to squeeze through the hole, but both were immediately wounded and slid back down the near sheer walls for 30ft (10m) or so. Gritting their teeth, both climbed back up for another go and this time they got through, followed by a file of Gurkhas, all on hands and knees. Desperate as this seems, it proved a tipping point. Enemy fire began to slacken, and men were seen abseiling down the far side and disappearing into a warren of buildings. The fight for the Jong was over.[54]

Grant's citation for his VC (the only one awarded in this campaign) reads:

> On the occasion of the storming of the Gyantse Jong on 6th July 1904, the storming Company, headed by Lieutenant Grant, on emerging from the cover of the village, had to advance up a bare, almost precipitous, rock-face, with little or no cover available, and under a heavy fire from the curtain, flanking towers on both sides of the curtain, and other buildings higher up the Jong. Showers of rocks and stones were at the time being hurled down the hillside by the enemy from above. One man could only go up at a time, crawling on hands and knees, to the breach in the curtain.
>
> Lieutenant Grant, followed by Havildar Karbir Pun, [both] 8th Gurkha Rifles, at once attempted to scale it, but on reaching near the top he was wounded, and hurled back, as was also the Havildar, who fell down the rock some 30 feet. Regardless of their injuries they again attempted to scale the breach, and, covered by the fire of the men below, were successful in their object, the Havildar shooting one of the enemy on gaining the top. The successful issue of the assault was very greatly due to the splendid example shown by Lieutenant Grant and Havildar Karbir Pun. The latter has been recommended for the Indian Order of Merit (first class).[55]

Despite this pounding most of the defenders withdrew in good order, but the road to Lhasa was now cleared. One of the Medical Officers (MOs), Major Wimberley, who had witnessed the earlier feat of storming the Dargai Heights, thought the Gurkhas' performance at Gyantse Jong surpassed even this. And to the victors the spoils; neither British nor Gurkha soldier was backward when it came to amassing loot and a great deal of it was indeed amassed. If senior officers were aware, as they must or surely should have been, they didn't interfere, turning a blind eye and probably not coming back empty-handed themselves. It was the nature of war.

They weren't quite done with fighting: the narrow pass at Karo La had to be stormed a second time with 8th Gurkhas repeating their successful mountaineering tactics to drive back Tibetan skirmishers from improvised *sangars*. From now on the march was pretty much uncontested; one fortress after another was abandoned, villagers fled and stripped the earth behind them, but fish and game were plentiful. On 3 August, the army entered Lhasa, the Forbidden City, which for the most part they found squalid and reeking beyond belief, a cramped warren of medieval rookeries with nothing resembling a sewage system. Even though the Dalai Lama had decamped to Mongolia, Younghusband bullied the administration and the regent into agreeing to his terms.

Barely a month later peace was agreed in the Treaty of Lhasa – and though Younghusband felt this vindicated his every action so far, it achieved little. The terms were largely unenforceable, and a tsunami of opprobrium was building at home. The Great Game was suddenly out of fashion and such swashbuckling colonial adventures, however Henty-esque, were beginning to lose their allure. Nonetheless it was a remarkable campaign. The British lost just over 200 men to enemy action, having killed several thousand Tibetans. The Gurkhas had covered themselves in even more glory. Yet, barely a decade ahead loomed their supreme test to date – and a hugely different kind of war.

Chapter 5

Over the Black Water

Fourth [Gurkhas] – an honourable number; I soon came to believe with a passion worthy of a religion that there was no regiment on earth like it. The 1st Gurkhas were earnest, the 2nd idle, the 3rd illiterate, the 5th narrow-minded, the 6th downtrodden, the 7th unshaven, the 8th exhibitionist, the 9th Brahminical [they enlisted high-caste Gurkhas] and the 10th alcoholic. As for the rest of the Indian Army – well, the Guides weren't bad, but even they were not what they used to be in the old days, when they had a Gurkha Company. The British Army, lock, stock and barrel, was useless but we – we were wonderful! We were stiff with battle honours.

John Masters, *Bugles and a Tiger* (1956)

When the tubercular Bosnian Serb Gavrilo Princip fired his two fatal shots in Sarajevo on 28 June 1914 hardly anyone would have guessed that this would trigger the most destructive war in history to date, and that Gurkhas with other regiments of the Indian Army would be thrown into the vast cauldron of the Western Front. So desperate had the situation in France and Belgium become by that autumn that the government of India lent a full army corps of two divisions to shore up the line. It was desperately in need of shoring as the soldiers, hardly any of whom had been to sea, 'over the black water', were rushed up from Marseilles to the bleak, shell-scarred morass of the front. They were neither acclimatised, nor trained to fight in an industrial war against the world's most formidable army without machine guns, mortars and heavy weapons.

The British Expeditionary Force first encountered the Germans at Mons on 23 August 1914 and then again at Le Cateau three days later. After the deliverance of the Marne and the beginnings of positional warfare one last chance for the combatants to potentially outflank each other arose at Ypres, a name then largely unknown but one which would resonate through thousands of British and imperial families.

Map 3. The Western Front, 1914–15.

The First Battle of Ypres raged through autumn 1914. The line held but only just, and at fearful cost. The 'Old Contemptibles' of the British Expeditionary Force (BEF) were terribly thinned, and then the cold, wet and mud of Flanders closed about the survivors. From now on, it was to be positional warfare with every yard of ground bitterly contested and paid for in blood.

Imagine a saucer and the city of Ypres in the depression, around, a thin, barely noticeable ring of higher ground to the east and south, like a gentle rim. That is the Ypres Salient. He who holds the rim dominates the saucer. By 1915, the Germans held this higher ground. The British position was horribly exposed. Wet, low-lying Flanders proved an uncomfortable and ungracious host. By the end of the First Battle of Ypres, the Germans held more high ground to the east, ending in the village of Passchendaele, a name to become synonymous with horror. They also held the significant pimple of Hill 60, 2 miles south-west of the ruined city, and the vital Wytschaete-Messines Ridge further south.

During the First World War more than 90,780 Gurkhas served in the British Army, suffering approximately 20,000 casualties, of which 6,168 were fatalities, receiving almost 2,000 gallantry awards. The number of Gurkha battalions was increased to thirty-three, and units were placed at the disposal of the British high command by the Nepalese government for service on all fronts. Many Nepalese volunteers served in non-combatant roles, in units such as the Army Bearer Corps and the labour battalions, but there were also large numbers who served in combat in France, Turkey, Palestine and Mesopotamia.

They fought on the battlefields of France and Belgium, at Loos, Givenchy, Neuve Chapelle and Ypres; in Mesopotamia, Persia, the Suez Canal and Palestine against Turkish advance; in Gallipoli and Salonika (one detachment did in fact serve with Lawrence of Arabia). During the Battle of Loos (June–December 1915) a battalion of the 8th Gurkhas fought virtually to the last man, hurling themselves time after time against the weight of the German defences, and the battalion, in the words of the Indian Corps commander Lieutenant General Sir James Willcocks, 'found its Valhalla'.[1]

The Western Front

At the outbreak of war, the Indian Army numbered some 155,000 officers and men. As early as 1911, consideration had been given to the use of Indian Army troops in a potential European war.[2] Little of a practical nature was undertaken and it wasn't until the end of July 1914, when war was clearly imminent, that the India Office agreed to commit two infantry divisions and a cavalry brigade. Mobilisation in India commenced on 8 August with the initial plan being to send two divisions to Egypt. This destination was changed to Europe, however, and the Lahore Division was the first to disembark at Marseilles on 26 September. Thus, it was that Indian troops arrived in time to take part in the desperate battle for Ypres which began in October – the death knell of the BEF 'Old Contemptibles'. The Indian Army formations were the only strategic reserve available as Territorial units did not begin to arrive in significant numbers until spring 1915.

It was early in October 1914 that the BEF advanced northwards. Sir John French hoped he would be able to strike a blow against the German exposed flank. He had already been reinforced by a further division to make good his earlier casualties. Encouraged by General Foch, Sir John believed the hinge of his successful blow would be the Belgian city of Ypres. At this point, the German high command entertained similar hopes. As the British felt their way towards Menin, they collided with large enemy forces. Flanders was about to become a major battlefield.

Trench Warfare

The Gurkhas came too late for the war of movement. They were plunged into a bloody stalemate. From now on they would live and fight from the trenches.[3] An officer described these early works, very much ad hoc:

> First and foremost, these were not the spacious and well-ordered works with which many became acquainted on the Somme and elsewhere. The very nature of the terrain precluded any system of mining excavation; water was seldom more than two or three feet below the surface even in comparatively dry seasons, so the trenches were in most places a compromise. A narrow, shallow ditch supplied the trench proper, above it to front and back were piled sandbags, usually in higgledy-piggledy manner … even if they were well laid the Boche gunner could be trusted to see that they did not long remain so. Rough traverses there were, very necessary when the Boche sniper commanded the flanks with enfilade fire.[4]

Beyond the parapet lay the wire, still in thin belts at this early stage and 'continually preyed on by enemy trench mortars and shells'. Life within was far from agreeable, the previous witness continues:

Before the days of revetting wire and frames, of iron and timber, even of duckboards, the painfully constructed trench was at the mercy of the weather. A heavy shower even in the heat of summer would reduce the interior to a quagmire. In the height of winter, conditions were unspeakable. An endless winding ditch, filled with glutinous mud of extraordinary tenacity, led past the support trench to the firing line proper – a rather wide, deeper ditch and consequently with the greater depth of water, not infrequently waist high. There the infantry would pass their tour of duty, harassed by enemy snipers, who seemed inevitably to command the weakest points of the system, and to a shell-fire to which their own batteries, for very lack of ammunition, were unable to respond.[5]

Within this stygian world of unceasing danger, of cold, wet and unending frozen misery there was, at this stage, little or no shelter:

… no dugouts, no mined dug-outs impervious to shell or mortar fire; not even the miserable shacks which passed for dugouts at a later stage … there was no material with which to build them, no iron, no planks, no surplus of sandbags, no surplus of men to build them. A wretched hole within the fire-bay above the level of the water, contrived often in the thickness of the parados, provided the only means of shelter, and a waterproof sheet the covering. There was no immunity from shell-fire; the parapet was not always bulletproof; often too after heavy rainfall or a thaw, the whole structure would collapse, burying the occupants in mud and water or exposing them to enemy fire.[6]

As the trench line began to harden, both sides had to try and hook around an open flank. Inevitably, the response was a steady thickening of the line northwards towards the sea. The hope for both was that they could outflank the enemy and then roll up his line. Such tactics had served commanders well in the past, but these huge armies of industrial age warfare were simply not agile enough. The vast coiling snake of supply, stretching so far behind, weighed too much for any lightning moves. Grand Napoleonic gambits such as the Manoeuvre of Ulm, which in 1805 had netted an entire Austrian army, were not likely to be repeated.

A Gurkha VC

Kulbir Thapa was born in 1889 in Palpa, Nepal; he was a 26-year-old rifleman in the 2/3rd Gurkha Rifles when he became the first Nepalese recipient of the VC. Thapa was at Mauquissart on 25 April 1915 taking part in a diversionary attack at the start of the Battle of Loos. He was in one of the leading companies attacking the German positions, and it was the first time he had been under fire. He found himself alone and wounded behind German lines. His citation reads:

> For most conspicuous bravery during operations against the German trenches south of Mauquissart: When himself wounded on September 25, 1915, he found a badly wounded soldier of the 2nd Battalion, the Leicestershire Regiment behind the first-line German trench and although urged by the British soldier to save himself he remained with him all day and night. In the early morning of September 26, in misty weather, he brought him out through the German wire and leaving him in a place of comparative safety, returned and brought in two wounded Gurkhas one after the other. He then went back in broad daylight for the British soldier and brought him in also, carrying him most of the way under continuous fire.[7]

He was personally awarded his Victoria Cross by King George V at Buckingham Palace and is still remembered by the Royal Leicestershire Regiment at their regimental museum. Kulbir Thapa survived the war and retired achieving the rank of havildar – equivalent to sergeant (see Glossary). He died in Nepal in 1956.

Baptism of Fire

When war was declared there were ten Gurkha infantry regiments in the Indian Army order of battle, all of which possessed two battalions. Until this point, as we have seen, the Gurkhas had been primarily deployed in operations on the Indian subcontinent, maintaining the peace and security of the British Empire. This was an entirely different type of warfare: fast, fluid, highly mobile and generally not involving heavy weapons larger than field or mountain guns. The regiments were not therefore trained to fight in the European-style battles that would characterise those of the Western Front. Of the two Indian Army divisions deployed to France and Flanders, the Meerut Division had four Gurkha battalions: 1/9th, 2/2nd, 2/3rd and 2/8th. The Lahore Division had two Gurkha battalions, 1/1st and 1/4th.

Indian and Nepalese troops were something of a novelty for the French, but 1/1st Gurkhas seem to have been an instant success. Major Aylmer and Indian Army officer in charge of mule transport saw that:

> The good people of Locon had not, so far, had any Indian troops billeted on them and were inclined to resent the idea. But the Gurkha at any rate soon succeeded in overcoming their prejudice against him, as is illustrated by the following anecdote related by an officer. He says that, on one occasion, he went on his rounds fully expecting to return to find strained relations between his men and the farmer on whom they were billeted, who had been openly hostile. He returned to find the host all smiles. He was telling the men to take what straw they wanted and, in apologizing for his former attitude, said that the Gurkhas had found several eggs in his barn and had brought them to him, 'Your men', he added, 'must be very good men; if they had been French soldiers, they would not only have kept my eggs but would be cooking and eating my chickens by now!'

It was the 2/8th which on 29 October went up the line and was immediately engaged in heavy fighting. By the end of the next day, seven British and four Gurkha officers together with 207 ORs had become casualties. But a few days after this savage blooding, 2/2nd and 1/9th were up in the line by Neuve Chapelle where they came under sustained enemy assault, supported by a heavy bombardment. When 2/2nd was at risk of being outflanked, 1/9th attempted to ease the pressure while 2/2nd counter attacked. Losses again ran very high: 2/2nd lost seven British and four Gurkha officers with 33 men dead and 99 wounded or missing.[8]

As autumn deepened and the dank Flanders mud clogged makeshift trenches, life was far from comfortable. For the Gurkhas their brief war of movement was very definitely over, and this would now be a war of attrition, lit by flashes of murderous action. At Festubert in late autumn 2/8th lost one Gurkha officer and twenty-two riflemen. In the course of this action, Subedar Shamsher Gurung, despite severe injuries, managed to rescue a number of other wounded men over an intense three-day period, winning the Order of British India. On 13 November, 2/3rd lost heavily during an abortive raid near Richebourg. Their comrades from 1/9th risked their lives by venturing into no-man's-land to bring in the many injured.

A British officer summed up the situation fairly accurately:

> They [Gurkhas] had been thrown into action and trench warfare, with which they were quite unfamiliar, at a moment's notice: there was no chance of letting them in by easy stages to get accustomed to the conditions and sending officers and parties up to work with seasoned troops in the line and learn from them the tricks of the game, as was the case later on with the New Army battalions. All that was learned was the result of bitter experience.[9]

From 10 March 1915, the British launched an offensive aimed at re-taking Neuve Chapelle and pushing on to Aubers Ridge behind; 2/3rd, part of the Garhwal Brigade, was deployed in the initial thrust. Charging with kukris drawn, they took the shattered remains of the village. As they dug in, the next wave, composed of the Dehra Dun Brigade with both 2/2nd and 1/9th, passed through and attempted to storm the ridge but were halted some distance short of the crest. In accordance with their tactical doctrine, the Germans counterattacked with a division-size force. Despite the odds, the embattled brigade clung to their tenuous gains and held firm, accounting for some 3,000 of the enemy. In the course of the battle, Rifleman Gane Gurung netted a fine haul of prisoners while engaged in clearing the village, winning an IOM.

Neither the British nor the French were able to batter through the ever-thickening German defences in that summer. In early autumn at Loos the British, supporting a major French push in Artois, attacked again in force. The Garwhal Brigade was again in the vanguard; 2/8th and 2/3rd took terrible casualties in the attacks. The 2/8th, having secured their objectives, found themselves isolated and forced back by relentless German pressure. Nearly 500 men were lost and a further 166 captured. The battalion virtually ceased to exist. Meanwhile 2/3rd found themselves stuck in the uncut wire and German machine guns took a fearful toll. A whole platoon, attempting to cut the wire, was shot down with only Rifleman Kulbir Thapa, mentioned earlier, surviving, though badly hit himself.[10] Later that autumn, after the battle for Loos had been closed down, the entire Corps was withdrawn from the Western Front.

Warfare in the trenches was hard, uncomfortable, dirty, exhausting and always extremely dangerous. Throughout the war the British and imperial forces lost several hundred men per day. Taking both sides together there were some 25,000 miles (40,000km) of trenches along the front. Big battles were relatively rare but daily hazards included sniper fire, rifle grenades, mortars and random artillery shells (both HE – high explosive – and shrapnel, latterly gas). Diseases such as trench foot and respiratory complaints claimed as many victims as enemy action. There was the comfort of a daily grog ration of naval rum which was increased before action; some men were too insensible to go 'over the top'.

It was British policy to dominate no-man's-land which necessitated nighttime trench raids. These could be at section, platoon, company or occasionally battalion level. Usually undertaken by volunteers, their purpose was, in addition to beating up enemy quarters, to gain intelligence and bring in prisoners for interrogation. As this involved close-quarter fighting, men carried knives and homemade maces or 'trench clubs' – truncheons studded with nails. One of the telling ironies of the wider conflict is that this vast industrial war was fought at one level with medieval weapons in a kind of fighting ancient warriors would instantly have recognised. This type of action required daring and nerve. Successful raids were a boost for morale.

In some sectors the trench lines could be awfully close, within grenade-throwing distance; in others they might be hundreds of metres or half a kilometre and more distant. Some sectors became known as 'quiet', where combatants on both sides preferred a 'live and let live' policy. In such famous instances as Christmas 1914, this led to an outburst of fraternisation.

Prior to any major offensive, artillery activity would increase dramatically. The guns were never completely silent but as an attack drew nearer, the bombardment would swell to a crescendo of biblical proportions, making it impossible to believe that anyone on the receiving end could survive. During the week prior to the Somme offensive on 1 July 1916, British guns fired over a million shells.

By 1915, both sides had developed sophisticated fire and movement tactics whereby squads in the attacking platoons would leapfrog across no-man's-land providing covering fire and staged rushes, using any cover available. The lack of portable automatic weapons – later, in 1916–17, remedied by the deployment of large numbers of Lewis Guns – was a major shortcoming. For the Somme battle it was felt the Kitchener battalions had insufficient training and should advance in four regular lines, almost shoulder to shoulder, relying on the bombardment to crush the enemy's front-line trenches. That didn't work.

As mentioned, a major obstacle was the wire, dense belts thrown out before front-line trenches. These coils of impenetrable wire were held down by metal stakes hammered into the ground. Impassable to attacking infantry, the wire had to be cut by shrapnel shells, fused to explode just above. This often failed and many hurriedly produced shells turned out to be duds.

Gas, first used by the Germans (in defiance of the Hague Protocols) in April 1915 heralding the Second Battle of Ypres, provided another deadly hazard. Chlorine gas was initially delivered from pressurised canisters, totally dependent upon wind direction. Latterly, mustard and phosgene gas were delivered by shell. Once the Germans had unleashed this unholy Pandora's Box, the Allies swiftly followed suit.

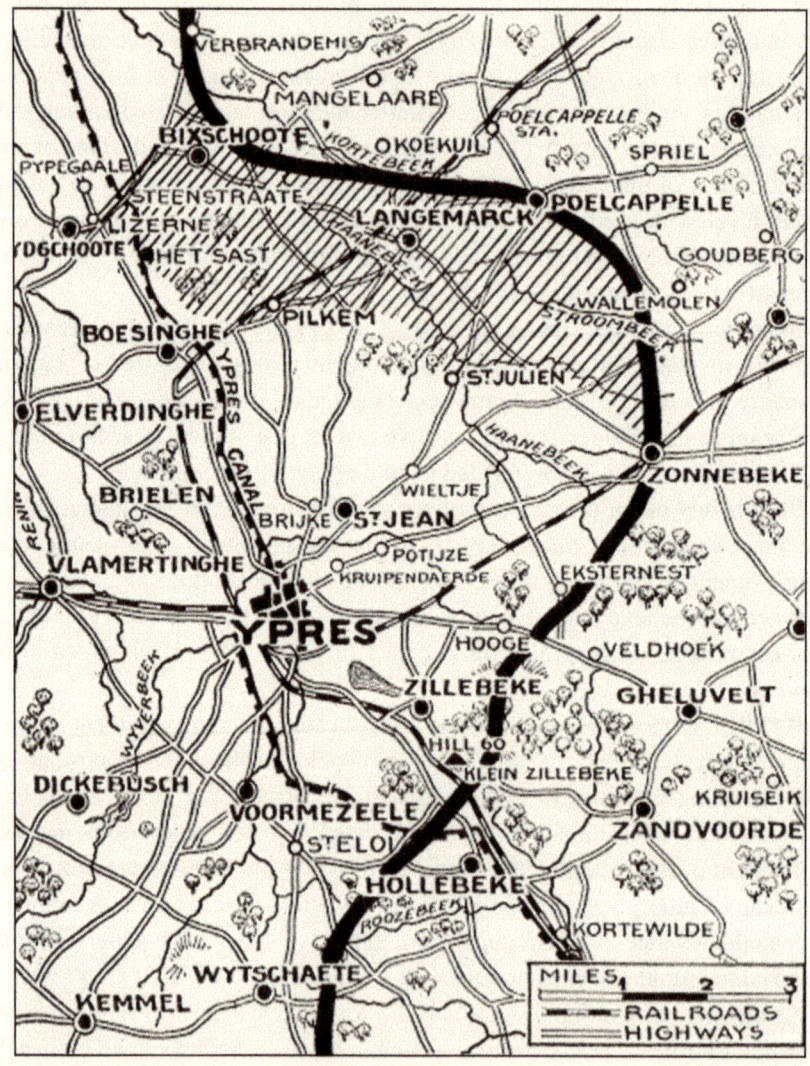

Map 4. The Second Battle of Ypres, 1915.

Neuve Chapelle and Givenchy

General Sir James Willcocks described 2/2nd Gurkhas as 'a regiment second to none in the Indian Army'.[11] Attached to Meerut Division, they had reached France in mid-October 1914. On the night of 29/30 October they moved up into the line just north of Neuve Chapelle.

The Gurkhas who, as mentioned, had no previous experience of fighting in trenches, had relieved a battalion of the Northumberland Fusiliers. This was to be a true baptism of fire. For several days they learned very much 'on the job' about trench construction and the daily rigours of trench life in dank autumn. The Germans were very close, no further than 160yd (150m) away and often less than a third of that. They had 1/9th Gurkhas on their right and Connaught Rangers on their left flank. They were organised as four double companies: 1. Lieutenant Lucas; 2. Major Becher; 3. Major Ross; and 4. Captain Barton.[12]

Overall, the trenches they inherited were scratch-built and inadequate, not even having proper communications trenches to the rear. Worse, the British trenches formed a bulge or salient in the line, with Germans on three sides. On 1 November, the enemy began digging saps (trenches which were prepared at right angles to the front line as jumping-off points for attack). As ever, the Germans opened with a terrific bombardment, inflicting casualties and severing the field telephone lines.

The Germans traversed the line with drenching fire targeting Nos 1 and 2 Double Companies. Survivors from both were forced to retreat a short way to an existing shallow ditch. Naik Padamhoj Guring fought a sole rear-guard action, holding back the enemy until he was finally forced out. This heroism earned him an IOM. No. 2 Company suffered heavily; both Lucas and Becher were killed. Major Ross led No. 3 Double Company in a counterattack. They regained ground but were themselves overrun in a German riposte. Major Ross and Subadar Major Man Sing Bohra were killed.[13]

Captain Barton of No. 4 Double Company was also dead, leaving Lieutenant Reid as senior surviving officer. He held on, sending to the Connaughts for help, but was, in turn, killed. Lieutenants Walcott and Innes from the survivors of No. 2 Double Company, having rounded up the few survivors, then launched another counterattack. Both perished, though Naik Rampershad Thapa earned the Indian Distinguished Service Medal for his dogged defence. Subadar Chet Sing guided the survivors back to the reserve position, losing his own life as he did so.[14]

By this time all that was holding the line were the survivors of No. 4 Double Company under Subadar Fateh Sing Newar, some additional remnants and a company from the Rangers. The odds were hopeless and the pressure relentless. The subadar attempted a fighting withdrawal but they were enfiladed by machine-gun fire. Even worse, they had to endure 'friendly' fire from British reserves mistaking them for the enemy. At last darkness and further reinforcement from the Rangers allowed the Subadar to get his men back. He survived and was awarded the Order of British India.[15]

The reserves comprised a company and a half under Subadar Karan Singh Rana. Colonel Norrie DSO had taken command and led this slender reserve forward at 8.30 a.m. They attempted to succour No. 1 Double Company but, in this maelstrom of fire, could make no headway. Two companies of 34th Poona Horse came up and they again moved up towards the left flank of the front line. Artillery and sustained small-arms fire forced them to fall back to a support position, 220yd (200m) behind the front line.

Colonel Swanston of the Poona Horse (fighting dismounted as infantry) was killed, and a German infantry attack followed, broken up by the defenders' rifles supported by accurate fire from the RFA. As the afternoon wore on the reserve position was strengthened by further reinforcements. At 5.30 p.m. Colonel Norrie used his fresh troops in a bid to retake the trench formerly held by No. 1 Double Company. Neither this nor an attack to recover the right flank positions succeeded but the Germans, shaken by their own heavy losses, did not attempt to consolidate their gains and vacated the front-line trenches. This gallant defence had been dearly bought. Casualties in 2/2nd were exceedingly high; not a single British officer survived.[16]

As 1914 drew to a dismal close and the 'Race to the Sea'[17] ended in stalemate, the war of manoeuvre morphed into one of largely static attrition. Neither side yet realised there would be no alternative to positional warfare for a long time to come, least of all the Allies, whose mission was to expel the Germans from French and Belgian soil. As a consequence, the Indian Corps in December was instructed to take an offensive stance across their sector of the front. The curtain went up on 16 December when Ferozepore Brigade launched an attack northeast of Givenchy. Meerut and Lahore divisions were committed to a further attack on 19 December. This was a confused affair; there was uncertainty as to whether the Indians were committing to a full-on offensive or making a demonstration to support attacks put in by two other corps. This ambiguity enabled Sir John French, unfairly, to blame Willcocks when the plan failed (though when things seemed to be going well, he'd supported the attacks).

Though gains on 19 December were both limited and costly, the Germans planned a counteroffensive for the following day. Rain, in biblical torrents, had reduced the miserable trenches to flooded field drains. Nonetheless, the dawn chorus of German shells came in fast and thick. Their superiority in guns and mortars quickly became evident and the tornado of fire was soon followed by co-ordinated infantry attacks along the line. At 9.00 a.m. the enemy detonated ten mines under the front line around Givenchy – the first time the Indians had experienced what was to become a feature of the war on the Western Front. By later standards these were quite small – a 110lb (50kg) of explosive, laid via saps. However, one double company of 1/4th Gurkhas suffered dreadfully and was very nearly wiped out.[18]

As the Germans swept over the shallow, rain-sodden waste of no-man's-land the other double company of 1/4th gave them a hot reception. Savage hand-to-hand combat followed in the water-logged ditches that passed for trenches. The Gurkhas exacted a high toll of their attackers, but force of numbers had by 1.00 p.m. pushed the survivors out of the first line, back through Givenchy village. With just a single company of Highland Light Infantry (HLI) on their right, 1/1st Gurkhas also lost men to the detonating mines and, possibly, to aerial strafing and bombing. The infantry, relying heavily on grenades, surged forward into a storm of fire; again, by sheer weight of numbers the defenders were forced out. Lieutenant Stewart of the HLI, with only 110 men, formed an ad hoc bastion in the support line and saw off all attacks.[19]

The 1/1st put up a tremendous fight but though they hung grimly to their battered, flooded trenches, the enemy was able to filter around their vulnerable flanks and force them to fall back to the support trenches. Soon, they had used up their meagre ration of bombs; they had no machine guns and were running out of ammunition. They suffered 160 casualties. The situation was becoming critical and could only be relieved by a successful counterattack. Such reinforcements as Willcocks had to hand were thrown in, including 2/8th Gurkhas. Givenchy itself, a key junction where the British and French positions abutted, was threatened. Much hard fighting was needed to stiffen the line and the enemy launched further counterattacks next day. But by nightfall on 21 December the position was, temporarily at least, secure. Both sides had run out of steam. Losses for both had been high.[20]

On 2 January 1915, Subadar Major Bhim Sing Thapa wrote to his officer Major Edwardes, who had been wounded during an attack on 19 December 1914. He was attached to the 2/3rd Gurkha Rifles with other officers and men of his battalion:

> Respectful Sir,
> I beg to acknowledge receipt of your kind letter dated 26-12-14 which I received this afternoon. I, with all of the men of

the 1/3rd Q.A.O GR, are always praying The God for your early recovery and have much hope that The God will very kindly send you soon to the field to command on us, and we all very anxious to fight with Germans with Kukris and Bayonets commanded by you.

I have shown your letter this afternoon to the men of the 1/3rd GR and every man was so pleased to see your letter that they have received the treasure of the whole world. We, the men of your Battalion are doing well and I will always try my best to maintain the good name of the 1/3rd Q.A.O GR.

He then lists seven wounded Gurkhas who came with Bhim Sing from the 1st Battalion and were casualties in the counterattack of 21 December 1914:

The above missing men with the exception of the Ran Santbira Gurung were killed but there being no sufficient proof, shown missing. I detailed Havildar Nawal Sing Rana with 3 men to pull out Ran Santbir from the mud but the Havildar informed me he tried his best, assisted with his 3 men, but could not get him out. When I was on the left we [were] ordered to retire so I was the last man to retire from the trench. Rn Bagat Bahadur Gurung [your orderly] says he helped you, not at the immediate place where you [were] wounded, but afterwards and a stretcher was also brought at that place for you. Sir, we all the men of your Battalion request you that you will very kindly favour us with a letter informing about your wound, I hope Maim Sahib and Babas are alright.

I conclude this with our best Salam and praying The God for your immediate recovery, I beg to remain Sir.
From your most obedient Servant
Bhim Sing[21]

In early April, the British had taken over a further 5 miles of French-held trenches, north-east of the battered ruin of Ypres, and it was here the blow fell on 22 April. This, the Second Battle of Ypres, witnessed the first use of poison gas by the Germans on the Western Front. French colonial forces, faced with this satanic yellowish mist, broke. Canadians, deployed around St Julien, did not and fought on in a display of sublime courage for which they paid a very heavy price.[22]

In the wake of this break-in the situation in the salient deteriorated rapidly, but despite the initial German successes, Ypres quickly became a slogging match. The enemy blundered forward, and the Allies blundered in riposte. General Horace Smith-Dorrien was one high-ranking casualty, not of German bullets but of Sir John French's animosity. He had been foolish enough to suggest shortening the line at Ypres and avoiding further piecemeal and bloody counterattacks. When General Plumer, his successor, suggested the same tactics, French concurred (the C in C was on poor terms with Smith-Dorrien and had worked hard to have him replaced).

On 23 April, the Lahore Division was moved up from billets into the line, a gruelling 19-mile march. After a 9-mile march the next day, they moved up to Wieltje on the 26th. At this stage the Sirhind Brigade with 1/1st and 1/4th Gurkhas was in reserve. Even as they moved up, they were subjected to long-range bombardment and suffered casualties. The map shows the start line at 11.00 a.m. on 26 April. The tactical problem was significant. The enemy was dug in, and in strength to the north along Mauser Ridge, roughly 1 mile (1.5km) distant with a rise of higher ground, Hill Top Ridge, in between at about ½ mile (0.75km) away. Ferozepore Brigade was on the left and Jullundar Brigade on the right (today La Brique Cemetery No. 2 lies on the line of approach of the left-hand brigade).[23]

There was little intelligence on the exact location and strength of the German position; no aerial reconnaissance had been undertaken. Equally, there was little preliminary artillery bombardment on the Allied side. There was a barrage at 1.20 p.m. with the attack to go in at 2.00 p.m.; the French on the left would leave their positions 5 minutes later. The attacking units were shielded until they passed the crest of Hill Top Ridge but were then faced with a further 600m, fully exposed to enemy fire. Both attacking brigades suffered heavy loss and got no closer than 200m to the enemy line.

Despite this costly failure, the Sirhind Brigade was sent in at 1.30 p.m. on the following day, 27 April, after the Germans had had a further 24 hours to consolidate their positions. Both Gurkha battalions were to lead the attack. Inevitably, the result was the same. Despite great gallantry no gains were achieved.[24]

The Battle of Festubert was fought from 15–25 May 1915. The offensive formed part of a series of attacks by the French Tenth Army and the British First Army in the wider Second Battle of Artois (3 May–18 June 1915). After the failure of an attempted breakthrough by the First Army in an attack at Aubers Ridge (9 May 1915), tactics of a short hurricane bombardment and an infantry advance with unlimited objectives were replaced with the French practice of slow and deliberate artillery fire intended to prepare the way for an infantry attack.

A continuous three-day bombardment by the British heavy artillery was planned, to cut wire and demolish German machine-gun posts and infantry strongpoints. The German defences were to be captured by a continuous attack, by one division from Rue du Bois to Chocolat Menier Corner and by a second division 600yd (550m) north, which was to capture the German trenches to the left of Festubert. The objectives were 1,000yd (910m) forward, rather than the 3,000yd (2,700m) depth of advance intended previously at Aubers Ridge. The battle was the first British attempt at attrition.

The attack was made against a German salient between Neuve Chapelle to the north and the village of Festubert to the south. The assault was planned along a 3-mile (4.8km) front and would initially be made mainly by Indian troops. This would be the first British Army night attack of the war. The attack was preceded by a 60-hour bombardment by 433 guns which fired around 100,000 shells. This bombardment failed to significantly damage the front-line defences of the German 6th Army, but the initial advance made some progress in good weather conditions.

On 16 May the attack was renewed and by the 19th the 2nd Division and 7th Division had to be withdrawn owing to heavy losses. On 18 May, the 1st Canadian Division, assisted by the 51st (Highland) Division, attacked but made little progress in the face of German artillery fire. The British forces dug in at the new front line in heavy rain. The Germans brought up reinforcements and strengthened their defences. From 20–25 May the attack was resumed and Festubert was captured. The offensive had resulted in a 2-mile (3km) advance.[25]

It was on 18 May that Sirhind Brigade was ordered to launch an assault on the Ferme du Bois, timed to go in at 4.30 p.m. The Guards Brigade on their right flank would attack the Ferme Cour d'Avoue. The British bombardment was due to commence at 2.00 p.m but the weight of German fire was so intense that the attacks could not hope to achieve any concrete results. During daylight on the 19th, the battered Sikhs and 4th King's who had been holding the line were relieved by the HLI and 1/4th Gurkhas. A fresh assault by the Sirhind brigade was planned for 22 May. This was a supporting assault timed to coincide with significant attacks by the Canadians and Highlanders south of Ferme Cour d'Avoue.[26]

The Sirhind Brigade attack involved, from left to right, 1st HLI, 1/1st Gurkhas and 1/4th Gurkhas. The preliminary bombardment lasted all night until 5.00 a.m. on the 22nd. During the hours of darkness at 1.00 a.m. the attack went in. On the right 1/4th fell foul of a sodden ditch barely 30m from the enemy line. The wire beyond was uncut. Sustained and telling fire brought the attack to a costly halt. Fortunately, the 1/1st fared better; their advance was shielded in part by rising ground and the ruined farm complex. Though they still had to negotiate the ditch, the wire in front of them had been successfully cut.

Both leading companies regrouped at the ditch then stormed the German front-line trench, driving out the surviving defenders who fell back on their support trench. This success came at a high price: all of the British officers involved had become casualties and Subadar Jit Singh Gurung assumed leadership. Though he called for reinforcements to consolidate this dearly won bridgehead, the failure of the attack on both flanks meant the precious gains had to be abandoned. This attack cost 1/1st Gurkhas a total of 121 casualties. HLI on the left had also withdrawn. Captain F.M. Douie and Sapper Jiwa Khan, both of the 1/1st's engineers, rescued an injured comrade under enemy fire. Douie was awarded a DSO and Khan the IOM.[27]

In total the British sustained 16,648 casualties between 15 and 25 May. The 2nd Division lost 5,445 casualties, the 7th Division lost 4,123, the 47th Division had 2,355 losses, the Canadian Division lost 2,204 and the Meerut Division suffered 2,521 casualties. The German defenders had $c.$ 5,000 casualties, including 800 men taken prisoner. French casualties during the Second Battle of Artois were 102,533 men and German casualties were 73,072.[28] The toll would continue to mount.

Gallipoli

For the Gurkhas, their Calvary on the Western Front was to be followed by the horrors of the Dardanelles. The Gallipoli Campaign was a disaster from beginning to end. The mission was ineptly commanded and poorly equipped. After nine months of deadlock and the loss of more than a hundred-thousand lives, the Allies eventually withdrew from their doomed attack on the peninsula. The offensive's ultimate aim had been to push through the Dardanelles Strait and capture Constantinople, the Turkish capital. If a breakthrough had been achieved, the Turks, who were allied with Austria and Germany, would have been unable to prevent Britain and France from joining the Russians in the war against Austria-Hungary and Turkey.

General Sir Ian Hamilton[29] was to lead this great invasion; the amphibious effort was almost an afterthought when the purely naval offensive faltered. The Allies fatally underestimated their opponents. For so long Turkey had been the

Map 5. Gallipoli Campaign, 1915.

'sick man of Europe', a tottering empire only held together by the glue of its monolithic bureaucracy. This was a big mistake: 'Johnny Turk' would prove himself a superb soldier, dogged and resilient.[30] Initially the troops deployed comprised the 29th (Midland) Division and the ANZAC Corps (one division each of Australians and New Zealanders). On 25 March, Hamilton petitioned Lord Kitchener for Gurkha reinforcements – 'a type of man who will, I am certain, be most valuable on the Gallipoli Peninsula'.[31]

He wasn't mistaken of course; the harsh terrain of Gallipoli, bare scrub-strewn summits, steep defiles, narrow unfathomable gorges, steep-sided cliffs, unyielding, disorienting, was just what the Gurkhas were used to. Before this 1/6th Gurkhas had been guarding the Suez Canal against infiltration[32] as part of 29th Indian Infantry Brigade, and it was six days after the initial assaults on Cape Helles. By then the early possibilities had been squandered and the chance to bull on to the top of the hill thrown away. There would never be another.

Gurkha Bluff

Further up the long tail of the peninsula, the ANZAC Corps was equally bogged, scarcely off the beaches, the blunt knob of Sari Bair looming above them and pinning them down. The 1/6th on the Allied left at Cape Helles was tasked with storming a feature on the extreme right of the enemy's line and were well dug in. This was a very risky assignment; previous attempts had all foundered with heavy losses. The Gurkhas' CO, Lieutenant Colonel the Honourable Charles Bruce, relying on a detailed recce undertaken by the very formidable Subadar Gambirsing Pun and additional information provided by the navy, braced his men for the attack.[33]

The ships' big guns added their Olympian barrage to the artillery overture. The Gurkhas, during the night of 12 May, succeeded in getting over their first major obstacle, a flat killing ground at the base of the hill. So far so good; next they swarmed up the slope and carried the summit. Turkish defenders were caught unaware, and the position taken. They soon woke up and put in a series of strong counterattacks but the 1/6th, and those big naval cannons, broke up every charge.[34]

Gurkha Bluff was taken and now held but the position, effectively a narrow salient, was still precarious. German General Liman von Sanders continued to throw in counterattacks, regardless of casualties, to pinch out the Gurkhas' toehold. Hamilton, for his part, was equally determined to capitalize on their success and committed the rest of 29th Brigade (1/5th and 2/10th Gurkhas) to enlarge the break-in and seize an additional feature known as Achi Baba which completely overlooked the beaches. This didn't go so well. Von Sanders wouldn't be caught napping twice: 1/6th was first in the attack again but got badly cut up. Despite the weight of Allied shells, the enemy wire stayed intact.[35]

It was now the turn of 1/5th, who fared no better. At this stage of the war the British relied on improvised grenades made from jam tins.[36] The Turks had plenty of real ones and it was this ready supply of bombs that enabled the attackers to 'bomb up the traverses'[37] and clear enemy trenches. Clearly, the availability of jam tins is largely dependent upon how much jam the troops are eating.[38]

On 28 June, 2/10th Gurkhas attacked the feature known as Gully Ravine. Here, again their speed, agility and relentless determination achieved wonders. Covered by a heavy naval bombardment, the battalion dashed forward, making good use of sheltering features and getting under the lee of a cliff, where the Turkish Maxims couldn't reach. The defenders stayed complacent, thinking the cliff face too steep an obstacle – at least until the Gurkhas came screaming over the top and hustled them back over 1,000yd (914m).[39]

A dispatch from General Sir Ian Hamilton, Commander in Chief of the Mediterranean Expeditionary Force, described the battles of May and June 1915, praising the Gurkhas:

> During the night of the 10th/11th May the 6th Gurkhas started off to seize this bluff. Their scouts descended to the sea, worked their way for some distance through the broken ground along the shore and crawled hands and knees up the precipitous face of the cliff. On reaching the top they were heavily fired on. As a surprise the enterprise had failed, but as a reconnaissance it proved very useful. On the following day Major General H.V. Cox, commanding 29th Indian Infantry Brigade, submitted proposals for a concerted attack.
>
> At 6.30 p.m. on the 12th May the Manchester Brigade and the 29th Divisional Artillery opened fire on the Turkish trenches and, under cover of this fire, a double company of the 1/6th Gurkhas once more crept along the shore and assembled below the bluff. Then, the attention of the Turks being taken up with the bombardment, they swiftly scaled the cliffs and carried the work with a rush. The Machine-gun section of the Gurkhas was hurried forward, and at 4.30 a.m. a second double company was pushed up to join the first. An hour later these two double companies extended and began to entrench to join up their new advanced left diagonally with the right of the trenches previously held by their battalion.
>
> At 6 a.m. a third double company advanced across the open from their former front line of trenches under a heavy rifle and machine-gun fire, and established themselves on this diagonal line between the main ravine on their right and the newly captured redoubt. The 4th double company moved up as a support, and held the former firing line. Our left flank, which had been firmly held up against all attempts on the 6th–8th, was now, by stratagem, advanced nearly 500 yards. Purchased as it was with comparatively slight losses (21 killed, 92 wounded) this success was due to careful preparation and organisation by Major General H. V. Cox, commanding 29th Indian Infantry Brigade, Lieutenant Colonel Hon. C. G. Bruce, commanding 1/6th Gurkhas.[40]

Sari Bair

Despite these successes, victory had come at an exceedingly high price and all three Gurkha battalions had lost heavily, so the brigade was pulled out for a spell of rest and recreation on the Greek island of Imbros. This was only a temporary reprieve as new attempts were being planned in an effort to break the deadlock. There would be another major landing at Suvla Bay, deploying three fresh divisions, and a major thrust to bust out of the ANZAC bridgehead aimed at taking the summit of Sari Bair, the most dominant local feature. The idea was to pinch out the defenders blocking Cape Helles and force the Turks back up the spine of the peninsula, bringing the dazzling prize of fabled Constantinople into Allied sights.

From Anzac Cove on 6 August 29th Indian Brigade with 4th Australians would form lead elements on the left flank of the attacking formations, pushing up two narrow valleys beneath the ridge line. It was to be a night assault, fraught with difficulties at best. And difficulties there were. On the left, the Gurkhas made good progress but were stopped tantalisingly short of the main feature. On the right, the attack stalled and 1/5th with 1/6th were both ordered to swing over to the right to lend their support. Even for Gurkhas, this broken ground proved a dreadful obstacle and while they kept going forward, they still ended up below the crest.[41]

Next day, the Allies tried again but the Turks had reinforced their threatened positions; any gains were measured in costly yards. Lieutenant William Slim from the Warwickshires (of Burma fame – see Chapter 9) was among those drafted in as reinforcements and it was here the future field marshal first encountered Gurkhas. His respect lasted a lifetime. Meanwhile, the offensive up from Suvla Bay just hadn't happened so the full focus still rested on Sari Bair. On the following day, they tried again.

Yet again, those huge naval guns sent their massive, screaming shells slamming down onto the defenders' positions, ravaging the shattered ground, a *Gotterdämmerung* for the Turks grimly clinging on. At first light on the 9th, 5.23 a.m. precisely, 1/6th Gurkhas with two companies of Lancashires went forward. They got into the enemy trenches and made up for their lack of grenades with bayonet and kukri. The Battalion CO, Major C.J.L. Allanson, was wounded by Turkish blades; Lieutenant le Marchant was killed. The fight lasted only 10 minutes. Dozens of defenders were cut down and finally the survivors broke. Gurkhas and Brits were masters of Sari Bair, the high ground.[42]

They chased the demoralised Turks clear off the summit and down the far side. That's when it was all thrown away, not by the 1/6th but by the simple fact that their brilliantly successful attack was completely unsupported. Those two full brigades intended to follow on were still lost in the maze of gullies far behind. There was no reinforcement and when the Turks halted to regroup, they realised just that. A strong series of counterattacks inevitably ensued, and the Gurkhas were forced back step by bloody step, back up the hill, back to the top and then back off again. They fought every foot of the way, losing virtually all their officers, command devolving onto Subadar Major Gambirsing Pun, a superb soldier who held what was left together – he didn't speak much English and needed the MO Captain Phipson to translate orders as they came in.[43] At Sari Bair they were the only troops in the whole campaign to reach the crest line and look down on the strait. There wouldn't be another chance.

Summer gave way to a dismal autumn, freezing wind and lashing rain; hastily dug trenches soon became foaming watercourses. The Allies clung on, like refugees abandoned in an earthly version of purgatory: cholera, dysentery, frostbite, trench foot and chest infections caused more casualties than the enemy. That day, 9 August, became the high-water mark, the great golden opportunity, the 'what if' or 'if only' of the Gallipoli Campaign.[44]

Fresh from the carnage on the Western Front, 1/4th Gurkhas were sent in as reinforcements. These were needed owing to the constant attrition from shelling, sniping and disease. When Kitchener himself came out in November, he decided on evacuation. Hamilton was sacked and replaced by Sir Charles Monro who organized the withdrawals – in the supreme irony of the whole tragedy, these were brilliantly conducted. Of the Gurkha battalions the order came too late for 755 officers and men, hundreds more being wounded.[45] It is said that Hamilton lamented he had not had more Gurkhas and that if he had, he would have won through. What is sure is that it was Gurkhas who took Sari Bair and who brought him to the very brink of a great victory – a victory that never was.

The Middle East

If asked to name the worst defeat of the Allies in the First World War, most people would probably answer 'Gallipoli' but they would be wrong, the British defeat at the Siege of Kut from December 1915–April 1916 was far worse.[46]

In December 2018, in the mellow, quintessentially English pastures of the Cotswolds, the author was introduced to Lieutenant Colonel Quentin Mathias, a retired gunner who had spent his career – as had his Huguenot ancestors

– as a professional soldier. His charming house was the very epitome of Miss Marple's retired brigadier with an impressive line of portraits: suitably stern young men in red coats, servants of the world's greatest empire. He has memoirs from the days of the Raj and Indian Mutiny and showed the author a folio of three slim, handwritten volumes which form an account written up by his father, Lieutenant Leonard William Henry Mathias DSO at the time; a day-by-day diary of the Siege of Kut al Amara (December 1915–April 1916), together with a further account of his captivity in the dreadful aftermath of the garrison's capitulation.

Nothing quickens the otherwise cool blood of the historian more than the scent of unpublished primary source material in the neat script of the original writer, meticulous, detailed and engrossing. The National Army Museum took a full copy in 1975 and their rather dry acknowledgement confirms it as the best and fullest account of the siege they have seen.

Lieutenant Mathias was a young, junior officer in the Royal Engineers and his skills as a sapper were at a premium as General Townshend's Division dug in around the ancient settlement of Kut, the wide and near mythical sweep of the Tigris running by on three sides. The Poona Division was short of all kinds of specialists, so a relatively junior sapper found himself virtually in charge of the defensive ring.

Mathias details the siege day by deadly day as the noose tightens. This is very much a soldier's view; grand strategy can be left to the editor. Nor was the defence passive. Deficient in all manner of kit, the sappers devised homemade trench mortars, periscope rifles and other gear, keeping the ring safe even as the vice closed, and relief efforts foundered. By nature of his role, Lieutenant Mathias was completely peripatetic, covering every section of the line, seeing no shortage of action as the Turks threw themselves forward time and again.

Mathias doesn't criticise his CO or any of the senior officers (happily, as editor the author is less constrained). The final capitulation was inevitable and while shameful, reflected no faintheartedness on the part of the defenders themselves who had fought long and hard, the victims as much of bad decision making as of enemy aggression. Lieutenant Mathias spent the rest of the war in the murderous confinement of captivity and was lucky, unlike about 70 per cent of his fellow European soldiers, to survive. In his personal memoir he recalls:

> Nobody thought the Turks would go down below Essin and there were some who doubted they would hold it. As it was they went down to Sheikssaad which lies 20 miles further down. Great mistakes were made at the beginning of the siege – the

> useless civilian population was not expelled from Kut, so we had 5,000 extra mouths to feed.

Gallipoli was bad but Iraq would be even worse. British troops campaigning during the West's ill-judged crusade against Saddam Hussein in 2003–8 were surprised to discover characteristic Commonwealth War Graves Commission cemeteries already established. These were the dead of the First World War, interred in a far flung corner of that titanic conflict, some at Kut al Amara by the banks of the eternal Tigris, the fertile crescent of antiquity and cradle of civilisation.

For any who knew their history, the First World War precedent would not have been encouraging: an epic siege concluded with the humiliating surrender of 10,000 British and imperial troops. The First World War throws up any number of disasters, yet Kut managed to be shameful as well as bloody and Gurkhas would suffer the full degradation. It was all about oil, of course. Britain had a vast refinery on Abadan Island, just across from Basra, and this would make it easy for Turkish vessels to intercept tankers on the Shatt-al-Arab passage. Once Britain and Turkey were at war Basra became a target and was seized in November 1914 by a brilliant little amphibious offensive. This appeared to augur well.[47]

Kut – the Deadly Refuge

Major General Sir Charles Vere Ferrers Townshend KCB, DSO (1861–1924)[48] was a product of empire. Born blue-blooded but cash-poor, he strove hard to forge a dynamic military career. He had been one of those who marched to the relief of Gordon at Khartoum, but his real chance arrived eleven years later when his remote outpost at Chitral on the North-West Frontier came under siege. This episode became the stuff of P.C. Wren or G.A. Henty, a regular epic of the sort Victorian newspapers loved and their readers applauded.

In spring 1915 Townshend was promoted to the rank of major general and given command of the 6th (Poona) Division in Mesopotamia, charged with protecting British oil-producing assets in Persia from Ottoman intentions. As he sailed down the Tigris in a steamer named the *Dwarka*, Townshend often wrote in his diary about his hero Belisarius, a late Roman commander of genius who took Mesopotamia from the Persians in AD 541. Townshend wrote: 'Who knows that I shall not eventually become governor of Mesopotamia?' It didn't quite work out that way.[49]

Townshend was instructed by his Corps Commander General Nixon to move his division up-river from Basra along the north-westerly course of the River Tigris in a large ad hoc flotilla made up of motley craft. 'The advance on Baghdad is perhaps the most remarkable example of an enormous military risk being taken, after full deliberation, for no definite or concrete military advantage.'[50] The strategic objective was for the division to capture the town of Amara and destroy all Ottoman forces present in Lower Mesopotamia. Townshend's relations with General Nixon were never cordial and within four days of their first encounter, Townshend was writing letters to their masters in India attacking him as incompetent and suggesting that he himself was a better man to lead Force D.

A costly battle at Ctesiphon beginning on 23 November shattered any illusions of another easy win. The Turks were well dug in and with 18,000 defenders outnumbered 'Charlie' Townshend's attacking force of 5,000 or less. Initially his attacks punctured the Turks' first-line defences but foundered against the second and recoiled in the face of strong counterattacks. Like the Spartans at Thermopylae, 300 Gurkhas from 2/7th, with a company of 24th Punjabis, staged a heroic defence and saw off repeated assaults. Even the official Turkish military historian recorded his respect for this gallant band. They were magnificent but it didn't change the outcome.[51]

Townshend now fell back upon Kut in the first week of December 1915. Despite losses, he still had some 11,000 fit troops under his command with additional cavalry. As the Ottomans began to mass before Kut, he made the key decision to dig in rather than attempt a further withdrawal.[52] The city with its 6,000 inhabitants occupied a sweeping bend in the Tigris which effectively acted as a wide moat on three sides, leaving only one landward flank exposed. Initially, after he had ordered his cavalry to stage a successful breakout, Townshend was confronted by a matching force of Turks led by Halil Pasha. These forces were steadily built up and a well-respected German officer, Baron von der Goltz, was given command of what was developing into a full-blown siege.[53]

To be fair, at this point Townshend wanted to break clear and retreat but Nixon ordered him to hold on – he saw advantage in tying down so many Turks. Efforts were being made to bring up a relief force by boats, but communication failures and delays proved fractious and damaging. Progress on riverine transport was slow as the vice steadily and inexorably tightened around the defenders at Kut.

It wasn't until January 1916 that Lieutenant General Aylmer led the first relief attempt, dangerously held back by internecine wrangling up the tortuous umbilical cord of the command chain. Meanwhile, Nixon was feeling the strain and had requested a replacement. An initial clash of arms occurred on 6 January at Sheikh Sa'ad. After several days' hard fighting the British prevailed, but atrocious weather imposed further delays. Having retreated only a relatively short distance, the Turkish forces dug in again but were once more ousted and pushed back.[54]

A mere 8km further on, the Ottomans established another block and efforts to dislodge them cost dearly. Both 1/1st and 1/9th Gurkhas took part in this fight. Medical arrangements throughout this campaign had proved woeful; wounded men were left for hours in awful conditions as there weren't enough ambulances or enough hospitals. Many of those injured endured agonising journeys in crashing, jolting wagons.[55]

Massive enemy reinforcements (freed up by the Allied failure at Gallipoli) were being pushed into the sector and the relief expedition ground to a halt. This settled Nixon's future and he was replaced by General Lake. He, in turn, pushed more troops up the line to support Aylmer who was leading the charge. Another breakthrough attempt foundered on 8 March with heavy casualties and Aylmer too was sacked. His successor General Gorringe tried again in what became known as the First Battle of Kut. Both sides were roughly equal in numbers, but the Turks clung to their redoubts and couldn't be budged. By 22 April, the British, despite a rapidly mounting death toll, were no further forward.

One helpful innovation of the rapidly stalling campaign was the first successful effort to supply a besieged garrison from the air. Planes from 30 Squadron of the RFC managed to drop both food and ammo into the ring at Kut but, inevitably, some drops landed in the Turkish lines. So far, in the campaign overall, the Allies had lost nearly 30,000 men, 3 times the butcher's bill on the other side and still with no relief in sight. Even the death of von der Golz from typhoid fever on 19 April didn't tip the scales back.[56]

Putting your faith in fortresses has been a risky proposition since Vercingetorix bottled himself up in Alesia facing Caesar in 52 BC. The Gallic leader could have told Townshend all about the dangers of handing the initiative over to the enemy – and the Turks knew a thing or two about sieges. This wasn't the North-West Frontier. Though he saw off attempts at storming the place, Townshend's position grew critical as the noose tightened and attempts at relief foundered.

In desperation a team of negotiators (including T.E. Lawrence) attempted to barter and stage a *Geltkrieg* ('Money-War') – buying the Turks off for, in today's money, £150 million. The bung didn't cut it; nor did an appeal to the

Russians who had large Cossack cavalry forces operating to the north in Persia. Townsend asked for terms on 26 April and surrendered unconditionally three days later. About 13,000 British and imperial soldiers went into the bag. Of these about 70 per cent of the British and perhaps 20 per cent of the Indian troops subsequently died in captivity, killed by hunger, disease, exhaustion and brutality.

For their general, captivity didn't prove too disagreeable. He was well housed in a substantial villa, treated more like an honoured guest than a POW, and even had the use of his own yacht. He became a friend of Enver Pasha and a fixture in the Ottoman social calendar. Meanwhile, his men were not enjoying quite such luxury. Nearly half died as a result of the neglect, indifference and outright brutality of their guards.[57] Of these, the Gurkhas from 2/7th, inspired by their first rate NCOs, fared at least slightly less badly; but as historian Christopher Bullock points out, many young men from Nepal would never see their high hills again.[58]

Kut itself was retaken at the end of 1916 but the tattered survivors of Force D remained prisoners until the end of the war. Townshend came home in 1918 but not to the popular acclaim he was expecting. His reputation was lost and it soon became clear the army had no further use for him. He resigned and tried politics but the ghosts of those he had abandoned continued to haunt him and he died in obscurity. Needless to say, the Gurkhas he had abandoned when surrendering fared far worse.[59]

Armageddon

After the Turks and their German allies had been seen off from the Suez Canal Zone in 1915, hostilities had been muted. The new Bavarian CO kept the pot boiling with pinpricks and the Senussi uprising kicked off in the desert, a forgotten mini-campaign worthy of P.C. Wren.[60] Meanwhile, Townshend had been left to surrender and there was a general stalemate. Both Gallipoli and Mesopotamia had ended in Allied failure, disastrously so. However, the war against Russia was going badly for the Sublime Porte, defeats for which the Armenian people would pay a heavy price,[61] and Turkey would now struggle to fight on two fronts.

At last, the British began a limited series of minor offensives into Sinai; a German-led response was rebuffed with losses. At the start of 1917 with Lloyd George desperately needing a win, any win, somewhere, the invasion of Palestine began with a narrow thrust at Gaza. With a clear superiority in

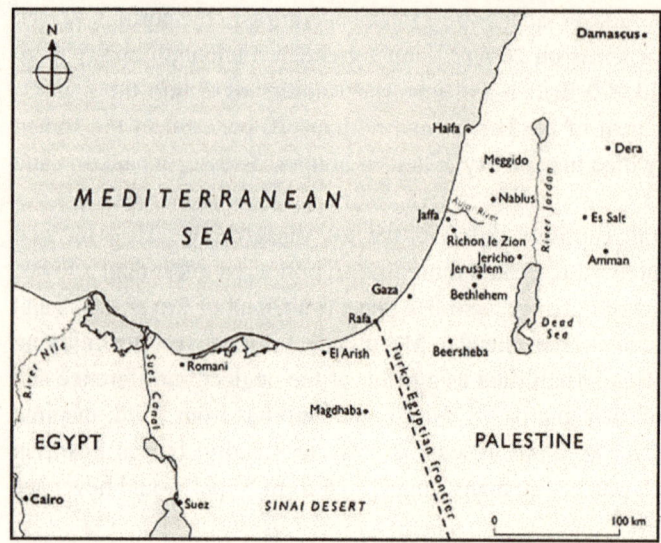

Map 6.
Palestine,
1917–18.

cavalry, the ANZAC mounted brigades outclassing anything the Turks could muster, Gaza could now be attacked. This still proved difficult and early attempts faltered.[62] A second attempt on Gaza cost many casualties for no gains and, once again, it seemed the Allies were going nowhere.

Things began to pick up in Mesopotamia with the appointment of the highly capable Sir Stanley Maude who, in December 1916, advanced up the Tigris to recover Kut. New and better kit for an army marshalled and led by a brilliant general achieved wonders and the Turks were soon in headlong retreat. Maude had six Gurkha regiments, a total of fifteen battalions under his hand.[63] He intended to force the Tigris at its Shumran Bend to outflank the Turks dug in on the east bank. Three battalions would each attempt the task; 1/2nd and 2/9th would form two-thirds of the attacking force. They would be rowed across by the 1/4th Hampshires, many of whom were ferrymen in Civvy Street so well suited to the job.[64] Just as well, since the waters were high, and the great river was flowing fast.

Major George Wheeler led the charge of 2/9th; of their thirteen lighters only ten made it over and they had to fight very hard indeed to win a narrow toehold.[65] If possible, 1/2nd had it even worse; drifting boats manned by dead or wounded, shot to pieces, slid downstream, the flotsam of war. Nonetheless, the aptly named Lieutenant Toogood got ashore on the far bank with just over fifty men and acted as a kind of impromptu beach-master, guiding other survivors in. They barely held on with only a slender fingerhold. It wasn't quite as bad for the third attacking unit, 2nd Norfolks, and together with the surviving Gurkhas, some of whom had been diverted to their crossing point, they clawed out a viable bridgehead, enough to allow construction of a pontoon bridge over which reinforcements soon flowed. It was, as Wellington might have observed, a very close-run thing.[66]

In March 1917, Baghdad was taken,[67] and 2/4th Gurkhas were among the first to enter the fabled city. Revolution in Russia and the Bolsheviks' peace with Turkey caused ripples of alarm and led to the quixotic adventures of 'Dunsterforce'[68] in a racing resumption of the Great Game. Before the blistering heat of summer laid a stifling blanket over operations, 1/2nd, 2/4th and 2/9th Battalions fought again at the confluence point of Adhaim on 30 April. The settlement itself was taken in the first rush but a fierce sandstorm, coming on just as the Gurkhas were attacking a key defensive position, 'The Boot', provided cover for elite Turkish units to counterattack. Desperate and costly fighting followed, and the day ended without any breakthrough. Next day, though, the Turks were found to have retreated and ceded their ground.[69]

Back before the un-breached walls of Gaza, a new player, General (later Field Marshal) Edmund Allenby, took the stage. His leadership would be decisive; just as well, since Prime Minister David Lloyd George was expecting Jerusalem as a Christmas present.[70] Maude, though a highly effective soldier, was not a cavalryman and yet the extensive use of cavalry in Mesopotamia and Palestine had great potential. Allenby was a horse soldier, and he would maximise the deployment of his cavalry. Maude died of cholera in November but before that he had launched another advance along the banks of the Euphrates. This meant 1/5th, 2/5th and 2/6th Gurkhas were again in action with yet another savage fight that September attempting to turn Turkish defences, well dug in as ever, at Ramadi. It was a very well-chosen position, one flank secured by the mighty river itself and the line bolstered by buildings and natural features. A night attack by the mainly Gurkha 42nd Brigade made gains, hotly disputed by counterattacks after dawn. Nonetheless, a successful encircling move held the defenders in a vice, and it wasn't long before white flags blossomed over enemy trenches. Once again though, the fight had been hard and costly.[71]

Allenby was making for Gaza, the key choke point. This was no easy matter, since the Turks had built up a hefty chain of defences bottling up all the land approaches. The general decided to pin the defenders of Gaza, too well dug in, to their trenches while he struck a blow at the less well defended centre inland which, if he broke through, would allow him to outflank the whole coastal belt. Von Falkenhayn, the brilliant former German impresario, sidelined after 1916 and the cauldron of Verdun, was sent to lead the defence and the Turks had managed to retrieve some elite divisions from other fronts to bolster their defence. For the moment they also had superiority in the air. Happily, for the Allies, the breakthrough at Beersheba was a complete success, glorified by the madcap charge of the Australian Light Horse which, against all odds, even all reason, succeeded spectacularly. Gaza was taken.

Von Falkenhayn was a wily and skilful opponent, even if his natural arrogance didn't endear him to his Turkish allies. If Allenby wanted Lloyd George to have a good Christmas he would have to keep moving before the rains came and Jerusalem, as from time immemorial, was still sheltered by the Judean Hills. Besides, he couldn't reduce the Holy City to a shell-ravaged ruin; it had to be taken intact. This meant another wide outflanking movement over hard ground and leaving his centre exposed. Falkenhayn tried but couldn't muster the strength or the will to strike back. Turkish resistance, which had been dogged, suddenly folded. Allenby, with due humility, walked through the gates on 11 December, more deliverer than conqueror – but he'd kept his promise to Lloyd George.[72]

This was just as well, as the prime minister wasn't going to have such a happy spring. The *Kaiserschlacht* offensives, which burst like a flood over Allied positions on the Western Front, neatly robbed Allenby of 60,000 troops, desperately needed as reinforcements. The outcome of the whole war hung in the balance. Allenby was at least bolstered by Lawrence's successes in the desert which, if a relative sideshow, were becoming legendary and significantly adding to the Sublime Porte's mounting catalogue of serious woes.

Despite being shorn of so many of his soldiers, Allenby was still thinking in terms of offence, striking up along the coastal plain. At first, he was checked: Liman von Sanders, victor at Gallipoli, had replaced the acerbic von Falkenhayn. He understood that the Turkish forces were nearing exhaustion and were naturally better suited to stubborn defence than active aggression.[73] He was right, but the pendulum was swinging inexorably against him, resources were dwindling and rations were scarce. The leadership in Constantinople appeared rather to have lost interest. Despite the attritional demands of the Western Front, Allenby had made up for this with fresh drafts from India. He was fully supplied and poised to strike. He had also achieved that vital mastery of the skies.[74]

On 10 April 1918, by the barren Plain of Sharon, Rifleman Karanbahadur Rana from 2/3rd Gurkhas charged enemy positions that had delivered a hail of fire and caused many casualties. He was part of a Lewis Gun team and when the leader was knocked out, braved bullets and bombs to take out a German machine gun and cover their withdrawal. He was awarded a well-deserved VC.[75]

Using his ad hoc Arab irregulars, now very adept in blowing up railways, Allenby planned to isolate the enemy in front of him by cutting off his line of retreat. He intended to blow a major gap in the Turkish positions, allowing his cavalry to flood through on to level ground where their superiority would be telling. A horde of 15,000 horsemen would seize the vital chain of railway links, channelling the Turks into shrinking avenues of retreat. Von Sanders might have seen the blow coming from the coastal sector, but Allied planes blotted out his view. The attack went ahead on 19 September and drove the Turkish outposts in, hurling their forces back into the Judean Hills. The cavalry burst through the kind of Napoleonic stroke Haig had so often imagined occurring on the Western Front but just as often failed to achieve.

So total was the rout that von Sanders' HQ was nearly overrun[76] and only the classic German ability to mobilise rear-echelon staff saved the day and allowed him to get clear. Harried by horsemen from the plain and planes from the azure blue above, the Turkish forces fell apart – such was the Battle of Meggido, 'The place which is called in the Hebrew tongue Armageddon.'[77] And Armageddon it was. During the fight all of Allenby's six Gurkha battalions, 1/1st, 2/3rd, 3/3rd, 2/7th, 1/8th and 4/11th, fought hard and well. Haifa fell and then, on 2 October, Damascus itself.

Not quite the last battle perhaps as there was another to fight by the Tigris, the Battle of Sharqat (28–30 October). Here 1/7th – like Caesar's mixed Germanic cavalry and light infantry – kept pace with their mounted comrades, covering an astonishing 36 miles in 26 hours. At the same time, 1/10th fought the Turks head on, until finally over 11,000 of them surrendered.[78] The adjutant encountered a motley group of high-ranking Turks anxious to surrender to somebody important:

> As the writer, who was Adjutant, was going forward in the half-light with orders for the forward companies, he met a small cavalcade of Turks led by a distinguished looking officer who asked, in French, to be directed to the headquarters of the British commander. This was the Turkish commander, Ismail Hakki Pasha, coming in to surrender, and thus the remnant of the Turkish army in Mesopotamia was destroyed after ten days hard fighting and relentless pressure in which, to quote the words of General Marshall's[79] final dispatch 'the fortitude and courage displayed by all the troops was beyond praise and was the main factor in the defeat of a stubborn enemy holding carefully prepared positions in a rugged and difficult country'.[80]

THE GURKHA WAY

This was more or less the end for Turkey and full and terrible retribution for the Allies' earlier defeats. The Gurkhas had played a key role throughout but had paid very dearly for it.

* * *

This had been a very new type of war for the Gurkhas, an industrial conflict on a titanic scale, never before witnessed. It was their greatest challenge and they had not failed the test, despite unbelievable odds and hardships. 'Tommy Atkins' and 'Johnny Gurkha' were two sides of the same coin. And, while life back in the Indian subcontinent on the fringes of Britain's still vast colonial domain might seem to have returned to normal, it hadn't: the world had changed, and the days of the old Raj were numbered. One officer was so inspired by the courage of the Gurkhas under him, he was moved to write:

> When God first chose a Gurkha,
> As a vessel of his own,
> He took a chunk of cheerfulness,
> And laid on flesh and bone,
> A face, well some deny it,
> But a smile that no-one could,
> For anyone who's seen it,
> Wishes his was half as good!
> I have seen him broken, mangled,
> With his life's tide running low,
> And the tears welled deep within me,
> As I watched the last thing go,
> But it triumphed 'ere it left him,
> And stifled every moan,
> 'Twas the little chunk of cheerfulness,
> Being gathered to its own.[81]

Chapter 6

'Ragged-Arsed Barnshoots' – Back to the Old Frontier

> Hail, soldier, huddled in the rain,
> Hail, soldier, squelching through the mud,
> Hail, soldier, sick of dirt and pain,
> The sight of death, the smell of blood,
> New mean, new weapons bear the brunt;
> New slogans gild the ancient game:
> The infantry are still in front,
> And mud and dust are much the same.
> Hail, humble footman, poised to fly
> Across the west, or any, Wall!
> Proud, plodding, peerless P.B.I. –
> The foulest, finest, job of all.
>
> A.P. Herbert, *The Poor Bloody Infantry*

My own ancestors, centuries back, came from the Anglo-Scottish Border reivers, those wild raiders who were the protagonists in three centuries of very nasty internecine border warfare between England and Scotland. They were light cavalry, 'hobilers', hard men on hardy garrons (small horses) who lived by cattle-stealing and owed no loyalty to any but their own kin and affinity. Modern-day concepts of nationalism and patriotism meant nothing to them. They generally made common cause with the 'riding' names over the line so the reivers[1] of Tynedale rode with those from Liddesdale, hardened criminal mafias happy to prey on anyone. They lived in strong stone towers and bastles,[2] knew no trade but war and seemingly revelled in the horrors of vendetta, the blood feud. Their dark and remote glens were a lawless tract of nowhere – the *threap*.[3]

Threapland

The 'Steel Bonnets' would have recognised much about the Pathans – that same wild addiction to your own version of freedom, awareness of and loyalty to your name, disdain for any external authority and the blind attrition of a decent feud. They too were feckless, wantonly cruel and frequently murderous. It's small wonder the British developed a wary respect for these uplanders, these savage, recalcitrant and totally untrustworthy hill-men, whose bellicosity and squalid little forts were the badges of their very identity and a two-fingered gesture to any form of authority beyond their own tribal laws. The official history (OH) of the 1919 Afghanistan Campaign rather romantically refers to the country as 'an Asiatic Switzerland'.[4] It isn't.

It was famously and fatuously said that the First World War was 'the war to end all wars'. That wasn't right either. Wars have a pernicious habit of begetting yet more wars and the First World War produced a few, intermeddling by the Western Allies in the Russian Civil War[5] being but one. It has been alleged that 'the last shot of that war was the first shot of the Second World War' – views on that may vary but it was certain the Gurkhas wouldn't be kept idle.

With hindsight, it can see that the bells were tolling, seemingly a long way off, for the Raj as the juggernaut of nationalism began to gather momentum and the cost of empire was easily outstripping the returns. The British Empire was going bust. But the old North-West Frontier so beloved of Kipling was still live – very much so.

Old Frontier, New War

In 1907 when tsarist Russia and the British Empire entered into the Triple Entente,[6] the Great Game which had raced across the top of the world for the best part of a century was postponed, potentially indefinitely. Indefinitely didn't, in the event, last longer than a decade when the Russian Revolution again shifted the dynamic and the hounds were off again. By 1919 Britain was backing (unsuccessfully) the Whites against the Reds and the underlying threat to India via the back door of Afghanistan seemed remote. That didn't mean there wasn't any bother – the Third Afghan War (May–June 1919) was about to kick off.

Since the end of the Second Afghan War relations between Kabul and the Raj had been, by local standards, almost cordial. Afghanistan maintained full independence, or very nearly full as it had been agreed that Delhi could direct

'RAGGED-ARSED BARNSHOOTS' – BACK TO THE OLD FRONTIER

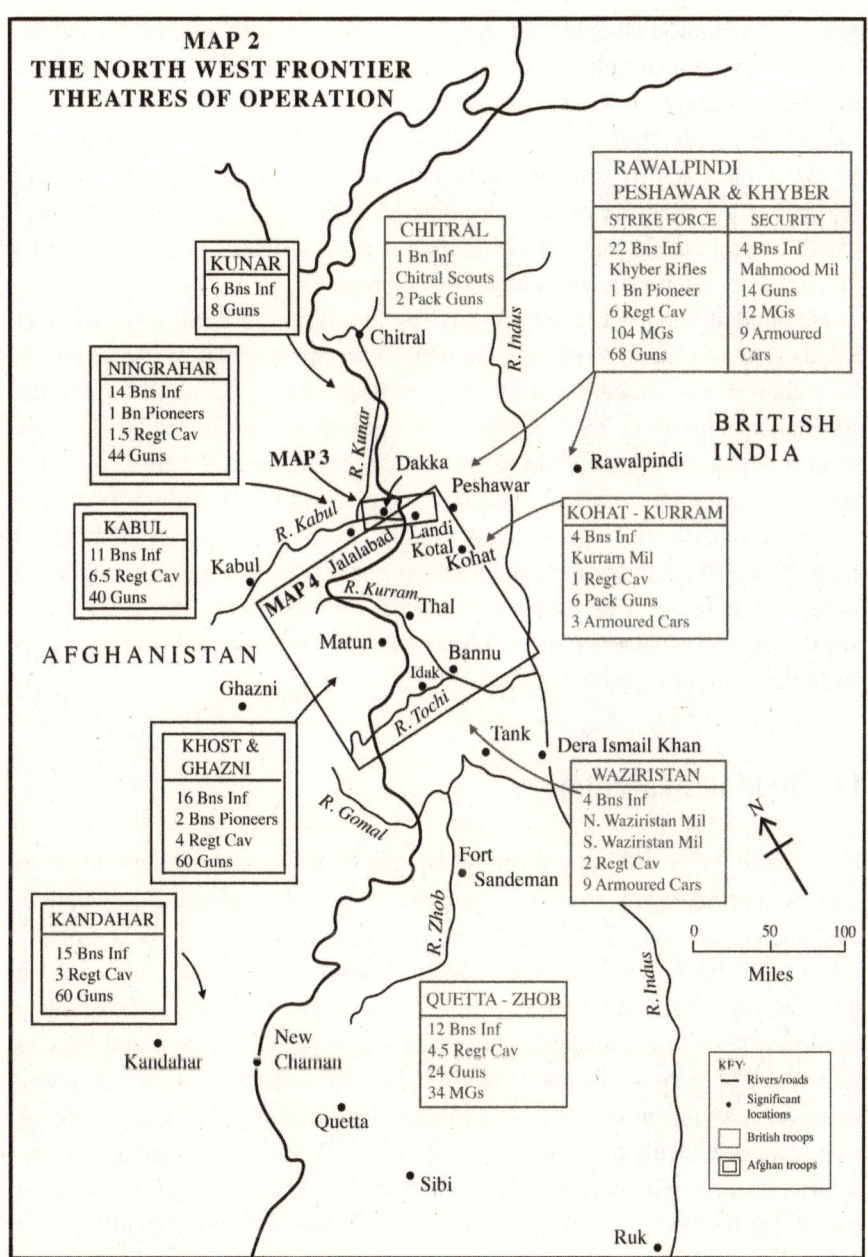

Map 7. Third Afghan War, 1919.

Afghan foreign policy. Not that the emirs had much in the way of external aims; internal survival was their general priority, and this at least meant Britain could be sure of keeping Russia at bay. Since 1901 the country had been ruled by the Emir Habibullah who had steered a clever path between Britain and the Central Powers, particularly Germany and Turkey. He had allowed these to establish a mission in Kabul and milked them for supplies.[7] The Turks were keen to stir up prospects for Jihad, but the emir was too canny to be drawn. At the end of the war, he considered he had in fact stuck with the winning side and had earned a seat at the peace talks. The Viceroy, 1st Viscount Chelmsford,[8] wasn't having any of that but Habibullah was assassinated in February 1919 which led, inevitably, to an internal power struggle.

Habibullah was succeeded, shakily, by his third son Amanullah who set out his stall as a kind of reformer, hoping to exploit stirrings of unrest within the Indian Army, exacerbated by the Amritsar Massacre,[9] to throw off the impediments imposed by the Treaty of Gandamack which had ended the Second Afghan War and allowed the British a measure of control over the nation's foreign policy in particular. Focusing attention externally was always one means of deflecting opposition internally. So, on 3 May, he invaded British India through the Khyber Pass and his forces seized the strategically important settlement at Bagh. This meant war. As the OH points out, the emir was a spiritual as well as lay ruler and as his people were 'bigoted Mohammedans' he could dress up his ambitions as Jihad.[10]

The Baldak Marching

This would be a different form of frontier warfare, something the emir, motivated primarily by an unfortunate blend of opportunism and desperation, had not appreciated. The First World War, that cosmic clash of competing industrial technologies, had spawned new weapons. Air power, control of the skies, was now a military reality. Britain had gone from a handful of string-bag motorised kites to a vast air fleet of swift scouts (fighters), light and heavier bombers. The hills would soon be alive with the sound of aircraft. It was a lot easier now to run out of hiding places; the dizzying heights and tortuous ranges were suddenly no longer so inaccessible. Tanks and armoured cars (see Appendix 6) were another new phenomenon. The frontier might not be good ground for lumbering tracked leviathans, but it was perfect for smaller, swift and well-armed wheeled terriers.

Now, three columns were sent out to meet the threat and turn the Afghans back. One moved straight up the Khyber and fought successful actions at Bagh, Landi Kotal and Dakka. A second took the fort at Spin Baldak (see below) but the third became pinned down at Thal until a relief force led by Dyer, coming up from Peshawar, saved the day. Tactically, the war was a British success, though in political terms the gains were muted.[11]

As the crisis loomed, 2/10th Gurkhas were based at Chaman, just over the border in India.[12] On 2 May, they were warned of the likely Afghan offensive – their responsibilities would be guarding water supplies and rail links. For a single battalion, this was quite a tall order and implied they would be strung out in penny packets on outpost duties. This didn't mean it wouldn't be dangerous; outposts were inevitably exposed and the Pathans very much liked an exposed outpost. In the event it didn't happen; most of the action took place further north, towards the Khyber.[13]

Here 1/4th Gurkhas formed part of the Quetta Division which, after concentrating at Chaman, moved out along the road to Kandahar aiming to take the strong fort at Spin Baldak, about 6 miles (9.6km) west of the border. Marching from Chaman in the cool dawn on 27 May, the force approached to within 1,000yd (914m) of the low ridge where tall towers, outriders of the big dun-coloured fort, stood out against a rising sun.[14]

British guns began their opening bombardment as the 1/4th Gurkhas surged forward against the main gate with 22nd Punjabis on their left, while two more infantry battalions attempted a flanking attack up the ridge. Breaching the gates won them a foothold but the flanking troops were bogged down by stiff resistance. Below, and drawn up on the now furnace-hot plain, the 2/10th had every hope they had be sent in to bolster the attack, but that job went to 1st Battalion, Duke of Wellington's, and the Gurkhas stood baking but safe. They remained so for the rest of the long, hot day as embers of resistance were finally extinguished.[15]

By late afternoon Gurkhas of the 2/10th were marching, very hot, dehydrated but without a whiff of adrenalin back towards Chaman. The Gurkhas derisively labelled their day the 'Baldak Marching', though it was enough for them to gain 'Afghanistan' as a battle honour.[16] The signing of a ceasefire on 3 June ended the war but didn't stop the shooting. Once the frontier was buzzing, it buzzed for a while. The Pathans weren't overly bothered about formality and sniping at any target of opportunity was just too good a chance to miss. High command decided on additional fortifications – a standard fall-back position when high command has run out of other ideas – so 2/10th stayed at Chaman. Strongpoints were to be built joining the base there to the important Bogra Reservoir, linked with trenches and wired in. It was thankless, broiling work with the constant risk of death from a patient sniper's bullet. To avoid escalation, Gurkhas were under orders not to fire unless fired upon; politic perhaps but adding extra frustration to danger.[17]

On 1 July, anniversary of the terrible first day of the Somme, both 2/10th and 1/4th were redeployed to the fortress at Spin Baldak where they remained for a fortnight. It was only on 8 August that a final deal was struck and 2/10th had the dubious honour of filling in all the defences they had just built.[18]

A Subaltern at War

One of Britain's most successful post-Second-World-War novelists was John Masters (1914–83; *Bhowani Junction*,[19] *Nightrunners of Bengal*[20] et al.). Masters came from a long line of soldiers who had spent their careers in India. So, for the most part, did he. After studying at Wellington School and the Royal Military College Sandhurst (now RMA Sandhurst), his first year as a subaltern was spent on secondment with the 1st Battalion Duke of Cornwall's Light Infantry, at that time serving on the North-West Frontier. He then transferred to 2/4th Gurkhas and in his superb memoir *Bugles and a Tiger*[21] recounts his experiences as a Gurkha junior officer in Waziristan during hostilities there in the late 1930s.

Gurkhas were no strangers to Waziristan having served there during the preceding century, yet the conflict there from 1936–9 would see 60,000 troops deployed and witness some savage fighting against the 'ragged-arsed barnshoots', as the local tribes were derisively known. After an earlier fracas, the army had established a forward base at Razmak, in one of the three districts of the more northerly region. It wasn't going to win any tourist awards.

Roman auxiliaries based on the cold remoteness of Hadrian's Wall at Housesteads or Great Chesters, high on the hard shelf of the granite Whin Sill, would have recognised the place immediately. It was a vast, plainly workmanlike fortress within a circuit of low stone walls around 5 miles (8km) in circumference. Squat, bunker-like barracks filled the compound; a ring of searchlights was mounted across the perimeter with dense belts of wire beyond. Razmak was built on a high plateau surrounded by jagged, primeval peaks and on top of a population whose lives had changed extraordinarily little, certainly not for the better, in centuries. The late and great George Macdonald Fraser, who had served in Burma during Slim's victorious campaign,[22] once summed up ultra-grim Hermitage Castle in Liddesdale as 'sod off in stone'. Translate that into Pushtun and it more or less sums up Razmak too.

Ghazi Mirzali Khan,[23] a Waziri tribal leader of some charisma, had been a long-term opponent of British involvement, his opposition fuelled by a sense that the Raj was losing its grip or at least the will to exert it. After a legal cause célèbre – the trial of a Muslim student charged with kidnapping a Hindu girl and forcing her to marry – he began to ratchet up the foment, alleging British intermeddling in what was a purely religious matter. Waziristan is about the size of Wales with Mahsuds living in the southern region and Wazirs further to the north.[24] Restoring the abducted and unwilling bride to her family particularly enraged the Wazirs for whom such perks had been an established custom. Resentment wasn't hard to channel.

Towards the end of November 1936, the British administration perceived that something needed to be done – ideally a demonstration of might, putting some stick about and persuading the locals that the lion still had teeth. A column would march out from Razmak (inspiringly badged as 'Razcol'), through the Khaisora Valley to the settlement at Biche Kashkai, where they would rendezvous with a second force from Bannu Brigade,[25] coming up from Mirali in the south. As this was essentially a flag-waving exercise, the troops weren't to go looking for a fight; in fact they couldn't, they were only able to fight if attacked. It is a limited and rather naive principle of war to assume that if you're not really serious the enemy will play the same game.

Mirzali Khan was in fact serious and staged a classic ambush in a narrow defile 10 miles (16km) from Biche Kashkai, forcing the British to fight for their objective and their lives. Force Number Two, 'Tocol', advancing north from Mirali was also shot up and all told about a hundred casualties were inflicted. Supplies were already running low and the combined columns had to stage a fighting withdrawal to Mirali, their rear-guard battling every foot of the way. As a show of force, this wasn't very impressive.

As a result of this poor showing Mirzali's star wasn't diminished; rather it rose into the heavens and brought forth chaos, lots of it. Trouble flared like brush-fire: Wazirs, Mahsuds, Bettanis[26] and inevitably Afghans, who could never keep out of a fight, dusted off their *jezzails* (long-barrelled flint or percussion rifles) and got ready. By next spring, April 1937, the British had to rush in another 4 brigades to bolster embattled garrisons at Razmak, Bannu and Wanna; nearly 60,000 troops all told.

Asymmetric Warfare

While the term hadn't yet been coined, the Waziri were old hands at this game of frontiers. The Waziris weren't daft enough to take on the British in open battle, resorting as they had always done to tried and tested asymmetric tactics. Large, conventional armies might not be vulnerable at the sharp end but the soft underbelly or rear echelon with significantly attenuated supply lines offered a range of tempting targets.

On 9 April 1937, in the narrow Shahur Tangi Defile, a long column of soft-skinned vehicles, supported at either end by armoured cars, was 'bounced' by a strong force of tribesmen, commanding the narrow glen from both sides. A classic ambush: troops were killed as their vehicles were jammed by those stalled front and rear, armoured cars hemmed in and unable to manoeuvre. Those at the very tip got clear and raced off for reinforcements while survivors clung on as best they might. They must have appreciated just how Custer felt. It wasn't quite that bad, but bad enough: nearly 50 soldiers were killed and as many more wounded.[27]

There were rules of engagement even in this savage war; 'Tommies' and Gurkhas both felt these were an unfair constraint and that the local politicos tended to lean rather too far towards an enemy who was bound by no rules at all. It was best not to be taken alive and the British, equally ruthless, took few prisoners. Those who were captured got short shrift:

> One wounded man ... had been overlooked. Both his thighs had been broken by grenade splinters. He was helpless and unarmed ... the senior officer got into a cold fury, but there was a prisoner whether he liked it or not. He had much the same idea of a good joke as the Pathans, so he ordered the prisoner to be pegged out, face up, in front of the quarter-guard. There was no shade, and the sun temperature was probably about 130. The further order was that every man who passed should kick the prisoner in the testicles ...[28]

Needless to add, the man didn't survive for long.

A captured Gurkha, Sikh or British soldier could expect far worse: castration and beheading or the inventive death of a thousand cuts, where grass or thorns were carefully pushed into each incision with the finesse of a seasoned inquisitor. Then, in exquisite agony, you'd have your mouth forced open, jammed with a stick, and be drowned in your captors' urine. It was often the women who perpetrated these atrocities, mercy and compassion tending to be in truly short supply on the frontier.[29] War, vendetta and atrocity were just the name of the game and the Pathans behaved exactly the same towards each other. After every bout of hostilities, when campaign medals were being dished out, many Pathans would apply, through the political residents, for theirs. After all they had fought, hadn't they?[30]

'RAGGED-ARSED BARNSHOOTS' – BACK TO THE OLD FRONTIER

Nasty as this war was for Masters, and his men of 2/4th Gurkhas, much of their energies were expended on routine 'RP' – road protection – dull, endlessly repetitive but vital and, at times, very dangerous. In this type of asymmetric fight, the guerrilla has the inestimable advantage of knowing just when and where he will strike, patient as the fox and deadly as the cobra. He will watch and choose his time, sensing any error, any forgetfulness, any shred of complacency. Every morning the Gurkhas would rise and move off in the cool of pre-dawn to sweep a given length of road, carefully scouting any handy ridge, rise or depression which could shelter an attacker. At each significant vantage a squad would be deployed and left as picquets. Only when the unit had reached the extent of its individual beat and linked up with the next formation could the all-clear be radioed back to HQ. One thing was always certain: you'd be watched every yard of the way.[31]

You never did things the same way for more than a couple of days; regular patterns were a clear invitation to those silent but ever-ready watchers and a mistake could kill you. Masters was fast learning the rules of this deadly game of shadows:

> The watcher might see that every day a piquet of half platoon strength left the road at milestone 27 and moved four hundred yards to the top of a hill. Every day two machine-guns waited among the boulders near the milestone, ready to support the moving men until they were in position. There was one little dip in the ground near the bottom of the hill, perhaps fifteen yards wide. The watcher never went near it, but his feel for country told him that the machine-gunners could not see into the dip.[32]

At first the picquets would cover this dip by having one squad cover the gap while the other passed through and they re-joined on the far side covered by the two Vickers. After a few days the troopers became just that wee bit complacent, plodding over the dead ground in a single bunched-up group. It only took 20 seconds to cross. That night a Pathan unit infiltrated the dip and hunkered down. They were very good at this, as quiet as church mice in bed-socks; even bladders and bowels were tightly disciplined. Just after 7.00 a.m. the Gurkhas walked into the dip and into the ambush; in that next few minutes twenty-six were killed and more wounded. That was the price of any carelessness.[33]

These weren't John Masters' men: 'the second fourth were not careless ... we never did the same thing in quite the same way twice running'.[34] Machine guns were sited just that bit differently every day; these Gurkhas would move up the hill by differing routes, or not occupy the hill at all. Next day a full company would tramp up. Pathans tended not to work nine till five and the real point of maximum danger was when the picquets withdrew. The enemy was already in position, having spent all the long, hot day creeping forward unseen by even the keenest observer. No sooner had the Gurkhas come back off the crest than they would be shot at, perhaps at close range. God help a wounded man – they would be on him faster than hyenas, his weapons their prize, his balls their glory.

But this was a game two could play at. 'When the moment came to withdraw, the rear party got up and trotted back over the crest and met the confident, rushing tribesmen with a blast of fire at point-blank range.'[35] Armoured cars and light tanks hull-down nearby would add a rain of shells to sweep the high ground just as the Pathans were taking possession; it was a constant game of cat and mouse where roles could, in a heartbeat, be reversed.

This attritional grind was enlivened by sharp moments of offensive action. The battalion was called out at night to interdict the retreat of an enemy force which was trying to escape the main battle zone. In fighting kit and with rubberised trainers rather than hobnails, the Gurkhas moved out from their fortified camp: 'The miles passed and though the tension in the column never completely disappeared it eased appreciably after we had moved for an hour and had our first rest, sitting down in the drainage ditch beside the road and holding up our feet to let the blood flow away from the congested soles …'.[36] By now they were hardened to the realities of this unforgiving frontier, scouting every hollow and hillock, even at night.

As dawn crept in the column was strung out along the northern flank of the Tochi River.[37] The battalion was ordered up onto both steep sides of the valley, mountain guns carried on mules going with them. It was seriously heavy going with no pathways and the need for constant vigilance. Moving upwards and forwards, leapfrogging to provide fire support, the lead elements reached the ridge line in the clearing light of a steel-grey dawn.

So far nothing, seemingly they were alone, but then Masters detected movement across on the far side, a platoon-sized group of tribesmen, filtering down towards the river. They were heavily armed. The Gurkhas opened fire, Lewis Guns spewing out rounds in rapid staccato bursts, a cascade of spent cases. As if in a chain reaction, the battalion's Vickers blazed from lower down and mountains guns added to this lively chorus with the dull thump of shells. It is difficult to say how many tribesmen had died in the storm (intelligence later reported eight dead).[38] By Waziristan standards this was a victory. More importantly, the Gurkhas had stolen a march on a brilliant indigenous enemy, their initiative beating him on his own ground.

Following that costly ambush and shootout in the Shahur Tangi, 2/4th Gurkhas was sent out again, very much on the offensive. On the evening of 5 May 1937, the brigade made camp on a windswept ridge above their old stomping ground of the Tochi River. Their arrival didn't pass without a typical form of local hello, a steady tempo of sniping: 'At two minutes after eleven something exploded in the air over my head with a sharp whip-crack slap. A second later a dull thump sounded from a dark ridge to the west.'[39] The sharpshooter was in no hurry, methodically quartering the camp and banging off a good thirty rounds. Someone asked Hamish, one of Masters' fellow officers, if he'd been hit; it sounded horribly as though he had but happily Hamish was able to confirm it was his inflated lilo mattress, not he, which had taken the hit.[40] Nine of the column's invaluable mules were not so fortunate.

Next day on the much-fought-over road towards Damdil (North Waziristan), they saw many more dead mules twisted grotesquely in ditches and large patches of dried blood, the stark hillsides further ravaged by artillery. They passed, just after the camp at Damdil, on the right of the road a hilltop *sangar*. Nothing unusual in this – but it had been here, weeks earlier, that an eight-man section from 2/5th Gurkhas had fought their own mini Rorke's Drift, through the long night of 20/21 March, surrounded by large numbers of enemy determined on their extinction. Two Gurkhas had been killed; the others each suffered multiple wounds. After running out of ammo, they relied on kukris but still held their ground until finally relieved,[41] the stuff of legends.

This new big push was to be the deciding round. Two brigades were attacking the Waziris around Dosalli (also in North Waziristan), advancing along the course of the Sre Mela stream, seeking to bring their elusive enemy to bay on the Sham Plains, his heartland. Easier said than done: the brook led upwards towards impressive ramparts of slab-faced cliffs with razor crests. These were held in force. High command decided to leave one brigade opposing the ridge lines to pin the Waziris whilst the other attempted a daring, not to say risky, flank march hooking around the enemy's right. This would involve a night approach over another precipitous crest, the Iblanke: '… it sounded like a hazardous proposition. It was.'[42]

With a screen of local scouts, the Gurkhas stepped off at 9.00 p.m., over the black waters of the Khaisora River, up to everyone's knees, and onto even blacker slopes beyond. The night air was balmy: odours of sweat and cardamom (Gurkhas chew the seeds); flashes of light on glinting fixed bayonets; iron-shod hoofs striking sparks from flint shards. Several mules slipped and loaded with hundreds of pounds of gear, plunged desperately down the hillside, crashing like boulders as they fell. Enough to wake the dead but not even the living stirred and for 8 hours of relentless, grinding, fumbling ascent they stayed undetected.[43]

By the time dawn's grey filtered light was spreading over the jagged peaks, gradually driving the pockets of darkness from the depths of the valley floor hundreds of feet below, the column was pretty much on top of 'their' ridge. But, and it was a significant 'but', they were in a mountainous realm of crowded peaks and the crest they were on was topped all around by others. A mere handful of riflemen dug in on any of these could have a field day. And shots there were, cracking through the thin, tepid air, the zing and whine of ricochets like rocket-fuelled fireflies. Up front, the native scouts and unreconstructed Pathans were already trading rounds. What the hostile tribesmen hadn't realised was that the scouts were the tip of an altogether larger iceberg.[44]

They were soon disabused – shells began falling and long rippling bursts of machine-gun fire raked the hillside. Elements of a Sikh battalion beefed up the scouts and both walloped forward, scattering all opposition. The Iblanke was taken, and the enemy flank had been turned – 'The boldest stroke in the history of the Frontier.'[45]

Now they had to fight for the valley. Marzali's lair was only a few miles east, located in a cave complex. Caught off-guard and now outgunned, the Waziris still weren't thinking about giving up or running. They didn't do surrender and had nowhere to run to. Masters was still able to be impressed by the great gallantry shown by both officers and ORs:

> Willie Weallens our second-in-command and Lance-Naik Dhansing ... rescued a wounded rifleman from certain mutilation. Willie had a pistol and Dansing nothing but a kukri – but then the man who had single-handedly attacked three hundred camels needed no other weapon ... they ran out under point-blank fire from forty Pathans and carried [the wounded man] to safety.[46]

A Gurkha, Rifleman Tilbahadur, was shot in the abdomen and killed. Pathans closed in on the casualty like vultures, disembowelling the dead man just to rip through his webbing for the loot; 'a counter-attack recovered the body, a torn and bloody sack that looked nothing like a man, shrunken, its hands rusty from dried blood ...'.[47] The dead were loaded onto specially adapted stretchers lashed to camels, a corpse bouncing on each flank for balance. The dead Gurkha began his final journey this way, jolting along till one limp hand came free,

'RAGGED-ARSED BARNSHOOTS' – BACK TO THE OLD FRONTIER

trailed and swung listlessly in tandem with the beast's uneven stride. Another soldier, seeing the hand, lifted the canvas cover to identify the late owner then shook the dead man enthusiastically by the hand before letting him go on his way. The Gurkhas found this hugely funny, their gallows humour on habitual good form.[48]

By the closing weeks of 1937, Mirzali Khan's gloss had begun to wear thin and his tribesmen were tiring of the game. Most of the Indian Army forces were pulled out shortly after. It wasn't over; the embers still glowed and frequently sparked into life. In July 1938, Bannu was attacked leaving many dead civilians and Mirzali enjoyed a brief comeback, but it was very brief and the frontier, by 1939, had pretty much returned to what passed for calm.

Another Breed of War

The Frontier, vicious and bloody as it was, remained a kind of virtual reality, a place rooted in the gloss of Kipling and the glory days of the Raj, now dipping towards sunset. In the West new and aggressive fascist dictatorships were rising, hungry for land and laurels. In the east an Imperial Japan, ruled by an equally aggressive military elite, was seeking to throw a vastly extended resource-rich cordon around the Rising Sun and had in 1931 already invaded China.

It was at 11 a.m. on 3 September 1939 that Britain entered a new era. The transition from peace to war was swift and dramatic. The country had put on uniform. The sky over the cities was dotted with balloons. Everywhere people were digging trenches, filling sandbags. Gas masks were given out. There was a rush for black paper and cloth to screen windows and skylights. Grim, grey vehicles thundered along the roads on mysterious errands. There was in the air a feeling of change – complete, inevitable and tremendous.

A generation before, war had come in cloudless August, greeted by vast, thronging crowds intoxicated with an almost transcendent spirit of patriotic fervour. Young men queued to volunteer in their tens of thousands. Their children, who listened to Prime Minister Neville Chamberlain's radio broadcast, greeted the business of war in an altogether different mood. The prime minister's voice, scratchy and somehow rather feeble over the airwaves, conveyed a sombre note of resignation. This time there would be no great rush of enthusiasts off to biff the 'Beastly Hun'.

That the 'Hun' was still beastly was beyond question: the Nazi regime's conduct in Poland, swiftly overrun and then murderously oppressed, hammered into a Dark-Age vision of servility, left no room for doubt. Appeasement was definitely out of fashion. An eyewitness from north-east England recounts the mood:

> I recall the bother with Czechoslovakia, and we thought there was going to be a war. My father certainly did – and we were quite prepared for it. Then of course it all blew over temporarily, and I remember Dad bought us a dolly each to celebrate, because it seemed as if it was going to be alright – and of course, it wasn't.
>
> I remember vividly 'Peace in our Time' – Neville Chamberlain coming back from Munich. We thought, 'Thank God, it's going to be peace, it's not going to be war.' But of course events proved [*sic*] wrong. I began thinking, 'Is it going to be like the First World War, when thousands of men were killed? In a way they were human fodder.' I thought, 'Is it going to be a repeat? What's going to happen to my brothers?'[49]

The war of 1914–18 had been billed as 'the war to end all wars' and Prime Minister David Lloyd George had promised a 'land fit for heroes'; both had proved illusory. The 'heroes' of the Western Front were seen begging on street corners and pawning their medals to survive, and now another war was brewing. Guernica had shown what indiscriminate horrors modern strategic bombing could unleash. The only thing certain about this war is that it would be very much worse than the last: 'Looking round, I could see that we were quite unprepared to enter a war of any magnitude – we just weren't ready. We never had the kit, and we never had the men. We never had anything – we had so far lagged behind.'[50]

Britain had 'won' the First World War but what was the face of victory? A whole generation of young men blighted in what seemed, in retrospect, a bickering between members of a dysfunctional pan-European royal family. There was a feeling that the huge, titanic effort expended during the war was somehow a one-off. The scale, suffering and sheer pointlessness of the whole ghastly mess had led to a view, not surprisingly, that such a thing could simply never again occur, must never be allowed to recur.

In India itself, the atrocity at Amritsar and the whitewash job that followed had further shaken the gilded throne of the king-emperor; elements within Bengal, led by Chandra Bose,[51] would actively side with the Japanese after 1942 and the tectonic shift of nationalism was already gathering momentum.

For the Gurkhas, this new world war would prove the greatest test of all.

Chapter 7

The Great Crusade – The Beginning

> I would say that I was fighting the war to rid the world of fear – of the fear of fear is perhaps what I mean. If the Germans win this war, nobody except little Hitlers will dare do anything. England will be run as if it were a concentration camp, or at best a factory. All courage will die out of the world – the courage to love, to create, to take risks, whether physical or intellectual or moral. Men will hesitate to carry out the promptings of the heart or the brain because, having acted, they will live in fear that their action may be discovered and themselves cruelly punished. Thus, all love, all spontaneity, will die out of the world.
>
> Richard Hilary, *The Last Enemy* (1997)[1]

Although few Gurkhas who fought in the desperate battles of the Second World War would have expressed their achievement in quite such Homeric tones, nonetheless, theirs would be a terrific but also very costly involvement. Gurkhas would fight in the heat and waste of the Western Desert, up the long blood-sodden spine of Italy and through the inhospitable jungles of Burma.

Throughout the first half of the war Britain remained on the defensive. One disaster followed another: Norway, France and Belgium, Greece, Crete, the fall of Malaya, Burma and Singapore. Cities were pounded during the Blitz, wolf packs stalked Atlantic convoys; defeat, starvation and ruin filled the horizons. It was not until October 1942 that the 'End of the Beginning' of the war heralded the 'Beginning of the End'.[2] Montgomery's great victory at El Alamein, though costly, ended Rommel's long run of successes, and disaster in the East at Stalingrad gave Germany a taste of what lay in store. Fortress Europe no longer seemed impregnable.

Gurkhas would first be blooded, in this campaign, in the Western Desert. 'Il Duce' ('The Leader') had swaggered into Egypt from Libya in 1940, sure the British Empire was a bankrupt estate just waiting for the receivers. He got a nasty shock, and his army was mauled and humiliated. Hitler, who wanted

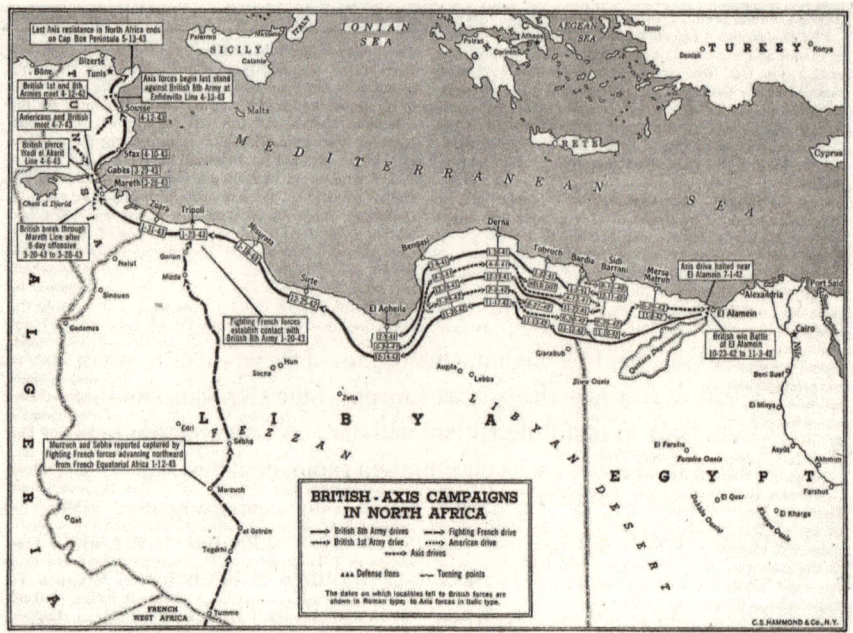

Map 8. The Western Desert, 1940–3.

no involvement in African adventures, sent out Rommel to stiffen the Italians' crumbling resolve. He did rather more and for three years the 'pendulum' of the Desert War would swing until the Axis was finally crushed.

'The Blue'

The great swathe of the Sahara Desert covers a vast expanse. It has an enduring aura of romance and exoticism, experienced by very few of those who fought in the Desert War. Armies have fought in desert conditions both before and after but never on such a scale and for such duration. Desert ('The Blue') warfare threw up a whole catalogue of factors to hinder military activity and increase the misery of individual combatants. For these, British and Dominion, Germans, Italians, French, Greeks and others, it seemed they had arrived in the very cauldron of a particular version of hell. A Durham Light Infantry (DLI) officer recalls his first impression of this strange, alien environment:

> ... my three strongest recollections are: the heat, sweat pouring and oozing from me, until I ached and itched with it ... the strange

lack of fear ... the seemingly endless hours of utter boredom, observing a low ridge about 2,000 yards away with nothing moving, nothing happening, except the sun beating mercilessly down and one's eyes straining (as I remember our gunner putting it) 'at miles and miles of f*** all'.[3]

The story of the Desert War from 1940 to the end of 1942 unfolds primarily in the Libyan Desert, a natural amphitheatre in which large armies wheeled and charged, stood at bay, gave and took ground. Men poured out their lifeblood over featureless, rock-strewn ridges barely showing above the scorched desert floor. Tanks, like dusty men o' war, cruised and fought, largely untroubled by the human landscape that defined other battlefields.

During the summer months, from May to October, the climate is scorching hot, a blistering and relentless sun, furnace-bright and searing dry. Only in the evenings before the dark cold of night, before the sun sinks, is the broiling fire of day mellowed into evening cool. Winters are dreary and damp with frequent heavy downpours. Torrents flow down the scree-riven wadis but water is soon soaked up by the parched and greedy desert. Mainly in spring the enervating wind shifts direction and can whip the sands into the abrasive fury of the khamsin. The land is harsh and gives nothing, shows no mercy to the unwary and punishes all who toil there. Yet, there is great beauty, and the desert can exert a powerful, almost obsessive pull. Dawn and sunset can be infinitely memorable and the stars glow with a clear, cold light that conjures biblical images. Soldiers were thrown back on their recall of heroic conflicts as depicted in Homer's epic poem *The Iliad*.

Gurkhas took part in the 'pendulum' battles in North Africa. General Rommel had described the desert fighting as 'war without hate' and the Eighth Army observed its prisoners to be 'a curious mixture of arrogance, belief in Hitler and surprise that the British had ever gone to war with them. They openly boasted that they were the finest soldiers in the world, and then added that the British were easily second best.'[4] The Germans were sometimes less punctilious toward Indian or Gurkha troops who might not conform to their notions of racial superiority. A DLI officer witnessed that '*krieg ohne Haas*' didn't apply to soldiers from Nepal:

> The enemy, having captured a Gurkha, shaved him and sent him back to the Gurkha lines. Shaving is, of course, against the Gurkha religion and is considered one of the greatest shames which can befall them. After telling his comrades what had

happened, the Gurkha is alleged to have committed suicide. For the whole of that day the British officers were only just able to restrain the Gurkhas from going out to the enemy. The British officers cajoled and finally threatened the Gurkhas with all kinds of punishment ... When night came the Gurkha lines emptied as though by the wave of a wand, and nothing was heard for some minutes. Then a great hullabaloo took place in the enemy lines, and the Gurkhas stole quietly back to their old positions. It was never known how many of the enemy died that night.[5]

Throughout the three years of intense fighting in the Western Desert, the see-saw nature of sometimes dizzying retreat and advance was referred to as 'The Pendulum'. Gurkhas would all too quickly understand what this meant. The further you advance, either east or west, the more attenuated your supply lines and the more vulnerable that vital connection became.

In the desert the Gurkhas would find themselves, as part of the Eighth Army, a formation that would emerge with near mythic status. In their time they would have three overall commanders, all remarkable characters. First up was General Sir Archibald Wavell, 1st Earl Wavell GCB, GCSI, GCIE, CMG, MC, PC (1883–1950). Wavell spent his formative years in India, studied at Winchester and Sandhurst, followed his father into an army career and was commissioned into the Black Watch. He served in the South African War, in Russia as an observer and then through the First World War, losing an eye at the Second Battle of Ypres in 1915. Having served in a succession of staff roles and in GSO1 appointments during the inter-war years, in 1937 he was promoted GOC (General Officer Commanding) British forces in Palestine and Trans-Jordan. His appointment to GOC Middle East came in August 1939.

Wavell successfully directed British forces to rout the Italians in Operation Compass, netting 130,000 prisoners. When he was replaced by Auchinleck he was sent to India where he commanded the hopefully named 'ABDA' (American-British-Dutch-Australian) forces attempting to stem the seemingly inexorable advance of the Japanese.

Next came Field Marshal Sir Claude Auchinleck, GCB, GCIE, CSI, DSO, OBE (1884–1981) – 'The Auk'. An Ulster Scot from Fermanagh, his father was a soldier and Auchinleck served initially in the Indian Army, commanding 62nd Punjab Regiment. In the First World War he saw hard service in Mesopotamia, the Middle East and Suez. He created a reputation for bravery, integrity and a deep concern for the welfare of the men under his command. In 1940 he inherited the poisoned chalice of the doomed Franco-British command in Norway, then commanded V Corps before being appointed as GOC of Southern Command. His subordinate was General Bernard Law Montgomery, who now had V Corps. The two men did not bond, as Montgomery recorded: 'I cannot recall that we ever agreed on anything.'[6] His contribution to victory in the Desert War has been steadily reassessed as time passes. 'The Auk' remains a revered figure.

Finally, there was 'Monty' – Bernard Law Montgomery, 1st Viscount of Alamein KG, GCB, DSO, PC (1887–1976). Born in London into a rather impoverished Anglo-Irish clerical family, he was commissioned into the Royal Warwickshire Regiment in 1908 and saw service on the Western Front where, in 1914, he was severely wounded by a sniper's bullet (to the extent his grave was dug in anticipation). During the lean inter-war years, when the army shrank dramatically, he held appointments on the Rhine and in Ireland.

In 1939 Montgomery had severe doubts as to Britain's preparedness for war, a view vindicated by the BEF's performance in France. After Dunkirk, where he served with some distinction, he did not endear himself by blunt criticism of his superiors. His frustrations often emerged as downright rudeness: tact and diplomacy were not among his qualities. In July 1940 he was appointed commander of 3rd Division where he soon fell out with Auchinleck and relations between the two men were never cordial. His ideas on the welfare of his troops, which were to earn him a huge following, often alarmed his exasperated superiors. A notion that army brothels for 'horizontal refreshment' should be provided was not untypical of his approach. He consistently failed to see why his bulldozer approach might ruffle feathers and he was not of a disposition that fostered compromise.

The Gazala Gallop

By late summer 1940, Britain was short of allies. Poland, Norway, Denmark, the Low Countries, Belgium and France had all fallen. There was no guarantee Nepal would stand firm. At the outset, British envoys in Kathmandu had approached the ruler Judha Shamsher, seeking his agreement for raising additional Gurkha units and for consent to their serving overseas. He could have said 'no'; this was post-Dunkirk and Britain's prospects looked bleak, but he responded warmly. The Gurkhas were to be built up to 30 battalions. Over the course of the war no fewer than 130,000 young men from the hills volunteered, forming a final tally of 46 battalions. They would fight in North Africa, in Italy, Greece and the Far East.[7] If there was no dearth of recruits there was a serious shortage of weapons and kit of all types. Losses of materiel at Dunkirk had been grievous and would take time to make good; armouries in India, like manufacturing capability in the Nile Delta, was soon being harnessed to the war effort.

* * *

It was in March 1942 that 2/4th Gurkhas found themselves in North Africa as part of the 'Gazala Line'. This was firmly in Rommel's sights. Hitler and Mussolini held a conference in April when their strategy for Axis moves in North Africa was on the agenda. It was concluded that the Afrika Korps should launch an attack on the Gazala Line at the earliest opportunity. So far so good, but this was to be a limited offensive; neither dictator would let the Fox completely slip the leash. Once the line was breached – and, as a major secondary objective, Tobruk re-captured – then the attack would be held until Malta was dealt with and the overall supply situation improved.

Rommel planned his attack for 26 May. Auchinleck was aware of his opponent's intention in terms of an offensive but not as to how and where he planned to deliver the main blow. The Eighth Army was thus braced to expect an attack in the centre with a diversion to the south. British armour was deployed accordingly.

Rommel, disobligingly, intended his main assault to be directed in the south swinging on the pivot of Bir Hacheim, which he expected to overcome without undue difficulty. The attacks in the centre and north would be, respectively, secondary and a mere feint. The Fox himself would lead the main armoured thrust in the south which would, having dealt with the Free French at Bir Hacheim, sweep around behind the Eighth Army and begin rolling up the line. Italian armour would attempt to batter through British minefields in the centre whilst General Cruewell would command joint infantry forces in the north. Despite a prophetic warning from Major General Tuker over the dangers of wide dispersion of Allied forces, no heed had been taken. Tuker commanded the Indian Division and thus also the Gurkhas. His C in C, General Ritchie, had deployed his forces both piecemeal and ill-advisedly. In the north 13 Corps was spread in a series of defensive 'boxes' with 30 Corps to the south disposed by brigades together with the bulk of available armour. Auchinleck, in all fairness, was not unaware of the current failures in British tactical doctrine.

Rommel's offensive and the Battle of Gazala, dubbed 'the Gazala Stakes' by the Eighth Army, can be divided into three phases:

1. Rommel launches his flank attack, 26–29 May, attempting to overrun British defences from behind.
2. Fighting in the 'Cauldron' – Rommel tries to resupply and consolidate his forces.
3. The reduction of Bir Hacheim, and the pounding of British armour, 11–13 June, followed by withdrawal from the Gazala Line.
4. The final phase of this battle was the subsequent storming of Tobruk.

In the fighting 100,000 Allied troops, 849 tanks and 604 planes would face some 90,000 Axis with 561 tanks (228 of which were of the inferior Italian sort) and 504 aircraft.

Bir Hacheim, the pivot upon which the Axis' southerly attack was to turn, proved a far tougher nut than Rommel had anticipated. General Koenig's Free French put up a spirited and resilient defence. The task of battering these defences into submission was entrusted to Ariete Division. Nonetheless, the Panzers achieved a series of local successes, swatting a succession of ill-coordinated Allied units. By mid-morning they had swept over General Messervy's HQ, netting the general and his staff. Though he soon made good his escape, the resultant confusion was disastrous. Rommel's two more northerly assaults both stalled against minefields and determined resistance. The new Grant tanks and heavier punch of the 6-pounder AT guns made their presence felt. Failure to eliminate Bir Hacheim spoilt the smooth execution of his plan; supply lines were attenuated, vulnerable to marauding columns of light armour and armoured cars.

Despite the Axis' potentially exposed position, Ritchie failed to concentrate his armour, an error which amazed his more nimble opponent: 'Ritchie had thrown his armour into the battle piecemeal and had thus given us the chance of engaging them on each separate occasion with just about enough of our own tanks; this dispersal of the British armoured brigades was incomprehensible.'[8] Many of the Allied tank officers had approached this battle with far greater confidence than before, believing the improved firepower of their Grants would even the odds.

Thrown in haphazardly, 2nd and 22nd Armoured Brigades, despite gallant and costly efforts, were insufficient to stem the onslaught. The Afrika Korps was now within an area known as the 'Knightsbridge Box'. British command failures permitted Rommel, whose position, hemmed in by mine marshes and Bir Hacheim, could and should have been dire, to concentrate his forces. During the 29th this consolidation proceeded with panzers massing between the Sidra and Aslagh Ridges, an inconspicuous span of barren desert soon to be dubbed, and with good reason, the Cauldron.

For Rommel this was the crisis. His armour was backed onto the British mine marsh; his support from the west had yet to penetrate. Bir Hacheim was not subdued and the supply situation critical. Resolute and concentrated attacks by properly directed British armour with artillery and infantry supports could have achieved success but no such concentration seemed possible. Instead, penny packet assaults without the necessary guns and men were fed into the mincer. The Germans too suffered loss: senior officers such as General Gause and General Westphal were wounded and Cruewell himself, recognised by both sides as a 'brave and energetic' leader, was captured on 29 May when his Storch spotter was shot down.

On 30 May, 150th Brigade, left terribly exposed, was overrun: 'Help did not arrive. At first light on 1st June the enemy attacked from all sides, and platoon by platoon the brigade was overrun and captured. The last sub-unit to go down was believed to be the platoon of the 5th Green Howards commanded by Captain Bert Dennis.'[9] It was not until 1–2 June that Ritchie decided to storm the Cauldron. As the OH tersely records: 'British operations on the night of 1st/2nd June were a fiasco.'[10] The subsequent attack put in before dawn on the 5th – Operation Aberdeen – was a tragedy. The 7th Armoured and 10th Indian Brigades stormed their objectives only to find they had missed the enemy and landed a blow in the air: 'evil consequences were to follow quickly'.[11] Exposed to relentless counterattacks, several regiments and their supporting guns were decimated.

For the Gurkhas it was exhausting, confusing and very frustrating. Moving in darkness, they were to shift to a location south of where 150th Brigade had been destroyed; but no sooner there, a sandstorm raging, and they were dispatched further south still to secure gaps through the dense minefields. Eventually with 2/4th Gurkhas in the lead, the remainder of 10th Indian Brigade caught up and hastily dug in. West of their current position lay the dreaded Cauldron and next morning they were to attack, with armoured support.

It all went very horribly wrong. The initial advance proceeded smoothly but 2/4th was soon caught trying to support the Highland Light Infantry who, without Allied tanks, were in difficulty. Next, supported by 25-pounders, they were ordered to dig in – easier said than done as the ground was rocky and the Royal Engineers (RE) officer who promised to return with equipment was never seen again.[12] They were in fact completely surrounded. Next day the Axis struck, rolling up the boxes. Their 2-pounder A/T guns were useless, and the bigger 25-pounders soon knocked out. That day, 6 June, was a long one for the Gurkhas; no tanks appearing, no guns left. The panzers inched closer to the perimeter, infantry following. It was hopeless and any who survived were captured.[13]

Once this minefield barrier was finally breached and Axis support came through, Bir Hacheim was further isolated as pressure ratcheted to an irresistible level. On 9 June, the survivors, battered but unbowed, fought their way clear of the trap. With this obstacle removed, Axis forces were freed for a further thrust, this time toward El Adem, with a demonstration to distract the British in 'Knightsbridge'. By dark on 11 June Rommel had attained El Adem having, once again, wrong-footed his opponents. Next day he moved in an attempt to surround the remnants of 2nd and 4th Armoured Brigades.

There was now a very real risk the largely static infantry formations to the north could be surrounded and heavy clashes occurred in the vicinity of Rigel Ridge. Here the Scots Guards fought tenaciously, earning high praise from Rommel, by no means an easy general to impress. Nonetheless, relentless pressure and mounting losses forced the British from the higher ground; 22nd Armoured lost two-thirds of its tanks. On 11 June Ritchie had been able to field some 300 machines, giving him a numerical superiority of 2 : 1. Within two days, ground down by murderous combat and poor tactics, only ninety-five runners remained, the odds having thus swung heavily in favour of the Korps.

Last Days of Tobruk

As the Axis held the field, they were able to recover many of their damaged vehicles with customary efficiency. The Eighth Army could not and those left broken were effectively written off. By 14 June, Ritchie was seeking permission to draw off, fall back to the frontier and save his forces from encirclement; Rommel was master of the central battlefield. This would imply the temporary abandonment of the Tobruk garrison which would again be isolated. Auchinleck was not yet ready to throw in the towel, insisting that further counterattacks be launched to deny the approaches to Tobruk. As C in C he had to answer to the prime minister who was already querying his intentions: 'Presume there is no question in any case of giving up Tobruk?'[14] Rommel felt a surge of confidence, which he transmitted in his daily correspondence to his wife on 15 June: 'The battle has been won and the enemy is breaking up …'.[15]

Withdrawal in the face of an aggressive enemy is never a smooth business and the retreat of the Eighth Army inevitably produced a semblance of rout. Rommel would not relinquish pressure and struck toward the airfield at Gambut. The rump of 4th Armoured sallied out but was again badly mauled; control of events had passed irrevocably beyond Ritchie's grip. For Rommel, there was now the matter of his unfinished business with the defenders of Tobruk.

As early as January 1942, the joint Middle East commanders, Auchinleck, Cunningham (navy) and Tedder (air force), had agreed that Tobruk, if isolated, should not once again be defended. Militarily, this was eminently sensible, but the place had become imbued with a great deal of political capital at a time when British arms had endured such a series of dismal defeats in Norway, France, Greece and Crete with such sharp reverses in the Western Desert. By 17 June, Rommel had secured Gambut airfield and beaten off the remnant of British armour. Tobruk was again invested.

Two days later there was still some ill-founded optimism that the perimeter could be held on the basis or in the pious hope that Axis forces would settle down for a lengthy siege. The situation now within the ring was very different from before. Hitherto strong defences had been denuded and pillaged to meet the exigencies of the now defunct Gazala Line and the garrison was badly placed to resist a sustained attack. The defenders comprised two South African brigades, one Guards Brigade and 11th Indian Brigade, of which 2/7th Gurkhas formed part.

Rommel, scenting this weakness, unleashed the *Luftwaffe* who began blasting the fortress on 20 June as the precursor to a determined attack from the south-east. By 7.45 a.m. the anti-tank ditch, equivalent to the medieval moat, had been breached and the perimeter was collapsing. There had been talk of a breakout should this occur but no escape route was viable. Auchinleck's report to London, late on the 20th, sounded a note of impending catastrophe:

> Enemy attacked south-east face of Tobruk perimeter early morning after air bombardment and penetrated defences. By evening all our tanks reported knocked out and half our guns lost ... Major-General Klopper commanding troops in Tobruk last night asked for my authority to fight his way out feeling apparently could not repeat not hold out. Ritchie agreed ... do not, repeat not, know how he proposes to do this and consider chances of success doubtful.[16]

First, it was the turn of 2/5th Marathas who were systematically and relentlessly ground down; then the Gurkhas, dug in as best they could, felt the flood. All day they fought against mounting odds and with white flags appearing all around were finally forced to throw in the towel – what bitter memories of the catastrophe at Kut in the last war.[17]

Tobruk fell; 35,000 Allied soldiers passed into captivity; 2,000 tons of fuel and as many vehicles fell into Axis hands.[18] It was a disastrous defeat. The debacles in Greece and Crete combined had not witnessed such fearful loss. Churchill was in the United States, within the sanctum of the Oval Office when the dread tidings arrived. The news could not have come at a worse time when Britain was struggling to instil some measure of confidence in its ally.

El Alamein

After Gazala came Mersa Matruh which proved yet another defeat. Despite this setback, Auchinleck had kept the army in being. This, as he and Brigadier Dorman-Smith ('Chink')[19] had identified, was the prime objective. Only by preserving mobile field forces could the British position in the Middle East be saved. He had now gone beyond Wavell's 'worst case' (i.e. retreat to the banks of the Nile) and was considering how best to defend the Delta itself should he be pushed that far. Meanwhile, there was the ground south of El Alamein, a strip of desert some 38 miles in extent that lay between salt marsh and sea to the north and the impassable Qattara Depression, where no tank could tread. Here was ground that favoured a defensive battle, to be fought by an army markedly inferior in armour and less mobile than its opponent, one that needed time to rebuild and replenish.

For the most part this ground is featureless, until one reaches the rock-strewn hills that flank the waste of marsh and dune announcing the depression. Even these are no more than 700ft above sea level, but much nearer the sea are the twin eminences, rounded hillocks or 'tells' of which Tell el Eisa and Tell el Makh Khad would prove significant. The terrain is everywhere barren; loose, deepening sand alternating with unyielding rock which emerges in the narrow lateral ridges Miteirya, Ruweisat and Alam el Halfa. These insignificant features would assume considerable importance in the fighting to come and blood would be poured out in torrents to secure them. Once taken, such features were heartbreakingly difficult to fortify, being horribly exposed. In places the ground dipped into shallow depressions ('deirs'), natural saucers. That Auchinleck and Dorman-Smith should focus on the potential here was nothing revelatory; the Alamein position had been identified as a natural defence line for the Delta for some years beforehand.

Efforts at constructing a line of fortifications had been begun in the early days but operational priorities had relegated the endeavour. Initially, the plan had been for the creation of three heavily defended localities at El Alamein and the coast, at Bab el Qattara (Qaret el Abd) and at Naqb Abu Dweis. By the coast some positions were completed, wired and mined; in the centre there was rather less completed and, in the south, very little. Water supplies were, however, on hand along the axis of the intended front.[20]

'Chink' prepared a detailed assessment of the strategic imperatives at this time which, though it offered little guidance to the tactics to be employed in the forthcoming battle at Alamein, established the Eighth Army's key priorities. Supply was acknowledged to be critical; defence of the Red Sea ports would facilitate rebuilding the army's strength and thus its future mobility. At the same time, increased activity from Malta could damage the Axis.

Dorman-Smith recognised that the Desert Air Force was becoming a force to be reckoned with and, for now, 'our only offensive weapon'.[21] That the army should fight at El Alamein was certain, but it was to avoid any risk of encirclement and be prepared to fall back again to defend Cairo and Alexandria. This brisk assessment, strong on objectivity, could not disguise the fact that Alamein promised to be yet another debacle followed by a panicked flight to the Delta with all the damage to rear echelon and supply this would entail. It left the question of whether the Egyptians could be relied upon unanswered. The overall effect upon morale could only be detrimental.

Auchinleck's key weakness was that he and Dorman-Smith were operating in a kind of vacuum. The army commanders could not readily divine his intent and 'The Auk' did not issue any 'backs to the wall' oration and rallying cry. With his Indian Army background, he did not possess the kind of informal but vital network that generally sustained the British Army. Employing 'Chink' as chief of staff, while a useful expedient at one level, created a further barrier, since he was universally detested by his fellow officers. That it was his intention to keep the army in being come what may was sound and logical, but this did not translate into language officers and men could understand and rally around. It seemed as if, outfought and depleted, they would once again be clinging to scratch positions in early expectation of a further, hurried withdrawal.

While the debacle at Matruh was unfolding, Churchill had again cabled the C in C to offer some helpful tips on generalship, tending to indicate how little the prime minister had learnt from the desert campaign thus far. He was incapable of understanding that the fluid and mobile nature of desert warfare was, above all, a battle of competing technologies. Put simplistically, the side which had the best tanks and in adequate numbers, together with commensurate strength in supporting arms, would win.

* * *

Any hopes that the swing of the pendulum would cause Rommel to simply grind to a halt proved groundless. His juggernaut, thin on supply, men exhausted, machines overtaxed, came on relentlessly. On 30 June, Rommel received confirmation, via an intercept from A.C. Kirk, the American ambassador, that the acerbic American observer Bonner Fellers felt the Axis could, within days, be at the very gates of Cairo.[22] In fulfilling this despondent prediction Rommel was only too happy to oblige. Victory, as it seemed, was very close indeed. Battered, ground down and in no small part bemused, the Eighth Army was still far from beaten. The Desert Rats[23] were down but not out and their morale, despite such repeated pummelling, did not collapse. This resilience was a disappointment to Egyptian nationalists hoping for signs of cracking.

In the summer of 1942, after 'The Auk' had beaten Rommel at the First Battle of El Alamein but been *stellenbosched* in turn by Churchill and after Gott, his preferred successor, died in a plane crash and General Bernard Law Montgomery had been appointed to command the Eighth Army, 1/2nd Gurkhas arrived in Egypt from Cyprus, Aphrodite's Island. Their introduction to the Desert War began, catastrophically, at Mena Camp near Cairo when a landmine went up during a demo and killed nearly seventy Gurkhas.[24] This shocking loss included many of the unit's specialists; barely recovered from this, they found themselves dug in along the bare backbone of Ruweisat Ridge.

Major General Francis Tuker,[25] as mentioned above and commanding 4th Indian Division (who had formerly led 1/2nd Gurkhas), was in charge. His job was to hold the northern flank, to tie down the enemy in front so they would not be able to interfere with Monty's grand offensive Operation Lightfoot which kicked off on the night of 23/24 October. Kukris were still drawn in anger when 1/2nd assaulted an enemy outpost at Point 62. This was real swashbuckling worthy of the Long Range Desert Group (LRDG) or SAS at their boldest. They bowled up to the Axis wire in Bren carriers (light, tracked personnel carriers), using grapnel hooks to get a grip and then drag clear. Ultimately the raiders had to withdraw but they had held the enemy's full attention.[26]

During the battle for France the BEF suffered due to a lack of sub-machine guns. The 9mm Sten Gun was an ad hoc response, 'cheap as chips' compared with the American .45 cal. Thompson but not without its quirks, prone to jamming and, worse, accidental discharge if dropped when cocked; this was particularly so with the earlier model. Far superior, the Bren (from BR – Brno and EN – Enfield), adapted from the Czech ZB vz 26; .303 calibre light machine gun, range 600–1,800yd and using a thirty round box magazine, was a robust, reliable and durable weapon, slower firing than the German MG 34 and MG 42 but produced for half to a third of the cost.

Pursuit

After twelve grinding and costly days of attrition, Rommel's line was finally broken and the remnant of his forces in headlong retreat. This wouldn't just be another swing of the pendulum; it had swung this time for good. Leading a mobile column, Lieutenant Colonel Osmond Lovett, 1/2nd Gurkhas CO, bounced a horde of fleeing Italians, mostly on foot, and the Gurkhas' Bren carriers soon shooed away enemy light tanks taking over 2,000 officers and men into the bag.[27] Even a few prowling panzers were seen off as they tried to intermeddle; the new 6-pounder A/T guns had a far more powerful bite than their predecessors. But chasing Rommel would never be a rout and the Fox would never be more guileful than when his back was against the wall.

Meanwhile to the west, on 8 November 1942, a joint Anglo-American fleet had made several landings on the coast of French North Africa, and the long-heralded liberation of Vichy provinces had begun. The Allies came ashore at Algiers, Oran and Casablanca. If Eisenhower, as C in C, was expecting a rapturous welcome he was sadly deluded. The French in fact resisted, treating the landings more as a hostile invasion than liberation. Memories of the sinking of French ships and the fight for Syria rankled. Even the presence of the Americans, who might be expected to be less tainted than the British, did not prevent stiff fighting.

Despite the mounting odds, Axis reinforcements were arriving in Tunisia and an active defence was underway. The country was mountainous and winter rains barely a month away. General Anderson, commanding the British First Army, made good progress, despite renewed activity from the Luftwaffe. Rommel continued to fall back, ignoring all and any pleas to make a stand. By the end of November Anderson's forces appeared to be closing in upon Tunis but deteriorating weather imposed its own check. Anderson's planned swoop down from the hills was met with determined resistance, the formidable Tigers (PzKw VI)[28] making their first appearance. Fighting hard and utilising interior lines, the German defenders could not be budged. Allied losses were mounting steadily, and the Axis were able to mount a series of sharp, local counterattacks. Then the rains began to fall in earnest turning ground into quagmire, bogging men and vehicles in a viscous sea of impotent misery. Tunis was not about to fall, and Eisenhower wisely decided to suspend further major operations.

An End to the Pendulum

On 15 February 1943, the Eighth Army moved against Rommel's positions at Beurat. Hopelessly outnumbered and outgunned, the Panzerarmee could only continue with a further withdrawal. A major conference was held at Casablanca where Eisenhower revealed his intentions for a further offensive in Tunisia, though Brooke felt such a move unwise. The potentially contentious question of who should exercise overall command once the First and Eighth Armies were united was settled in favour of Eisenhower, with Alexander as his subordinate and Tedder having direction of all Allied aircraft. De Gaulle had been persuaded or browbeaten into a makeshift accommodation with General Giraud (at the time Roosevelt's favourite). Rommel had retired behind the relative security of the Mareth Line which afforded him a respite and the opportunity of striking a fresh blow in the west.

As ever, the Desert Fox chose an ambitious and risky strategy while his fellow officers, von Arnim commanding the Fifth Panzerarmee in North Tunisia and, equally predictably, Kesselring, favoured a less perilous course. The result was an inevitable compromise. The Germans made initial gains. The Americans, facing these battle-hardened desert veterans, were caught off-guard and suffered losses but the offensive soon began to run out of steam. Von Arnim had severe doubts, and these translated into lukewarm support. Rommel's assault on the Kasserine Pass, spectacular and rapid, ran into a thin screen of Allied guns and stalled. With resources depleted and the Allies recovering, the attack was abandoned.

On 23 January 1943, the Eighth Army entered Tripoli; in the three months since El Alamein Montgomery's forces had advanced some 1,400 miles. Rommel fell back across the Tunisian border and prepared to hold the old Mareth Line, originally constructed by the French as a buffer against their Italian neighbours. By mid-February the Allies were at Medenine, where a vigorous thrust by the Axis was seen off with loss. The Eighth Army, having cleared the way, must now assault the formidable barrier Rommel had bequeathed his successor at Mareth.

Alexander had been pretty appalled by the unprepared state of his American allies but the crisis in the western sector had passed. Rommel was ordered to launch a blow in the east, despite his misgivings, exacerbated by failing health. This attack, hurled at Eighth Army positions at Medenine in early March, ran into a well-prepared and concealed gun line; both tanks and infantry were badly shot up as they struggled to come to grips. Rommel's last attack was a total failure. He left North Africa for a final attempt to talk sense into Hitler but the Führer still wasn't listening. The Desert Fox had seen the last of North Africa; he was placed on mandatory sick leave. Von Arnim was left to oversee the final *Götterdämmerung*.

It was to be no picnic; the Germans were not yet defeated, and the ground favoured the defender. One of the pursuers from the DLI noticed:

> Except for a few tracks running through narrow passes, these rugged, broken hills formed a natural barrier to wheeled transport and at the same time dominated the whole western end of the defence system. In the coastal sector the line had been based on the Wadi Zigzaou, a horrible obstacle, widened and deepened to form a tank trap and covered by enfilade fire along its whole length by a complicated system of concrete and steel pillboxes, gun emplacements and blockhouses. The strongpoints, formidable affairs of concrete two or three feet thick, were supported by a well-revetted trench system, linked with deep dugouts and funk holes.[29]

Monty deployed Tuker's 4th Indian Division to attack the Matmata Hills on the landward flank to land a left hook. Both 1/2nd and 1/9th Gurkhas participated in this assault. It was heavy going, un-gapped mines and conflicting orders slowed the pace and when the blow was finally delivered on 28 March, events had been overtaken by British tanks breaking through nearer the coast.[30] The Axis had fallen into the earlier French belief that the Mareth position could not be outflanked on the landward side. However, Monty had LRDG, and the Axis did not. These indefatigable raiders had cracked the key to a turning movement so the division of New Zealanders under General Freyburg appeared as though by mysterious alchemy on the Axis's flank. The battle was still not over but, by 27 March, the enemy had pulled back, the Germans' turn now to quit the ground across Wadi Zigzaou that had cost both sides so dear.

The Italian General Messe, beaten at Mareth, now fell back to another potential Thermopylae at Wadi Akarit, flanked inland by a formidable range of hills, the Fatnassa Mountains. Monty planned to kick in their front door while Tuker's 4th Indian Division attempted a right hook. Tuker, who wasn't afraid of Montgomery's vitriol (the general didn't care for dissenters), objected, asserting that his troops would do better to scale the heights at Rass-es-Zouai which, due to their steepness, were only lightly held and not by Germans. He knew his Gurkhas and their capacities as mountain men.

THE GREAT CRUSADE – THE BEGINNING

It was well and thoroughly planned, studied and rehearsed right down to section level; every man knew what he was about. They, four companies from 1/2nd, would have to cover 3 miles (4.8km) before getting in sight of their objectives, their progress made easy by tapes. Then they could see where they were headed and at 11.30 p.m. on 5 April they attacked. Only a single Italian sentry lived just long enough to shout the alarm before a swinging kukri did for him. Fire erupted like a tropical storm, flame and the fireflies of tracer zinging through the balmy desert air.

Subadar Lalbahadur Thapa of D Company led the charge that resulted in his Victoria Cross, as his citation in the *London Gazette* confirms:

> On the night of 5–6 April, 1943, during the silent attack on the Rass-Ez-Zouai feature, Subadar Lalbahadur Thapa was second in command of D Company. The Commander of No. 16 Platoon was detached with one Section to secure an isolated feature on the left of the Company's objective. Subadar Lalbahadur Thapa took command of the remaining two Sections and led them forward towards the main feature on the outer ridge, in order to break through and secure the one and only passage by which the vital commanding feature could be seized to cover the penetration of the Division into the hills. On the capture of these hills the whole success of the Corps plan depended.
>
> First contact with the enemy was made at the foot of a pathway winding up a narrow cleft. This deep cleft was thickly studded with a series of enemy posts, the inner of which contained an anti-tank gun and the remainder medium machine-guns. After passing through the narrow cleft, one emerges into a small arena with very steep sides, some 200 feet in height, and in places sheer cliff. Into this arena and down its sides numbers of automatic weapons were trained and mortar fire directed. The garrison of the outer posts were all killed by Subadar Lalbahadur Thapa and his men by kukri or bayonet in the first rush and the enemy then opened very heavy fire straight down the narrow enclosed pathway and steep arena sides.
>
> Subadar Lalbahadur Thapa led his men on and fought his way up the narrow gully straight through the enemy's fire, with little room to manoeuvre, in the face of intense and sustained machine-gun concentrations and the liberal use of grenades by the enemy. The next machine-gun posts were dealt with, Subadar Lalbahadur

Thapa personally killing two men with his kukri and two more with his revolver. This Gurkha officer continued to fight his way up the narrow bullet-swept approaches to the crest. He and two Riflemen managed to reach the crest, where Subadar Lalbahadur Thapa killed another two men with his kukri, the Riflemen killed two more and the rest fled. Subadar Lalbahadur Thapa then secured the whole feature and covered his Company's advance up the defile.

This pathway was found to be the only practicable route up the precipitous ridge, and by securing it the Company was able to deploy and mop up all enemy opposition on their objective. This objective was an essential feature covering the further advance of the Brigade and of the division, as well as the bridgehead over the anti-tank ditch. There is no doubt that the capture of this objective was entirely due to this act of un-surpassed bravery by Subadar Lalbahadur Thapa and his small party in forcing their way up the steep gully, and up the cliffs of the arena under withering fire.

The outstanding leadership, gallantry and complete disregard for his own safety shown by Subadar Lalbahadur Thapa were an example to the whole Company, and the ruthless determination of this Gurkha officer to reach his objective and kill his enemy had a decisive effect on the success of the whole operation.[31]

Driven by such magnificent elan, the attack was a total success, fully vindicating Tuker's vision and unswerving faith in his Gurkhas.

Though 1/9th attacked on their right and made good progress, ½nd found themselves exposed and overlooked as the Axis attempted to wrest back this vital high ground. All through the next day they fought off counterattacks, heavily shelled, often hand to hand against infantry and armour. Only when the divisional artillery could turn its guns, pounding enemy reserves, did pressure on ½nd finally slacken. By now Messe was in trouble all along his line and finally pulled back again. His final redoubt was the ring of hills which encircled the ancient coastal settlements of Tunis and Carthage. It was Indian soldiers from 4th Division that shook hands with Americans from Patton's 2nd Corps. By 10 April Sfax had fallen; Sousse followed two days later. The Axis grip was more than shaky, it was crumbling. Mussolini's North African Empire was about to go into liquidation.

Despite these triumphs, Alexander had decided the final blow must fall further north and thus be delivered by the First Army, though the Eighth Army was to assault the remaining Axis bastion at Enfidaville. This was essentially a sideshow. In part it was due to recognition that the Enfidaville position was an extremely strong one. Nonetheless, the orders were subsequently modified, perhaps in consequence of matters in the north proving more strenuous than anticipated. Several army commanders had grave doubts over the attack on the Enfidaville defences, fearing the price paid in casualties would be exorbitant. Montgomery, as ever, was aggressive and fully confident.

On 18 April, Monty sent in 5th Indian Brigade to bash through and take Djebel Garci which would uncork the defensive ring, clearly inspired by the brilliant success of 1/2nd Gurkhas at Wadi Akarit. Monty had thought this sector only lightly held. He was wrong. Patrols sent out by 1/9th soon found an alert and well-dug-in enemy. One recce ended in disaster, the Gurkhas trapped in a minefield and shot to pieces.[32] Montgomery's plan of attack was for 1/4th Essex to seize a significant pimple at the base of the massif, allowing 4/6th Rajpatana Rifles to storm the near ridge line with 1/9th Gurkhas passing through to take the next high ground. Essex boys would then link up with the Gurkhas to assault the final summit.

There's an old military maxim that no plan ever survives contact with the enemy. This one certainly didn't. The Rajpatana Rifles were caught in murderous fire and mercilessly winnowed. Very soon none of their British officers remained alive and unwounded. All the Gurkhas could do was to bypass this carnage in an attempt to grab their own objective whilst it was still dark. If they didn't, the dawn would bring fearful retribution.

Captain Jones led D Company which was soon engaged hand to hand.[33] Jones lost an eye but continued to fight (becoming CO of 1/9th in 1961). Captain Donovan brought up A Company which waded into the tight melee. Nobody was planning to give up easily and clearing the position cost 1/9th over forty casualties.[34] Jemadar Diwansing Basnet went forward to recce but ran into a German sentry – not good news for him, since Basnet accounted for him and another quartet. Seriously wounded in the melee, he might have ended up dead or in the bag, but the remainder of his platoon surged forward, bombing the Axis foxholes, saving him and taking the ground. Despite his wounds he remained in command of his men throughout.[35]

In that third week of April, fighting in this sector reached an intensity and fury easily the equal of the worst which had gone before. Men scrambled, fought and died on scarred and rock-strewn slopes, pounded by artillery and small arms, a soldier's battle of rifle and bayonet. Battered and clinging to their gains, 1/9th Gurkhas held out for three long, hard days until they were pulled out. As this attack stalled (through no fault of the Gurkhas) similar difficulties were experienced in the north, where Axis formations bitterly contested each foot of mountainous ground. Montgomery, not to be denied a victor's crown, renewed his attack on 25 April. Both sides fought with great skill and valour, losses again were high, every inch of ground contested. The result was a temporary stalemate.

On 6 May, Alexander planned a final, overwhelming blow in the north. To add irresistible weight to Anderson's assault, two veteran Eighth Army units, 4th Indian and 7th Armoured Divisions, were detached in support, together with 201st Guards Brigade. Thus, two units which had endured the whole gruelling campaigns in the Western Desert, including the original 'Desert Rats', would take part in what promised to be the last battle. Von Arnim knew the plight of his exhausted survivors, some 135,000 Germans and nearer 200,000 Italians, was desperate. Despite the odds, Axis defenders continued to fight long and hard as the onslaught began. After intensive bombardment and a successful break-in, dusk found the leading British units 15 miles (24km) from Tunis. Next morning British armour and armoured cars rolled into the city.

It fell to 1/2nd Gurkhas, on 12 May, to win one final accolade – it was they who captured von Arnim himself.[36] General Messe also formally surrendered his command. At 2.15 p.m. on 13 May Churchill finally received the telegram from Alexander he had waited so long to read: 'Sir, it is my duty to report that the Tunisian campaign is over. All enemy resistance has ceased. We are masters of the North African shore.' The Gurkhas had crossed over the Dark Water again and fought as ever with honour and distinction in yet another immensely hostile landscape, but their war was very far from over.

Chapter 8

The Great Crusade (2) – The Beginning of the End

> ... Locked in close combat with a large German, a Gurkha takes a swipe at him with his kukri. The German says, 'Ha – missed'! To which the Gurkha replies, 'Shake your head ...'.
>
> T. Gould, *Imperial Warriors* (1999)

Flung like a triangular boulder into the Mediterranean, separated from the heel and toe of Italy by the Straits of Messina, Sicily has been a stepping stone from Africa to Europe for a catalogue of conquerors from Carthaginians, Romans, Arabs and Normans to, in 1943, the Allies. The land is rugged and harsh, dominated by high, sharp-fanged ridges. In summer, the air is furnace-hot, scorching hills and terraces, oven-like on the plains. The planned Allied invasion, Operation Husky, hit the beaches on 9 July and officially ended on 17 August. It was the first major blow directed against the Axis heartlands after victory in North Africa and formed a curtain raiser for the subsequent invasion of the Italian mainland, hammering nails into Il Duce's political coffin and heralding the demise of his regime. The island would not be easily won.

The decision to target Sicily had been taken at the Casablanca Conference early in 1943,[1] even before the Tunisian Campaign was finally confirmed. The objectives were to knock Italy out of the war and oblige Hitler to move troops out of Russia and away from France. Stalin, with his titanic losses, was clamouring insistently for the Western Allies to launch a second front and take some pressure off the Soviets. He did have a point; Russia was bearing the brunt of the world war and his paranoia led him to suspect the Allies weren't entirely unhappy with the vision of Nazi Germany and Communist Russia bleeding each other out. He probably wasn't far wrong.

The decision to invade the Italian peninsula, previously and famously described by Churchill as 'The underbelly of Europe',[2] was a backstairs child of compromise. After the North African campaign and the subsequent invasion of Sicily, strategic thinking between the Allies was sharply divided. The United States, moving up to become lead partner, favoured an immediate opening of the Second Front against Fortress Europe:[3] the invasion of France. Britain, as ever, preferred a more peripheral strategy. The bastard spawned became the Italian campaign. This was to last from summer 1943 to the capitulation of Germany in May 1945 and would claim the lives of 60,000 Allied soldiers. Axis casualties were in the region of 434,000.[4]

Allied Forces Headquarters (AFHQ) under the direction of General Harold Alexander, comprising the US Fifth and British Eighth Armies, would undertake the forthcoming campaign. The perceived benefits were that an assault on the peninsula would finally knock Mussolini's tottering regime out of the conflict. This would guarantee the Royal Navy complete hegemony in the Mediterranean and force Germany to shift reserves from the Eastern Front. Mussolini's regime might have collapsed but German resistance was always ingenious, fierce and determined. Conditions in Italy veered from oppressive heat to freezing mud and sleet. It was here that Gurkha units were bloodied in a series of savage actions that frequently recalled the horrors of trench warfare.

Once the invasion of Sicily got underway, Il Duce's shaky throne quickly collapsed; he was deposed and imprisoned in July. A new provisional government established under Marshal Pietro Badoglio[5] wasted no time in opening up a line of communication to the Allies. While the campaign in Sicily had been successful the bulk of Axis forces had got clear, their overall losses quite light. This meant the battle for the Italian peninsula would be that much harder – perhaps much harder than anyone had realised.

Hitler responded, as intended, by rushing up another sixteen divisions. This might denude his lines elsewhere but under the notably able direction of Field Marshal Kesselring ('Smiling Albert')[6] the Axis would give a very good account of themselves. They had to; air bases in Italy would bring south German cities within range and threaten the vital Ploesti Oilfields in Romania; no oil, no war. On 9 September 1943, American troops came ashore at Salerno and were very nearly dislodged by a swift Axis counterattack. The fight would be a long and gruelling one, more like an extended form of trench warfare – a *materielschlacht*, or battle of attrition.

Kesselring had an enormous advantage in ground which more than compensated for having fewer resources. The narrow strip of the peninsula with its high, jagged spine of the Apennines was ideally suited to defence, both flanks secured by the seas beyond. This allowed the Germans to set up a series of defensive lines running west–east and one of the most challenging was

THE GREAT CRUSADE (2) – THE BEGINNING OF THE END

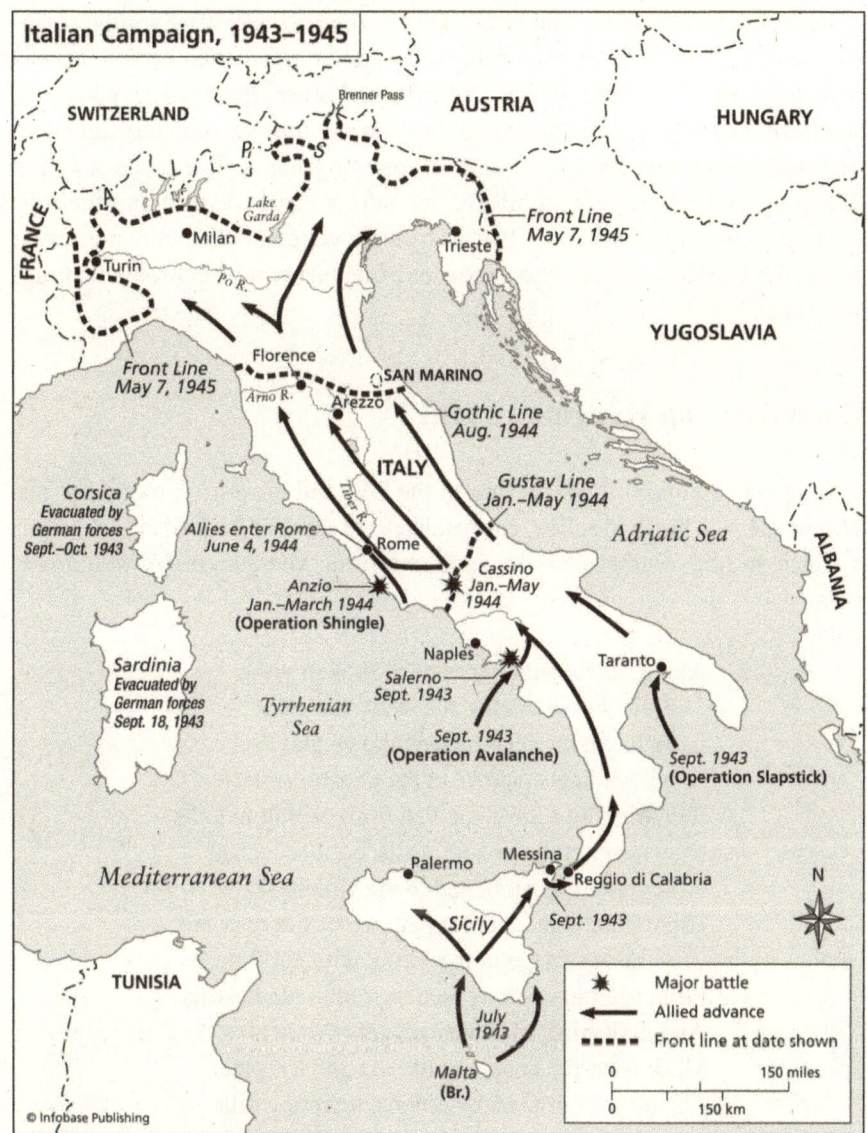

Map 9. Italian Campaign, 1943–5.

the notorious Gustav Line.[7] Running from just north of Monte Cassino, this would bleed the Allies nearly white in a quartet of major battles. An attempt to outflank the position by further amphibious landings at Anzio[8] appeared to offer dazzling prospects but faltered and finally got bogged down as Kesselring enclosed the beaches in a steel vice.

Losses in North Africa had been high but the Gurkhas were soon thrown into the long, hard slog up the unforgiving Italian peninsula. First to arrive in theatre was the 1/5th which disembarked after the main landing in October 1943. By 27–28 November they were thrown into the fight for Mozzagrogna, a wonderfully romantic sounding name. But it wasn't; the village was on a par, geographically, with Anzio and Cassino and the toll was high. All of the battalion's British officers were knocked out and it was the senior Gurkha officer who extricated the survivors of three attacking companies.[9]

Martyrdom on Hangman's Hill

E. Yates was a junior officer serving in the DLI and his poetry, tragically cut short by his own death in action, encapsulates the spirit of the Italian Campaign in which so may Gurkhas would serve and from where so many would not return:

> Along the twisting terraces of broken view
> The silent colonnades, the shattered arch
> Look down on dust-masked things that pass
> Tired, waving shadows in the ghostly streets,
> Stumbling in rubble spewed from gaping mouths
> New torn in tall, smooth walls, cool-drenched
> I' the moon, up-stretched to the violent sky
> Night blue with layering patterns of fire overlaid
> Cool scent of sage in the scrub, with acrid fumes
> From roaring, vicious flames, mix in the nostrils
> And darkening, climbing pillars of dust
> Mask from the cool, smooth sea and the plain
> The placid farms and ominous, towering hills.

The Gurkhas' particular Calvary was the assault on Monte Cassino – 'martyrdom on Hangman's Hill'. The seemingly impregnable Gustav Line was one of the major barriers to an advance by the US Fifth Army on the western side of the Italian peninsula, and the heavily fortified monastery at Monte Cassino was the chief obstacle in the drive to the Rapido River. All attempts to capture this key feature failed. An Allied aerial bombardment reduced the monastery to rubble, but this actually improved the defensive capabilities of the place.

THE GREAT CRUSADE (2) – THE BEGINNING OF THE END

In fact, Monte Cassino wasn't one battle but four, collectively one of the toughest fights of the Second World War. The first attack, launched on 17 January 1944, was when British X Corps attacked with two divisions astride the River Garigliano, followed by a second phase involving 46th Infantry Division near the confluence of the Garigliano and Liri rivers. Axis reinforcements were rushed in just in time to counter a big push by the US 36th Division aimed at getting across the Rapido River. These attacks failed. Towards the end of January fresh American-led assaults with French *Goumiers*,[10] highly adept mountain fighters, clawed out a bridgehead and the Germans fell back towards Cassino.

Inch by precious, bloodied inch the Americans crept forwards, the Axis fighting for every scrap of ground. Attacks against Monte Cassino itself[11] faltered in early February. Both sides took tremendous casualties; so costly was the defence that Kesselring was being urged to abandon this western flank of his line and pull back northwards. He decided to hang on instead. Operation Shingle – the Anzio landings – had gone ahead on 22 January and so Operation Avenger, a renewed attempt on Cassino, went ahead too.

Tuker's 4th Indian Division had not reached Italy until the previous December and entered the fray at Cassino on 11 February. It was pretty terrifying. The ancient monastery clung to the high summit in front of them while below the crest a lower pimple, Hangman's Hill,[12] rose not quite as high. Right of this was Castle Hill, while Snake's Head Ridge was actually more elevated than the monastery. Below these massifs was what remained of the once agreeable town of Cassino; little of it was left standing.

The Americans had battered their way onto Snake's Head but could get no further, any additional advance blocked by another swell of high ground. At this point Tuker fell ill and was casevaced.[13] General Bernard Freyberg VC[14] commanded the New Zealanders who, with the British 78th Division, would try to succeed where the United States had failed. Tuker's plan, drafted before he was stricken down, preferred a peripheral strategy, effectively pinching out the high salient of Monte Cassino and avoiding a head-on charge. This was a particularly good idea.[15] The alternative plan of kicking down the front door was not. His three Gurkha Battalions, 1/2nd, 1/9th and a revived 2/7th, would have cause to agree.

It would fall to 4th Indian Division to renew the attack from Snake's Head, take the intervening hillock (Point 593), secure the monastery and clear the ground so the New Zealanders could capture what was left of the town. Both 1/2nd and 1/9th Gurkhas, from 7th Indian Brigade, would be in the vanguard. On 17 February they attacked, inching up the slopes, something the defenders did not fail to spot. All their guns and mortars, and they had plenty of both, were already registered and a tsunami of shot flayed the Gurkhas. It was hideous ground, bare and spare, very little in the way of cover; stone chips flew like yet more shrapnel as though the air was alive. At the same time Allied bombers blasted the monastery,[16] not that the infantry had been made aware, as though there were competing strategies.[17] Initially, the assaults achieved nothing.

Brigadier Lovett, the Brigade Commander, decided to commit his whole force in a night assault with the two Gurkha battalions being thrown against the now bombed-out monastery, an advance of 800yd (732m) across open ground. Every inch was covered by intense machine-gun fire; the Germans had cunningly extended an outpost line ahead of the main defences; scrub and bushes which might have offered meagre cover were sown with mines. It was a massacre: casualties were appalling.[18] Both battalions were forced back, and the remnants tried to dig in. C and D companies from 1/2nd lost nearly 100 men.[19]

It was back to the drawing board for a new Plan B. This time the New Zealanders would, as before, have another crack at the town while Tuker's men would attack along a different axis and attempt to secure Hangman's Hill[20] before trying to take the monastery. It was here that the 1/9th endured their protracted sacrifice, clinging on for sixteen days (starting 17 March) in the shadow of the great monastery. Initially, the New Zealanders, first-class fighting men, got onto Castle Hill then swooped down onto the ruined streets, but *Fallschirmjager* (paratroopers) contested every inch and had burrowed like troglodytes into the rubble to create a network of mini strongpoints. Increased bombing couldn't dislodge them but did prevent Allied armour from getting close.[21]

Inching ahead, under continual fire, 1/9th seemed to have stalled but, almost miraculously, C Company actually made it up onto Hangman's Hill. This feat gave new legs to the divisional assault so that, despite intense fire, the remainder of 1/9th reached the top, in the nick of time, as C Company had just seen off a determined enemy counterattack.

The Germans, having failed to win back the ground, tried to cut off all communications and supplies and very nearly succeeded. Allied troops there could only take out their casualties and bring in supplies at night; even then they were under near constant shellfire. An attempt to airdrop supplies was only partially successful; half the containers rolled down the mountain out of reach. Men were killed trying to retrieve them. For a time, Hangman's Hill became a focal point for the battle, both sides striving with all their strength over this tiny slice of terrain.[22]

Here, the Gurkhas' opponents were the German 1st Parachute Division,[23] which has been described as 'one of the greatest fighting formations ever to take the field'.[24] The Gurkhas were taking daily losses, they were on short rations, and it was obvious that they could not advance. Efforts by a New Zealand unit to relieve them failed. Even so, Gurkha morale remained high. When told that they were going to pull out, some asked, 'But who is going to relieve us?'

To effect a safe withdrawal, or as safe as it was likely to get, every effort was made to deceive the enemy. During the day an air drop was made. With the help of a rum ration, the last to leave sang and played music while their comrades stole away. Then it was over. Only 8 officers and 177 other ranks survived out of nearly a thousand.[25] General Tuker, still commanding 4th Indian Division if *hors de combat*, said of this battle that 'it will go down to history as one of the most stubborn ever fought'.[26] Today, into a giant boulder near Hangman's Hill is carved the badge of 9th Gurkha Rifles.

With the line finally breached in May after a magnificent charge from the Poles (actually relying on Tuker's original idea), the Allies could advance in massive bounds, hoping to cut off Kesselring's retreat by a decisive thrust from both Cassino and the refreshed bridgehead at Anzio. It was now that American General Mark Clark,[27] no favourite of the British, decided to swing north-west and seize the Eternal City – more PR than strategy while Kesselring's forces survived to keep on fighting. Rome might appear a stellar prize, but its fall was more symbolic than pragmatic.

Rome fell on 4 June 1944. Two days later, Operation Overlord, the D-Day landings and the beginning of the end for Hitler's thousand-year Reich burst along the Calvados coast: the greatest, most daring and ambitious amphibious invasion since Troy. Italy was relegated to a sideshow and six full Allied divisions were stripped out to join in the fight for Normandy which raged till the remnants of German forces were pulverised in the Falaise Pocket. Those left in Italy became a half-forgotten army – 'the D-Day Dodgers' as grossly unfair as grossly unfair can get.

Once autumn came, the tourist dream of a sun-soaked landscape quickly went sour, cold and biting rain turning ground into a morass worthy of Flanders. Denuded of troops, the objectives narrowed. Alexander's job was now more purely attritional: just keep as many German divisions pinned down as possible.

The Gothic Line

It was during that dismal autumn that 43rd Gurkha Lorried Brigade[28] deployed in Italy; this comprised 2/6th, 2/8th and 2/10th Gurkhas with have half a dozen armoured regiments, gunners, signallers and so on supporting them. Next up after the Gustav Line was the Gothic Line and anchoring this was the tiny state of San Marino. On top of Passano Ridge, above the frothing Fossa del Valle River, 26th Panzer Grenadiers[29] were well dug in. The Germans were incredibly good at digging in and they certainly hadn't lacked practice during this campaign.

On the balmy late summer's evening of 12/13 September 1944 2/8th and 2/10th were sent in. A heavy barrage and salvoes from British tanks might have softened up the position but didn't dislodge the defenders who fought back with customary zeal and vigour. Still, the enemy positions were carried with the Gurkhas' habitual elan and the ridge was taken; enemy machine guns were taken out one after the other along with two Mark IV Panzers.[30] As the Gurkhas dug in to withstand the inevitable counterattacks, Axis guns pounded their captured positions, blowing down the Bailey Bridges over which their armoured support was arriving. They held on, nonetheless.[31]

San Marino still wasn't fully in Allied hands. As well as going in by the front door, 4th Indian Division was tasked with a broad flanking sweep around the northerly foothills of the great massif. It fell to 1/9th Gurkhas to have a crack at San Marino town, clinging to the face of the hillside in a succession of terraces. With two companies dug in, on 18 September, A and C companies moved into the settlement itself. This prompted a tornado of enemy fire, big guns and mortars backed by an abundance of small arms. As ever, the defenders had burrowed into the rubble, improvising minor fortresses worthy of Tolkien. Both forward companies were in trouble: no support, ammunition running low, no serious prospects of advancing.

At least the British guns could lay down a smoke barrage which helped C Company to exfiltrate successfully. A Company were less fortunate: Axis troops were pretty much on top of them, rounds coming in thick and fast, bright fireflies of tracer arcing, seeming deceptively lazy. It was at this critical juncture that Rifleman Sher Bahadur Thapa swung into action:

> In Italy on the night of 18th/19th September, 1944, a Battalion of the 9th Gurkha Rifles was fighting its way forward into the State of San Marino against bitter opposition from German prepared positions dominating the river valley and held in considerable strength in depth. Rifleman Sher Bahadur Thapa was a number one Bren gunner in a rifle Company, which just before dawn came under heavy enemy observed small arms and mortar fire.
>
> He and his section commander charged an enemy post, killing the machine gunner and putting the rest of the post to flight.

THE GREAT CRUSADE (2) – THE BEGINNING OF THE END

Almost immediately another party of Germans attacked the two men and the section commander was badly wounded by a grenade, but, without hesitation, this Rifleman, in spite of intense fire, rushed at the attackers and reaching the crest of the ridge brought his Bren gun into action against the main body of the enemy who were counterattacking our troops.

Disregarding suggestions that he should withdraw to the cover of a slit trench, Rifleman Sher Bahadur Thapa lay in the open under a hail of bullets, firing his Bren gun which he knew he could only bring to bear on the German emplacements from his exposed position on the crest of the hill as they would not have been visible from the slit trench.

By the intensity and accuracy of the fire which he could bring to bear only from the crest, this isolated Gurkha Bren gunner silenced several enemy machine guns and checked a number of Germans who were trying to infiltrate on to the ridge. At the end of two hours both forward Companies had exhausted their ammunition and, as they were by then practically surrounded, they were ordered to withdraw. Rifleman Sher Bahadur Thapa covered their withdrawal as they crossed the open ground to positions in the rear and himself remained alone at his post until his ammunition ran out. He then dashed forward under accurate small arms and mortar fire and rescued two wounded men, who were lying between him and the advancing Germans.

While returning the second time he paid the price of his heroism and fell riddled by machine gun bullets fired at point black range. The great bravery of this Gurkha soldier was instrumental in saving the lives of many of his companions and his outstanding devotion to duty contributed largely to the severe reverse which the enemy eventually suffered when our troops counter attacked. His name will live in the history of his Regiment as a very gallant soldier.[32] Rifleman Thapa won a posthumous VC and his mother came down from Nepal to receive the award from the Viceroy at the regimental depot.[33]

In all, nine Gurkha battalions would fight in that long slog up the 'boot' of Italy. Despite having secured the Passano Ridge, 43rd Lorried Brigade still wasn't through the Gothic Line. Ahead lay another summit, the Ripabianca Ridge, still in enemy hands. At dusk on 15 September, both 2/6th and 2/8th went into the attack and, brilliantly supported by a drenching bombardment, took the ground. So far so good: this success engendered the hope (by way of wishful thinking) that the Panzer Grenadiers had had enough. But they hadn't, and a follow-up charge put in by two infantry divisions plus armour got a very bloody nose.[34]

Crossing the Rubicon

It wasn't over. The late Brigadier Peter Young, a man who knew a great deal about fighting, answered a question about which opponent he rated most highly with: 'If you haven't fought the Germans, you haven't been to war …'.[35] Any riflemen from any of these nine battalions could have told you that. Soon, in the cool, late summer pre-dawn on 23 September, 2/8th and 2/10th Gurkhas were back in action. The Germans were dug in now at Santarcangelo and while the attack was successful, the price was fearful. A single company of 2/10th took 90 per cent casualties.[36] With the whole brigade sent in and 10th Hussars bashing through with Shermans, the line fractured, the high ground was cleared and the survivors poured down the reverse slope to the river – the Rubicon. In this instance the die had been cast some time ago and whether any of these young hill-men from faraway Nepal got the classical allusion is not recorded.

Nobody can quite agree on the derivation of the name Apennines; it is probably Celtic, insofar as anyone can now agree on what that means. A southward extension of the Alps, these epic limestone ridges run for 750 miles (1,200km) down the thin spine of Italy, with parallel ridges folding on either side of the main frame. They are beautiful and rise at their highest point, Como Grande ('Big Horn'), to 9,500ft (2,192m). But once across the fateful Rubicon the Gurkhas, as part of the Allied armies, would be fighting to drive the Germans from their high, bristling eyries among the jagged labyrinths of peaks and gullies. It would be very tough going.

This was the last redoubt between the Allies and those fertile northern plains, but the local Masada was Monte Chico. Here the primeval terrain ruled out tanks and the Germans, as ever, made full use of every defensible feature, another fight for the infantry. It was at 10 p.m. on 13 October that 2/6th Gurkhas attacked. Fighting flared, desperate and hand-to-hand; a feature dubbed 'The White House' formed a plug and no progress could be made until it was prised free. Yard by yard, the Gurkhas struggled toward the summit 1,300ft (400m) up. They got there but dawn left them dreadfully exposed to the inevitable rush of counterattacks, down to bayonet and kukri once their ammo was exhausted. Two more battalions, 2/8th and 2/10th, clawed their way up in support, finally

THE GREAT CRUSADE (2) – THE BEGINNING OF THE END

creeping forward to find that the Germans had had enough and fallen back, unlocking a crossing of the next wet gap: the River Ronco.[37] Those broad, sunlit plains were finally in sight.

On the right flank of Eighth Army, 8th Indian Division was inching towards Monte San Barolo, a heavily defended massif at the very junction of British and American forces. Yet another well-defended hilltop position that needed storming. The preliminary recce fell to 1/5th Gurkhas which sent out a platoon-sized patrol to investigate a narrow saddle below the main peak.[38] The tactical importance of this had not escaped the Germans who were, as ever, well dug in. One of these Gurkhas was 20-year-old Rifleman Thaman Gurung. His citation as featured in the *London Gazette* tells the story of what happened next:

> In Italy on 10 November 1944 a Company of the 1st Battalion 5th Royal Gurkha Rifles (Frontier Force) was ordered to send a fighting patrol on to Monte San Bartolo, an objective of a future attack. In this patrol were two scouts, one of whom was Rifleman Thaman Gurung.
>
> By skilful stalking both scouts succeeded in reaching the base of the position undetected. Rifleman Thaman Gurung then started to work his way to the summit; the second scout attracted his attention to Germans in a slit trench just below the crest, who were preparing to fire with a machine gun at the leading section. Realizing that if the enemy succeeded in opening fire, the section would certainly sustain heavy casualties, Rifleman Thaman Gurung leapt to his feet and charged them. Completely taken by surprise, the Germans surrendered without opening fire. Rifleman Thaman Gurung then crept forward to the summit of the position, from which he saw a party of Germans, well dug in on reverse slopes, preparing to throw grenades over the crest at the leading section.
>
> Although the sky-line was devoid of cover and under accurate machine gun fire at close range, Rifleman Thaman Gurung immediately crossed it, firing on the German position with his Tommy gun, thus allowing the forward section to reach the summit, but due to heavy fire from the enemy machine guns, the platoon was ordered to withdraw. Rifleman Thaman Gurung then again crossed the sky-line alone and although in full view of the enemy and constantly exposed to heavy fire at short range, he methodically put burst after burst of Tommy-gun fire into the

German slit trenches, until his ammunition ran out. He then threw two grenades he had with him and rejoining his section, collected two more grenades and again doubled over the bullet-swept crest of the hilltop and hurled them at the remaining Germans.

This diversion enabled both rear sections to withdraw without further loss. Meanwhile, the leading section, which had remained behind to assist the withdrawal of the remainder of the platoon, was still on the summit, so Rifleman Thaman Gurung, shouting to the section to withdraw, seized a Bren-gun and a number of magazines. He then, yet again, ran to the top of the hill and, although he well knew that his action meant almost certain death, stood up on the bullet-swept summit, in full view of the enemy, and opened fire at the nearest enemy positions. It was not until he had emptied two complete magazines, and the remaining section was well on its way to safety, that Rifleman Thaman Gurung was killed.

It was undoubtedly due to his superb gallantry that his platoon was able to withdraw from an extremely difficult position without many more casualties than were in fact incurred and that some very valuable information was obtained which resulted in the capture of the feature three days later. The rifleman's bravery cost him his life. The deceased rifleman was awarded a posthumous VC and interred with comrades in the Rimini Gurkha War Cemetery.[39]

Breaking out onto the plains might have seemed like a relief – it was not really. No more mountains perhaps, but the sodden paddies and flushed meadows were swept by well-sited bunkers dug into raised banks or levees, holding back the rivers. These were akin to First World War redoubts, swaddled with wire and mines. These lines were almost impossible to outflank. The only realistic tactic was to get in close, burrow through and fight your way along using flame-throwers; not quite bombing up the traverses but close enough.[40]

Through the first dismal, freezing and soaked two months of 1945, 43rd Lorried Brigade battered away at the Senio River Line. In its own way this was as deadly and sapping as fighting for the hills. Despite now being issued with 'Kangaroo' armoured personnel carriers,[41] the toll continued to mount, almost to the very bitter end. Once they had punched a 3-mile-wide gap in the Senio River Line, the brigade barrelled on to the next barrier, the River Sillaro. Now, in this northern region of Italy, the Germans might have expected some

THE GREAT CRUSADE (2) – THE BEGINNING OF THE END

interference from the Luftwaffe, but the Allies still had dominance over the winter skies and the Germans were finding themselves bombed and strafed off the roads. Next objective was the town of Medicina, a mere 15 miles (24km) east of the great metropolis and industrial/rail hub of Bologna (the nemesis of Joseph Heller's fictional American aircrew in *Catch-22*).

Towards dusk on 16 April, 2/6th, racing in their Kangaroos and beefed up with the tanks of 14th/20th Hussars, burst into the town (this feat is still commemorated by strong links between the Hussars and RGR).[42] As ever the dogged *Fallschirmjager* fought hard, despite being caught, for once, before they had fully dug in. By dawn, the place was fully in Allied hands. There were still numerous rivers to cross and next up was the Gaiana, defended by German 4th Parachute Division. This was another nightmare, the banks bristling and bolstered by drainage ditches, running into the main river – all eminently defensible. Once again 2/6th Gurkhas went in first and paid a heavy price. Cracking this particular nut required a full divisional attack put in by the New Zealanders with massive air and artillery bombardment. The enemy positions were successfully assaulted on the night of 18/19 April.[43] The end was almost in sight.

It was on 2 May 1945 that Kesselring finally threw in the towel. By then the Allies had pushed over the wet swamp of the Po Valley. Those D-Day Dodgers had fought a terrific fight in dreadful conditions against a world-class enemy. Their overall and largely unsung sacrifice had been a major contribution to a final Allied victory. It was felt by many who served in Italy, including Gurkhas, that they were somehow second rate as attention moved to Normandy; that they were seen as shirkers (which they certainly were not). This anonymous rendition, sung to the tune of 'Lili Marlene', trumpets:

> We are the D-Day dodgers out here in Italy,
> Always drinking vino, always on the spree,
> Eighth army skivvies and the Yanks,
> We live in Rome and stuff our pants,
> We are the D-Day dodgers out here in Italy.
> We landed at Salerno, a holiday with pay,
> Jerry sent the band to cheer us on our way,
> He showed us the sights and gave us tea
> We all sang songs and the beer was free
> We are the D-Day dodgers out here in Italy.
> Naples and Cassino were taken in our stride
> We didn't go to fight there; we just went for the ride,

> Anzio and Sangro were just the same,
> We did nothing there to prove our fame,
> For we are the D-Day dodgers out here in Italy.

Greek Interlude

Greece has always had a place in the hearts of many Britons, the land of Homer and Leonidas. To be fair, many Germans were also under the classical spell. The Greeks were less enamoured, and the occupation had been harsh. Churchill was a great Greco-phile and was determined, as the war swung inexorably in favour of the Allies, that one of his allies in particular, Joseph Stalin, wasn't getting his hands on Greece. He was certainly in with a chance – unrest followed the German withdrawal. Furthermore, tensions between the Communist partisans of ELAS[44] and the newly returned government-in-exile were running high. Insofar as British troops such as the Geordies of 16th Durham Light Infantry (DLI), who ended up there, gave much thought to the internal politics, there was a measure of empathy with the left. Socialism was a doctrine which most espoused and even Churchill's epic wartime leadership had failed to convince the men who fought that it was time for a major shift. The Gurkhas probably didn't care much either way.

Many British soldiers had some initial sympathy with ELAS, as a DLI soldier records, though for most Gurkhas the politics were not relevant. It's that distance which helps make Gurkhas good peacekeepers:

> All of the army by that time was pretty well socialist. Everyone was of the view that the Conservatives were to blame for all sorts of ills that we had in the war, the general level of the economy and the way that people felt about the future, so that, by and large, they were all pretty well Labour. Even though people admired Churchill for his ability to lead the country, his politics were completely suspect – he was a Conservative. We felt that what the government was trying to do in Greece was to restore the monarchy, which we all surmised was really not what the people wanted but was going to be imposed upon them. Therefore, in the beginning there was a fair amount of favourable feeling towards this insurgency.[45]

Such sentiments tended not to survive contact with the realities.

THE GREAT CRUSADE (2) – THE BEGINNING OF THE END

> The ELAS tended to use women; they had women coming along the street, just as though they were housewives having a demonstration, followed by armed men behind them using the women as a shield, or even children, having children around so that you couldn't fire at them. So it got very dirty in that sense. This is about the time, as will always happen in these situations, that the soldiers' attitudes changed from being politically favourable to being militarily against them ... Churchill was trying to re-impose the King, the Communists were trying to impose Communist rule so that really in effect one was almost as bad as the other – and we were somewhere in between, I guess!

What of 'Johnny Gurkha'? He wasn't likely to be quite so impressed with the classical past and 4th Indian Division with its three Gurkha battalions was soon in the middle of a quite different kind of simmering climate. Gurkhas, as versatile and agile as they are and immune to intimidation, managed this switch to uneasy peacekeeping with their customary panache. This was as considerable an achievement as any attained in warfighting; stopping wars is as important as winning them.

There would still be civil war in Greece[46] but that was no fault of 4th Indian Division. Used to the arrogance, casual brutality and sneering of the Aryan master race, the Greeks, even the most disaffected, found these outwardly alien soldiers from a distant sub-continent neither threatening nor controlling, just calmly authoritative, endlessly patient and always so damn cheerful. If this was a respite of sorts, they had certainly earned it.

Meanwhile, way beyond Europe, there remained the Empire of the Sun, straddling the Far East, a colossus of tyranny and cruelty. For the Gurkhas, this might just prove the hardest test of all.

Chapter 9

The Great Crusade (3) – A Forgotten Army

> Why does your pointing finger accuse,
> your black arm, swollen (skin stretched tight
> as a surgeon's glove) point, accuse?
> Was your cause just
> that you accuse me, your enemy?
> You the aggressor, I the defender?
> Why do you stink so, fouling the air, the grass,
> the stagnant pool in the creek?
> No other animal stinks so in putrefaction.
> Why do you vent your protest against life itself?
> Is it seemly for the dead to fight?
> Charles McCausland, 'Dead Japanese'

Few British veterans I have interviewed show much rancour towards the Germans; it was not necessarily war without hate but there was generally a measure of mutual respect. The same cannot be said of those who fought in the Far East. For them, the Japanese are still perceived as vicious and bestial beyond words. One of my own uncles by marriage, who served in the Royal Army Medical Corps, refused for the rest of his life to have any Japanese products or electrical goods in his house or surgeries. He married late and his intended bride, at that point, drove a Japanese car – there could be no wedding until the offending vehicle was disposed of and another acquired, any nationality bar Japanese.

Burforce

Burma: a campaign where fighting was murderous, no quarter asked or given and frequently up close and very personal, as Sergeant McLaine of 2 DLI savagely records:

THE GREAT CRUSADE (3) – A FORGOTTEN ARMY

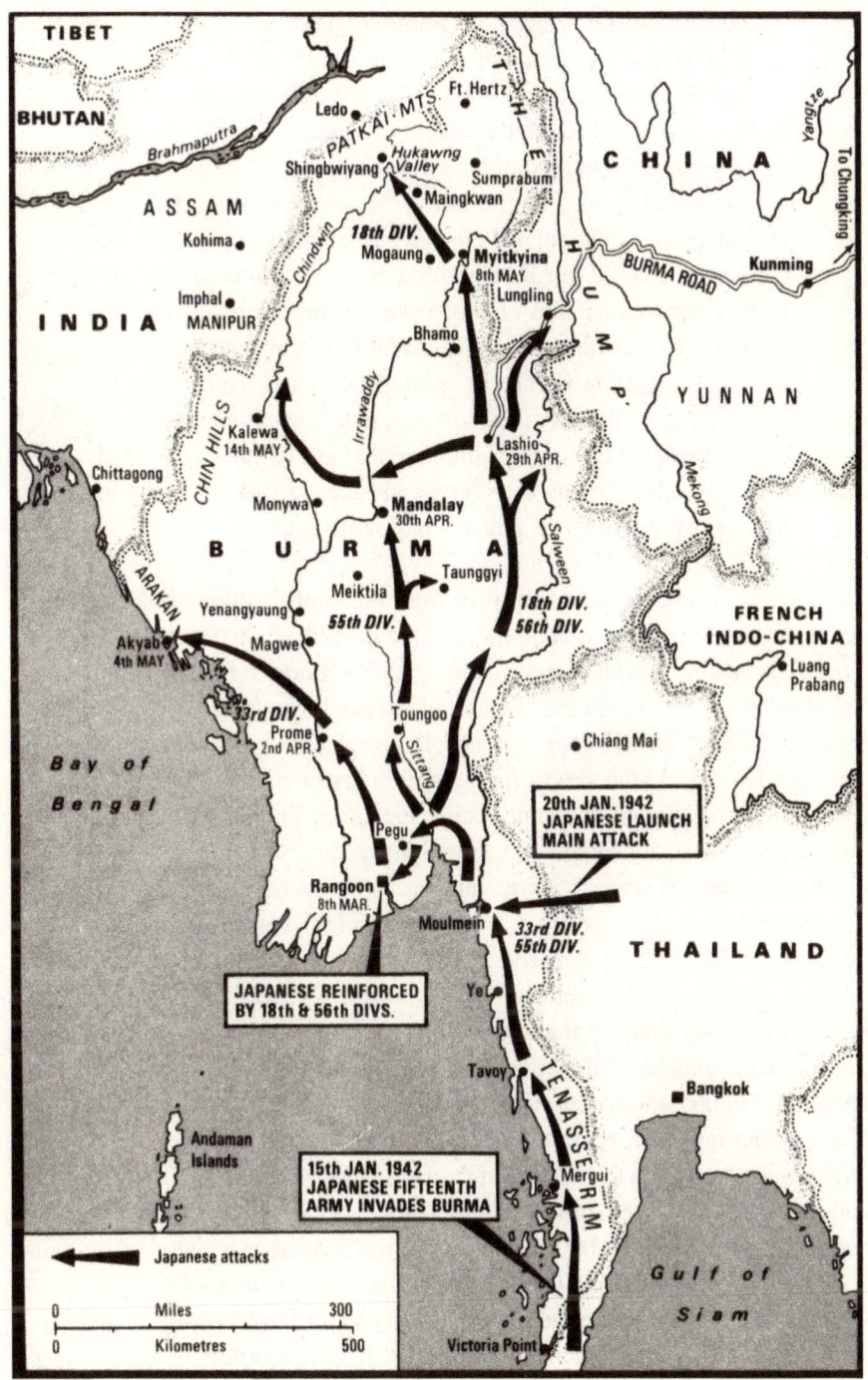

Map 10. Burma Campaign, 1942–5.

At the next bunker, a Japanese soldier rushed out. He knew if he stayed there he was going to get a grenade in, so he came out of the back door, which was behind me. I didn't see him when he fired. He got me through the side of my face. It felt like being hit by a clenched fist but it didn't hurt as much as a really good punch in a fight. I spat out a handful of teeth, spun round and he was a few paces away, facing me. He had a rifle and bayonet. I pressed the trigger but I'd got no ammunition. As he came towards me I felt it was either him or me. I was an instructor in unarmed combat, so I let him come and threw the light machine-gun in his face ... Before he hit the ground I had my hand round his windpipe and I literally tried to tear it out. It wouldn't come – if I could have got his windpipe out I would have twisted it round his neck. We were tossing over on the ground. I managed to get his bayonet off his rifle and finished him with that.[1]

Burma was an exceedingly long way from the conflict raging in Europe and, for the British public, possessed none of the immediacy. Eyes there were fixed upon Italy and the inevitable assault upon Hitler's 'Fortress Europe'[2] upon which the outcome of the war in the West would depend. Nonetheless, this Forgotten Army in the Far East was coming of age. British, Indian Army and Gurkha forces had endured defeat after defeat from a seemingly omnipotent foe, yet that was changing. Orde Wingate's vaunted raids, though of limited strategic value, did much to restore badly dented morale and the tactical value of air-supply would further transform Fourteenth Army's prospects. The warriors were British, Indian, Gurkha and Sikh. Of the score of VCs won during the campaign, fourteen went to soldiers of the Indian Army and three of these to a single Gurkha battalion.

It is fair to say that neither side would have chosen to fight in Burma, a country where high, tree-clad mountains plunged into dense, almost impenetrable jungle; suffocating heat, cloying humidity, disease-ridden and infested swamps alternated with baking plains of near-desert savannah. For the Imperial Japanese, conquest offered two enticing possibilities: the first was the means of severing the lifeline of the Burma Road[3] over which vital military aid was trekked to the Chinese Nationalists fighting under Chiang Kai-shek.[4] Secondly, Japan held the belief that if its armies were to cross into British India, the oppressed masses there would welcome them as liberators. This might seem unlikely but a turncoat Bengali politician, Chandra Bose, formed an effective fifth column and his inducements had succeeded in suborning many thousands of Indian Army soldiers captured in the debacle at Singapore.[5]

THE GREAT CRUSADE (3) – A FORGOTTEN ARMY

At the outset, as noted earlier, it wasn't clear to what extent Britain could rely on its traditional support from Nepal. Shamsher Rana[6] whose pro-British stance in the First World War had been significant had, on his demise and that of his successor, been replaced by Judha Shamsher.[7] The rise of nationalism across the Indian subcontinent had put pressure on him to withdraw cooperation but he stuck to the 'auld alliance' with Britain. In 1940 – the darkest hour, with a cross-Channel invasion seemingly inevitable – the British representative in Nepal had to ask Judha for consent to raise those other ten battalions of Gurkhas. The Nepalese would be hitching their cart firmly to what might very well be a doomed empire and a number of the ruler's advisors were hostile. Happily, he concurred, in the circumstances a choice both bold and shrewd.[8]

Pearl Harbor was the cataclysmic game-changer.[9] The Allies had been blind to the rising Japanese leviathan. The Japanese military, very much in control, had planned to raise a vast imperial shield around the Rising Sun, creating an impenetrable ring and securing all those natural resources, oil and rubber, which the homeland lacked. This was a very well-armed, major industrial power with huge pools of manpower and a fanatical code of adherence.

Sir Archibald Wavell, hero of early operations in the Western Desert, was now in charge of India. His policy of pushing his slender and ill-trained forces forward to meet the Japanese head-on proved unfortunate. Lieutenant General William Slim found himself conducting a desperate retreat up the long spine of Burma; 'Burforce'[10] was outnumbered, outgunned and outfought. Slim fell back along the gash of the Irrawaddy River towards the gates of India, where a bitter stalemate ensued.

In late January 1942, 48th Brigade from 17th Indian Division arrived at Rangoon. There were three Gurkha battalions in this order of battle: 1/3rd, 1/4th and 2/5th. In less than three weeks the Bushido whirlwind, brilliantly executing a series of wide outflanking movements, had worked around this brigade together with 1/7th and 3/7th battalions. To complete their plans the Japanese had to capture the Sittang Railway Bridge over the wide, slow-moving river. It was equally imperative for the British to withdraw from the trap and blow the bridge.[11]

Defeat

A detailed record of these frantic days has been left to us by Lieutenant Colonel W.P.A. Lentaingne, CO of 1/4th. The British 48th Brigade had retreated some 30 miles (48km) from its previous line along the Bilin River and footsore 'Tommies' and Gurkhas trudged into Kyaikto in the small hours. It was a moonless night and dawn revealed the battalion bivouacked amid an old rubbish dump. The rising sun was chorused by distant gunfire, rattling in ominous thunder. There was much confusion but no rations. 'We Gurkhas got food at 08.00 which partly restored flaky morale. I was called to brigade HQ and ordered to move to Sittang Bridge.'[12]

This would be a leap-frogging withdrawal. The men deployed in marching order, mules and baggage at the back. The first leg was a relatively short hop to the Mokpalin Quarries, only 6 miles from the bridge. The march was enlivened by strafing from RAF Blenheims. 'Friendly fire' is a relative concept; it doesn't feel that friendly on the ground. However, nobody got hit and the battalion escaped the arid plain for the cover of rubber plantations; from then on and into scrub jungle, it was hellish difficult going, as recorded by Lentaingne: 'Lots of rear echelon forces were clogging the road with little discipline.'[13] More heat and dust and more unwelcome RAF attention – this was rebuffed with sustained Bren gun fire and two Blenheims were brought down. That does nothing for morale. Lentaingne continues his narrative:

> At 1730 hours I got to Divisional HQ at the Quarries, the 1/4th was deployed to defend our HQ. Meanwhile RAF liaison denied they had been shooting at us – they claimed the Japs were using captured planes! The men had a late evening meal but orders were to move at 0415 hours as we feared the Japs might try and seize the west bank and the bridge using paratroopers. We had to get over by first light at 0600 and deal with any enemy paras. We had no maps – just had to follow the wheel tracks of Divisional HQ who were in vehicles. We had one and three-quarter hours to cover the six miles.[14]

In Mokpalin village the Gurkhas barged into a huge traffic scrum – a truck had got wedged on the bridge, skewed right across and blocking the roadway. The Gurkhas had to skirt the obstacle using the dew-slimed steel access catwalk, treacherous in the half-light of dawn. At last, they were all safely over and soon digging in, platoons strung out in a broad defensive arc. Sappers dragged the broken-down truck clear and released the pent-up flood of fleeing vehicles. That first day then settled down into the tedious business of waiting. Nothing happened; one of those weird lulls. There were no enemy paras. Next day dawned with bursts of heavy firing ominously near and the Japanese tightened their vice around the perimeter. Lentaingne records:

There was still heavy firing going on in the direction of Mokpalin village which was just over the hill that ran by a curved railway cutting running from the bridge and was heavily wooded. North of the cutting was a large pagoda and a huge stone Buddha, whilst to the south of it and nearer to the river was a railway inspector's bungalow held by the Burma Rifles. The Gurkhas were in possession of the pagoda but their positions curled back just west of the Buddha. Heavy clouds of smoke came from over the crest in the direction of Mokpalin which I learned was on fire together with much of the transport. It was apparent that the Japs were closing on over a wide front against the rest of the division withdrawing down the road from Kyaikto.[15]

Colonel Lentaingne's battalion was still patiently awaiting enemies dropping out of the sky but none came. He was sent by his 48 Brigade Commander to undertake a recce over on the east bank to assess if the perimeter there needed shoring up at all. The timing was inopportune as an artillery barrage bracketed the bridge as they were crossing. This heralded a mass retreat by those on the east bank. Next, the brigadier ordered a counterattack to restore the situation before it crumbled beyond redemption. Sappers were already wiring the structure as A and C companies filed over. It was in fact British guns that were firing, the unpredictable fog of war swirling around. Japanese infantry soon appeared nonetheless but were seen off with relative ease. It seemed that the enemy were pretty much in the dark too, both sides probing.

Once darkness fell, the Japanese attempted to infiltrate with the Gurkhas clinging to both ends of the span. Stragglers filed over during the whole night spreading tales of woe and defeat, a noose that was tightening irrevocably. The brigadier still had control over the bridge, now fully wired for demolition. The decision to blow it was a heavy burden: the risk of a determined Japanese thrust against a possibility of leaving hundreds or thousands of men marooned on the wrong side. The colonel's feet were covered in blisters, his men worn out, tracer fire spinning from the steel beams as Japanese machine guns crept closer.

By dawn their aim was improving, and something had to be done. The sappers needed to trip their fuses if, or rather when, the bridge was to go. They couldn't get near under such accurate fire, so improvised breastworks of sandbags were thrown up around the firing points before first light. The stalemate continued throughout that day, but the Gurkhas could almost feel each twist of the garrotte. That evening's conference agreed that the bridge would be destroyed at 6 a.m. next day to give those remaining on the east bank a chance to get clear under cover of night. Lentaingne records: 'At the west end we collected in sandbagged redoubts, a series of terrific explosions, a blinding flash, a blast of hot air and a shower of fragments.'[16] Such was the Sittang Bridge's thunderous elegy. A great gap now yawned where two spans had collapsed; the bridge was a bridge no more.

At about 9.30 a.m. the colonel reported to brigade HQ. It wasn't a happy time. Fatigue and hopelessness were ratcheted up when the brigadier, realising he'd blown the bridge too soon, entered a state of near collapse: 'My God, I've lost the whole division.'[17] Large, Allied forces had been left isolated and now cut off on the east bank. Their last hope was blown sky high. All that could be done generally was to request an air drop of all available life jackets while all the Gurkhas could do was to hang on until ordered to withdraw to Pegu – still with no maps. The colonel set his men off in three marching columns, picking up waifs and strays: some Baluchis, local gunners from Rangoon with some old Italian pieces and a Bombay Pioneer outfit.

All was confusion. The Japanese, at this stage, seemed far better at jungle fighting than the Allies. It seemed (wrongly) that they could move through dense bush with consummate ease. Of the Gurkha battalions, 1/4th got clear over the bridge, while 1/3rd and 2/5th did not. Then it was blown. Cut off, the two battalions fought hard to reach the rear-guard from 1/4th clinging to the east bank. It was a shambles; four battalions were now trapped in a shrinking pocket. The only way to get over was to swim for it, and Gurkhas are not natural swimmers. Some of their British officers swam across and, collecting such random rivercraft as they could find, managed to ferry out at least some of their soldiers.

This phase of the retreat to Pegu was at least carried out by train. The men de-trained about half a mile from the village with tree cover, which was just as well; the Japanese bombed the place mercilessly. Overall, the colonel was unimpressed with his force's showing and just glad he got his men away: 'the division fought in uncoordinated penny packets, owing to a complete lack of knowledge of what was afoot … the Japs were as tired and hungry as our troops, but they knew what they were doing'.[18] Allied losses in the action were about 2,500 of whom two-thirds were Gurkhas.[19] These were far worse Gurkha losses than on the Western Front in the previous war when about 350 had been killed.[20]

What was left of 1/3rd and 2/5th formed a scratch battalion, as did the survivors of 1/7th and 3/7th. In March, in time to see Rangoon lost, 1/10th also arrived in theatre. Lieutenant Colonel R.G. Leonard the of 1/10th was shot up during an ambush which saw 63rd Brigade's commanding officer also wounded, and two battalion commanders killed. Leonard was casevaced back to an advanced dressing station set up in a school but the ambulance he was in was also bushwhacked – the Japanese were no respecters of red crosses.

One Japanese soldier with a captured .45 calibre Thompson sub-machine gun raked the interior of the vehicle. This was a looted weapon, and the soldier firing didn't really know how to handle it – happily so for the colonel as the rounds missed him. Almost immediately he was rescued by a timely counterattack sent in by 1/4th Gurkhas. While he'd been unlucky at the outset, he was more fortunate now and survived, despite a staggering total of nearly seventy wounds.[21]

Withdrawal

Field Marshal William Joseph ('Bill') Slim DSO MC (1891–1970) is often and with justification regarded as the best British senior commander of the Second World War. He was born in Bristol, but the family moved to Birmingham where he was educated. Falling on hard times, they could only afford to send one, the elder, son to university, so the young Bill became a teacher. He did get into Birmingham University's OTC, and this was enough after 1914 to elevate him to temporary gentleman status[22] and a commission in the Warwickshires. He was blooded and wounded at Gallipoli, where he first met the Gurkhas and then again in Mesopotamia where he won the MC, transferring to the Indian Army where he was a major (later adjutant) in 6th Gurkhas before moving up to command 2/7th. By 1939 he was a colonel but with temporary elevation to brigadier.

During the East African Campaign, he commanded 10th Indian Infantry Brigade of 5th Indian Division and was again injured fighting in Eritrea. While he was recovering from wounds he was temporarily assigned to the staff at GHQ Delhi before serving again in Iraq and Syria as a major general, leading 10th Indian Division. He was given command of Burforce in March 1942, rising to lieutenant general two months later. His leadership of the Fourteenth Army would be both masterful and decisive, firstly extracting a defeated corps but then holding it together and then patiently transforming defeat into a magnificent victory.

American historians Alan Millet and Williamson Murray described Slim thus:

> A hardened field soldier who had learned his trade on the Western Front and in the Indian Army, Slim combined troop-leading and

training skills with personal and moral courage as well as charm, a sound grasp of soldiering, and a solid appreciation of Asian warfare and the excellence of the Japanese Army. He had experienced the catastrophe of the 1942 retreat from Burma and the abortive attack on the Arakan. His honesty and character made him the obvious choice to reshape the Fourteenth Army, a force built on the Indian Army but including the ever-dependable Gurkha Rifles of Nepal, unproven infantry battalions from East and West Africa, and infantry battalions and supporting arms from the British Army.[23]

The late, great George Macdonald Fraser, then serving as a teenage private in the Border Regiment, was one who became a convert:

> But the biggest boost to morale was the burly man who came to talk to the assembled battalion ... it was unforgettable. Slim was like that: the only man I've ever seen who had a force that came out of him ... British soldiers don't love their commanders much less worship them; Fourteenth Army trusted Slim and thought of him as one of themselves and perhaps his real secret was that the feeling was mutual.[24]

Gurkhas had tasted the bitter dregs of defeat but, as ever, the Nepalese hill-men were fast learners. They would learn how to out-fox and out-fight even the Japanese in the deadly, sapping business of jungle patrols. British officers began to note the effectiveness of Gurkhas, soldiers the Japanese must learn to fear, as one recorded:

> These patrols came back to their regiments with stories of success ... as did the Gurkhas who presented themselves before their general, proudly opened a large basket, lifted from it three very gory Japanese heads, and laid them on his table. They then politely offered him for his dinner the freshly caught fish which filled the rest of the basket. The buzz went round each unit ... 'We rushed them as they were cooking, Havildar Bhupsingh bayoneted three. Rifleman Gingerbir crept up "luki-luki" behind him with his kukri. The Yellow-belly's head bounced three times before it stopped rolling.'[25]

On 15 February 1942, the Singapore garrison capitulated with 130,000 British and Commonwealth troops marched off into terrible captivity. It was a massive blow, far worse even than the fall of Tobruk. Japan's 18th Division, which had taken part in the brief siege, stormed forward and attacked again at Kyaukse, held by the now all-Gurkha units of 48th Brigade. In a fierce battle on 28/29 April 7th Gurkhas met the Japanese tsunami head-on, breaking up multiple attacks in a moonlit battle. With the enemy rebuffed they then put in a very successful counterattack on the 29th. They lost 10 men, the Japanese 500.[26]

This withdrawal through Burma which Slim's genius, within two years, would transform into a magnificent victory was the stuff of nightmares, unquestionably even worse than the road to Dunkirk. Getting back over the Chindwin River in early May was a particularly good example of the sum of all these many hardships. Two full divisions of Burforce would cross the mighty river at Shwegyn. This marked the border with Assam, effectively India. The place was a dreadful bottleneck and Slim was haunted by three principal terrors:

1. The Japanese might succeed in cutting the British off.
2. Food and supply might run out.
3. The imminent arrival of the monsoon could lead to catastrophe.[27]

On the evening of 8 May 7th Gurkhas were sent forward to reinforce the rearguard established by 48th Brigade, a couple of miles north-east of Shwegyn. It was here the general had his comic encounter with the subadar major (recounted in the Introduction) as a firefight erupted. Slim was blinded temporarily by the fog of war but it turned out the Japanese had attempted a turning move, landing troops amphibiously, and that 7th Gurkhas had become involved in a messy and confused fight. They were soon fighting a soldier's battle, split into smaller sub-units as they clawed their way backwards.

More and heavier attacks followed, the Japanese making good use of their handy 3in mortars.[28] The British position on the vital escarpment shielding the crossing was under immense pressure, with the enemy infiltrating between the strung-out defenders. A spirited counterattack put in by 7th Gurkhas restored the situation. It was still very much touch and go. Steamers crowding the riverside jetties were conspicuous targets and enemy pressure never slackened. Nobody was feeling this more than 7th Gurkhas at the front of the rear, who had not managed to dislodge a body of Japanese troops occupying a key feature, 'The Basin'.

As there was little prospect of getting all their 25-pounder ammunition away, the gunners decided to simply shoot the lot off. This was the biggest barrage so far in Burma[29] and plastered the Japanese forward positions, allowing surviving Gurkhas to get back unmolested. Those weary, bloodied and hungry soldiers could be excused for not having appreciated this was, in effect, the end of the campaign. The British had been beaten, Singapore had been lost, vast quantities of materiel destroyed – but it wasn't total defeat, not quite.

Getting the bulk of Burforce back over the Chindwin River before the onset of the monsoon, which effectively cancelled out any prospect of serious campaigning by either side, had, in fact, averted total disaster. A year on, in May 1943, as the very final remnants of 17th Indian Division were falling back, 2/5th Gurkhas were holding a line on the Tiddim Road. Their losses to date in the campaign had been dire, nearly half, yet to hold the line they would have to attack and clear the enemy from higher ground in front.

It was here that Havildar Gaje Ghale, of 5th Gurkhas, won his VC on 27 May 1943:

> In order to stop an advance into the Chin Hills of greatly superior Japanese forces it was essential to capture Basha East hill which was the key to the enemy position. Two assaults had failed but a third assault was ordered to be carried out. Havildar Gaje Ghale was in command of one platoon: he had never been under fire before and the platoon consisted of young soldiers. The approach for this platoon to their objective was along a narrow knife-edge with precipitous sides and bare of jungle whereas the enemy positions were well concealed. In places, the approach was no more than five yards wide and was covered by a dozen machine guns besides being subjected to artillery and mortar fire.
>
> While preparing for the attack the platoon came under heavy mortar fire but Havildar Gaje Ghale rallied them and led them forward. Approaching to close range of the well-entrenched enemy, the platoon came under withering fire and this N.C.O. was wounded in the arm, chest and leg by an enemy hand grenade. Without pausing to attend to his serious wounds and with no heed to the intensive fire from all sides, Havildar Gaje Ghale closed his men and led them to close grips with the enemy when a bitter hand to hand struggle ensued.
>
> Havildar Gaje Ghale dominated the fight by his outstanding example of dauntless courage and superb leadership. Hurling hand grenades, covered in blood from his own neglected wounds, he led assault after assault encouraging his platoon by shouting the Gurkha's battle-cry. Spurred on by the irresistible will of their leader to win, the platoon stormed and carried the hill by a

magnificent all out effort and inflicted very heavy casualties on the Japanese.[30]

Chris Bellamy comments that it seems most unlikely the Gaje Ghale, who had joined up in 1936 and served with the battalion throughout this dreadful time, had apparently not seen combat before, but there is no evidence to contradict the words of the citation. In any event, he was a very brave man.[31] What remained of 1/3rd, 1/4th, 2/5th, 1/10th and the ad hoc 7th Battalion gained a respite to recover, re-form and replace. Happily, Gaje Ghale survived.

The First Arakan Offensive

Wavell had devised a plan to strike a major blow – the Arakan offensive – to clear the foe from the Mayu Peninsula and seize Akyab Island. It was thought the Japanese had no more than a single regiment and 14th Indian Division would sweep down the mountainous spine of the peninsula, allowing 6th Brigade to mount landings on the island. On paper this looked feasible but conditions in the Arakan were fearsome, the hills high, rugged and difficult, cut with sharp ridges and deep, scrub-filled gullies. The thin strip of coastal plain is laced with small tidal rivers, or *chaungs*. This was bad ground for attackers, well suited to tenacious defence. The Japanese knew all about tenacity, and their capacity to construct highly efficient improvised lines of defence was impressive. They were ferocious and fanatically brave. Later, much later, the Allies would notice that, as morale declined, more would surrender but the Arakan defenders were not yet at that stage. They had faith in their capabilities, and it wasn't misplaced.

Initially the offensive produced some gains and 14th Division managed to advance almost as far as the aptly named Foul Point opposite Akyab Island, but a subsequent hiatus allowed the Japanese to regain their composure and prepare suitably strong defences. Attempts to wrest the village of Donbaik, key to securing the landward side, failed and a stalemate ensued. This could not endure as it was now mid-February 1943 and the dreaded monsoon was due, a continuous downpour of biblical fury that would choke further operations. It became the turn of 7th Indian Division to attack down the length of the Kalapanzin Valley on the far flank of the central ridge. This went well until a battalion of the King's Own Scottish Borderers ('KOSB') ran into a well-defended hilltop position. The advance was stalled and not even nearly point-blank fire from a massive 155mm gun could shift the Japanese. Nor, for once, could the Gurkhas. Overall, the first Arakan Campaign was a failure.

While fighting in the Arakan was to demonstrate that the Japanese were mere flesh and blood and scarcely superhuman, they remained a most formidable enemy. The Allies enjoyed superiority in the air and with artillery and armour. Japanese commanders squandered the lives of their men in reckless, suicidal, human-wave attacks yet, in defence, they proved infinitely subtle. Their bunkers were ingeniously constructed and brilliantly sited, impervious to much that Allied guns could throw at them. Even when British attacks overran their trenches they could shelter in dugouts while their own mortars deluged the attackers above.

Unquestionably, the vast cultural gap between the British and Japanese fuelled the latter's demonic reputation. A British officer confesses:

> I was quite scared of the Japs, myself. I thought they were very nasty people. They would die but they wouldn't lie down. They literally did hold their positions absolutely to the last man and the last round. They were immensely determined; we used to come upon pockets of these Japs, all lying dead under a tree or something. They had either died of complete starvation, or in some cases they had committed suicide by holding a grenade to their bosom and pulling the pin out, rather than be taken prisoner; we found that their food consisted only of an old sock full of rice and some bits of raw fish – terribly smelly and nasty ...[32]

F. Spencer Chapman put his experiences in Malaya into his celebrated narrative *The Jungle is Neutral*.[33] And indeed, this was so; despite contrary myth, the British suffered no more in jungle conditions than their adversaries. What was true, certainly at the outset, was that the Japanese had learned to fight better in such conditions; they used infiltration tactics and cover far more effectively. Those large-scale tactical manoeuvres religiously practised by British forces were ill-suited to such close terrain.

Part of the Japanese mystique is that they were frequently invisible, their foxholes and bunkers so carefully dug and sited, so well camouflaged, the unwary might not realise imminent danger until it was rather too late. Sound tactical skill at junior leadership level proved critical. British forces had to learn not just to cope with the physical demands of such hostile terrain but how to meet the dual tactical challenge of ground and a skilled foe. They learned that encirclement only meant defeat if your forces thought in strictly conventional terms. Where those surrounded could be sustained from the air and an all-round, all-arms defence established then the fight was far from lost.

This important realisation would be the gift of a very eccentric and highly contentious officer, one of those brilliant and uncompromising mavericks the British Army has also been so good at producing. Love him or hate him, Orde Wingate would become legend.

Wingate

One of the most celebrated if controversial sets of operations in Burma was the Chindits, brainchild of the mercurial (some allege psychopathic) Brigadier (later Major General) Orde Wingate. Taking the fight to the Japanese and using the jungle as it was believed they could use it, captured imaginations at a time when successful aggressive action was in short supply. In reality, the PR value exceeded any actual gains and casualties were extremely high. One anecdote that circulated about Wingate was that, during the first operation, he appeared at reveille one day at 5 a.m. stark naked and wearing only an alarm clock around his neck, advising his no-doubt astonished soldiers that he'd realised, during the preceding night, he was actually a re-incarnation of John the Baptist! A single Gurkha battalion, 2/3rd, took part in the first Chindits expedition. For the second, more ambitious plan three more, 3/4th, 3/6th and 4/10th, took part, earning high praise from Wingate's successor.

Orde Charles Wingate (1903–44) DSO and 2 Bars was, by turns, brilliant, impossible and unsound. He had seen the Long Range Desert Group being so successful in the Western Desert and at one point he had even proposed his own version, significantly beefing up Bagnold's original,[34] but this was wisely ignored. He originally conceived of what would become the Chindits (named after the Goddess Chinthe, a mythical creature which stands guard outside Burmese temples) as 'Long Range Penetration Groups'[35] – surely a nod to the LRDG? Wingate, alongside 'Mad' Mike Calvert,[36] had been briefed by Wavell to facilitate behind-the-lines resistance as the Japanese overran Burma.

Wingate was born in India into a military family. Educated in the UK at Charterhouse and then the gunnery school at Woolwich, commissioned into the Royal Artillery in 1923, he was noted as being a brilliant horseman and an advocate of 'Special Forces' type warfare – a novel concept at the time. Most of his fellow officers detested him but he benefited from the patronage of an older relative, General Sir Reginald Wingate, under whose aegis, in 1928, he transferred to the Sudan Defence Force. He relished the life even if his fellow officers failed to relish him.

When he was subsequently attached to UK forces stationed in Mandatory Palestine, Wingate quickly identified with the Jewish settlers and Zionism, becoming a convert to their cause and creating British-led Jewish commando units to fight against insurgent Arabs. This was the genesis of the Israeli Defence Force and Wingate has attained totemic status. His obvious pro-Zionist bias got him into trouble, and he was *stellenbosched*.[37] Never destined to be popular with his peers, the outbreak of war nonetheless gave him scope and he served with distinction against the Italians in Ethiopia. Destined to be contentious not just in his relatively short life but thereafter, his Chindits became national heroes at a time when heroes were desperately needed, and they have been heroes ever since.

It had been Wavell who had listened to Bagnold in 1940 when he dreamed up the LRDG, and he listened to Wingate three years later. What the major, soon to be brigadier, suggested was a re-working of his desert ideas and he was given 77th Indian Infantry Brigade to get the job done. The brigade consisted of one British Battalion (13th King's Regiment), one of Burma Rifles, 3/2nd Gurkhas and some attached commandos.[38] Chris Bellamy makes the valid point that Wingate didn't understand the Gurkhas; the bizarre mystique and wild egocentricity he flaunted was rather lost on them.[39] Many of his superiors were equally unimpressed.

Wingate's plan was to split his command into seven marching columns, each centred on an individual rifle company. Four of these companies would be drawn from 3/2nd Gurkhas. This sat badly with the men from Nepal and their British officers who saw their battalion effectively being broken up and used, not just in penny packets but without their customary unit cohesion, and the men, in some circumstances, relegated to the rather menial if important job of mule-handlers.[40] Even for the most ardent animal enthusiast, the mule is generally unlovable. Gurkha recruits had little experience with them and rather less affection for them. Gurkhas do like other Gurkhas; they're not used to being part of units they don't know and whose ways of doing things are different.

Wingate's remote and unsympathetic methods of command led him to order that any wounded should be left at the nearest native settlement. Gurkhas don't abandon their comrades; the lessons of the North-West Frontier were still recent, and the Japanese treatment of Allied wounded was easily as murderous. To leave a man behind was tantamount to a death sentence.[41] The plain fact was that Wingate did not understand the nature of these men under his command. Worse, he didn't seem to care.

Operation Longcloth kicked off on 6 February 1943. In all, some 3,000 men were deployed, of whom rather less than half were Gurkhas.[42] Once back over the significant wet gap of the Chindwin they pushed 150 miles (240km) into enemy-held territory. This was intended to be a two-pronged offensive with American impresario 'Vinegar Joe' Stilwell attacking with Nationalist Chinese units from the north. Vinegar Joe was a marked Anglophobe, as dour and sour as his handle implies. But like Wingate he was both brilliant and erratic and about as popular. At the last minute, his part of the joint offensive was called off. Probably, as Chris Bellamy suggests, Wingate's mission should also have been cancelled. It wasn't.[43]

Gurkha regimental historians were not altogether impressed by their unpredictable brigadier:

> There can be no doubt that the Gurkha sections of 77th Brigade were used by Wingate as a 'feint' to confuse the Japanese about the real route to be taken by and intentions of the Northern Section and their demolition squads. Gurkha Columns 1 and 2 were sent off in a southerly direction as the operation began in February 1943, with the direct instructions to make themselves known to the enemy and the local village spies, as they moved openly toward the rail station at Kyaikthin. Some commentators have remarked upon the callous nature in which Wingate used the Gurkhas as a diversion and suggested that he would never have dared use the 13th Kings in the same way. There is no doubt that Gurkha casualties were high from these two columns, but when you analyze the overall casualties for the operation, they do not stand out as overly exceptional, with similar numbers of British troops being lost. The ultimate commitment and bravery of the Gurkha Rifleman on Operation Longcloth cannot be called in to question and the men of the 3/2 Gurkha Rifles upheld the traditions of the regiment.[44]

The raiders did succeed in cutting the vital Japanese umbilical cord of the Mandalay–Myitkina railway line, essential for the Japanese to maintain their front against Stilwell. Having reached the Irrawaddy, Wingate might have gone a river too far and the Japanese were quick to recover and strike back. He then split his columns into sub-columns to facilitate exfiltration and escape. This was, with hindsight, a mistake as those enemy units setting off on the chase were individually larger.

It was an awful experience. Naik Devsur Ale was with Chindit Column One, which found itself further east than any other Chindit unit after dispersal was called. The journey home would be long and arduous. Around the third week in

April, the Column attempted to cross the Irrawaddy River near a village called Singyat. Naik Devsur Ale was given the task of setting up a rear-guard position to protect the men as they crossed. Subadar Major Siblal Thapa recalled:

> The last boat with Naik Devsur Ale's platoon was only about 50 yards from our side of the river when we were attacked from all angles. The enemy fired on the boats; the only survivors were Devsur and one other Rifleman. A few men from that last platoon were left on the far side with Subadar Padanbahadur's party and did not cross the river that day.[45]

Subadar Kumba Sing Gurung IDSM was the senior Gurkha Officer with Column Three. Lieutenant Harold James described him as 'a short but broad-shouldered man, keen on smart appearance and self-discipline, he was a perfect soldier'.[46] The subadar not only took care of the young Gurkha Riflemen from Column Three in 1943, but the young British subalterns too.

At the Battle of Nankan, 'Mad' Mike Calvert placed Kumba Sing in charge of blocking the main road into the railway station while the demolition squad went about their business. The subadar succeeded in holding off a large patrol of Japanese for several hours and was duly awarded an Indian Distinguished Service Medal. After dispersal was called in late March, Calvert gave Kumba Sing command of one of the teams. He got the job done and led the group out of Burma, onto the Chinese Yunnan Borders and eventually to safety.

Calvert put in for Kumba Sing Gurung's IDSM in August 1943:

> On 6th March 1943, at NANKAN Railway Station, Subadar KUM SING was detached with one section and an anti tank rifle to guard a track while demolitions were being carried out on the railway. Two lorry loads of Japanese infantry arrived and drove straight into the ambush which he had laid. The majority were killed at the outset, but the remainder were reinforced. Subadar KUM SING continued to fight the enemy for two hours, gaining complete immunity from interruption for the parties engaged in demolishing the railway. He himself shot two of the enemy, on whom 15 casualties were inflicted without loss to our own troops. During the whole of the campaign as Senior Gurkha Officer with his column he maintained the morale and discipline of his men under trying circumstances and upheld the finest tradition of the Gurkha Officer.[47]

Premsingh Gurung, a young Gurkha NCO, was with Column Two, a machine-gunner in a platoon commanded by Lieutenant Ian MacHorton. Column Two had a hard time and disaster beckoned on 2 March at the railway station town of Kyaikthin, where they were ambushed by a large Japanese force.

MacHorton described the fierce nature of that battle in his book, *Safer than a Known Way*:

> We shuffled to a halt as the guides probed forward. There came the sound of just one bang up front then an inferno of noise engulfed the world around me. There came the high-pitched staccato scream of a machine gun, then overwhelmingly many others joined in, the crash and ping of rifle bullets, the banging of grenades as the battle reached a fearful crescendo. Men and mules were lying, twisted and contorted, twitching and writhing, others were still erect, stark in the moonlight, heaving and jerking in the midst of this chaos. Then a sinister scuffling noise made by men of all kinds in close combat: the close combat of bayonet and kukri, the fanatical, personal laughter with blood-dripping cold steel.[48]

After the guns fell silent that night MacHorton took stock of his situation and found he was alone with a small group of Gurkha Riflemen, one of whom was Premsingh Gurung. The naik was seriously wounded and could not walk unaided. On closer inspection the officer realised that his thigh bone had been smashed and the flesh around the entry wound badly burned. MacHorton ordered the group to retire to a small copse on top of a hillock just a few yards or so from the railway.

After dressing Premsingh's leg and placing splints in support, the group settled down for the night, always wondering when the enemy might pay them an unwelcome visit. At dawn the men prepared to move out, MacHorton having decided during the night to attempt to make the previously arranged dispersal rendezvous by heading east towards the Irrawaddy River. He knew the young naik would never be able to make the trek to the Irrawaddy; he would have to be left behind.

> My mind was made up now. The way ahead was clear. I would lead my little party to the rendezvous and join up with the rest of the survivors from the ambush. I stood up to call the others to their feet. It was good to be on our way again.

> But was not there something else, something unpleasant, before I gave the order? Yes. There was the problem of Naik Premsingh to solve. I realised it with a sinking of spirits. I knew all too well what I had to do about Premsingh, but with someone as close as he had become during our weeks behind the Jap lines it was going to be hard.[49]

Orders were clear: wounded men who could not move without help had to be left. This was a death sentence; one any officer would dread. MacHorton knew he would have to tell Premsingh he must be abandoned, a decision made even worse by the knowledge the man's wounds could be easily treated and he could soon be fighting fit. It was a hard and emotional parting, made more poignant by the fact the injured man accepted his fate with an almost cheerful stoicism.

Wingate's after-action report was pretty scathing about his Gurkhas, making the blindingly obvious point that only seasoned soldiers with good British officers were suitable for such arduous work – he could well have said the same for his British units.[50] In reality he just wasn't attuned; his temperament and aloofness were far removed from most officers who had served with Gurkhas. This was not an ideal union.

Before this, as mentioned above, the Japanese had still appeared as some form of diabolical supermen, impervious to the dreadfulness of jungle warfare – in fact they were not and suffered equally. During 1943 Allied morale was raised by the costly success of Wingate's Chindits which began to demonstrate that they could fight in these conditions as effectively as the Japanese and, crucially, could use their air power and capacity for air supply to achieve an advantage. George MacDonald Fraser found: 'It seemed a terribly old-fashioned kind of war, far closer to the campaign my great-uncle fought when he went with Roberts to Kandahar, (he's buried somewhere in Afghanistan; I wore his ring in Burma), than to what was happening in Europe; compared to that or the electronic campaigns of today, it looks downright primitive.'[51]

Wingate's first foray cost 1,000 casualties, a third of his entire order of battle.[52] But the psychological impact vastly exceeded the tactical. Ever since the Japanese had first attacked in 1942, the Allies had known nothing but defeat: Singapore and Hong Kong lost, Malaya and Burma overrun, the British pushed back to the very gates of India. Now they were hitting back, taking the Japanese on and beating them, showing their men could do whatever the Japanese could do and actually do it better. Wingate, in terms of morale, had turned the tide.

THE GREAT CRUSADE (3) – A FORGOTTEN ARMY

'Turn You to the Strong Hold, Ye Prisoners of Hope'

These words from Zechariah, 9:12, were quoted by Wingate. Churchill loved derring-do; his tactical stance often owed more to G.A. Henty or Dumas than Clausewitz. Wingate attended the Quebec Conference[53] and the prime minister convinced the Americans, who were less sure, of the rich harvest to be reaped from special operations. This next one would be bigger and involve what had not occurred last time round: a joint assault launched by both Slim and Stilwell. Wingate moved up to major general (to the chagrin of many) and to command of 3rd Indian Division, though this wasn't any regular unit as such but his 'Special Force'.[54]

Despite his unhappy experiences with Gurkhas last time, he would have four battalions under his command: 3/4th, 3/6th, 3/9th and 4/9th. What would be different was the huge amount of air support, critical to resupply, and the fact that by now the Allies were definitely gaining the upper hand in the air. Chindits would be ferried in by air and establish redoubts – 'strongholds' which could, if necessary, be prepared against siege.

Before Wingate's new mission got underway, the Allies had another crack at the Arakan, this time with greater success, Slim making good use of comprehensive air cover and supply. Time was running out for the Empire of the Sun which seemingly couldn't adapt to these re-invigorated Allied attacks delivered by a resurgent enemy they thought they had had on the ropes. Another four Gurkha battalions, 4/1st, 4/5th, 3/6th and 4/8th, were deployed as part of 7th Indian Division and, as ever, saw plenty of action. At a significant hilltop, codenamed 'Abel', 1/4th mounted a superbly sustained defence against the inevitable waves of Japanese. They won the day, but it cost them a third of their strength.[55]

Operation Thursday got going on 5 March 1944 with three brigades attacking, two of which, 77th and 11th, came in by glider, targeting locations that were suitably remote but adjacent to water and where ground was sufficiently level to allow rapid construction of a serviceable landing strip. The strips formed a rough semi-circle around Indaw, and were named Aberdeen, Piccadilly (where there was an early attack of panic, as it seemed the enemy had already built timber bunkers but it turned out to be only locals felling trees), Broadway and Chowringee. As ever with air-landing operations, these did not pass without incident: drops were spread out and now and then in the wrong place. Brigadier Calvert, commanding 77th Brigade, had 3/6th and 3/9th while Brigadier Lentaingne, promoted since the Sittang Bridge debacle, led 3/4th and 3/9th at Chowringee as lead elements of 111th Brigade.

From early March, more men and beasts, together with stores, were flown in. Quite quickly the Chindits had 12,000 men in the zone. Fighter cover was provided, and these flew sorties against Japanese bombers. This was serving a significant strategic purpose, diverting enemy efforts to prepare for their anticipated blow against Imphal and Kohima (see below). The raiders actually outnumbered the immediate opposition by about 2 : 1.[56] On 24 March, Orde Wingate was killed in an air crash[57] and while he might be short of mourners, his eccentric dynamism was largely irreplaceable.

Partly, perhaps largely, as a consequence Slim changed tack, diverting Calvert's Brigade northwards to help Stilwell and ease some of the mounting pressure at Kohima. This, as Chris Bellamy ably points out, is an early use of what we would now call 'force-multiplier';[58] the disproportionate effect well-directed Special Forces can exert over the conventional battlefield. The brigade objective was the nodal point of Mogaung. The Japanese realised this too and had 3,500 defenders ready. On 11 June, Captain Michael Allmand, leading the point platoon from B Company 3/6th Gurkhas, took part in the attack on the Pin Hmi road bridge which controlled entry to the town. His citation in the *London Gazette* chronicles his astonishing heroism:

> Captain Allmand was commanding the leading platoon of a Company of the 6th Gurkha Rifles in Burma on 11th June 1944, when the Battalion was ordered to attack the Pin Hmi Road Bridge. The enemy had already succeeded in holding up our advance at this point for twenty-four hours. The approach to the bridge was very narrow as the road was banked up and the low-lying land on either side was swampy and densely covered in jungle. The Japanese who were dug in along the banks of the road and in the jungle with machine guns and small arms, were putting up the most desperate resistance.
>
> As the platoon came within twenty yards of the Bridge, the enemy opened heavy and accurate fire, inflicting severe casualties and forcing the men to seek cover. Captain Allmand, however, with the utmost gallantry charged on by himself, hurling grenades into the enemy gun positions and killing three Japanese himself with his kukri. Inspired by the splendid example of their platoon commander the surviving men followed him and captured their objective.
>
> Two days later Captain Allmand, owing to casualties among the officers, took over command of the Company and dashing

thirty yards ahead of it through long grass and marshy ground, swept by machine gun fire, personally killed a number of enemy machine gunners and successfully led his men onto the ridge of high ground that they had been ordered to seize.

Once again on the 23rd June in the final attack on the railway bridge at Mogaung, Captain Allmand, although suffering from trench-foot, which made it difficult for him to walk, moved forward alone through deep mud and shell-holes and charged a Japanese machine gun nest single-handed but he was mortally wounded and died shortly afterwards. The superb gallantry, outstanding leadership and protracted heroism of this very brave officer were a wonderful example to the whole Battalion and in the highest traditions of his regiment. His selfless heroism was sufficient to earn a posthumous VC.[59]

Astonishingly, this sublime courage was matched in a complementary feat from Rifleman Tulbahadur Pun who was serving in one of Allmand's sections. The rifleman's citation in the *London Gazette* tells of what he did:

In Burma on 23 June 1944, a Battalion of the 6th Gurkha Rifles was ordered to attack the Railway Bridge at Mogaung. Immediately the attack developed the enemy opened concentrated and sustained cross fire at close range from a position known as the Red House and from a strong bunker position two hundred yards to the left of it.

So intense was this cross fire that both the leading platoons of 'B' Company, one of which was Rifleman Tulbahadur Pun's, were pinned to the ground and the whole of his Section was wiped out with the exception of himself, the Section commander and one other man. The Section commander immediately led the remaining two men in a charge on the Red House but was at once badly wounded. Rifleman Tulbahadur Pun and his remaining companion continued the charge, but the latter too was immediately wounded.

Rifleman Tulbahadur Pun then seized the Bren gun, and firing from the hip as he went, continued the charge on this heavily bunkered position alone, in the face of the most shattering concentration of automatic fire, directed straight at him. With the dawn coming up behind him, he presented a perfect target to the Japanese. He had to move for thirty yards over open ground, ankle deep in mud, through shell holes and over fallen trees.

Despite these overwhelming odds, he reached the Red House and closed with the Japanese occupants. He killed three and put five more to flight and captured two light machine guns and much ammunition. He then gave accurate supporting fire from the bunker to the remainder of his platoon which enabled them to reach their objective. His outstanding courage and superb gallantry in the face of odds which meant almost certain death were most inspiring to all ranks and beyond praise.[60]

Incredibly, this was not the last Victoria Cross to be awarded during this operation. The third, also posthumous, was won by Major Frank Blaker, then commanding C Company 3/9th Gurkhas, though he was actually on detachment from the Highland Light Infantry. Their job had been to take part in the northward move to assist Vinegar Joe. His Nationalist Chinese forces had got as far south at Taungni. The enemy was well dug in on Hill 2171 and a two-company attack was planned, one to go in by the front door to get Japanese attention while the second worked around the flank. Major Frank Blaker was to earn a posthumous VC, as the citation in the *London Gazette* describes:

> In Burma on 9th July, 1944, a company of 9th Gurkhas was ordered to carry out a wide, encircling movement across unknown and precipitous country, through dense jungle to attack a strong enemy position on the summit of an important hill overlooking Taungni. Major Blaker carried out this movement with the utmost precision and took up a position with his company on the extreme right flank of the enemy, in itself a feat of considerable military skill. Another company, after bitter fighting, had succeeded in taking the forward edge of the enemy position by a frontal assault, but had failed to reach the main crest of the hill in the face of fierce opposition.
>
> At this crucial moment Major Blaker's Company came under heavy and sustained fire at close range from a machine gun and two light machine guns and their advance was completely stopped. Major Blaker then advanced ahead of his men through very heavy fire and in spite of being severely wounded in the arm by a grenade, he located the machine guns, which were the pivot of the enemy defence and single-handed, charged the

position. When hit by a burst of three rounds through the body, he continued to cheer on his men while lying on the ground.

His fearless leadership and outstanding courage so inspired his company that they stormed the hill and captured the objective, while the enemy fled in terror into the jungle. Major Blaker died of wounds while being evacuated from the battlefield. His heroism and self sacrifice were beyond all praise and contributed in no small way to the defeat of the enemy and the successful outcome of the operation.[61]

The Gurkhas now had the full measure of their Japanese opponents. General Tuker noted the changes:

In early 1944 they were fighting for their airstrips. These were small affairs. Once a platoon surprised thirty-five of the enemy, closed with them and in a vicious melee, slew nineteen with kukri and bayonet for the loss of two of their own. By patrol and ambush the tables were completely turned on the Japanese.[62]

They had mastered the art of the concealed ambush, as Tuker and others confirmed:

There was an ambush on the Bhamo–Myiktyina road. The first lorry arrived at two o'clock, travelling steadily with its headlights. The plan was to let the convoy pass well into the killing area before we opened fire, but just then something very untoward happened. The lorry fouled an overhanging branch and stopped to clear it. It drew up a few yards from a Bren gun loaded with armour piercing rounds; if the Japanese debussed, they could scarcely avoid treading on it. Already, there was movement in the lorry; a second lorry drove up and joined the first and a third was approaching.

The Bren gunner, finger on trigger, was intently watching no. 1; he needed no indication what to do. The platoon commander, Thamabahadur Guring directed his PIAT gunner onto no. 2; there was a shattering explosion and the lorry burst into flames. Immediately the Bren opened up on no. 1. The PIAT then engaged the third lorry, destroyed it and turned to the 4th but the range was too great, and he missed it. However, the 4th was not allowed to escape. Such Japanese as survived leapt into a hollow and were there killed with grenades. This action blocked the road so that the bombers caught a long convoy next day, head to tail behind the wreckage, and destroyed it.[63]

This second, much bigger raid achieved far more success and definitely served a useful, if by no means decisive, purpose. 'Special Operations' have always punched above their weight in terms of PR value and in the end Slim wasn't really a fan; most senior officers even today aren't. However, the psychological and morale boost should not be under-estimated. The Chindits became legendary. For the first time in the Burma Campaign, Wingate took the fight to the enemy in a most audacious manner. Mistakes were made but valuable tactical lessons were also learned, and the Japanese were thrown onto the defensive at the very moment they were putting all their remaining impetus into one last giant gasp. What is sure is that any man, British, Commonwealth or Gurkha, who fought as a Chindit would hold his head up high for the rest of his life, 'he that outlives this day, and comes safe home, will stand a tip-toe when the day is named, and rouse him at the name …'.[64] And this feat is commemorated by the Chindit Statue outside the MoD in Whitehall.

New Blood and Hollywood Style

General Slim in an 'order of the day' to the 17th Indian Light Division[65] both praised his men's efforts and recognised their contribution to final victory:

> In my last Order of the Day I told you, you had defeated the Jap armies opposing you and that it remained to destroy them. The extent to which you have done that is shown by the fifty thousand Japanese left dead on the soil of India and Northern Burma, the great quantities of guns and equipment you have captured, the prisoners you have taken, the advances you have made and the flight of the remnants you are still pursuing.
>
> To the 15 Corps in the Arakan fell the unique honour of being the first British-Indian formation to hold, break and decisively hurl back a major Japanese offensive. Theirs was an example of tenacity and courage which inspired the whole army. The 4 Corps met the main weight of the Japanese Assam offensive, and, in one of the hardest fought and longest battles of the war,

Above left: 1. Forerunners of the 6th Gurkha Rifles, early nineteenth century.

Above right: 2. Gurkha rifleman armed with the Snider conversion of the Enfield percussion rifle, *c*. 1880.

Below: 3. Gurkha and British soldiers on the North-West Frontier, 1880s.

Left: 4. A native officer of the 48th Regiment of Bengal Light Infantry, 1880.

Below: 5. Recruits for 44 Gurkha Rifles, also with Sniders, 1884.

6. Another group of recruits for 44 Gurkha Rifles, 1886–93.

7. A group of Gurkha officers, *c.* 1890.

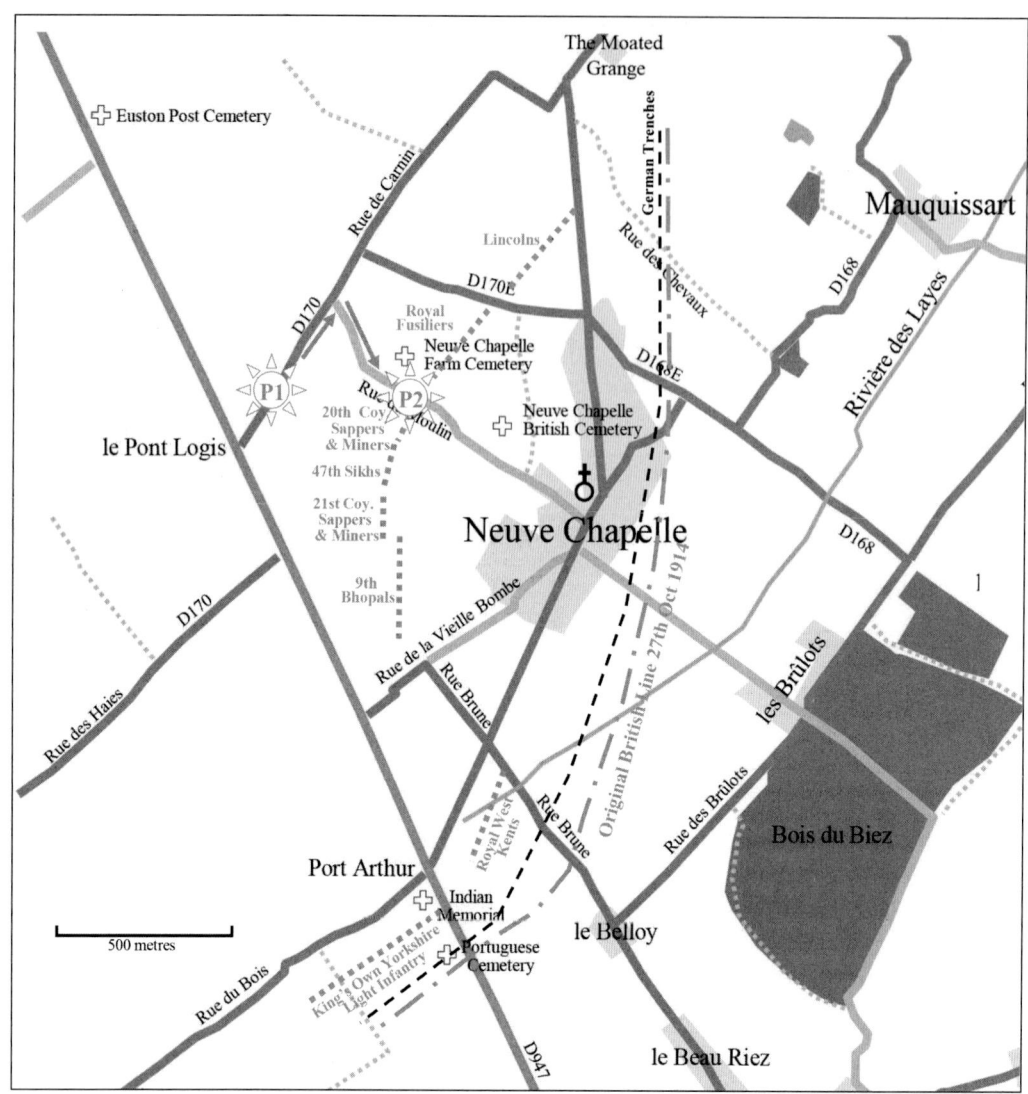

Above: 8. 2/2nd Gurkhas' action at Neuve Chapelle, 1–2 November 1914.

Opposite above: 9. Action at Neuve Chapelle, 2 November 1914.

Opposite below: 10. 2/2nd Gurkhas at the orchard and 1/1st Gurkhas in defence, Givenchy, 20 December 1914.

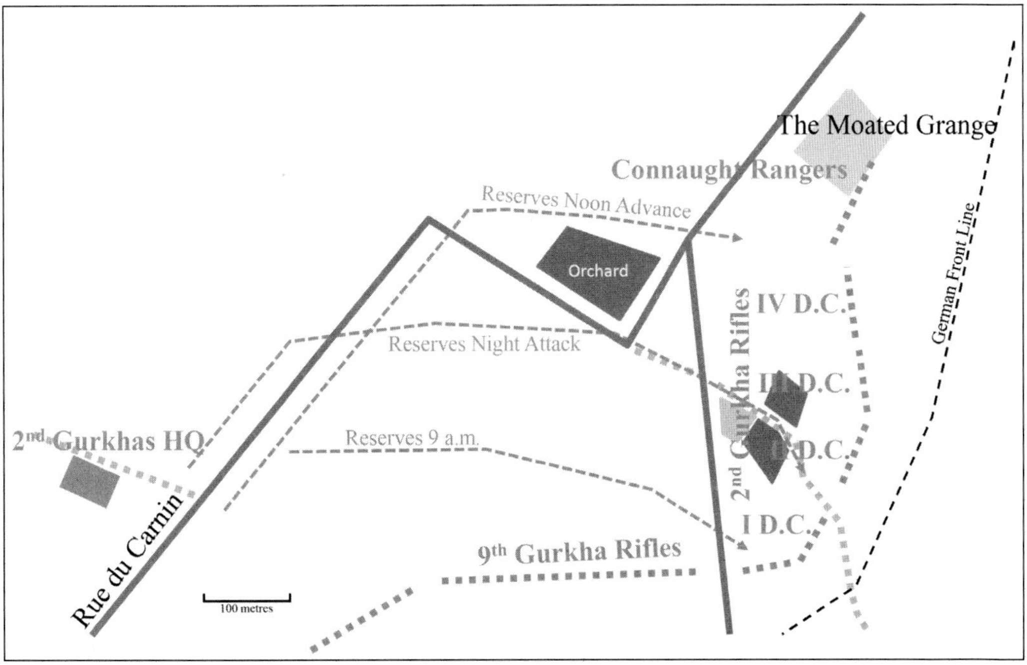

The Moated Grange
Connaught Rangers
Reserves Noon Advance
Orchard
IV D.C.
III D.C.
II D.C.
I D.C.
2nd Gurkha Rifles
German Front Line
Reserves Night Attack
2nd Gurkhas HQ
Reserves 9 a.m.
9th Gurkha Rifles
Rue du Carnin
100 metres

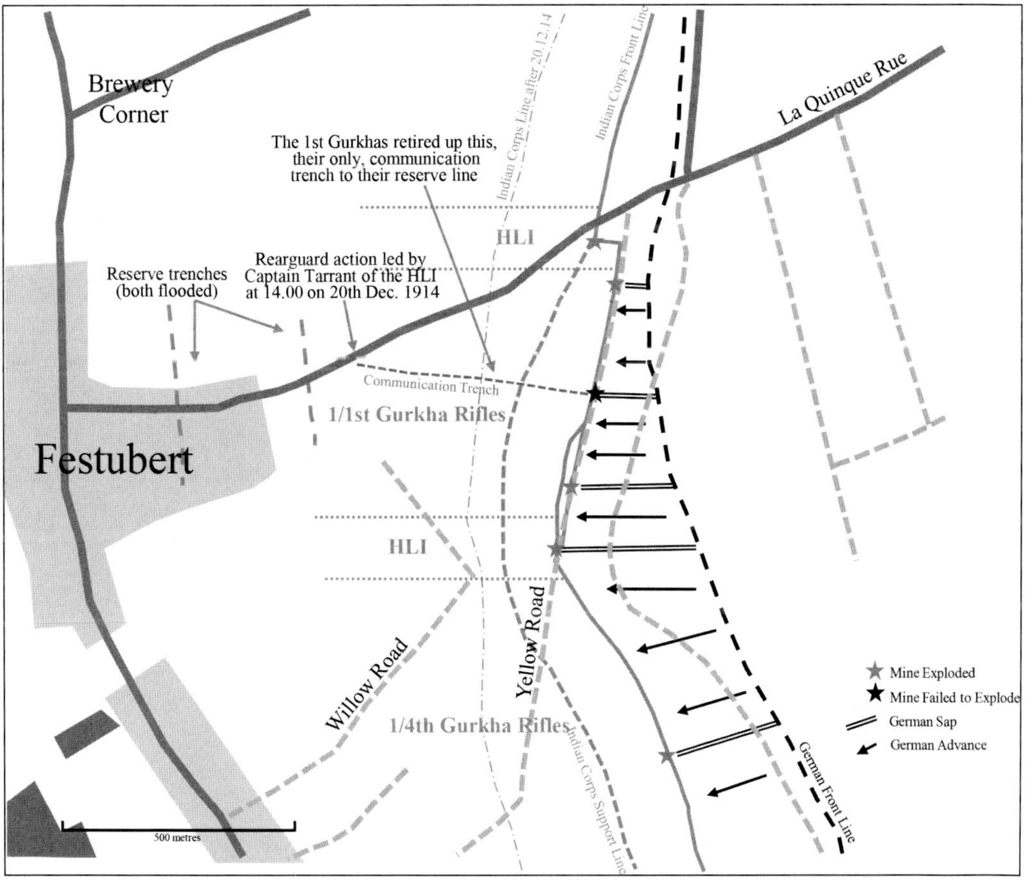

Brewery Corner
Indian Corps Line after 20.12.14
Indian Corps Front Line
La Quinque Rue
The 1st Gurkhas retired up this, their only, communication trench to their reserve line
HLI
Rearguard action led by Captain Tarrant of the HLI at 14.00 on 20th Dec. 1914
Reserve trenches (both flooded)
Communication Trench
1/1st Gurkha Rifles
Festubert
HLI
Willow Road
Yellow Road
1/4th Gurkha Rifles
Indian Corps Support Line
German Front Line
Mine Exploded
Mine Failed to Explode
German Sap
German Advance
500 metres

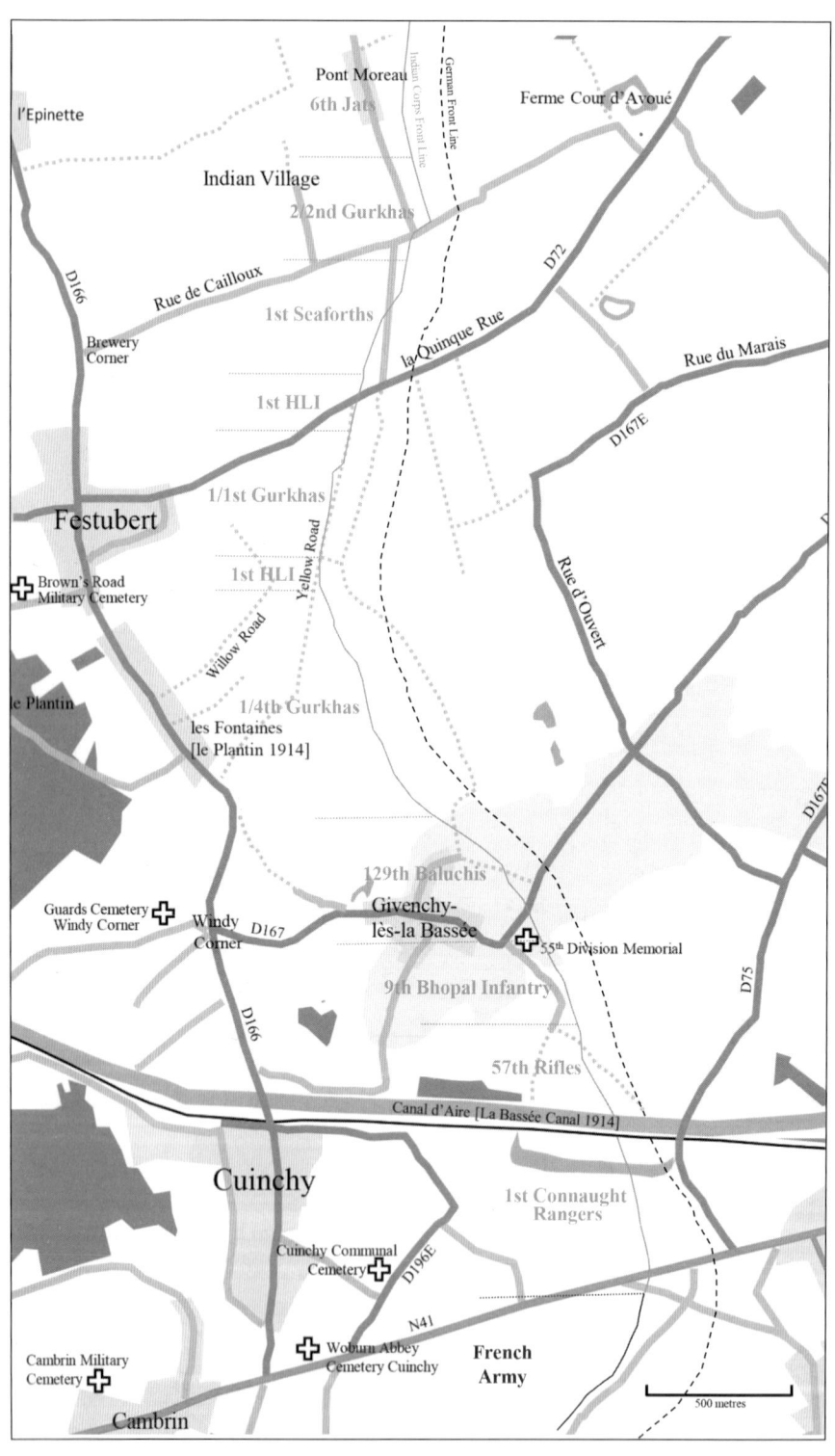

11. Givenchy, 16–22 December 1914.

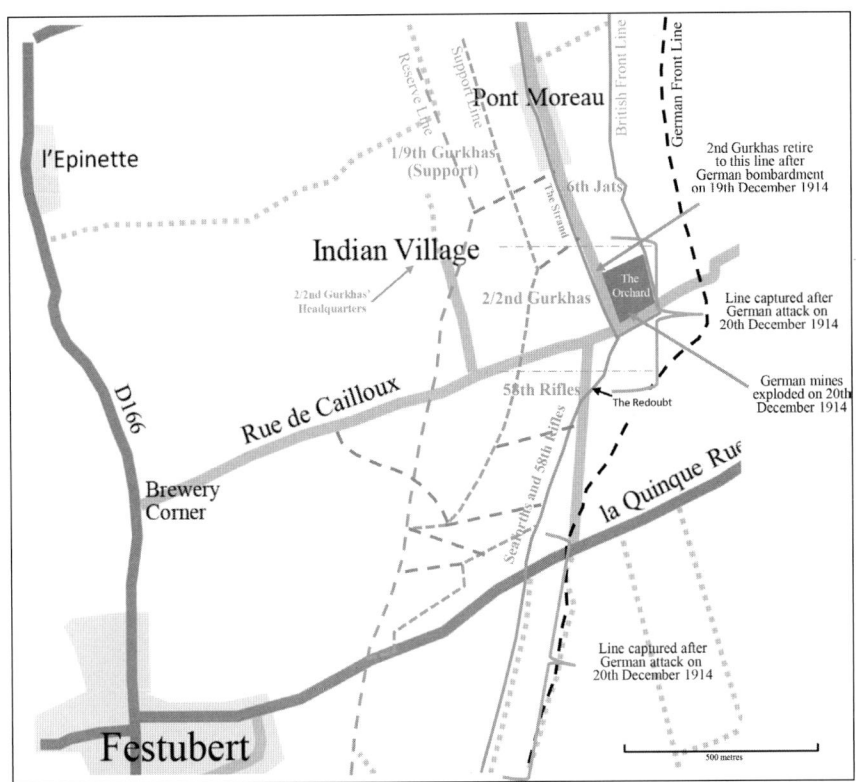

12. Festubert and the Indian Village, 19–20 December 1914.

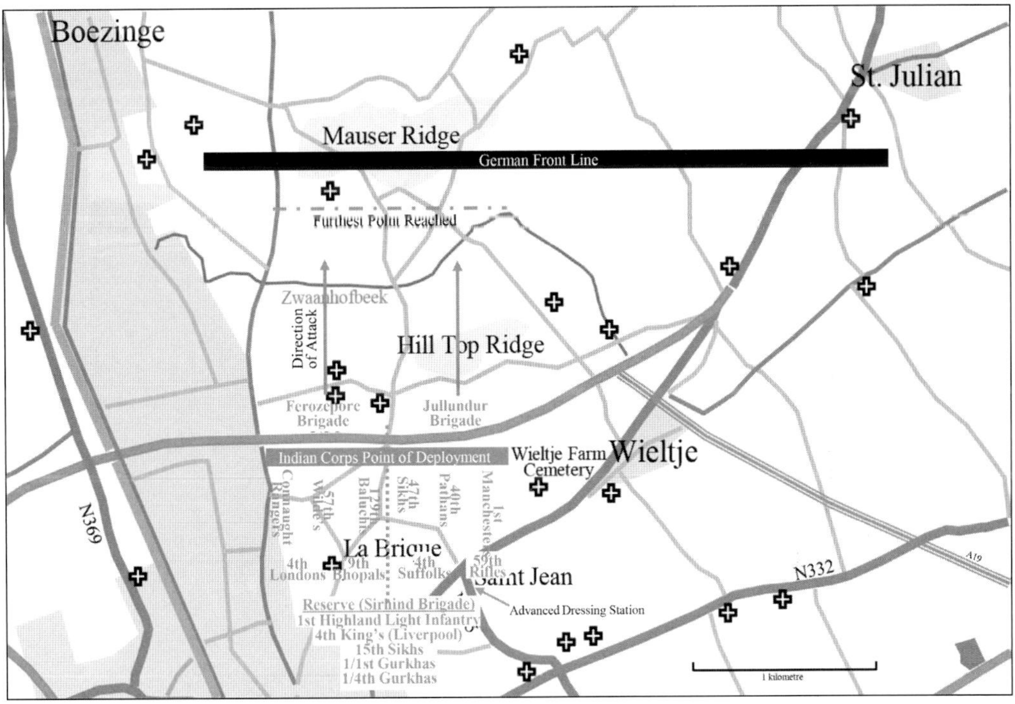

13. The attack at Mauser Ridge, 26 April–1 May 1915.

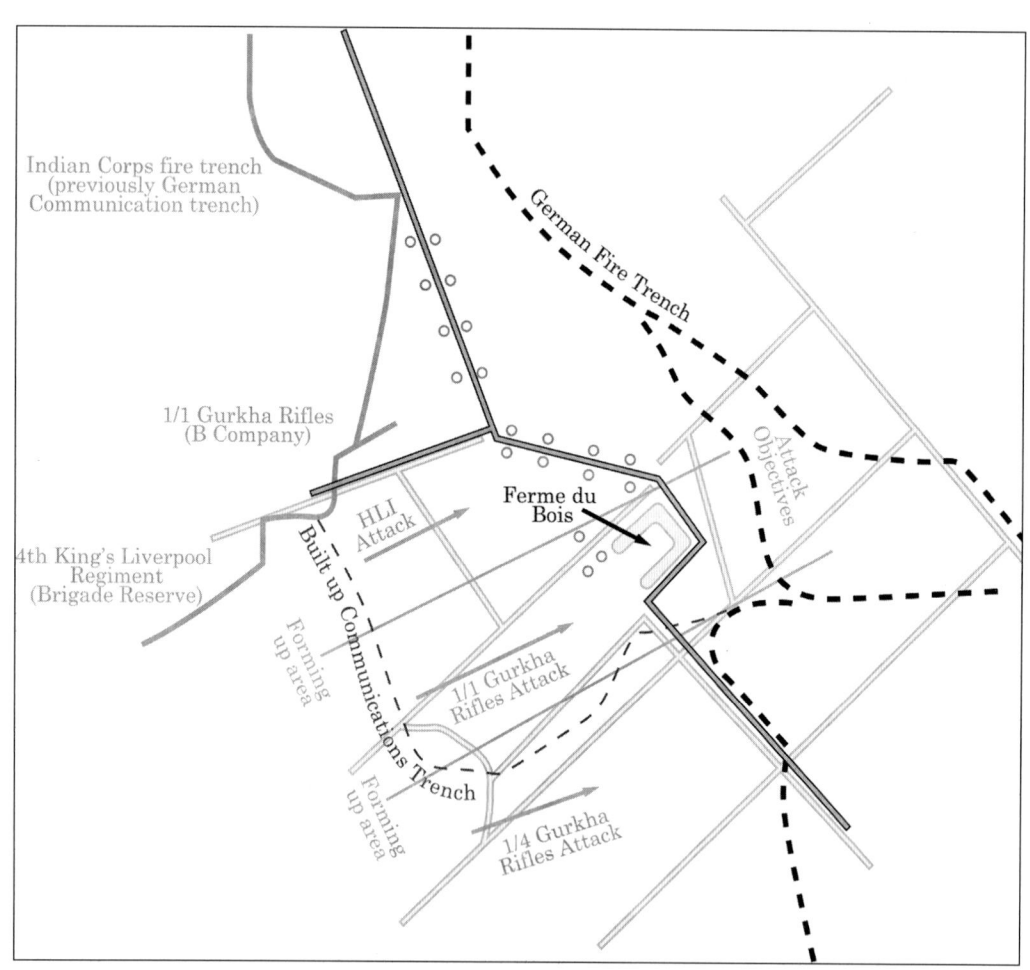

14. The actions at Festubert, 15–27 May 1915.

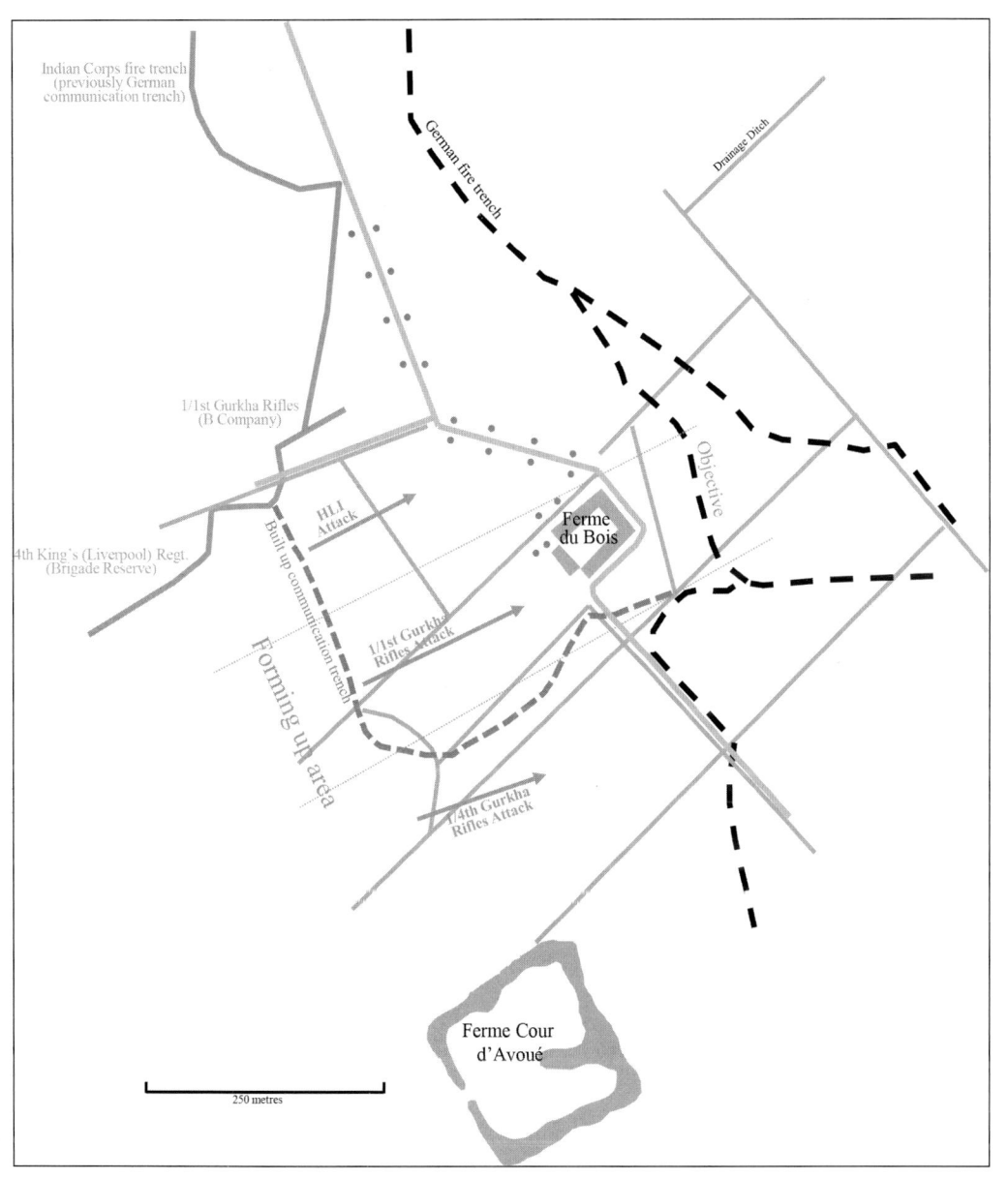

15. The attack on the Ferme du Bois, 22–23 May 1915.

Above left: 16. A Gurkha VC, Gaje Ghale, havildar (later captain).

Above right: 17. A Gurkha VC, Lachhiman Gurung, 4th Battalion 8th Gurkha Rifles.

Left: 18. A Gurkha VC, Netra Bahadur Thapa, subedar, serving with 2/5th Gurkhas.

19. Corporal Sachin with Rifleman Aita, Rifleman Chiran and Lance Corporal Arjun.

20. Rifleman Aita and Captain Meadows.

Above: 21. Group 2, Silicon 13, just prior to Operation Panther's Claw, June 2009.

Left: 22. Nepalese Limbu woman, May 2009.

23. Live mortars firing during Operation Herrick 14 pre-deployment training at Castlemartin, 2014.

Above: 24. Corporal Pradeep sacrificing a goat during Dashain festival in Kabul, 2015.

Right: 25. Colour Sergeant Yogendra Rai in the highlands of Sutherland during pre-deployment training for snipers for Operation Toral in Kabul, 2015.

26. Mortar Platoon conducting training for Operation Herrick 14, Stonehenge, 2010.

Above: 27. Operation Zafar, a view from Gurkha positions.

Right: 28. Rifleman Chiran with the LMG.

29. Rifleman Khagendra.

Left: 30. Rifleman Prakash.

Below: 31. Rifleman Pralon.

shattered it. 33 Corps in their brilliant offensive from the north not only drove a large Japanese force from what should have been an impregnable position, but destroyed it. Together the 4th and 33rd Corps have swept the enemy out of India ...

You of the 17th Indian Light Division were under me in the original Burma Campaign, where, in the darkest days, you never lost that outstanding morale which has always distinguished you. You have always been where the fighting has been hardest and the bravery of your units has inspired us all ...[66]

When Admiral Lord Louis Mountbatten replaced Wavell, the resurgent Fourteenth Army, led by Slim, took on a refreshed and invigorated aspect. Mountbatten understood the value of air drops. No longer would Allied troops be defeated by Japanese encirclements. They would hold their positions and be sustained from the air, grinding down their attackers whose own supply lines were over-stretched. By this time in the war principal strategic direction among the Western Allies was coming from the Americans, who were assuming a more pivotal role in the overall conduct of operations.

That Japan would finally be defeated by the campaign in the Pacific rather than by any initiative undertaken purely by the British was an undoubted reality. Burma would become the last of the great imperial adventures, the twilight of Britain's vast overseas dominion. It was estimated that the Japanese had suffered no more than 2,000 casualties when they conquered Burma; to stay there, fight and suffer eventual defeat would cost them very nearly 50,000 more.[67]

Mountbatten had Hollywood looks, an easy and urbane charm and a close connection to the royal family. He was an ideal choice for 'front of the house' in diplomatic terms but possessed few qualities required of a senior theatre commander. His fellow officers were scornful of his strategic grasp and limited intellectual capacity. General Henry Pownall, his chief of staff, observed:

> There are so many paradoxes ... his charm of manner ... is one of his greatest assets; many is the time I've gone to him to have a really good showdown ... he would apologize, promise to mend his ways – and then soon afterwards go and do the same thing again! [He] has great drive and initiative ... He is however apt to leap before he looks ... His meetings are overlong because he likes talking ... And he likes a good big audience to hear what he has to say.[68]

'Bill' Slim was a different matter altogether. He had served with distinction during the First World War and exhibited that bulldog tenacity Churchill so admired in his officers, though, in the event, he proved no friend to Slim or the Fourteenth Army. The disastrous retreat through Burma was rightly considered no fault of his. Down to earth, pragmatic, unassuming and reliable, he was to lead British forces in Burma from the brink of defeat to the pinnacle of success.

Kohima and Imphal – A Great Blooding of Kukris

Finding themselves checked, the Japanese command decided to attempt a major and crippling blow by driving deep into Assam and capturing two key bastions at Imphal and Kohima. These settlements, the former being the principal town of the hill region of Manipur, would witness some of the most savage fighting of the war and would become the crucible in which the Fourteenth Army would be truly tested. No wonder soldiers fighting in Burma regarded themselves as a 'forgotten' army as attention in Europe fixed on the forthcoming invasion of France and titanic struggles being fought in the East. Yet, Kohima was to be decisive; neither side could afford to give ground and whoever won here must triumph in the contest for Burma. For the Japanese, this would be both their high-water mark and the rock against which their prospects for final victory were dashed.

General Mutagachi, commanding the Japanese Fifteenth Army, was an aggressive if erratic commander who did not permit logistical difficulties to interfere with his ambition. He had already sacked his own chief of staff for highlighting these obstacles too pointedly.[69] Assam was not the place to fight if it could be avoided. The province could claim to be the wettest on Earth, with some 800in (20,000mm) of rain annually. Supplies had to be moved by four-legged transport, long, snaking bullock trains, tenuous, slow and vulnerable. The Japanese had a slang term for Burma, *jigoku* – 'hell'. A posting there was equivalent to being *stellenbosched* or, as the French would say, *degomme* – essentially a punishment.

Kohima was an unlikely battleground in that it stood high in this majestic, unspoilt hill region of Assam. Politically, the settlement was the base for the district commissioner, whose neat bungalow, summer house and tennis court became key tactical features. This agreeable domestic arrangement would not have looked at all out of place in the Home Counties, yet the hitherto tranquil tennis court would witness some of the most savage combat of the entire desperate defence. At about 5,000ft (1,524m) above sea level, the long single road from Dimapur clambered up the saddle of Kohima Ridge before cutting across the dipping crest at right angles. The ridge was banana-shaped, with civilian buildings at one tip: beyond lay Kohima village. Running away from this first eminence were a series of summits or hillocks, the whole lot just a few miles in length.

One key feature was the tennis court, the perfect reminder of more civilised days, which became the fulcrum of much very close-quarter fighting, a charnel house of biblical proportions where only the reassuring patter of racquet and balls had been heard before. Movement in daytime was impossible due to Japanese snipers and darkness brought no respite. It was then that the enemy came on, wave after fanatical wave. Water was scarce and precious in the sapping, humid heat. Air drops, as for Wingate's Chindits, were vital and without them the place couldn't have been held, even though a lot of the kit fell wide and bolstered the hungry Japanese. Losses were very high. A British officer describes the extremely close-quarter fighting where the previously serene tennis court, a symbol of English calmness, became its own front line:

> The battle took place on the tennis court – we shot them on the tennis court and grenaded them on the tennis court. We held the tennis court against desperate attacks for five days. We held because I had instant contact by radio with the guns, and the Japs never seemed to learn how to surprise us. They used to shout in English as they formed up, 'give up'. So we knew when an attack was coming in. One would judge just the right moment to call down gun and mortar fire to catch them as they were launching the attack, and by the time they were approaching us they were decimated. They were not acting intelligently and did the same old stupid thing again and again. We had experienced fighting the Japs in the Arakan, bayoneting the wounded and prisoners. So whereas we respected the Afrika Korps, not so the Japanese; they had renounced any right to be regarded as human, and we thought of them as vermin to be exterminated.[70]

Manipur region was inhabited by native hill-men, the Nagas,[71] who did the Allies tremendous service acting as stretcher-bearers and porters. Their physical hardiness enabled them to perform feats of endurance Allied fighters could not, in the circumstances, have hoped to emulate. The Burmese generally were no particular enthusiasts for British rule; the British had come as conquerors originally, as now did the Japanese. The sheer savagery of the occupiers, however, soon alienated the locals, who even formed ad hoc militias armed with ancient muskets and liberated Japanese Arisaka rifles.[72] Allied soldiers recuperated by the hill settlement of Jotsoma, a quiet sector untrammelled by enemy action. Lieutenant Greenwell of the DLI found the local fleas every bit as aggressive as the Japanese[73] while Sergeant Hogg, also from the Durhams, became a sure hit with the young women of the tribe, practising the hairdresser's art.[74]

All the while fighting continued, resupply was a major logistical nightmare, as the legendary Gurkha officer Lieutenant Colonel John Cross OBE describes:

> The rain poured down upon this jungle and its narrow tracks. The mud deepened, the branches dripped in melancholy rhythm, and progress towards the ... box [defended area] was slowed down most seriously ... Anxious and confused men slithered on the slopes, sweated and swore as they struggled to drag their frightened obstinate mules uphill. So slippery was the muddy surface of the tracks that even when the mule loads had been taken off the saddles and laid in the slush, the mules still stumbled and kicked in their game efforts to mount the slope, mule drivers fell to their knees and held on to the saddle ropes to stop themselves from rolling down to the bottom.[75]

Even when there was no intense fighting in progress, there was always the nerve-shredding danger of patrols. Handy hints for young officers offered a view straight from Kipling. Cross continues:

> Jungle warfare should be regarded as a game, healthful, interesting and thrilling; the men should feel at home in the jungle and regard it as a friend. They must realise the absolute necessity for jungle training as a means to defeat the Japanese who come from one of the most highly industrialized countries in the world and have no natural advantages as jungle infantry.[76]

Practical experience tended to assume a less cheery note, as a British officer tells:

> Any Tommy will tell you that next to making a bayonet charge, the thing he hates most are patrols ... I took part in many patrols, but the one I will always remember was a listening patrol just outside of Mogaung. On a listening patrol you are away from

the main body of troops, listening and noting any movement of enemy troops. On this occasion there were just four of us; lying by the Mogaung Road ... It was pitch black. Time was dragging. All we wanted was to get back to the main body of troops ... Suddenly there was a movement, a sound. The usual challenge was shouted: 'Halt, who goes there?' There was just a lot of muttering. The password was shouted. More muttering; then the Bren gunner opened up, hand grenades were thrown. One could not see a thing, just flashes of bursting hand grenades. We were all lying flat on the ground. Suddenly I got the urge to urinate. To stand up was out of the question. I could not hold on any longer, so I just lay there and pissed myself; next morning we found one dead Jap who had taken the full burst from a Bren gun magazine.[77]

Three Japanese divisions were thrown into the attack that spring and even if the Empire of the Rising Sun was going down, it wasn't finished yet. The fanatical fighting spirit of the Japanese soldier had not dimmed; nor, it seemed, had his officers' carelessness with his life. Heavy and intense fighting sparked along the Tiddim–Imphal road, the Bishnapore–Silchar track and as far as Ukrul in the north. Gurkhas were very soon in action taking on repeated Japanese assaults at Shenam, the curiously named positions Scraggy and Gibraltar.[78]

The Gurkhas and other Allied units were supported by American-manufactured M3 Stuart light tanks. These four-man vehicles were produced in significant numbers between the years 1941 and 1944, primarily by General Motors. Light, handy and reliable, these 'Honeys' as the British called them, with their 37mm turret-mounted gun and .30-06 Browning, served initially in North Africa where, while useful, they were outclassed by the German Mark III and IV Panzers. With the crisis in Burma, 2nd Royal Tank Regiment and 7th Hussars with Honeys were withdrawn from North Africa and shipped to the Far East where they did good service in the initial phases of the Imphal/Kohima battles before gradually being replaced by heavier M4 Shermans.

On 15 April, a tremendous scrap kicked off 8 miles (13km) north of Shenam, at Sita. Here, Minbahadur Rana, serving with 3/1st Gurkhas, performed prodigies of valour, single-handedly taking on a whole platoon of the enemy as he struggled to get a Bangalore[79] into place. Despite having the full and undivided attention of thirty odd Japanese, he kept at it and killed most of them with a succession of well-thrown grenades. Amazingly, he lived to tell the tale. It was a long day's fighting at the Gurkhas' Malaun Post position, but it stayed theirs and 300 dead Japanese lay around in broken, mute and contorted testament.[80]

This was very much war with hate, as Tuker observes:

> The hours of daylight were ours. We could do what we liked and gave the Jap much trouble. The whole of this period is characterized by the ferocity and determination with which the men dealt with the enemy whenever they met them, and this was particularly so when we would sortie out by day. One episode best illustrates what I mean. A patrol reported about eighty Japanese resting half a mile away. Lalbahadur Limbu took his platoon out to deal with them, stalked them, surprised them and killed at least forty. He put a section behind the Japs and was in among them with bayonet and kukri before they realised what was happening. They ran into the arms of the waiting section. There was a great blooding of kukris on this occasion.[81]

Next fight up was for control of the Bishnapore–Silchar route. During April, the key high ground of (locally named) Wooded and Wireless Hills was taken. The Gurkhas were vastly assisted by light tanks (Honeys) which crawled up 2,000ft (610m) to deploy both guns and searchlights to support the assault. Fierce counterattacks inevitably followed which, while they took an inevitable toll on the defenders, were seen off with tremendous enemy losses.[82] On 13 May, 1/3rd and 1/10th Gurkhas with armour and artillery support attacked a strongly held enemy position at Potsangbam. The fight cost them dear: 1/10th lost over 200 men by the end, some from 'blue on blue' (so-called 'friendly' fire as Allied forces are generally coloured blue and enemy red on operational maps) when artillery rounds were dropped short during a morning assault. A second night attack, launched with 1/3rd battering at the front door while 1/10th went for the flanks, succeeded.[83]

During this fighting, one of the Gurkha platoon commanders asked for a volunteer to try and get over a narrow, wet gap virtually in front of the Japanese. Step forward Rifleman Jagardhan Rai, a diminutive (even by Nepalese standards) Gurkha. Off he went; delving into his grenade pouch for a Mills bomb, he could only produce a whole inventory of distinctly unwarlike accessories. His officer was not impressed, roundly cursing his incompetence. But at last, he did find a grenade which he then used to impressively deadly effect. Now fully into the swing, he kept going and knocked out another half-dozen enemy emplacements, carving out a vital bridgehead.[84]

Wave after suicidal, frenzied wave of Japanese was thrown into murderous counterattacks. At the very sharpest tip of the sharp point, Mortar Bluff, Netrabahadur Thapa of 1/7th fought his own Thermopylae. For a long, dark night, 8 hours of savage hand-to-hand melee, he and his dwindling section saw off assault after assault. He was killed just as dawn was breaking, kukri in hand, buried in the shattered skull of a final adversary.[85] He gained a posthumous VC.

These battles have something of the First World War Western Front about them: fearful conditions, a relentless enemy and grinding attrition. In June the Allies went on to the offensive, looking to drive the Japanese from a salient they hammered into the line. Stymied by enemy tanks,[86] 19-year-old Ganju Lama of 1/7th crept forward with a PIAT (Projector Infantry Anti-Tank) and a sack of grenades. Hit in both arms and legs, he still destroyed the two leading tanks and accounted for their crews. Despite his wounds he went painfully back to stock up on bombs and proceeded to knock out a third tank. This cleared the way for his comrades to advance. His Victoria Cross citation reads in the *London Gazette* records:

> On 12 June 1944, near Ningthoukhong, India, 'B' Company was attempting to stem the enemy's advance when it came under heavy machine-gun and tank machine-gun fire. Rifleman Ganju Lama, with complete disregard for his own safety, took his PIAT gun and, crawling forward, succeeded in bringing the gun into action within 30 yards of the enemy tanks, knocking out two of them. Despite a broken wrist and two other serious wounds to his right and left hands he then moved forward and engaged the tank crew who were trying to escape. Not until he had accounted for all of them did he consent to leave to have his wounds dressed.[87]

The two battles at Imphal and Kohima, whilst immensely costly for the Fourteenth Army, had decided the course of the campaign in Burma. The Japanese, like the flood tide, had run to their high-water mark; from now on theirs would be the ebb and the inexorable road to certain defeat: 'General Grover reckoned that the fighting on Garrison Hill at Kohima was worse than the Somme, where he had fought in the First World War.'[88]

Defeat into Victory

With the battle won, it was time for Slim to strike. Yet, time was not on the British side. Already that herald of monsoon, the *chota bersaht*, was opening nature's annual offensive: a chorus of hammering, unending wet, rising to the full crescendo as the monsoon proper got under way. Slim had taken the bold decision to fight on despite the season. If IV Corps, advancing now from Imphal, could join with the troops from Kohima, the Japanese line of withdrawal to the Chindwin could be successfully interdicted, dealing a major blow and turning the enemy's retreat into catastrophe. Now, 2nd Division was to advance straight down the road towards Imphal, a major undertaking in itself.

The British advanced by stages, one platoon leapfrogging over another. It was slow, dangerous and most uncomfortable:

> The rains had now started in no mean fashion, and what with the Jap, the thick jungle, the hill and the weather, life was pretty unpleasant. However, having got practically to the top, some other units of the division got behind the Jap, who very obligingly pulled out and saved us what would have been a most bloody battle on the crest. In spite of the fact we didn't see a great deal of fighting on the way up, I liked this part of it least of all, as the jungle was very dense and you never quite knew where anybody else was; and wherever we went the Jap was always uphill, which is a beastly sensation.[89]

Mutagachi's survivors were falling back but the ground as they withdrew towards Imphal, the single ribbon of road, swooped and ducked along precipitous cliff-sides, great soaring peaks crowding around. The Japanese were in retreat but still full of fight. At Khuzama, what would now be termed a suicide bomber with a magnetic mine strapped to his chest flung himself upon the hull of an Allied tank. The advance was complicated by a series of small but highly dangerous 'search and destroy' type operations, but day by day the tempo of resistance began to slacken, until it could be termed a total rout: 'It really was great fun, just like walking up partridges. We got them absolutely on the hop, the whole battalion and attached troops were plugging away for dear life at the Japs, who were making off sideways up over the hill towards the Chindwin.'[90]

Alex Wilson of the DLI took part in the pursuit:

> We met the Imphal Garrison coming north. We were clearing road blocks quicker than the Japs thought we could. The Japs would blow the little culvert between two ridges, and sit on the other side – there were no bunkers but foxholes and they fought

hard. The technique was to fix them in their front and climb above them, and outflank them. The Japs were getting short of men. Artillery support was very important. Sometimes the guns fired direct over open sights; Jap artillery was very sparse – they were an army in disarray ... but it didn't mean they didn't fight.[91]

For the Japanese, as Brigadier 'Tubby' Lethbridge, Slim's chief of staff, noted, the rout:

> ... must have been worse than Napoleon's retreat from Moscow. The whole jungle stinks of corruption. I counted 25 dead Japs on the side of the road, between two successive milestones. There must have been hundreds more who had crawled away into the jungle to die; in some places there are Jap lorries with skeletons sitting in the driver's seats, and a staff car with four skeletons in it.[92]

Such sights were commonplace on that Road of Bones. 'Tubby' Lethbridge continues:

> The air was thick with the smell of their dead. The sick and wounded were left behind in hundreds ... We saw dead Japs all along the road, some in their stockinged feet, and where the hills were highest and most exhausting, they lay huddled in groups. They carried only a mess-tin, steel helmet and rifle. Some lay as though asleep, while others were twisted and broken by the bombs which had rained down on them. Five hundred dead lay in the ruins of Tamu. The pagoda was choked with wounded and dying. They had crawled here, in front of the four tall and golden images, to die. Hand grenades littered the altar. In the centre of the temple was a dais, and carved into this was a perfectly symmetrical pattern of the foot of Buddha. It was littered with blood-soaked bandages and Japanese field-postcards.[93]

After this dreadful slogging match, the offensive now became something of a triumphal march. Everywhere Mutagachi's survivors were in retreat, their losses disastrous. Another anonymous songster penned a regional version of 'Bye-Bye Blackbird':

> Wrap up all my care and woe,
> Here I go swinging low,
> Bye-bye Shanghai!
> Won't somebody wait for me,
> Please get in a state for me
> Bye-bye Shanghai!
> Up before the colonel in the morning,
> He gave me a rocket and a warning:
> 'You've been out with Sun-Yat-Sen,
> You won't go out with him again,'
> Shanghai, bye-bye![94]

Slim was ready for a general advance over the Chindwin and the Irrawaddy, towards Meiktila and to Mandalay, then on to Rangoon to the banks of the Sittang River of such evil memory. In the second month of the final year of the war, 20th Division fought its way over the Irrawaddy, dug in at Myinmu and prepared for an inevitable counterattack; the Rising Sun hadn't quite sunk yet. As ever Gurkhas were in the vanguard and a brace of enterprising Nepalese established a crow's nest high in the trees, pelting the enemy below with judicious showers of grenades. Despite shrapnel wounds in their nether regions from fragments of their own bombs, they bagged a respectable total.[95]

They fought for Mandalay: the ancient fortress like a Kipling relic was stormed in the pre-dawn on 8 March by 4/4th Gurkhas. Damar Singh, who had served there before the Japanese invasion, led his company into the maze of foxholes and bunkers tenaciously held by Japanese 15th Division. They killed many and then they killed more at Tawma near Meiktila, then more again at Pyawbwe and yet more at Myingyan.[96] This was payback time for 1942, and payback with overdue interest.

In the course of May 1945, Lachhiman Gurung would win the VC: 'There is a story told in the Himalayan foothills village of Dahakhani of how a man sent out his son to buy some cigarettes at the village shop one morning in 1941. The son returned five years later, blind in one eye, minus his right hand and wearing the Victoria Cross – but without the cigarettes.'[97] On the night of 12/13 May, his platoon from 4/8th Gurkhas were dug in forward at Taungdaw. They were attacked by at least two companies of Japanese infantry, showering them with grenades. The first two he successfully chucked back but the third exploded in his right hand, taking off most of his fingers; he suffered additional, severe facial wounds and damage to his right leg. The two mates in his foxhole were badly wounded. For 4 more hours he kept fighting, loading and shooting with his left hand.

As his citation in the *London Gazette* reads:

> Of the 87 enemy dead counted in the immediate vicinity of the Company locality, 31 lay in front of this Rifleman's section, the key to the whole position. Had the enemy succeeded in overrunning and occupying Rifleman Lachhiman Gurung's trench, the whole of the reverse slope position would have been completely dominated and turned. This Rifleman, by his magnificent example, so inspired his comrades to resist the enemy to the last, that, although surrounded and cut off for three days and two nights, they held and smashed every attack. His outstanding gallantry and extreme devotion to duty, in the face of almost overwhelming odds, were the main factors in the defeat of the enemy.[98]

History hadn't done with this particular hero, as an article later published in *The Times* relates:

> It was more than 60 years later, after actress Joanna Lumley took up his and the other Gurkhas' cause, that he was allowed to live – and die – in the nation he had largely fought for, Great Britain. Havildar (roughly equivalent to Sergeant) Gurung was at the forefront of Lumley's campaign of the past few years to ensure that Gurkhas who had served Britain and the Commonwealth should have the right of residence here. Despite his age, the diminutive, multi-medalled figure – missing one eye and most of his right arm from a Japanese grenade – was often by her side during her campaign. Commenting on his death, Lumley said: 'Although he was small in stature, we shall all walk in his shadow.'[99]

It was obvious the end in Burma was now in sight. Slim's swinging pincers had been highly effective; Japanese veterans who had charged so seamlessly triumphant over this same ground only two years before must have wondered just how it had all gone so badly wrong and how badly they had underrated British and imperial soldiers. It still wasn't quite over: a Gurkha section commander called Kishanbahadur, despite what would turn out to be a mortal wound, charged Japanese encircling their position, blazing away with a Thompson, throwing grenades and making a final, suicidal charge with his kukri. He killed about a dozen Japanese and the company broke out next day.

THE GURKHA WAY

Gurkhas had bad memories of the Sittang River where they had lost so heavily in 1942. This time it would be very different. The Japanese Twenty-Eighth Army would have to get back across the Sittang to survive but British 17th Division was between them and the river. 'The Twenty-Eighth Army came on with orders to do or die ...'.[100] For the most part it was to die. It was horrible ground, a wet delta-type maze of channels and ditches, sodden rice paddies, soon crowded with heaps of Japanese dead, bobbing limp and broken in the eddies. Rifleman Ujirsing Limbu won the IOM when he led a section against Japanese machine-gun posts and killed all their crews.[101] As General Tuker pithily commented, 'The Jap will not forget the Nepalese highlander.'[102]

Max Hastings, for whose analyses I have the greatest respect, takes the view that the campaign in Burma was always going to be difficult, and would not bring the defeat of Japan a day closer, but British and Indian soldiers must die so that Churchill's people were seen to pay their share of the price for victory in the Far East.[103] The prime minister was no stranger to realpolitik, yet this view is overly cynical. The Japanese had trounced British armies in Malaya and Burma, and the fall of Singapore was a humiliation and catastrophe of unparalleled dimension; not since the debacle of the First Afghan War[104] had British arms been so shamed. To prove that the Japanese were not invincible was essential in restoring British pride; Kohima was the obverse of Singapore and final triumph in Burma both vindication and restoration. They simply had to do it. British commanders, Slim in particular, were not impressed by 'Vinegar Joe' Stilwell's obsession with Nationalist China or his rampant Anglophobia.

The Kohima and Imphal battles, though never as much in the public eye as the campaigns in Western Europe, showed that the British, Indians and Gurkhas could take on the best of the Imperial Japanese armies and not just win but ultimately rout them. The names of men carved into the memorial on Garrison Hill tell a very different story to the disgrace of Singapore. Their stand brought about the collapse of the Japanese position throughout the whole theatre and contributed considerably to their final defeat.

During the whole of the Second World War 182 VCs were awarded and 9 of these were won by Gurkhas. In an echo of the classical dedication to the 300 Spartans at Thermopylae, the Kohima Memorial sombrely and poignantly reminds us:

> When you go home
> Tell them of us and say
> For your tomorrow
> We gave our today

Special Forces?

These are defined as 'elite highly trained military forces selected to work on difficult missions'.[105] That's quite a broad definition and Chris Bellamy, in his superb study of the Gurkhas, when writing of paratrooper operations in Burma,[106] sees the Gurkhas as filling a special operations, therefore Special Forces, role. This is sound sense yet Gurkhas probably shouldn't be defined as Special Forces in the sense that bespoke Second World War outfits like the LRDG or SAS were. These commando-type formations were set up with the specific aim of operating behind enemy lines in small numbers. They are different from assault infantry units like the Paras or Royal Marine Commandos. Gurkhas are riflemen and light infantry; a commando-type function, in certain circumstances, is a natural extension. The contentious Robert Rogers was perhaps the first to develop light infantry and frontiersmen into Rangers during the Seven Years War in America and their more daring raids look very much like commando operations.

Paratroopers were a novelty in the Second World War. Britain, beset in the grim inter-war years by the pacifist reaction, had been slow to pick up on the potential for airborne operations. Soviet Russia, on the other hand, in an unlikely entente with Nazi Germany, was much quicker off the mark. Former First World War flying ace Kurt Student developed and led the new Aryan elite *Fallschirmjager* and showed just what they could do when a single company effectively took out the vast Belgian fortress complex of Eban Emael and nearly captured the Dutch royal family in a daring *coup de main* which involved landing men in a football stadium. It nearly worked and scared the devil out of the Allies who had nothing similar in their arsenal. Fear of paratrooper landings plagued homeland defence in Britain as the threat loomed large after Dunkirk.

Then Student, recovering from a severe head wound, was allowed to attempt his masterpiece – 'aerial envelopment' – a complete airborne invasion, destination Crete and codenamed Operation Mercury. This didn't quite work out and at best resulted in a very expensive pyrrhic victory. Losses were so bad that Hitler wrote off any further such attempts. Despite this salutary lesson airborne operations were in. These come in two shapes:

1. Air-troop landings which involve the use of gliders.
2. Actual paratroopers who jump individually from planes.

There are pros and cons with both.

Nobody would necessarily have seen Gurkhas as natural paratrooper material. The society they came from was unsophisticated by European standards and few had any experience with aircraft, let alone jumping out of them. Nonetheless, the 50th Indian Parachute Brigade had been formed in late 1941[107] but nothing serious happened before the middle of 1944. There would be three airborne battalions: the 151st (British), 152nd (Indian) and 153rd (Gurkha). The 151st was diverted and replaced by another Gurkha outfit, the 154th, which was raised from the depleted remnants of 3/7th.[108]

The recruiters would need some 750 volunteers, not helped by a confusion of recruiting reels which showed how to defend against airborne attack and that the paras might be virtually wiped out by vigorous measures. The New Zealanders had demonstrated that ably on Crete; or as Corporal Jones from *Dad's Army* might have expressed it – 'They don't like it up 'em!' But the recruiting worked and a recce team from 153rd Gurkha Parachute Battalion, Operation *Puddle*, was dropped ahead of the first Chindit raid in July 1942 and spent six useful weeks spying on the Japanese. Next month a second small team was air-landed ahead of a full company deployment to prepare a landing strip; again this mission was successful.[109]

It was in October 1942 near New Delhi that Gurkha para training began, followed by large-scale exercises.[110] Ironically, their first time in the field wasn't as airborne but as heavy infantry defending the twin bastions of Imphal and Kohima. They also carried out long-distance reconnaissance into the largely blank but inhospitable canvas of the Naga Hills, a role that demanded many of the characteristics of Special Forces, though this does not necessarily equate with the LRDG/SAS role as they were extending their normal deployment but returning immediately, a moot point admittedly.[111]

It wasn't until March 1945, almost at the war's end, that the Indian Army parachute units got the coveted red beret, when three battalions were formed into a single Indian Parachute Regiment. Now the old 153rd became 2nd Battalion and 154th the 3rd Battalion. Five months earlier high command had decided upon creating a full Indian Army Airborne Division, the 44th, with two brigades – 50th and 77th – each of which would have a single battalion of Gurkhas as part of its core establishment. The 154th went to 50th Brigade and the 153rd to the 77th.[112]

Their chance came in the final stages of the battle to retake Burma. The Japanese had suffered tremendously but had no intention of giving up. This wasn't their way and whatever is thought about their brutality, their courage and motivation was never in question. In mid-April 1945, Slim was contemplating crossing the significant wet gap of the Rangoon River. The Japanese were equally determined he should not and had mined the water extensively as well as throwing up strong defences on the west bank, with a major redoubt at Elephant Point. There was no prospect of any amphibious operation until these strongholds were taken out.[113]

Airborne might be the answer, but a lot of the Gurkhas were on furlough back home and the division as a whole in flux. Slim would have to pull together an ad hoc unit from what could be found from both battalions. Concentrating at Chakala, the new hybrid was beefed up with the necessary support units to form an independent if somewhat improvised formation. Worryingly, their airborne taxi service would be supplied by American allies with forty transports; worrying because their crews had never dropped paras before. The unfortunate results of such inexperience had been seen on the night of 5/6 June 1944 when the American air drop over the Cotentin had gone so horribly adrift with men being scattered in penny packets across the Norman countryside. Happily, a brace of Canadian jumpmasters who could speak to the Americans but also had experience with Gurkhas were conscripted into the mix.[114]

There wasn't a lot of time for training and the lead elements lifted off bright and early on 1 May. This was part of the wider Operation Dracula, though it must be wondered how many Gurkhas had heard of the fifteenth-century Wallachian 'Vlad the Impaler'. They would probably, however, have approved of the sentiment; they were to be a deadly stake in the heart of this final Japanese bastion.

Their objective was Elephant Point and the drop some miles from the target went well, no mean achievement in the circumstances. Collecting their gear, the Gurkhas marched to within a couple of miles of the position just to let Allied bombers provide a final softening up. This proved too close for comfort as a lead company was shot up by their own side – 'blue on blue' as it is called today, plain bad luck in the fog of war. Undeterred, the brigade pressed on and took the objective, dealing with the Japanese platoon holding the place.[115]

When it comes to Special Forces, a number of Gurkhas had, as volunteers, been seconded to the Special Operations Executive (SOE). The body charged with 'setting Europe ablaze' had extended its remit to the Far East where the rather pedestrian-sounding Force 136 had been active against the Japanese. The future star of cinema Bill Travers, actually Major William Lindon-Travers, had led a platoon-sized unit after the retreating enemy in the wake of their defeat at Imphal-Kohima. Their brief was to ascertain if the Japanese were in fact retreating or simply withdrawing to regroup. This was a Special Forces role and a very risky one, as dramatic as anything Bill Travers would subsequently enact on screen.[116]

THE GURKHA WAY

Field Marshal Slim wasn't overly keen on Special Forces:

> We had commandos, assault brigades, amphibious divisions, mountainous divisions, long range penetration forces, airborne forces, desert groups and an extraordinary variety of cloak and dagger parties. The equipment of these special units was more generous than that of normal formations ... we employed most of them in Burma, and some, notably the Chindits, gave splendid examples of courage and hardihood. Yet I came firmly to the conclusion that such formations, trained, equipped and mentally adjusted for one kind of operation only, were wasteful. They did not give, militarily, a worth-while return for the resources in men, material and time that they absorbed.[117]

Slim goes on to point out – and this is an understandable and oft-heard refrain from senior officers – that such units had a romantic pull for the best of those serving in conventional units; a chance for glory, less Blanco and bollocks: 'The result of these methods was to lower the quality of the rest of the army, especially of the infantry.'[118] Gurkhas cannot be seen as Special Forces within this overall envelope. They are recruited to serve as infantry yet they have, in two centuries of service, shown a remarkable adaptability, able to flex and extend their skills as circumstances may have demanded. They have fought against past masters at irregular warfare, Pathans and Wazirs, who operate as Special Forces by way of their birthright.

Gurkhas adapt to the military needs of a given tactical and strategic situation, yet they remain Gurkhas. As riflemen, their flexibility doesn't transform them into something else: it consolidates what they already are. It is certainly fair to describe them as 'elite' which means, in a military context, beyond the norm as in today's British Armed forces Royal Marines Commandos and paras are undoubtedly elite.

Chapter 10

End of Empire

> If you're not prepared to pay the price of peace, you'd better be prepared to pay the price of war.
>
> Harry S. Truman (1945)

The end of the war and the retreat from empire saw swingeing cuts in overall army numbers. Some Indian Army units, post-independence, remained with that army (six out of ten Gurkha battalions). Some of the Gurkha units, forming a much-reduced brigade, continued to serve beneath the Union Flag.[1] While the current brigade may be a pale shadow of its wartime strength, the Gurkhas have stayed at the cutting edge (pun intended).

London, 6,036 Miles

The Partition of India could have been the end of the Gurkhas in British service. Those long years of the Raj slipped into history, but the birth of a new independent India was hard and bloody. Possibly as many as a million people died in inter-religious and ethnic violence; enmities which still endure. The Raj may have given birth to the Gurkha battalions, but its obituary wasn't also theirs. They had proved themselves on too many battlefields and, in the years of uneasy peace since 1947, would go on to prove themselves on many more.

For some, however, during that post-war epoch when the Raj finally lost its grip on the Indian Subcontinent, it seemed initially as though life would continue much as before. One of those was Lieutenant Anthony Ford who served with 6 GR in India. A native of Northumberland, he was commissioned as a second lieutenant just in time for the end of the war but saw no action against the, by then, defeated Japanese. In July 1945 he found himself at a transit camp at Deolali:[2] 'I remember being horrified at the beggars lining the railway as we left Bombay, many of the children were maimed and I'd been told they were sometimes deliberately maimed to make them better beggars.'[3]

Ford was 19 and newly elevated to full lieutenant. In the mess one evening he was told volunteers were needed and, as much from boredom as by any conscious decision, he stuck his hand up and discovered he had just joined 6 GR. This wasn't really any kind of light-bulb moment. He soon found himself up in the hills at Abbottabad (now in Pakistan). The camp was 4,000ft (1,219m) up and the nearest major town was Rawalpindi some 70 miles (113km) distant. Outwardly, not much had changed since John Masters' time during the pre-war years:

> The mess was very like a good hotel or London Club, uniformed orderlies served dinner on regimental silver and it was always a four-course affair – a piper came around with the port.[4] VE day was celebrated but the newly recruited lieutenant along with his pal 'Plum' Warner got into bother for wearing green, jungle fatigues rather than khaki. The adjutant was incensed – only those who had actually fought in the jungle were allowed to wear green![5]

Having arranged for the monthly hire of a bicycle, Anthony was assigned to training duties attached to a company based further up the valley at Khakul. Here he saw the sign some wag had put up informing that London was a mere 6,036 miles west. The track terminated 10,000ft (3,050m) up where there was a government rest-house. Many of the officers were just waiting to be demobilised. Anthony spoke neither Urdu nor Gurkhali; most of his soldiers were Gurungs and Thapas who had little English.[6]

This brand of soldiering was not that glorious. The war was over, and the fag end of empire was more bureaucracy than action. It could almost seem like nothing had changed. Anthony's duties were pay and defaulters, sorting out endless admin, supervision of cooks, cleaners and sweepers (the lowest of the low). 'I remember noticing that one rifleman who had been a lance-naik had lost his stripe – "You did that", he exclaimed. "It was for not having my trousers on after sunset when you inspected the barracks (an anti-malarial precaution). In fact, they fell down when I stood to attention as you came in!"'[7] Ford felt immediate twinges of guilt.

Another of his allotted tasks was to auction off the kit of any poor sod who had copped it; even peacetime has its casualties: 'On one occasion there was a rather odd, shaped kukri, to be sold off but nobody bid. It had a smooth curved back instead of the usual angle. I put in a bid myself to encourage others and ended up with it! After I got married, we used it as a poker for many years.'[8]

John Masters had by now turned to fiction and his *Bhowani Junction*, as previously mentioned, was a bestseller and successful film. Ford expressed his own opinion: 'I felt Masters got it about right. Muslim clerks were despised, sweepers barely visible. Anglo-Indians were looked down upon and their daughters considered fair game; servants and waiters were treated with little respect.'[9]

The hill station might seem unaffected by the seismic events breaking loose all around but tentacles reached out even into this relative haven of tranquillity. There was a fire in the bazaar, clearly arson, and the Gurkhas were called in. Both Hindus and Muslims had been burned out yet no stock seemed to have been lost in the Muslim shops. Even more tellingly, busloads of Hindu refugees were on the roads, and many were murdered wholesale. Despite the Gurkhas' essential role in providing security for such displaced people, the imminent handover to independence meant the 6th was to be rapidly scaled down and moved to a new HQ in Malaya (see below).[10]

One officer serving with 2/9th, R.N.P. Reynolds, wrote a series of letters home to his mother from the east Punjab during 1947. He also was 19:

> 3rd September, Jagadhi: I arrived in time to avoid absolute chaos, because just as the head of the column was about to pass a Muslim village, 200 yards from the road Sikhs and Hindus decided to attack the village from the other side, so heavy rifle fire was coming from the village, while refugees streamed out towards us. I stopped them with great difficulty just in time – collected them together and made them wait until the end of the column where they tacked on. Five villagers had been killed I believe; as we drew away a column of smoke rose from the village – just the end of one more Muslim village in the area.[11]

The region was branded as a 'dangerously disturbed area'. This was a classic understatement if ever there was. The battalion then moved up to camp at Ludhiana:[12]

> As we moved into camp we could hear the continuous rat-tat-tat-tat of MG fire from the city which had been going on all day and every day since the trouble started. When we had made camp I was told there were two wounded children among the refugees whom

I went to see. They had been horribly slashed about by knives so I put them and a wounded man into a truck and whipped them off to the civilian hospital in Ludhiana. On the way the streets were practically deserted, as the place was under curfew. Whole streets were burning and piles of mutilated bodies lay about the place – I saw 22 dead in one small space alone; they lay along the Grand Trunk Road, along the railways line and in the city.[13]

Reynolds wrote a further letter on 3 November 1947:

On Wednesday the whole company moved here to Jagadhi relieving Nobby Clarke and his platoon from B Company which went down to Panipat in Karnal District, where trouble was expected. We left one platoon in Pipli which is on the Grand Trunk Road where we branch off for here – trouble was expected there too. On Thursday morning we were informed that a village had been attacked during the night. So I took a section and went with the magistrate there. Total casualties were 12 killed, one missing believed dead, 7 wounded. Three quarters of the village was burnt down and about a dozen cattle roasted. We inspected each of the dead to determine the nature of weapons used, and we received definite info that the attackers had been Sikhs from Kalsia State, only a few miles away. Even where small settlements were forcibly evacuated, people desperate, returned to their homes hoping the storm might pass them by and that the madness might end; all too often it ended for them in death or mutilation.[14]

Lieutenant Stanley Roberts OBE served with 2/10th GR during Partition with 43rd Gurkha Lorried Brigade. His battalion and 2/8th were tasked:

(a) To shepherd the Hindu and Sikh refugees moving from the newly created Pakistan, to collecting points north of Lahore; (b) To protect them from attacks by local Muslims as they moved south; (c) To assist them on their journey by rail and by convoys of 3-ton lorries and in the case of the vast majority, moving on foot with their slow moving bullock carts and animals, along a specially selected route which ran west of Lahore, across the Indian border to an area west of Amritsar.[15]

The final doleful column to struggle towards the idea of safety was over 80,000 strong and stretched, straggled for mile after mile:

> Those scenes on the refugee route were ghastly. Hundreds died from sickness, exhaustion and hunger as did many animals. Wild dogs were so bloated they could hardly move, kite-hawks and vultures could barely lift off the road. I saw more dead in one day than I had done during the whole of my time in the war ... A rich Indian merchant came to see me in our Lahore HQ and begged me to allocate a 3-tonner to him for carrying his possessions to Amritsar. When I pointed out that, if I did so, at least 30 refugees would be left behind, probably to die, he replied – 'they are poor and have nothing to lose but I am rich and have much to lose.'[16]

The merchant didn't get his truck. Roberts continues:

> One Gurkha officer, patrolling the toiling endless flood, saw a woman in the final stages of exhaustion leave her baby by the side of the road. He stopped the vehicle to entreat her to pick the child up and she said 'Why, we'll both be dead soon.'[17] Such horrors were the norm. Hindu refugees were being directed towards the column's route, often by Muslim police. In fact, a whole flock were simply misdirected into a defile where 500 Muslims were eagerly anticipating another atrocity. Happily, in this instance, a Gurkha officer from 2/8th witnessed what was about to happen while on a routine jeep patrol with only his driver and batman in the vehicle. The Gurkhas, all three, waded into the fight with a Tommy-gun, Bren and rifle, saving the bulk of the refugees and killing or wounding at least 50 of their attackers.[18]

Emergency in Malaya

Attlee's post-war Labour government romped home with a sizeable majority; out went Winston and the old order. That included empire. Imperialism was fast acquiring the dirty name it has today and Britain was looking to divest itself of its vast colonial portfolio which had been lurching significantly into the red for decades. This wouldn't be easy, and Attlee's socialists would be confronted by diehard communists, firstly in Malaya – the 'Emergency'.

Why an 'emergency' when it was a war? All to do with 'insurance' it seems: if your property gets blitzed in a 'war' you can say goodbye to your insurance

Map 11. Malayan Emergency, 1948–60.

cover but not if the same damage occurs during an 'emergency'. That isn't so bad and doesn't void your cover. Such things matter; they matter a lot if it's your property that has gone up, and loss adjusters would be very busy indeed in Malaya between 1948 and 1960.

During the years of Japanese occupation, the British had supported indigenous resistance groups such as the Malay People's Anti-Japanese Army (MPAJA). They had a common enemy if not necessarily a common purpose. One brand of empire can look much like another, and many fighters were not too keen just to swap flags back from the Rising Sun to the Union Jack.[19]

After the final defeat of the Japanese in 1945, all the Malay states with the exception of Singapore were brought together as the Malay Union, which had colony status with a British administration. Brunei too opted to remain independent, Singapore changed to this position late on in the proceedings.

From February 1948, this earlier structure was re-configured as the Federation of Malaya, headed up by a High Commissioner. Many who wanted to see a communist-style tyranny – the Malayan Liberation Army, branded by the British as Communist terrorists (CTs), or even more simply just as plain 'bandits'[20] – had in fact been trained by the British for the clandestine war against the Japanese occupier. Theirs would be a nasty war of attrition, attacks on rubber plantations, assassinations, plain murder and intimidation.

Initially, the British were grossly unprepared. Their enemy was well trained (ironically by the people they were about to fight), well equipped, highly motivated and fully able to operate freely in difficult jungle. It would be a long, hard and attenuated process to beat the CTs and it would see the rebirth of the SAS, disbanded after the end of the Second World War. Gurkhas would more than play their part. It was on 18 June 1948 that the High Commissioner declared a state of emergency in response to a series of particularly nasty murders. Leading the insurgency was Chin Peng, a dangerous and highly astute character who had actually been given an OBE for his services in the war, though still only 25 in 1948 – whether he ever displayed this award in any of his jungle bases seems unlikely. Chris Bellamy quotes one Gurkha officer witness:

> Gradually, like the widening ripples of a stone thrown into a pond, the influence of the communists would spread to swathes of territory which would then be taken over and become 'liberated zones' in which the government had no influence except when it sent in large numbers of troops. As these zones increased in size and number, so the third phase of revolutionary warfare would emerge, the Counter-Offensive phase (so called, presumably, because by then the communists were in a position to counter the government's security forces successfully).[21]

This was the Maoist blueprint, and it came close to succeeding. In fact, the CTs had seriously over-estimated their own in-country support and failed both to appreciate the robustness of the response and to up their game sufficiently.

In all eight Gurkha battalions, starting with 1/6th, were transported by sea to Malaya. While they were almost up to strength and fresh recruits were coming in steadily from Nepal, what was lacking were sufficient trained officers and NCOs. Their jungle experience would, for many, be a baptism of fire. Most Gurkha soldiers arriving in Malaya might have thought they were experiencing a taste of paradise, a haven of exotic tranquillity; those seismic tremors beneath the surface only beginning to bubble. The original intention had been that Gurkhas would form the principal building block in a whole new division, the 17th (in tribute to the Burma Campaign).[22] Part of the process would be to create additional supporting arms, Gurkha gunners, engineers and signallers (which continue to this day). Some of these ideas worked better than others: Gurkhas could make good gunners, but it was infantry that was needed.[23]

At the outset they were unready and lumbered with a palpable shortage of experienced jungle hands. Major Ronald Barnes, in January 1949, leading a platoon-sized patrol from A Company 1/6th Gurkhas, walked into a well-laid ambush and was killed along with ten others. Another ten soldiers were gunned down when a lorry load of new recruits intended for 2/2nd was ambushed and shot up at Sungei Siput, north of Ipoh.[24] As Christopher Bullock recounts:

> When the 1st Battalion arrived in Malaya it was little more than 300 strong with no specialists except a handful of drivers, and no signallers, so grave had been the disruption caused by the referendum ... The task of building up the Battalion to strength and the training of specialists had to go on concurrently with the chasing of terrorists but it was done and by the beginning of 1949 the Battalion was itself again.[25]

In 1950, realising the current deficiencies, Colonel Walter Walker[26] set up a jungle warfare training school at Kota Tingii and Gurkhas were soon both learning and instructing there. It was needed; too many raw recruits were being flung into the fiery pit of jungle warfare against an enemy who knew every trick in the book. Long ago the basic engineering skills which Gurkhas possess had been recognised and their engineering unit performed superbly in Malaya. Julius Caesar had during his Gallic Wars (58–51 BC) overawed the Germanic tribes by bridging the Rhine, a prodigious feat, and successful engineering has always been a war-winning factor. Herod's fortress eyrie at Masada was impregnable till Flavius Silva built a vast ramp in the desert. British and Gurkha engineers had built roads and bridges through every imaginable terrain. Jungles cease to be impenetrable if you can build ways through.

Gurkhas would become ruthless virtuosos in those deadly games of hide, seek and destroy which soon developed, pitted against savagely determined CTs, as Rifleman Dal Bahadur Pun witnessed: he recalled a constant, lethal game of cat and mouse. The enemy would set ambushes, or the Gurkhas would try to ambush them. If they escaped the net bandits would flee into the villages where they had sympathisers, but it was impossible to tell 'good' from 'bad'.

Villages were moved to frustrate the bandits and often people had to leave much behind. Even in training when forces were armed only with blanks, they could still be vulnerable to attack by deadly hit and run, only a few casualties at a time but desperately morale-sapping.[27]

Corporal Dal Prasad, who served from 1948–64 and was an expert with the light machine gun, had similar experiences. Life in the jungle was hard, it was never a major war but a small-scale guerrilla-type conflict: they would try to bushwhack the Gurkhas or the other way round. You always had to be on your guard. He saw friends die and they set up a lot of their own ambushes; sometimes these worked, sometimes not. They could be out in the bush for a day a week or a month, kept going by regular air drops.[28]

For those dozen years of asymmetric warfare, the brigade was based at Sembilan, in Negri State; that is, six out of eight battalions; one remained in Singapore and the other went out to Hong Kong. 'Jungle-bashing', as it was dubbed, became their daily fare. It was tedious, energy sapping, often dangerous. This was as cunning and skilled an enemy as they had faced in the older days of the North-West Frontier. It was humid, unhealthy and pestilential, and leeches were a persistent irritant: 'there were several varieties, including a green and yellow monster, which I discovered one night on my leg and showed it to my orderly. He was neither sympathetic nor impressed ...'.[29]

Like those frequent tales of lost Japanese soldiers emerging from remote bush, 1/10th Gurkhas, on patrol in October 1949, discovered a hooch, deep in thick jungle where they discovered, not any CTs but Naik Nakan Gurung of 1st Gurkhas who, weakened by disease, had been abandoned during the retreat through Burma seven years earlier. He had rallied, managed to dodge the Japanese and had been surviving as a kind of latter-day Alexander Selkirk in his hideout, imagining the war was still going on.[30] His relief was considerable.

In April 1950, Lieutenant General Sir Harold Briggs arrived as new director of operations. This proved a significant turning point. He grasped it was necessary to sever the umbilical cord between the insurgents in the bush and their covert civilian collaborators whose efforts sustained theirs. This was a Sisyphean task, rounding up the suspects and effectively banging them up in 'New Villages' – compounds effectively where they would be watched and corralled. This, the 'Briggs Plan', proved a game-changer.

So too were the Gurkhas: those initial setbacks had engendered a new professionalism and Major Peter Richardson of 1/2nd led an attack on the 'Labis Gang', a very nasty bunch who terrorised the district they were named after. In January 1950, the gang beat up the night mail train from Singapore prompting a contact with a platoon from 1/2nd who had driven the bandits from their fortified lair, though they lost their company commander in the fight. Richardson had intelligence from police who had pinpointed the gang's new hideout, and, under cover of darkness, he moved B Company up into a mosquito-infested rubber plantation, waiting for dawn and a sudden sweep of the place, beating the line like a grouse shoot.

Skeins of mist hung like shrouds, cutting down visibility, giving rise to spectres till one took solid shape, bolting from a shanty. Rifleman Bombahadur Gharti loosed off a burst. All hell immediately broke loose as more bandits burst from cover, shooting and chucking grenades. Rifleman Gharti shot several and Richardson another brace. The major swung round in time to see an insurgent hacking at one of his wounded men with a native machete, or *parang*. He killed the attacker, though the wounded Gurkha later died. As they fled the bandits were neatly cut off by the left-hand platoon, which threw them back into a deadly crossfire. In all, thirty-five were killed. Richardson won a DSO and Sergeant Major Bhimbadur Pun a DCM.[31]

Such battles were, however, pretty rare in Malaya. An average jungle soldier would be likely to endure 700 hours of patrolling before he even glimpsed his enemy. It took on average 64,000 man hours to bag an insurgent.[32] In the mid-1950s the declared rule of engagement was to shout a warning, giving the CT a chance to surrender. While humane and leaning firmly towards the rule of law, this tended to give suspects an opportunity to decamp before any shooting started. To what extent this requirement was honoured more in the breach than the observance cannot be said, happily perhaps.

In today's wars, Western populations tend to expect fast results, an almost arcade-game type of war with decisive results slotted between commercials. It isn't like that, of course, but public attention, obsessed with soundbites, spin and the vortex of social media, soon fades. Enthusiasm for the recent war in Afghanistan quickly waned, until only the sombre reminders of shrouded, flag-draped coffins coming into RAF Brize Norton managed to grab any headline space. The strategic objectives were long shrouded. Malaya, one of the classic counterinsurgency campaigns, was long drawn out, expensive and draining. There would be no major battles, just steady attrition; bribery was often as effective as force and, bizarre as it may seem, usually cheaper. But gradually the Gurkhas, as a spearhead of the UK's overall response, began to gain the upper hand.

They would be in the bush for several weeks at a time, giving the bandits no rest and no chance to regroup or consolidate. It took a heavy toll; soldiers developed horrible jungle sores, suffered from those omnipresent mosquitoes and leeches, endured rations that were often cold and patrolling always monotonous. Even their time out of line would be harnessed by energetic COs like Walter Walker for more training; but it all helped ratchet up the score of dead insurgents. It would be a long fight. Briggs, terminally ill, returned to Britain and in October 1951 Sir Henry Gurney, the high commissioner, was killed during an ambush. The subsequent appointment of General Sir Gerald Templer, who would hold dual office as high commissioner and head of operations, proved another game-changer – earning him the accolade 'Tiger of Malaya'. He integrated security and counterinsurgency operations. He was also totally ruthless.

Graham Greene came out to Malaya in January 1952 and was briefly attached to 1/10th Gurkhas even venturing out on patrol with 1/7th. He found the jungle work hard going and needed stimulation from brandy and ginger ale which had to be dropped in from the air.[33] Like the later Vietnam War, in a war where winning or holding ground, even taking strategic targets, counts for very little, 'kill' ratios become the principal yardstick of success: a tally of dead enemy establishes victory. This is imprecise and of questionable reliability. Today, such scoring would be politically incorrect and considered reprehensible, but battalions naturally competed with each other to ramp up their tallies, breaking out the beers when they scored a century.

In the course of August 1952, one platoon from B Company, 2/10th Gurkhas, was operating in the Muar River vicinity of West Johore, something of a hot spot and where bandits had ambushed and wiped out a team of Malay Special Constables. Corporal Makarpal Tamang, leading a patrol group comprising two sections tracked a lone insurgent they had spotted. He led them to a hilltop encampment. Tamang sent one section round to bolt the back door while he with the remaining Gurkhas probed along the cliff edge to reach the front. This cost them six dead and nine wounded,[34] three of whom were caught. The Regimental Journal recorded the fight:

> Early on Friday, 15th August, a party of bandits ambushed some special constables, of whom one was killed. Within half an hour a platoon of B Company was on their tracks. Another patrol of two sections – sixteen men in all – under command of Cpl. Makarpal Thamang, set out to head the bandits off, and at about two o'clock in the afternoon, seeing a lone bandit making off through the jungle in rather a hurry, they gave chase. The chase led them to a hill which was obviously occupied in some strength. Sending one section to work round the back of the hill, Makarpal led the other section up the hill until finally they got so close to the top that

the defenders could not, owing to the steepness of the slope, fire at the attackers without standing up, thus giving the Bren gunner who was covering the advance a glorious target of which he took full advantage.

The bandits now assumed an ostrich-like head down posture but, unfortunately for them, by now the other section had got in behind them and was presented with the sort of target that the boy with the catapult dreams of. Within minutes the bandits were in full flight, leaving six dead behind. Three wounded ones were captured in the follow-up and they gave information that six more had been wounded and that the total strength on the hill had been about thirty-nine. We had only one casualty, Lance-Corporal Abirdhoj Rai, who was killed by LMG fire early in the fight.[35]

Major Neill of 2/2nd, who had served with the Chindits and also in the Arakan, racked up an impressive personal score of twenty-one confirmed kills.[36] Attrition was taking its toll on the CTs. Others were succumbing to a government bounty, selling out their chums for cash rewards as disillusionment deepened. With the containment policy instigated by Briggs now biting deep, the bandits had to retreat further into the bush with their supply lines fractured or, at best, uncertain.

In February 1953, 2/7th Gurkhas, who had endured many months of barren patrolling, benefitted from intelligence gained by low-altitude spotting over the bush. They, with 1st Gordon Highlanders – old friends from the North-West Frontier – would attack a CT base, concealed in deep jungle. The Gordons would go in by the front door and Captain John Thornton's C Company of 2/7th would set up a series of ambush points to catch bandits as they fled. This meant they had to approach silently under cover of darkness and drenching rain, some distance from their objective. Quiet as proverbial church mice the recce patrols crept forward until they actually detected signs of enemy activity: a pair of CTs taking a bath, blissfully unaware.[37]

Alerted by his patrol, Thornton edged closer, throwing a cordon around the bandits' base, tipping a nod to the Scots then going in with an assault team, all guns blazing, brassing up the camp and driving survivors, like partridges, onto the guns of the ambush teams. Eight bandits died. Perhaps they hadn't heard the warnings.[38]

At about the same time 1/7th was on the trail of a particularly nasty character: Goh Sia, who had instigated a reign of terror in the Segamat region directly between Kuala Lumpur and Singapore. Corporal Partapsing and his section hid in their ambush spot for three tortuous days, tormented by local wildlife and subsisting literally on bread and water. Their patient endurance was rewarded when Goh Sia and his henchmen finally put in an appearance. The corporal shot dead the insurgent.[39]

At the beginning of 1953, 1/10th Battalion was working the tricky Kulai District of South Jahore until they handed over responsibility to 2nd Battalion that February. So far they had accounted for 217 bandits killed and 26 captured. The Gurkhas had lost 6 men dead and 35 wounded.[40] After more training out of the line, the 1st again handed over to the 2nd Battalion and then returned to operations in the Pengarang Peninsula (the very south-east tip of Malaysia). The Gurkhas had a six-month tour based here with HQ at Kota Tingi and company firebases spread over the area. Bandits were active and patrolling: 'an indication of the stubbornness of some of the insurgents was the finding by A Company in the Mersing District of the bodies of bandits who had preferred to starve rather than surrender'.[41]

In all a score of kills was racked up during the battalion's tour and that October they shifted to the Cameron Highlands to take part in Operation Valiant. This was a dense, remote area inhabited by aboriginal tribes who had been intimidated by CTs since the start of the conflict. Not too much 'jungle-bashing' to begin with:

> The battalion was transported in outboard motor-boats to a police post 10 miles up the River Medang and from there was taken by helicopter to a Landing Zone called 'Net' ... this was the battalion's first large-scale move by this modern method of transport, which has proved itself of such inestimable value in difficult country such as it now encountered.[42]

The Cameron Highlands rise up to 7,000ft (2,130m) along a jagged spine of the country, a steep and hard slog uphill through dense belts of bamboo thicket – pure hell. Even hardened riflemen who had fought in Burma described the terrain as 'sheer agony'.[43] Resupply was by air drop, an inestimable blessing, and the Gurkhas had ample cause to be grateful for the skill and dedication of RAF pilots who could drop their loads with great accuracy in such difficult country. One chute which failed to open nevertheless descended with perfect precision onto the CO's bivvy.[44]

Contacts were scarce but deadly. A confusion of orders exposed one patrol from B Company who were bushwhacked and had three riflemen injured. That same month, November, D Company suffered similarly but didn't get off as lightly: one man was killed in action and another succumbed to wounds. The ambush party was tracked and scattered but escaped retribution.[45] It was hard, dangerous and tedious by turns, always physically exhausting. Vast tracts of impossible ground were covered without any significant gains.

When a particularly notorious enemy, like Goh Sia, was 'taken out', the successful hunter could become an instant celebrity. The regimental journal *The Kukri* featured a photo of Rifleman Bharnabahadur Rai from C Company 1/10th when he shot a 'most wanted', Manap Jepun.[46] Or, from the Summer 1955 edition:

> In April, May and June, A, B, D, and Support Companies [of 2/10th] killed five bandits between them, whilst their company commanders successfully reduced their handicaps on the Bahau Estate Golf Course ... October 1952 proved to be the battalion's best month since the beginning of the Emergency, seventeen bandits were killed ... [In the 2/6th] we rounded off our R & R by killing six out of six terrorists whilst the Battalion cocktail party was in progress.[47] When the 1/2nd notched up a double century of kills, a civilian administrator donated half a dozen silver beer tankards to the mess as trophies. It was a really big day when the Brigade claimed its 1,000th kill.[48]

It was still a hard slog; a dozen years of fighting were needed to end the threat.

A total of nearly 40,000 British and Commonwealth troops were engaged, with 25,000 Malay Home Guard, 37,000 special constables and 24,000 Federation Police; about 3,500 of the Malay security personnel were killed with as many as 5,000 civilians. Late in 1955, when the tide was clearly turning in the Cameron Highlands region, a bandit gang blitzed a settlement, killing Home Guard, stealing weapons and causing devastation.

Major Harkasing Rai, leading C Company of 1/6th Gurkhas, was swiftly on their trail and tracked them to a hideout where, on 9 January 1956, he killed four. The rest got clear but Major Rai was soon back on their tails, closing in again four days later. Again, the quarry escaped. More Gurkhas were on the scent and shot two additional insurgents; a platoon from the Malay Regiment joined the chase and accounted for another brace. Three of the dead bandits were high in the CT hierarchy.[49]

Malaya, 'the War of Running Dogs',[50] has rightly been hailed as an extraordinarily successful counterinsurgency campaign even if it got off to a shaky start. Over 500 UK military personnel were killed but some 10,000 CTs, dead, wounded or captured, were accounted for. There were further sporadic flare-ups between the years 1967 and 1989 but the main threat had been defeated by 1960 and the Gurkhas, effectively acting as a very efficient hybrid fusion of regular and Special Forces, had played a major role. This would stand them in very good stead for the second round in South-East Asia – Borneo.

Confrontation in Borneo

In December 1962, an insurgent group the TNKU (North Kalimantan Liberation Army), kicked off the Borneo Confrontation when they rebelled against the sultan angered particularly by his decision to join the Malaysian Federation (which he did anyway). Even after the end of hostilities a battalion of Gurkhas remained stationed there in Tuker Lines (named, obviously, after Major General Francis Tuker).

It was in November 1965 that Lance Corporal Rambahadur Limbu, who was then 26, fought in the action where he won a VC. He had joined the 2/10th Battalion in 1957 and had gained experience in Malaya. His unit had

Map 12. Borneo Confrontation, 1965.

been deployed to take and hold a position 5,000yd beyond the border in the Bau district of Sarawak. His platoon came into contact with a strong enemy force well dug in atop a commanding, steep-sided hill.

Leading his section forward toward an outpost, he and they came under heavy fire. He was only 10yd away and rushed the slit trench, disposing of its occupants. As the advance continued the group came under increasingly heavy fire. Men went down; two were badly hit. Both were lying in no-man's-land in front of the enemy's many guns. Limbu crawled forwards to try to bring his men in but intense fire drove him back each time.

Undeterred, he tried again, reaching one of the casualties and with his section laying down suppressing fire, managed to get him back alive. Next, he went back for the second one, rounds ripping up the ground around. Picking the injured man up, he pelted back, a storm of fire chasing. He wasn't done. With the wounded safe it was time to resume his attack. The fight raged for an hour until the enemy survivors fled leaving two-dozen dead behind. For this action Lance Corporal Limbu was awarded the Victoria Cross.

Borneo was one of those little wars of peace that get forgotten about, yet it was a significant British victory and a triumph for the Gurkhas. Like Malaya, it was never called a war, rather a 'Confrontation'. President Sukarno of Indonesia had cast covetous eyes on the Sultanate of Brunei together with the colonies of North Borneo and Sarawak. It was feared at the time that this could lead to a 'domino' effect throughout the region and this 'Confrontation' occurred as the United States was scaling up its presence in South Vietnam. Obviously, the result there was very different. During four years of conflict, at every level the Gurkhas honed their already formidable counterinsurgency skills and formed strong partnerships with both SAS and SBS.

Denis Healey, defence minister during the Confrontation, described the British response to Borneo as a 'textbook demonstration of how to apply economy of force, under political guidance for political ends and in the history books it will be recorded as one of the most efficient uses of military force in the history of the world'.[51] Britain, her Commonwealth allies and Malaysia fought an undeclared war to counter the Indonesian strategy of *konfrontasi*, or confrontation, designed to destabilise the newly formed Federation of Malaysia between 1963 and late 1966, in what became the UK's single largest operational commitment post-Second World War involving 54,000 servicemen.[52] The Indonesian strategy utilised political, military and economic means to undermine the embryonic Malaysian state in a bid to annex Sabah, Sarawak and Brunei.

The Indonesian Foreign Minister Dr Subandrio stated in a press conference on 20 January 1963 that: 'Confrontation does not include war, because it can be carried out without war'.[53] Conflict halted in August 1966 with the Indonesian government recognising Malaysia as an independent and legitimate state arguably, at least in part, due to an internal coup rather than to military operations.

Lieutenant General Sir Walter Walker, Commander of British Forces in Borneo from 1962–5, viewed the effort as a 'decisive victory' and that such 'claret' (offensive cross-border raiding) operations were the 'secret knock-out weapon'[54] within this (although one should perhaps be wary of politicians and military commanders evaluating their own success).

To link tactical and operational success as determinants of the strategic outcome in Borneo risks drawing skewed conclusions over the utility of military force and the political realities of conflict resolution. Instead, the Confrontation is a good example of where tactical and operational success provided time and space for the political elements of conflict resolution to play out as part of that comprehensive approach so popular in the modern military lexicon. If military success lies in achieving the overarching political intent, the Borneo Confrontation was a success.

Britain had, since 1945, undergone a specific and unique retreat from empire. This wasn't decline and fall but a phased withdrawal aimed at securing a democratic and oppression-free future for its former colonies. India, Malaya, Kenya, Cyprus and Aden all witnessed significant fighting and bloodshed. To fully understand the Borneo Confrontation, it's imperative to grasp the full context, viewed through a prism of British decolonisation and the Cold War. Malaya and Singapore had been granted independence in 1957 and 1959 respectively but the island of Borneo consisting of Sarawak, North Borneo (Sabah) and Brunei hadn't yet been incorporated into Greater Malaysia.

In fact, Brunei did not join the confederation and Singapore left in 1965. Malaysia was finally born in 1963. With the spread of communism and a growing deployment of American forces in Vietnam, the Borneo Confrontation took on a more important role. The Brunei Revolt of December 1962 can be seen as the embryonic stage, when the North Kalimantan National Army sought to annex Brunei as a separate communist state. The formation of Malaysia in 1963 was the catalyst for an increase in the Indonesian policy of swelling confrontation evidenced by an upsurge in traditional cross-border raids, limited sea and airborne incursions.

Leadership was critical to providing clarity in line with this broader political objective of protraction. General Sir Walter Walker had commanded at every level and more importantly had started his career during a counterinsurgency operation on the North-West Frontier, had fought during the Second World War as a battalion commander and in Malaya had trained the irregular and short-lived 'Ferret Force'. He had set up the Jungle Warfare School to train British units before commanding the 99th Gurkha Infantry Brigade and defeating those remaining communist insurgents, working closely with Field Marshal Sir Gerald Templer. The operational challenge facing Walker was complex.

Demanding geography meant that there were few navigable roads and aviation became the centre of gravity. As an example, between November 1964 and October 1965 in each month, 19,000 troops and 2 million pounds (907,000kg) of materiel were moved by air.[55] The threat consisted of an internal clandestine communist organisation (CCO) and an external threat comprising Indonesian trained guerrillas with regular army and marine units. This varied threat from both regular and irregular forces, controlled centrally by Indonesia, enabled freedom of action, deniability and did not risk open war in much the same manner as Commonwealth Forces practised a comprehensive approach to operations.

At the operational level General Walker issued a clear directive in December 1962 consisting of six measures of success: unified operations; timely and accurate information; speed, mobility and flexibility; base security; and domination of the jungle.[56] The final element was winning the hearts and minds of the people, a direct lift from Templer's tenets in Malaya. This principle became the cornerstone of the way Walker expected his forces to act at the tactical level. This involved British forces, in particular SAS units, embedding within local communities to share in their fear and danger. British forces worked tirelessly to improve the standard of life for the local population and provide health-care provision. In Walker's own words: 'winning the hearts and minds of the indigenous inhabitants is not just a question of direct aid. People must be given the will to help themselves and the necessary expertise to do so.'[57]

This COIN campaign was initially modelled on Walker's experience in Malaya (see above) through a hedge of reactive defences fronted by a series of forward patrol bases from which Commonwealth forces[58] could launch reactive or offensive action. At a tactical level, this strategy of defensive attrition was achieving some success; Christopher Tuck notes in his detailed study that by November 1963, of the twenty Indonesian raids, casualty rates of 5 : 1 were in favour of Commonwealth forces. A good example of such tactical success is provided from the 10th Gurkha Rifles archive. In December 1963 an initially successful attack by a force of 200 North Kalimantan National Army (TKNU) guerrillas and regular infantry against various outposts in Kalabakan were whittled down to barely 20 through skilled ambushing by Gurkhas.[59]

These tactical successes did not prevent Indonesian forces from continuing their incursions. That long jungle border and overall paucity of Commonwealth forces made safe extraction to Kalimantan simple. Walker provides a good overview of his thought process in *Fighting On* and as quoted by Gregorian:

> The sanctuary of camps just out of reach of the security forces was for us an insuperable problem and as long as the Indonesians retained this immunity, they could strike at will knowing that an escape route was assured. This led to the creation of top secret clandestine raids across the border into Indonesia, which regained the initiative from the Indonesians by making Indonesians themselves feel insecure everywhere.[60]

These operations enabled an offensive mindset at operational level ensuring that the tactical level could continue utilising those principles detailed within Walker's original directive.

Claret operations have to be viewed in the wider geo-strategic environment, meaning that authorisation has to be at Cabinet level.[61] It was envisaged that Claret would starve the CCO insurgency of external support and deter Indonesian forces from conducting cross-border raids. These were targeted and not intended to escalate the conflict into the international arena but, more importantly, Claret operations were initially authorised to a depth of 3,000yd (2,750m) into Kalimantan; this was later extended to 5,000yd (4,500m) and then 10,000yd (9,000m).

A deterrent effect would be achieved by a comprehensive fusion of intelligence from various sources to identify suitable ambush locations for attacking Indonesian forward bases and lines of communication. Detail of each operation was subjected to General Walker's 'Golden Rules' and authorised by him personally, as Gregorian confirms: 'Only trained and tested troops will be used; depth of penetration will be limited; no air support; every operation must be planned and rehearsed for two weeks; each operation will be planned and executed with the utmost security and secrecy and no soldier taking part can be captured by the enemy – alive or dead.'[62]

The Indonesian response to these raids was illuminating; information gleaned from signals intelligence suggested that local Indonesian commanders were not reporting the Claret operations within Indonesian but rather within Malaysian territory.[63] At the tactical level, knowledge of this false reporting further emboldened British and Commonwealth forces to continue operations safe in the knowledge that Sukarno would not therefore seek to escalate the

Confrontation. Conversely, it suggests that those operations are likely to have had limited impact on Indonesian strategic thinking as the very decision makers were unaware of realities on the ground.

By August 1964, the conflict was escalating. Britain and Malaysia continued to pursue a comprehensive approach with cross-government co-operation encouraging dissident movements within Indonesia together with the military campaign. In response, Indonesia kept building its military presence along the border while it was itself conducting clandestine activity to encourage instability along ethnological divides.

Indonesian Independence Day, 17 August 1964, marked an upsurge in activity with President Sukarno announcing the 'Year of Living Dangerously'[64] to coincide with amphibious landings in west Malaysia and an airborne assault two weeks later onto Labis. Although both elements were unmitigated military disasters, they demonstrated a shift in policy.[65] The British riposte was to prepare contingency strategies: Plans Mason and Addington, one for amphibious landings onto the Riau Islands and Sumatra and the other for the destruction of Indonesian Air Force capability.[66] The inherent threat of escalation was mitigated by an upsurge in the use of Claret operations and the extension of operational depth to 10,000yd (9,500m).

Tactically, these operations were achieving great success. Analysis of the war diaries of 2/10th Gurkha Rifles, in particular Operations Super Shell and High Hurdle, a simultaneous two-company attack against Indonesian supply bases and associated resupply routes, resulted in the Indonesians 'surrendering 10,000 yards [9,000m] of border jungle to the Gurkha patrols'.[67] Indonesian units charged with securing these base areas thereafter lost their offensive spirit as self-preservation tied them to base locations;[68] essentially the Gurkhas were out guerrilla-ing the guerrilla. The net operational effect of these was a marked drop in Indonesian cross-border attacks and a change in the mindset of Indonesian forces from offensive to defensive.

This symbiotic link between tactical success and policy outcome was not straightforward. Wider regional discontent between the Tunku and Lee Yun Kuan led to the secession of an independent Singapore in August 1965, dealing a further blow to British strategic interests in South-East Asia. This, coupled with the spiralling costs of confrontation, ensured that despite tactical and operational success, Britain was, by September 1965, seeking a resolution.[69] Fortuitously, on 30 September 1965, the Partai Komunis Indonesia (Indonesian Communist Party) launched a coup. This was quickly countered by General Suharto who eventually displaced Sukarno as nominal president. The purge that followed cost the lives of half a million Indonesian communists and inevitably caused the Indonesian military to switch focus toward internal affairs.

British policy makers were acutely aware of the careful balance needed to maintain regional stability, so reduced Claret operations in what came to be known as the 'be kind to the Indos' period.[70] This further demonstrates how the tactical, operational and strategic decision making were all intrinsically linked, with political considerations reverberating down to tactical level.

Claret operations were resumed following a large Indonesian incursion into Sarawak in November 1965 with a punitive series of sorties to a depth of 10,000yd (9,500m) that saw 'every rifleman in C Coy 1/2nd Gurkha Rifles spend at least half of his tour living in Kalimantan'.[71] Despite this clear tactical success, the Commander in Chief Far East commented in 1965: 'Our current military policy of containment has had some tactical success but has had no strategic effect in that it has not changed Indonesia's aims, nor ... her capability to sustain or even escalate the present level of confrontation'.[72]

This protracted Confrontation endured into March 1966, maintaining the use of Claret operations including a two-company ambush laid along Indonesian lines of communication by 1/10th Gurkhas resulting in thirty-seven Indonesian fatalities.[73] By late March, General Suharto (the second President of Indonesia who held office for thirty-one years) realised that the Indonesian expansionist aims were not achievable and began to realign the country away from China towards the West. The British strategy of protraction had been successful with tactical and operational victories providing space and time for a political outcome. The internecine struggle within Indonesia and ensuing purge of communists were undoubtedly important contributory factors. However, the careful strategic design of operational and tactical actions combined with the shifting political situation in Indonesia, a polity approach, provided the foundation for a successful counterinsurgency operation.

Connolly[74] analysed regimental archives from 2/2nd Gurkha Rifles during these Claret operations – one of the few complete sets of post-operational reports for this period – focusing particularly on August–December 1965, to draw lessons and provide a metric of success. He was able to identify four key lessons that contributed to the tactical success of British forces: planning and intelligence; marksmanship; timely and effective coordination of fire support; and leadership.

This complements Walker's post-operational report of 1969 which details six elements of success: specialist fighting skills; close air support; lightweight weapons for the infantry; secrecy; small groups giving effect to unified command; and political-military cooperation.[75] The effectiveness of Claret operations has been a point of contention in recent years between traditional and revisionist schools. Analysis of the 2/2nd Gurkhas' operational reports demonstrates that of 11 Claret operations, 8 achieved their mission of disrupting lines of communications, and 2 had chance encounters with Indonesian forces. If the casualty rate is examined those 11 operations resulted in 113 Indonesians killed in action for the loss of 1 Gurkha killed and 3 wounded.[76] The deniable nature of such operations ensured that commanders necessitated low casualty numbers, thus ambushing was the key tactical action.

It isn't ever that objective in the bush, of course. In East Africa how Masai tribesmen detect a predator's approach is very revealing. The stealthy killer is dead silent, but the tempo of birdsong rises; it's the chatter that gives the game away. The bush is, in a strictly modern sense, silent. There are no irritating and raucously intrusive man-made noises: no annoying electronic bleeps, no reversing vehicles, no mobile phones, no traffic hum. The sounds are strictly those of nature, but they have their own symphony, and the jungle soldier is as attuned as any conductor. His is the intrusion; to stay undetected he must blend in seamlessly, his progress measured, silent, always focused. A mistake, a second of casual carelessness, the flare of a match, will inform those other predators for this is a game where the hunter can very easily become the hunted. Rifle and machine-gun bolts edged back with great care, lines of fire identified and then waiting, and waiting, patience his most potent weapon.

It's easy to talk in objective terms but the costs of 'winning' are always high. Gurkha soldiers and officers know that only too well. On 20 April 1964, the late Major General Patrick Crawford, then a young captain, was serving as MO to 1/7th Gurkhas and flying in a helicopter alongside Major Eric ('Birdie') Smith DSO and a squad of Gurkha riflemen, intending to drop in on a company outpost north of the Indonesian Border. The chopper was about 100ft (25m) above the tiny helipad hacked out from the bush when the motor failed and the aircraft plummeted, landed tail-end first, thrashing the grass with its dying spasm, then rolling onto its side and toppling over and into a rocky defile.

The wrecked helicopter bounded downhill until it slammed into a hefty tree which smashed through into the cabin, trapping Major Smith by the arm and fracturing his hip. Crawford, miraculously, was unhurt, as were the soldiers. He took charge and got them out through the broken-off tail section. At any second the whole thing was likely to go up like a Roman candle. Crawford, however, climbed back through the fuselage to reach Smith, still trapped, hanging literally by his broken arm. For an hour Crawford supported him to take the weight; the pain would have been indescribable.

He had no medical kit, and the cabin was filling with noxious fumes and baking heat. Smith, against the odds, remained conscious. Crawford applied an improvised tourniquet and then performed an in situ amputation without anaesthetic, using a pocketknife borrowed from one of the riflemen; he had sharpened the blade to a razor before handing it across. He cauterised and dressed the stump, before improvising an ad hoc hoist to lift the casualty clear. At last, a stretcher party got through and Smith was casevaced on a relief chopper back to a base hospital at Simmanggang and Kuching where he underwent further operations. The patient survived and even continued his career in the Gurkhas, rising to command a battalion. Captain Crawford was awarded the George Medal.[77]

The Borneo Confrontation is an excellent example of a COIN operation where, following years of campaigning in Malaya, the British and Commonwealth forces were attuned to the vagaries and complexities of operating in a jungle environment among the people. On the other hand, the nature of the conflict meant adapting COIN principles from Malaya to develop an offensive spirit to counter regular forces acting in an irregular fashion.

Development of Claret enabled British forces to dominate the border areas of Kalimantan to a substantial depth to such a degree that one Indonesian commander wrote to the British: 'I will not disturb you. I've withdrawn back to this village. I'm carrying out no more offensive operations against you. Please leave me alone.'[78] The tactical success of these COIN operations established conditions for Malaysia to survive as a viable nation state, developing indigenous forces that would form the backbone of Malaysian security post-British withdrawal west of the Suez. Superior training, weaponry, intelligence and good leadership from the lowest tactical level ensured that when contact was made with Indonesian forces, the outcome routinely favoured British and Commonwealth troops.

Fort Bravo

On a very warm Mediterranean afternoon in September 2017, Captain Graham Trueman and I drove along the main road in eastern Cyprus which links the two cities of Larnaca and Famagusta – the latter the setting both for Shakespeare's *Othello* and an epic siege of the Venetian fortress by Ottoman armies in 1570. There is a fine hint of historical irony here because the journey involves far more than just bowling over the well-laid tarmac; it means crossing an armed frontier. I have not done that in Europe since the fall of the Berlin Wall and this one shows no sign of going away. It has been in place since 1974 but its origins go back to that long and very bitter siege, ending in wholesale massacre and atrocity, which pretty much set the tone for Greek/Turkish Cypriot relations since.

'Aphrodite's Island' has seen its fair share of conquerors, aside from the goddess of love herself: Phoenicians, Mycenaeans, Assyrians, Greco-Romans and the Ptolemies, Byzantines, Richard Coeur de Lion, then Lusignans/Knights Hospitaller, Genoese, Venetians, Turks, more British, more Turks and latterly Russian gangsters.

In July 1974, Turkey launched the well-named Operation Attila – the Hun would have approved. This was a dynamic response to a deteriorating situation on the island where the Turkish minority was being freshly oppressed by a Greek majority. Now, when in doubt blame the Brits and, to be fair, they did employ the old 'divide and rule' trick when they took over from the faltering Ottomans in 1878. After the Second World War, a groundswell of Greek Cypriot opinion wanted independence from the UK and union, *enosis*, with Greece. The British were not too keen: Cyprus was perceived as strategically vital in the Great Game of Cold War. It may even be that the UK helped Turkey in 1974, though this remains mere rumour.

What followed from 1955–60 was a very nasty asymmetric struggle with General Grivas and his *Eoka* partisans. This left hundreds dead on both sides and ended, inevitably, in a compromise which satisfied nobody. There was independence but no union; the political head, Archbishop Makarios III, presided over a new, generally moderate, state but the far right never went away and, in 1974, the ageing cleric was sent packing in a military coup which set alarm bells ringing in Ankara.

Britain still had boots on the ground. The original peace deal ceded two tracts of land in perpetuity to Britain: Western Sovereign Base Area, including what is now RAF Akrotiri and Episkopi, together with Eastern Sovereign Base Area, the Dhekelia Cantonment. Several generations of UK servicemen and women have served in Cyprus – as an overseas posting it could really be an awful lot worse.

Driving along the UN-policed Green Zone, just the silent observers in their rival watchtowers scanning each other across the narrow, dried-up defile, is an oddly eerie feeling. You can't get to Famagusta without crossing the border at the atmospherically named 'Black Knight' checkpoint, Cyprus' answer to Checkpoint Charlie. In the 1990s a couple of British gunners were wounded there in an exchange of fire.

Back up the dusty road and very easy to miss is what's left of Fort Bravo, just a forgotten sign by the verge, almost lost among the scrub and the remains of a platoon outpost. My friend and guide who had served on the island in the 1980s with UK forces got quite excited, as you would – the place still has a real feel to it, a forgotten slice of history that practically none of the modern army of British tourists would begin to understand. But this is Europe's last fighting frontier and anyone over 40 in Cyprus will remember the invasion. Sporadic talks about re-unification get lost among the chatter of cicadas and the watchtowers stay put.[79]

This is still history's unfinished business but the Gurkhas more than 'did their bit'. The original treaty document was signed in 1960 but tension between the two communities never went away. It kicked off in late 1963 then again, spectacularly, in 1974 when Archbishop Makarios was deposed by a paramilitary coup which next triggered attacks on Turkish enclaves by the Greek National Guard. Survivors barricaded themselves into Famagusta and Nicosia and held out until invasion forces broke the sieges.[80]

On 6 August 1974, 10 GR, deploying from the UK and including many soldiers who had served in both Malaya and Borneo, landed an advance detachment at Akrotiri, then moving on to Dhekalia. Over the following weekend, 600 men, 37 Land Rovers, 31 trailers, 2 water trailers with all supporting arms, kit and materiel were flown in.[81] A fragile truce had been brokered but this soon collapsed as Turkish forces moved on Famagusta. This induced panic among civilians who flooded in large numbers into the base area. While this, from a Gurkha perspective, wasn't war fighting as such, it was the dangerous end of peacekeeping in a small country with centuries of racial hatred finessed to boiling point. For Greek Cypriots a full-scale Turkish invasion was their absolute nightmare.

The distinctive slouch hat of the Gurkhas, Lieutenant Colonel John Cross believes, awakened memories of Gurkhas at Gallipoli and earned respect among the Turks. This may perhaps be a shade fanciful but what did impress was their cool efficiency and cheerful even-handedness. One of their more bizarre local challenges while controlling generally chaotic traffic was to make signals in both Greek and Turkish – no mean achievement. With Turkish units advancing on Famagusta the National Guard retreated, falling back into an enclave east of the base, labelled the 'Triangle'. Two companies of Gurkhas, A and C, were deployed to process the militia, disarm them, move them through the base area and then return their weapons to them. There were 800 of them crammed in 60-odd vehicles, nervy and trigger happy, not readily inclined to hand over their guns.[82]

Aside from these truculent partisans there were another 25,000 displaced refugees to be cared for, to be housed and fed, administered and calmed, a

Sisyphean task in itself; a tented city, Athna Forest, sprang up from scratch. The war had its moments of dark farce. The Greek militia, cocky at first, were totally outclassed by their Turkish enemy who could deploy armour and guns and were soon closing in on Famagusta – though not before a squadron of their tanks ran out of fuel just outside the base perimeter and had to draw on fuel supplied by 10th Gurkhas. While these were halted, random squads of Greeks swarmed up onto their hulls thinking this was their relief. Turkish officers quickly disabused them and they shifted off very rapidly. The fun wasn't over – next morning another armoured column appeared to have failed to see the boundary stones and had to be warned off by a British officer landing his helicopter directly in front.[83]

Another ramshackle ceasefire was cobbled up which provided time for the invaders to dig in. As they had cleared the Greeks from beneath the walls of Famagusta and the adjacent area this meant they were consolidating literally up to the perimeter. As Colonel Cross wryly observes, 'their map reading was not always correct' so the Gurkhas had to provide assistance by digging in the line of the boundary, just to add clarity.[84] This was needed: being on a roll, the Turks might have felt they could just gobble up the base. Gurkhas manned checkpoints, searched for weapons and didn't budge an inch. Any compromise would have been instantly perceived as weakness and exploited. The Turks might see the Gurkhas as peacekeepers, as cheerful and approachable (as ever), but still an elite group of soldiers, not the sort you push too hard or take liberties with.

As the air cooled, any immediate threat to the Sovereign Base Area began to recede and only 10th Gurkhas were left on deployment, effectively in charge of security. Tensions remained high of course; forty-five years on they are still palpable. Detached companies were sent out on outpost duty while the recce platoon carried out active patrolling and 'tracked goats and Turks, catching and eating the former while merely capturing the latter'.[85] The Turks still needed watching; there remained a possibility that they might yet decide to have a go at annexing the base territory.

Much of the work was hearts and minds; 10 GR proved very adept and the head of the International Peacekeeping Force, Indian Army General Prem Chand, was an ex-Gurkha and a lot of patience was required. Feelings were running very high, tension like electricity as the new frontiers were being drawn. Just when it seemed things were calming down it kicked off again at Ayios Nikolaos when the arrival of the acting president of the island clashed with the appearance of Turkish soldiers who had lifted some innocuous shepherds just across the boundary. A crowd of locals gathered to pelt the

Turks who responded by forming up and cocking rifles. Gurkha B Company also turned up and effectively pushed the two factions apart, interposing their calming yet authoritative presence. The politician was persuaded to clear off and all hostages were released.[86]

Next flashpoint was west at Akrotiri and Episkopi where Greek Cypriots vented their fury against the British and it fell to 1st Royal Scots to keep the lid on with just a platoon from B Company 10 GR in support. Even the normally tranquil heights of Mount Troodos Ski Centre came under attack and Gurkhas there on a mountain course found themselves in the front line. Hatred between Greek and Turk raged like a swirling cyclone and the British, in the middle, caught it from both sides as proxies.

The battalion's proposed leaving do was enlivened by fears of a Turkish attack, happily one that didn't materialise. By 27 February 1975 10 GR had said goodbye to Aphrodite's Island and were back in the cold drizzle of a wintry UK. It was a good job well done: 'If it had not been for the complete military competence, impartial steadfastness, untiring efforts and obvious fearlessness shown by 10 GR, the Turkish Army would most certainly have occupied the major Greek Cypriot City and post of Larnaca and might well have overrun the Eastern Sovereign Base Area ...'.[87] Any doubts the Foreign Office may have felt over the deployment of Gurkhas to Cyprus were clearly fatuous; they did a very fine job in extremely difficult circumstances. Since then, they have helped restore and keep the peace (however shaky) in Sierra Leone, East Timor, Bosnia and Kosovo (see below).

South Atlantic – *Los Barbaros Gurkhas*

Nobody really expected the Falklands War; even the Argentinean junta apparently only made the final decision to invade the day before. But once lost, the islands who many in Britain had only barely heard of had to be recovered. It is equally unlikely that anyone in the Brigade of Gurkhas had ever thought they would be serving in the South Atlantic, the most remote and, in some ways, most alien environment the hill-men from Nepal would encounter in their two centuries of service.

On 2 April 1982, in overwhelming force, Argentina invaded and seized the Falkland Islands or, as they optimistically named them 'Las Malvinas', not that Argentina had ever exercised sovereignty. The then uninhabited and inhospitable islands had been ceded to England by France as far back as the Treaty of Ryswick in 1697. The UN was impotent. If Britain wished to recover the Falklands it would have to be done by force using the biggest armada the UK had assembled since D-Day in 1944, travelling very much further away than the Calvados coast.

When Prime Minister Margaret Thatcher heard that General (later Field Marshal) Sir Edwin Bramall (who'd served alongside the Gurkhas in Borneo) proposed to send only a single Gurkha battalion, she was surprised: 'What Dwin, only one?' Prior to embarkation, the Gurkhas allowed media access to Church Crookham in Hampshire, to film them in training for the forthcoming campaign. Images of them zealously sharpening kukris and doing bayonet drill went, in the modern sense, 'viral'. After the Argentine defenders of Goose Green had surrendered, many had copies of their home-grown version of *Soldier* magazine which featured lurid claims about these Asiatic berserkers the British were about to unleash – who would apparently be high on drugs and taking heads rather than prisoners. So terrible was the Gurkha reputation, it had a serious effect on enemy morale and was said to have influenced their final capitulation at Port Stanley. That was before they had fired a shot or struck a blow.[88]

At the outset Gurkha participation in the task force didn't seem likely. There were fears that Kathmandu wouldn't be happy, but these proved groundless; both the king and his government were perfectly amenable to the idea. In consequence 1/7th would form part of ad hoc 5th Infantry Brigade serving alongside two Foot Guards Battalions; in fact, the Gurkhas led by Lieutenant Colonel David Morgan were far more ready, equipped with new weapons, Milan anti-tank launchers and latterly with captured Browning .50 cal. heavy machine guns. On 12 May, the brigade sailed south aboard the liner *Queen Elizabeth II*. Nobody thought this might be a luxury cruise.

Touching first on South Georgia, the men transferred to the P&O ferry *Norland* for their onward passage into South Carlos Water. It was rough and Gurkhas don't like the sea; this was very black water indeed and everybody was glad to get ashore, however inhospitable it might be. Probably not since their forebears had climbed to the roof of the world in Tibet had men from Nepal encountered such a bleak and forbidding place. At Goose Green they came too late for the fight which had cost the Paras sixty-seven casualties, including their commanding officer Lieutenant Colonel H. Jones who had won a posthumous VC. Rather oddly, it was the exhausted red berets who had deployed forward again while the Gurkhas were left to mop up and guard 500 dispirited POWs.

Tactically, their role was to secure and guard the area, the southerly part of East Falkland known as Lafonia: barren, dreary and largely featureless, it was not somewhere ever likely to appear on any holidaymaker's bucket list. It was thought that groups of enemy commandos, squad sized, were lurking and waiting to fire ground-to-air missiles at British helicopters. One of the first incidents nearly led to a blue on blue incident when a downed crew of army broadcasters was only just identified as friendly.[89] When an actual Argentinean unit was discovered, they threw up their hands at the sight of a single drawn kukri.[90]

By 3 June Fitzroy and Bluff Cove of evil repute had been taken so D Company of 1/7th would go ahead as a recce in force aboard a venerable coastal steamer, *Monsunen*, which would then bring up Battalion HQ and Support Company. This move was scheduled to take place in daylight hours, but Lieutenant Colonel Morgan opted, wisely, for caution, since enemy planes were still active, and delayed their passage until dark. Given the disaster which overtook the Welsh Guards on RFA *Sir Galahad* this was a sound precaution. The ancient vessel still wasn't really up to the job and most had finally to be transported by helicopter.

The final, hard-fought battles to secure the ring of hills surrounding Port Stanley and fought over on 13/14 June were about to begin. Royal Marine Commandos would assault Mount Harriet, 3 Para Mount Longdon, 2 Para Wireless Ridge, the Scots Guards would take Tumbledown, and Morgan's Gurkhas would storm Mount William. With these thrusts the ring around the capital would be punctured. If successful, the attacks would make Port Stanley untenable and effectively end the war. Needless to say, the defenders were equally aware of this.

Timings proved tricky; even in this modern era of conflict, the fog of war consistently billowed. A disrupted timescale for coordinated assaults – 'no plan ever survives contact with the enemy' – meant 1/7th was exposed in their forming-up positions and had four soldiers wounded by enemy artillery fire. When they finally, on 14 June, slogged forward, it was in broad daylight and under the gunners' noses. Para sappers were ahead gapping mines and the Gurkhas' Milans and .50 cals went into action. Still, another eight men were injured. Captain Keith Swinton, the Gurkhas' FOO, was hit squarely in the chest by a rifle round but miraculously survived. As they closed to contact the Argentineans began capitulating in increasing numbers. Fearful of their own propaganda and intent on keeping their heads, most preferred to surrender to the Scots. It was the Dargai Heights again.[91]

It appeared that 1/7th had gone through the entire campaign without any fatalities. By one of those dreadful ironies of war the only man lost died after hostilities had ceased, a lance corporal killed by an unexploded grenade, which he bashed inadvertently with a shovel during clearance operations at Goose Green.

Hong Kong

As mentioned before, Gurkhas are not distinguished solely by their courage and stamina in combat; they are also remarkably effective and even-handed as peacekeepers. Perhaps this is in part recognition of their fighting prowess and that they are best kept on-side, but they genuinely do have a flair for the patient discipline and diplomacy of what is effectively police work, a role which demands a rather different if complementary skill set.

Hong Kong, after India and Singapore, was one of the great gems in Britain's imperial diadem, a hugely wealthy and successful trading entrepôt, prised from the Chinese as the spoils of colonial aggrandisement. When the Chinese Civil War ended in a clear-cut victory for Mao Zedong, Hong Kong was more than just a historical anomaly; it was a tangible reminder of hated foreign domination and exploitation. The Gurkhas would come to know the place well, moving there from Malaysia in 1971[92] in time to share the last declining glow of Britain's imperial twilight.

Britain's major Defence Review, conducted in 1967, promised a gradual withdrawal from 'East of Suez'. This was a bitter pill for the Gurkhas whose overall numbers were to be significantly reduced, many of those who'd fought so well in Malaya and/or Brunei would find their services and their service redundant. By 1971 the brigade would be shrunk to a total of 6,000. By then Gurkhas had got used to Hong Kong as the first to arrive had been 26th Brigade in 1948 – following Indian Independence, based at Whitfield Barracks (Kowloon Park). Two years later, these were replaced by 51st Infantry Brigade, a rather more mixed bag of Gurkhas and Scots, who'd see action in Brunei. Next up was 48th Gurkha Infantry Brigade which arrived in 1957, latterly and two decades later re-badged as Gurkha Field Force, before yet another twenty years on reverting to their original title. During this period, the total numbers deployed were about 8,000 and Gurkhas saw action in April 1966 calming the so-called Star Ferry Riots (a carefully orchestrated set of protests, ostensibly triggered by increased fares).

Though the UK's overseas commitments might be shrinking, domestic troubles were escalating. The Troubles in Northern Ireland – Operation Banner, which was to splutter bloodily on for over a generation and soak up much of Britain's defence capacity – were just getting into their internecine and murderous stride. At the same time the ageing despot in China, having killed millions through reckless economic policies, now unleashed his Cultural Revolution, which was not revolutionary, merely a savage restatement of a pernicious authoritarianism.

All who might have strayed or were even daring to think about it were targeted. Even before this the colony had been a magnet for those desperately seeking escape. Though the Portuguese didn't hand back Macau until December 1999, they saw Hong Kong Island and Kowloon as a collective imperialist ulcer in the very innards of the People's Republic. Britain's lease wasn't due to expire until 1997. From late spring and early summer 1967, China tried to hasten the UK's departure, unleashing a carefully orchestrated plan for riot and civil unrest, topped with a string of border provocations. These were bolstered by a strong Chinese military presence and Gurkhas had to be deployed to bolster the outgunned civilian police. One of the nastiest and trickiest of these flashpoints was the Sha Tok incident in 1967, when several hundred carefully choreographed 'rioters', bolstered by communist militia, swarmed over the border and stormed a police station. They killed five officers and left another dozen injured. As a rapid response, Major General Ronald McAllister led 500 soldiers from 10 GR and, after a tense 10-hour siege, regained control without casualties on either side.

It got nasty: several members of the security services were injured and others killed. D Company of 1/7th Gurkhas had to be sent in to reinforce the police who were effectively under attack, just short of the border line. As ever, the hillmen from Nepal acquitted themselves with courage and, in the circumstances, forbearance, supporting the beleaguered police who suffered several fatalities but avoided sparking a full-scale battle which could easily have escalated into war.[93] Typically, during this fraught era of the Cultural Revolution, six Gurkha battalions comprising 1/2 GR, 2/2 GR, 6 THGR, 1/7 GR, 2/7 GR, 10 THGR, together with transport, signals and engineering battalions and a training depot at Shek Kong, were deployed. As a rule, four battalions would be in the Territories with one more in Brunei and another in the UK.

Steadily the screws were tightened, and tensions stiffened. The cross-border needling was incessant, always backed up by naked might. Infiltrators playing rebellious and disgruntled locals were sneaking through by the vanload and it was the job of 1/10th Gurkhas to interdict the flow. At the same time the tide of genuine refugees continued to surge. The old tyrant's death in 1976 merely stimulated the flow, by land and sea. Despite being convinced landlubbers, Gurkha engineers manufactured ad hoc craft to effectively patrol the inshore waters and round up a large number of fleeing hopefuls. Many craft loaded with Vietnamese boat people also attempted the crossing.

Throughout this difficult and dangerous time, the Gurkhas behaved with firmness, efficiency and also humanity, showing their levels of tolerance and forbearance. Those who fled in terror from *los Gurkhas* might have been surprised. When the Union Flag was finally lowered in 1997 it was with assurance and dignity; the British withdrew but were never ejected.

Nasty Little Wars of Peace

> They were kneeling in a small box shaped pit sunk into the stone floor, huddled together in fear, their arms and hands entwined in support. Normally the hold would have been used to store grain and covered with the wooden trapdoor that now lay upright on its hinges behind their backs. It would have been the ideal place to hide. Close the lid and the pit would be nearly invisible. There would have been just enough room for three people to lie beneath it. What gave them away? I wondered. A cough? A sob?
>
> Two of the women were in their twenties; the third was an old lady. Someone had shot her in the mouth and her shattered dentures cascaded with her own teeth down her front like mashed melon pips. One girl had been shot repeatedly in the chest. It was difficult to tell if the other had had her throat cut or been shot; a great gash of blood crescented her neck. The expression on their faces had survived the damage. It was so clear. A time valve that opened directly onto those last moments; so you saw what they saw; I hope beyond hope that I never see it again.[94]

This vivid and sombre description relates to the Balkan Wars of the 1990s. Gurkhas have form too in this fractious and violent region. In June 1999, as part of the NATO force intervening in Kosovo, they took part in the invasion: 'The biggest peacekeeping operation in history involving 30 countries and 50,000 troops gets under way in Kosovo today, led by British mine-clearance specialists who will be the first across the frontier, while paratroops and Gurkhas leapfrog ahead by helicopter to seize the first open ground beyond the border'.[95] Once established, the Gurkhas conducted a fraught mission to disarm Kosovo Liberation Army (KLA) fighters. This could have led to fighting but, as ever, the Gurkhas conducted their mission with firmness and fairness, very probably KLA activists knew who they were dealing with and chose the safe option.[96] In Bosnia itself Gurkhas were deployed during October 2019 as elements of a joint exercise, part of the European Force (EUFOR) annual exercise aimed at ensuring EUFOR's readiness for action and as a reminder to any who might seek to reactivate old hatreds.[97]

The author was able to interview Captain Krishna Pun QGE, EngTech MIsntRE, Ops Officer, 69 Gurkha Fd Sqn, 36 Engr Regt on 15 December 2020:

> My first operational tour, as a young sapper, came with Kosovo in 1999 where we engineers were deployed to counter a perceived threat created by soviet mines. Though the threat was less widespread than feared a lieutenant and NCO died in UXB incident, a terrible reminder of how dangerous the work can be. The war had just ended, and the capital Pristina was like a ghost town, nobody around, in a military vehicle you drove along deserted roads and streets. Gradually, as security was restored, the place began to fill up and volumes of traffic returned to the roads. I have to say I found the locals generally friendly even though my Battlegroup was involved in security measures including dousing fires in buildings targeted for arson on ethnic lines. The coffee people provided was always extraordinarily strong!

Again in 1999, old enmities re-surfaced in East Timor. This had been seized and annexed by Indonesia in 1975 but voted in August 1999 to seek independence. This decision was unpopular with their former masters who deployed squads of gangsters to terrorise the populations. Gurkhas, 300 of them, flying to Darwin from Brunei, formed the nucleus of the UK's commitment to the peacekeeping mission International Force for East Timor (INTERFET) and deployed alongside Australian soldiers already in theatre.[98]

A year later in July 2000 during Operation Kukri, Indian Army Gurkhas (5/8 Gorkha Rifles) formed a key element in a UN Assistance Mission to Sierra Leone (UNAMSIL) being besieged for a period by strong forces belonging to the Revolutionary United Front (RUF). Their eventual success was a huge boost to the mission overall and grateful citizens erected the Kukri Memorial by the banks of the Moa River. Four years later, during November 2004, Gurkhas, 120 in all, took part in a fraught evacuation of civilian refuges from Ivory Coast. With two RAF Hercules and a C17 Globemaster, a shuttle lasting 50 hours delivered 300 people to safety. Gurkhas secured the route from Abidjan to the airport and maintained a defensive cordon and did so while avoiding any civilian or military casualties.[99]

Gurkha units were involved in both Gulf Wars against Saddam Hussein's regime in Iraq. During the first clash in 1991 (Operation Granby), members of the (then) Queen's Own Gurkha Transport Regiment (now the Queen's Own Gurkha Logistic Regiment) were deployed. This mission was to eject Iraqi forces from Kuwait which they'd invaded, terrorised and pillaged. A dozen years on, in 2003, they were back to bring Saddam's bloody and oppressive rule to an end:

> The British involvement was codenamed Operation *Telic*. Brigade of Gurkhas involvement in the initial Op *Telic* deployment included the 69 Gurkha Field Squadron of the Queens Gurkha Engineers, 248 Gurkha Signal Squadron of the Queen's Gurkha Signals and 8 Transport Squadron of the Queen's Own Gurkha Logistic Regiment, as well as D (Gurkha Reinforcement) Company of the Royal Irish Regiment.[100]

Krishna Pun was one of those deployed for Telic 1, Second Gulf War in 2003 as a combat engineer driving an AVRE and followed the armoured thrust into Basra:

> As engineers we saw our first relatively small columns of Iraqi POWs and were soon constructing internment camps for the flood of thousands which followed. Whilst on Telic 4 in 2004, I experienced the full drama of being on the receiving end of mortar fire – men were under canvas and one tent, a few down from my section's was hit, causing casualties. As a result, we sappers had to shift to a more solid building where we were confined for five days with no facilities while the threat level remained high; days were long and hard, the heat stifling!

Peace can be as nasty as war and, as evidenced by their experiences in Cyprus and Hong Kong, Gurkhas make good peacekeepers. Sapper Ishwor Gurung was deployed during 2017 on Operation Trenton in South Sudan, a member of the UK's commitment to a UN mission. He recounts:

> It was challenging to leave civilian life behind and become a soldier. It was even harder to become a Gurkha. Eventually after completing the Combat Engineers course and the Bricklayer and Concreter course I was posted to 36 Engineer Regiment, home of the Queen's Gurkha Engineers.
>
> I am currently deployed to an operation in Malakal, South Sudan as a part of Op TRENTON 3 attached to 32 Engineer Regiment. South Sudan is the youngest country in the world, gaining independence from Sudan in 2011. Since then, disagreements between the president and Vice President have led to a new civil war.

Thousands have been killed and millions have been internally displaced or have fled the country. There are around 30,000 internally displaced personnel (IDP) in the Malakal Protection of Civilians (POC) site. The UK Engineering Task Force has been deployed to support UNMISS in its mission to protect civilians. We are now over halfway through the operation.[101]

This author has been privileged to speak to a number of officers serving with the Gurkhas, including a telephone interview with Major Mike Gledhill Royal Engineers (RE) – Officer Commanding 69 Gurkha Field Squadron the Queen's Gurkha Engineers (QGE), on 14 December 2020, one who has served in South Sudan:

I'm a Royal Engineer, was appointed to lead 69 Gurkha Field Squadron in July 2019 for a two-year term. I'd not thought particularly of being a Gurkha officer and indeed am and will remain a Royal Engineer! I've now served with the Brigade of Gurkhas for over a year, nearly a year and a half in fact and have served with them on deployment in South Sudan. I've been mightily impressed with the Brigade – Gurkhas are of course selected after a rigorous process and remain with their unit for most if not the whole of their service which they enter on a full career rather than a sort or medium time basis.

Throughout my time with Gurkhas, I've continually been aware of their high levels of skill and professionalism, competence and capability, self-discipline, task orientation and ability just to get on with the job. Moreover, I find I've been drawn to their family and cultural ethos, the importance and conviviality of family and mess nights.

Operation Kabrit – the NATO mission to deter Russian pressure on the Baltic States also involves Gurkhas. Corporal Vijavsingh Gurung deployed as part of 60 Squadron Queen's Own Gurkha Logistic Regiment: 'After a month of pre-deployment training 19 personnel from 60 Squadron deployed on *Kabrit* 4 "B" on 8 July 2019 to provide logistical support to the King's Royal Hussars who were in Estonia to provide Enhanced Forward Presence as part of the NATO deterrence deployment'.[102] Since the Russian invasion, or 'Special Military Operation', launched against Ukraine in February 2022, the strategic position has undergone a seismic shift and the Baltic States are now a new front line.

Chapter 11

On Infidel Hill

> Start off nice; if you start off nasty, you've got nowhere else to go.
>
> Military wisdom

> Barking dogs do not bite.
>
> Phastu proverb

The eve of war is universal, unchanged since Homer's time. Roughly 3,250 years after the siege of Troy, 2 RGR were getting ready to deploy to Afghanistan. Captain Sam Meadows would be one of those deploying and his eve of battle was particularly affecting:

> 1st April 2009: On the eve of the deployment, we went into the temple in Sir John Moore Barracks to undertake a 'purja' or blessing from the regimental pundit. This lasted about 45 minutes, but you could see in the boys' faces that this meant a great deal more than a British Officer could understand. Despite much of the service being conducted in Sanskrit the boys seemed engrossed and this is when I saw the mood change from the smiles in camp to the serious, determined look of a soldier on his way to a war zone.[1]

This time the enemy was the Talib(an). The word means 'student or seeker after truth', and Taliban members are the product of an Islamic religious school, or *madrasah*, of which some 40,000 exist in Pakistan. Their roots lie in the anti-imperialist Deobandi schools founded after 1867. The Deobandi (named after that particular town) were conservative, anti-Raj and anti-Shi'a Muslims. Islam as previously practised in Afghanistan was more tolerant. Other faiths such as Buddhism have now been suppressed and monuments defaced.[2]

Map 13. Helmand Province ISAF 101.

Afghanistan is familiar territory to the Gurkhas; they have got form there and the rules of war in such a harsh land remain as brutal as ever, although now UK audiences are perhaps too squeamish for the more graphic realities.

On 17 October 2011 the *Daily Mail* posted a feature referring to an incident in Helmand in the vicinity of Babaji where a rifleman from 1 RGR had beheaded a Taliban he'd killed. This might prove too rich for the folks back home so the incident was nicely disposed of as having been due to an erroneous belief that enemy heads were needed for DNA identification.[3] War, especially in Afghanistan, is up close, personal and immeasurably savage. The Gurkhas, however, left no man behind, as a Gurkha officer caught in an ambush describes:

> When a squad of troops was ambushed out in the open in Afghanistan in 2008, one soldier, Yubraj Rai, was hit and fatally wounded. But Captain Gajendera Angdembe and Riflemen Dhan Gurung and Manju Gurung carried Rai across 325 feet of open ground under heavy fire. At one point, one of the soldiers resorted to using both his own rifle and Rai's rifle at the same time to return fire on the enemy.[4]

Into Afghanistan

British intervention in Afghanistan as part of a United States-led coalition was prompted by the 9/11 terrorist attacks on the World Trade Centre in New York, by members of Islamist militant group al-Qaeda. The United States accused the Taliban, the dominant faction in strife-torn Afghanistan, of sheltering the prime suspect, Osama Bin Laden, and instigated hostilities. Britain deployed ground forces in November 2001. The opening stages of the campaign were characterised by massive aerial bombardment of Taliban and al-Qaeda targets, while Special Forces were inserted to fight alongside the Afghan Northern Alliance, already resisting the Taliban. Kabul was the first city captured by the Northern Alliance, on 13 November.

Kandahar, their spiritual home and final redoubt, was taken from the Taliban on 7 December. The then British prime minister, Tony Blair, hailed it as a victory, calling it a 'total vindication of the strategy we have worked out from the beginning.'[5] This may have owed more to spin and wishful thinking than realities on the ground. Meanwhile, Afghan groups agreed a deal for an interim power-sharing government, and Hamid Karzai, a former spokesman for the mujahedeen, was sworn in as its leader.

The UK (Operation Fingal) became a part of NATO-led operations – the International Security Assistance Force (ISAF) – in 2002. The first contingent of foreign peacekeepers comprised personnel from eighteen different countries.

This force's mandate extended only to helping the Afghans maintain security in Kabul and surrounding areas; it was not a primarily military function. By April 2002, UK forces were concentrated in Kabul, with 1,700 troops working alongside other coalition units.

After the initial successful intervention phase, Coalition, and particularly American attention shifted toward the hunt for Bin Laden and then the invasion of Iraq. By 2003, the Taliban had used this breathing space and regrouped. While the world was largely focused on events in Iraq, Taliban fighters began to infiltrate across the porous border from Pakistan into southern Afghanistan. The group recruited new members in the Pashtun heartlands and small training camps sprouted along the mountainous border. This resurgence was supported by various tribal groups and gained momentum after ISAF air strikes led to civilian deaths.

'Stay Low, Move Fast'

In 2015 the Directorate of Land Warfare produced an analysis of the British experience this time around in Afghanistan:

> Land forces must be careful in acknowledging what Operation HERRICK was not – where context at TTPs [techniques, tactics and procedures] have no or limited utility. Though a demanding COIN operation, Operation HERRICK presented no air threat, limited logistic risk, no threat to air lines of communication, no deep air battle, and an opponent, regardless of his agility and adaptability, offered no combat arms threat enabled by sophisticated capabilities. From a dynamic early stage where land forcers struggled to blend MCO ('Main Communications Office') drills with stabilisation, land force TTPs became bespoke to the specifics of the geography, the threat and the discretionary nature of any of the operations. TTPs exploited dominance in ISR [intelligence, surveillance, reconnaissance] and fires were enabled by a network of well found infrastructure.[6]

The attacks that came to be known as 9/11 on 11 September 2001 killed 2,977 people from many countries, including 67 Britons. This atrocity, perpetrated by al-Qaeda, was the product of several years of planning and was in part co-ordinated from Taliban-held areas of Afghanistan where al-Qaeda had established itself. If the United States and its allies wanted to wreak vengeance on Osama Bin Laden, they were left with little choice but to invade Afghanistan, supported by a UN Resolution which called for the handover of the al-Qaeda leader. Their declared grand tactical objectives were to destroy training camps and replace the Taliban regime that was supporting terrorism. The invasion was considered legitimate by the international community as al-Qaeda had directly attacked the United States.[7]

Within days of 9/11 advance reconnaissance teams from CIA Special Operations Group (SOG) were in theatre, essentially intelligence gathering and distributing bribes. They were followed by teams of Green Berets, Special Advisers to prepare Northern Alliance warlords to take the fight to the Taliban; these were joined for reconnaissance and target acquisition by SAS/SBS who had far greater experience of such operations. At the time of 9/11 the UK was conducting Exercise Swift-Sword off and inside Oman – deploying 22,000 personnel, 6.500 vehicles, 20 warships and close air support; the United States already possessed a substantial forward base in Uzbekistan. The West had to respond swiftly once the initial ultimatum to the Taliban, demanding they give up Osama Bin Laden, expired. Ground operations thus began on 7 October – essential so as to gain as much ground as possible before the onset of winter.

The Taliban (*c.* 50,000 strong plus several hundred al-Qaeda fighters) and the Northern Alliance (*c.* 15,000 strong) had been fighting sporadic conventional warfare with massed forces on the ground, fortress complexes and extended trench lines; the early phase of the war was thus an industrial battle for which the Taliban was neither ready nor equipped.[8] As the Taliban was attempting to fight a conventional war, they were massively outgunned and quickly routed; airburst munitions and strategic bombing by American B-52 bombers resulted in the destruction of fixed defences, supply depots and command and communications networks. Special Forces were directing and leading the campaign, doing 'hearts and minds', looking at target acquisition; overall the Taliban put up a poor showing.

The United States' response was Operation Enduring Freedom, which began on 7 October 2001 with American and British aerial bombing of Taliban positions and known terrorist training camps. This weakened the Taliban, who were then, seemingly, defeated by the Northern Alliance. The American military subsequently took control of much of the country and began the process of establishing a democratically elected government, starting with the Bonn Agreement in December 2001. Crucially though, the Taliban had not been completely defeated and as a result the insurgency that Afghanistan is facing today took hold and began to undermine the democratically elected government that had been installed.

The Coalition mission to Afghanistan was channelled through the medium of the NATO-led International Security Assistance Force (ISAF). This was led at one point by General Sir David Richards, Chief of Defence Staff, latterly Lord Richards. From 2003, UK troop resources in Afghanistan were about 300, mainly involved in training NCOs of the Afghan National Army (ANA).

At the same time ISAF was putting together hearts and minds programmes led by individual Provincial Reconstruction Teams (PRT). Late in 2003, ISAF took over from the United States in the north of the country while the American effort switched to the south; the UK role in the north was eventually handed to Norway and Sweden, while the UK prepared to accept the responsibility of Helmand as a PRT exercise. The comment by Dr John Reid's (then the Labour government's defence minister) that, in their three-year rotation, it was unlikely the British would fire a single shot in anger was unfortunate and naive.[9]

The British military presence was calculated at 5,700 to begin with, reducing to 4,500 joined by contingents from Canada, Estonia, Holland and Denmark. Helmand Province is essentially dominated by a central valley corridor running the length of the Helmand River, with the provincial/political capital Lashkar Gah at the southern end, then the crucial river and road intersection at Gereshk, more the economic hub, with Sangin in the north. The British Camp Bastion, with forward operating bases Price and Robinson, formed the major British concentration.

Initially, UK troops were deployed to assist in stabilising the capital Kabul and its environs (Operation Fingal). This was twinned with a counterterrorist/insurgency push (Operation Jacana).[10] By 2004 the focus had shifted towards the delivery of the PRT centred in Mazar-e-Sharif in the north. However, strategic priority had shifted after 19 March 2003 towards Iraq (Operation Telic). This was unfortunate: it is a key axiom of war that you don't try to fight on two fronts at once, as both Bonaparte and Hitler could have testified. The Coalition chose to do so, erroneously believing the situation in Afghanistan to be fully under control. It wasn't. Their underestimation of the resilience of Afghan fighters was a blunder, a lesson they could and should have learned from the Russians (who, needless to say, found this highly gratifying).

By 2006 the UK's attention had moved into Helmand Province turning 'the UK's commitment to Afghanistan from a "military operation" into a "war"'.[11] Taliban resistance to the Government of the Islamic Republic of Afghanistan (GIRoA) led to British forces being deployed, with their focus being on prosecuting a counterinsurgency campaign in the six key districts within the province, namely Lashkar Gah, Gereshk, Sangin, Musa Qaleh, Now Zad and Garmsir.

Helmand is the largest of thirty-four separate provinces in Afghanistan, covering 20,000 square miles (58,584 square km), home to nearly 880,000 people and watered through its dusty length by the river of the same name. The region is subdivided into a baker's dozen districts and the provincial centre is the town of Lashkar Gah.[12]

Settled since the Bronze Age, the place has seen its fair share of conquerors, though its main fame prior to British intervention in 2006 was as probably the world's largest single producer of raw opium (Myanmar comes second), contributing about 42 per cent of the world's crop.[13] In the 1960s Helmand was given a makeover, or the beginnings of one, with a substantial United States-led aid programme which created a development agency, the Helmand and Arghandab Valley Authority. Lashkar Gah got a 'little America' look with new tree-lined boulevards, an irrigation programme with new canal networks and a large hydro-electric dam. Soviet infiltration after 1978 brought this good work to a dead halt.[14]

The campaign was to prove a bruising and challenging experience for British forces, as the 2015 study points out:

> The challenge of understanding what kind of war the British military was now in became the priority, set against a backdrop of depictions of small groups of soldiers from the 3 Para Battlegroup fighting off an increasingly determined and capable adversary; a dysfunctional command structure; a campaign plan kicked way off course and casualties at a level which increasingly disturbed both political and public opinion.[15]

Gurkhas were naturally among those British units deployed early on: 'naturally' because this was just the type of warfare they were trained for and, after all, their ancestors had fought over the same ground in two previous Afghan wars. Corporal (latterly Warrant Officer and then Captain) Kailash Limbu was pretty soon up at the sharp end, and it was very sharp indeed: 'The Taliban fighter crawled silently across the alleyway almost within reach of the Gurkha position. Even in the darkness of the early hours, Limbu's night vision goggles showed clearly that the man silently crawling like a leopard was armed with an AK47 assault rifle'. His first reaction was pure anger: 'My strongest memory is when I saw that leopard crawl in the alleyway, seeing someone is within 10m and trying to kill you,' he recalled. The Gurkhas were there to aid the people not to oppress them and this flagrant challenge heated the young Nepalese warrior's blood.[16]

Limbu opened fire, clearly hitting the Taliban who was dragged clear by his comrades. Such actions were typical of the early days in Helmand during 2006, fighting reminiscent of Kipling and the Thin Red Line. Now Zad became a regular Alamo as the Gurkhas fought hard to maintain their toehold in the beleaguered police compound. Kailash Limbu is one of the first Gurkhas to actually write up his experiences; generally what is published about Gurkhas is written about them rather than by them.

> No sooner had the sound of the heli started to fade than I heard machine gun fire. Aayo! We were being engaged but where from? First you hear the TAK TAK TAK of the rounds as they fly past, then the TUM TUM TUM of the report. 'Contact wait out!' I screamed into the PRR: if you hear the rounds in the air before you hear the sound of them being fired, you can be fairly certain they're being fired at you.[17]

One major difference was that these Afghans weren't using flintlock jezails but modern automatic weapons, meaning a lot more lethality in the air. Peacekeeping had turned into war making and a desperate bid for survival. They say you never hear the one that gets you, but Limbu heard plenty more, lit by fireflies of hot tracer.

Attack after attack burst against the defences, men finding they stood ankle deep in spent rounds. Massively outnumbered, the Gurkhas were so few they couldn't patrol the streets or move over to the offensive. Limbu remembers in interviews for the *Telegraph*: 'We were totally fixed. We wanted to go out, to clear and fight, we were so frustrated; all the time, day and night, they attacked.'[18]

All civilians fled; only the enemy stayed, like ghosts among deserted alleys and compounds. Taliban fighters were highly motivated and well equipped. They thought they could win. They and their fathers had been at war for a generation and had seen off the Soviets whose numbers dwarfed those of the British. They had plenty of heavy weapons and deployed their mortars effectively; such men command respect: 'They were very good fighters, and they were brave men, but I didn't have any regrets about trying to shoot them because they were first trying to kill us.' Limbu won a Mention in Dispatches (MID) for exposing himself to heavy fire and twice firing shoulder-launched missiles into a school building harbouring a score of insurgents. To deaden the deafening blast of the weapon, he stuffed an empty bullet casing in each ear.[19]

They weren't alone in the defence of the compound, joined by a contingent of Afghan National Police who, not being local, were generally trustworthy. The actual local coppers were far less dependable: one was caught red-handed feeding coordinates to the Taliban via his mobile phone. The instinct was to shoot him on the spot but all that could be done was to impound the phone.[20] As related by the *Telegraph*:

> WO2 Limbu, who is now 33 [in 2015] and regimental quartermaster sergeant with 2nd Battalion Royal Gurkha Rifles in Folkestone, describes himself as a 'simple hill boy' who did not see a car until he was fifteen. The exploits of his grandfather and uncle who were also Gurkhas left him with a desire to join up from as early as he can remember. He said: 'When I was growing up, my grandfather used to say, "If you want to become a man, you have to join the British Army."' In Nepal the Brigade of Gurkhas still retains a high level of prestige. When Kailash Limbu applied to join only 230 out of 32,000 recruits were taken on that year.[21]

In 2009 the Coalition forces' uplift saw the United States taking responsibility for the majority of Helmand Province including Garmsir. One who served in Helmand was Captain Chandra Pun, 2IC D (Kandahar) Company. They were stationed at Forward Operating Base (FOB) Delhi and responsible for two checkpoints: JTAC HILL and BALACLAVA. These were sited at either end of a gravel track running west–east. The road formed a border between the 'protected' community to the north and a no-man's-land lying south and east. At that time they could engage anyone within their arcs under Rules of Engagement No. 429A. This meant they could engage the identified enemy while the men in the air were on 'Card A' which permitted them to fire only in self-defence. This was because these areas were only used by the enemy, either to attack their positions or for smuggling arms and explosives into the sheltered zone.

Pun recalls the difficulties of their assignment:

> It was a dangerous time with little respite from fighting – we even took over the check points from the Coldstream Guards under small arms fire contact [It was 1RGR who took over from the Coldstreamers in the south on Herrick 12, April–November 2010, the Guardsmen were deployed on Herrick 11]. There was

a high threat of accurate Small Arms Fire (SAF), Indirect Fire (IDF) attack (107mm), RPG and a very low threat of Improvised Explosive Devices (IED) during that period.[22]

At that point they were not focusing on Counter Insurgency (COIN) operations; mainly on holding their ground and fighting Taliban. Nonetheless, they did support the locals by constructing a water pump and distributing warm clothes. Looking at the overall pie chart across the whole Area of Operation (AO), Garmsir was the most contacted AO within Helmand province during Herrick 7 with up to forty-seven contacts sparking daily, with a mixture of SAF and IDF being fired at their positions.[23]

An article in the *Telegraph* (14 March 2017) goes on to describe the living conditions: 'Daily life was quite basic; we operated with very limited welfare facilities and without fresh rations however we used to have messing every 2 days. Although we were only one Coy Group operating in Garmsir, we managed to establish three further new Check Points to the south and east before we conducted our TOA [transfer of authority].' They deployed in WMIKs (modified Land Rovers with special Weapons Mount Installation Kits) with Pinzgaurs (high-mobility 4WD vehicles built by BAE in the UK) acting as ambulance vehicles.[24] These were open vehicles devoid of any armour and with a 7.62mm or .50 calibre machine gun mounted up top.[25] Survival was dependent on good soldiering rather than heavy protection.

Pun continues: 'A number of times IDF and RPG landed inside the FOB, which was only 150 x150 m. We were very lucky that no one was injured as on one occasion 3 x 107-mm rockets landed inside.' Finally, they completed their six-month tour with only three men seriously injured. This could and would have been far, far worse had it not been for the outstanding skills and endurance of their riflemen. 'During *Herrick 7* I had the honour of serving with Harry Saheb (Prince Harry), when he was appointed as FAC (Forward Air Controller) to control air assets for us. We looked after him very well, and we taught him how to eat curry by using his hands.'[26]

Captain Pun was later sent some photos of the bazaar in Garmsir. Now, the old gravel track was properly black-topped, and the bazaar was crowded (there were solar-powered streetlights there too), full of people in an area where they had previously patrolled with weapons locked and loaded. Pun was heartened that his men's sacrifice and efforts at creating a secure environment had clearly had a significant effect.[27]

Soviet intermeddling in Afghanistan had lasted for a decade, from 1979–89, and had ended in defeat: Russia's Vietnam, one that ushered in the final collapse of the old communist hegemony in Eastern Europe. In all over 600,000 Russians were committed during the course of the struggle and 15,000 failed to return. The campaign achieved nothing.[28] The Western Coalition assumed it could do better and history has yet to record a final verdict, yet, increasingly all that the UK public saw of the fruits of British involvement was the sad procession of flag-draped hearses passing through silent crowds in Royal Wootton Bassett, each a poignant reminder of the real cost of war.

'Stay Low, Move Slow'

The 2015 report attempts to define the tactical objectives:

> The tactical mission on deployment to Helmand and Kandahar Provinces reflected the strategic assessment and objectives which underpinned the decision to deploy south to 'conduct security and stabilisation operations within Helmand and the wider Regional Command (SW) jointly with Afghan institutions, other government departments and multi-national partners in order to support Government of Afghanistan and development objectives'.[29]

The UK deployment was proceeded by the United States-led Operation Mountain Thrust aimed at attacking al-Qaeda and Taliban bases in the south. This stirred the hornet's nest and fostered a Taliban resurgence in Helmand, where the British found themselves in a full-scale shooting war for which they were under-equipped.

Since 1945 preparation for UK military campaigns had been predicated on the basis of a major conventional threat requiring large conventional forces and a viable nuclear deterrent. The situation in Afghanistan found the British therefore under-equipped for an asymmetric war. Vehicles particularly Snatch Landrovers, designed for police operations in Northern Ireland, were ineffective and dangerous to the occupants. A new breed of armoured personnel carriers was to be spawned by the war, specialist transport like the six-wheel-drive Mastiff which can take two crew members and eight soldiers, attain speeds of 90kph and traverse particularly rugged terrain. It is heavily armoured against IEDs with one 7.62mm GPMG (General Purpose Machine Gun) and a 12.7mm heavy machine gun or 40mm grenade launcher. The Land Warfare Directorate report stresses the logistical achievement:

> Operation *Herrick* is a story of the successful delivery of extensive quantities of equipment delivered under UOR [urgent operational requirement] procedures with clear evidence that this saved lives and enhanced operational effectiveness; with a total UOR outlay of £5–6 billion (with an annual average spend of £800 million) some have argued that the core equipment programme failed, that predictions of equipment requirements were wrong, that sufficient depth of capability had not been preserved and that it took time to realise that existing capabilities were not good enough ...[30]

Asymmetric warfare is a wholly different proposition where reliance falls upon 'boots on the ground' rather than high-tech solutions on a conventional battlefield. Consider the situation in Vietnam where the United States required thirty support personnel behind every 'grunt' in the field; the North Vietnamese and Viet Cong by contrast required only one support personnel for every two in the field, an efficiency ratio of 60 : 1 in their favour. Such efficiencies go a long way toward offsetting a technical superiority and the same is true of the Taliban. Gurkhas are in part a remedy for this. Yes, they have a full conventional requirement but are far more adaptable to difficult conditions. It was often noted during Herrick operations that Gurkhas, returning from lengthy periods on patrol, were at times in better shape than their comrades. They had an ability to live off the land, rather than relying on composite rations (though 'Tommy' in general has always demonstrated genius for creative foraging).

In any UK troop rotation, the mix comprises infantry, logistics, artillery, engineers, signals and medics, say a ratio of five in support to one in the line. Allowing for rest, rotation and so on there are probably no more than 400–500 boots on the ground in the front line (wheresoever that may lie). Helmand is twice the size of Wales in area. As a comparison, at the height of the Troubles in Northern Ireland the UK deployed 47,000 troops in the province, and more now remain there than were at any single point serving in Helmand.

The prime difficulty lies not in taking ground – the army can always defeat the Taliban in battle – but in holding it, having the resources to hold on to what has been won (known as 'mowing the lawn'). In numerous instances the British have taken ground only to withdraw once the fight is over allowing the Taliban to re-infiltrate. The switch towards a mix of guerrilla and insurgency tactics enabled Taliban fighters to maximise use of IEDs or roadside bombs. New vehicles provide better protection for crews, but an IED is cheap and potentially devastating. Every UK vehicle, such as the Panther,[31] retails at £280,000, heavier vehicles, Mastiffs, Wolfhounds and Huskies, a great deal more – the Taliban use a cheap motorbike with a captive child strapped to the front.

Aside from the main forward bases the British occupied a series of local strongpoints in towns and villages, usually ex-police or government compounds, strong mud-walled mini-forts. These, like bees to honey, drew Taliban attention. Perhaps the most notorious was the Red House in Sangin ('Sangingrad'). Here for the whole of July 2006 the Paras, in platoon strength and virtually cut off, fought a Rorke's Drift-type fight against huge numbers of enemy who besieged the post for five weeks of near continuous combat. This was a British victory but cost ten dead (six from the Paras and four Marines). Hundreds of Taliban died.[32]

Captain Sam Meadows of 2 RGR deployed 'in-country' in spring 2009 (Operation Herrick 12):

> 6 April 2009: An early start today, getting up at 05.00 to catch a Chinook CH47 from Camp Bastion to Lashkar Gar at 06.30. When the flight took off sweeping low across the desert I was surprised to see sprouts of greenery from the desert and numerous small streams running across it, this was also being capitalised by numerous nomadic groups of which one in particular struck me, with a large herd of camels, a scene unchanged for hundreds if not thousands of years in this part of the world.[33]

In terms of tactics the Taliban will engage defenders at long range with 12.7mm machine guns and heavy mortars. Fighters infiltrate through the canals and ditches to within small-arms range for LMGs and RPGs (Light Machine Guns and Rocket-Propelled Grenades), then move closer to launch an assault with automatic rifles and grenades. The defenders respond with .50 calibre machine guns, then mortars and 7.62mm GPMG. A cheap supply of .50 calibre ammunition, defective and clearly untested, caused severe difficulties for the defenders at Red House.[34] Sam Meadows tells us that:

> 1RGR Battlegroup deployed to the Nar-e-Saraj AO in Helmand province in a ground holding role. As I entered PB3, I was stunned to find that all the soldiers were living in tents. Clearly there was no IDF threat. As A (Delhi) Company 2IC, I took over the Ops room (from where all operations were controlled) from the Coldstream Guards. As the Company started to conduct Ground Defence Area (GDA) patrols, we realised there was a high threat

of SAF, IEDs and suicide bombers. Our ground patrols focused on Biometric Enrolment and ex-spray link analysis [hidden data connections], hearts and minds, and Counter Insurgency (COIN). The ISAF mentoring team started to teach weapon training, medical skills, basic map reading and use of radios to the Afghan National Army and Police.

We encouraged them to conduct Vehicle Check-Points, foot patrols and compound searches. Wherever possible we conducted joint planning and preparation prior to conducting joint patrols and operations with the ANSF [Afghan National Security Forces]. We started to encourage them to share our ops room, in contrast to HERRICK 7 where ops rooms would have been completely out of bounds to the ANSF. On patrols we encouraged them to take a lead, or at least put an Afghan face on Operations. For example, whilst they were conducting compound searches ISAF would be providing flank protection for them. Compared to HERRICK 7 it was different in terms of Rules of Engagement (ROE). Card A for self defence was used throughout the tour due to increased risk of civilian casualties. The IED threat was extremely high and therefore vallons [proprietary detectors] were used on every occasion.

After the first three months of the tour there was a 'green on blue incident' [where Afghan National Army recruits turn on their supposed mentors], which occurred in PB 3 and resulted in 3 x Killed in Action (OC -Maj Bowman, Pl Comd- Lt Turkington and Sect comd- Cpl Arjun Purja) and 4 x Wounded in Action. Immediately after this incident we moved further south west to establish new check points which helped to push bad memories of PB3 out of our minds. Meanwhile, one of the Coys from 1 Lancs took over PB 3.

Initially, we found it was quite hard to establish new check points in RAHIM KALAY (it was an area known as an insurgent stronghold) and check points were constantly hit by Under-slung Grenade Launchers ('UGL'), RPGs, SAF and grenade attacks. However, we managed to establish a number of positions in forward locations in order to dominate the ground. Despite the various threats, the ground call signs regularly patrolled in and around the village to protect the community. Gurkhas were known as 'Black Rats' in HERRICK 12 because we never stopped or moved backwards during contacts, but instead kept pushing towards Insurgents' firing points. This made it difficult for the enemy to withdraw or hide their weapons inside the compounds. Village Elders and Local Nationals of RAHIM KALAY village praised our hard work prior to our departure from their village. All typified by the term 'courageous restraint'.[35]

In Country

It's glorious to die for your country but more glorious to make someone else die for his.

General George S. Patton

Meadows, like T.E. Lawrence before him, started as an archaeologist before making the transition to soldier:

[Back to] 6th April 2009: As I sit in bed at 22.30 I have finished preparing my kit and equipment for my first operational patrol in Afghanistan which starts tomorrow morning and I have feelings both of trepidation and great excitement for what lies ahead both tomorrow when I will be acting as a rifleman and in nine days time when I will be in command of my men with little or no guidance which, in itself, is a slightly daunting thought.

8th April 2009: Another day of familiarisation patrols today into Kartolagen Chirmitiri and Mukhtar districts of Lashkar Gar – these areas are narrow urban spaces with a maze of roads and junctions that do not relate very well to the map! As the district centre becomes more peaceful, new people are building in the open areas. The patrol was led by Sergeant Hemanta Limbu and was controlled very well from the start. Similarly, the relationship he had developed with the ANP [Afghan National Police] was excellent and he used his grasp of Urdu to facilitate this. We visited various ANP CPs where the local people looked generally happy to see us and morale seemed good.

Interestingly, a socio-political problem is currently playing out in Lashkar Gar at the central police CP [command post] in the bazaar area of the city. A group known as the Shah Korez militia who 'belong' to the governor or Musa Qala have been staying in the city causing various minor theft and extortion problems. Today, the leader of this militia's brother had been taxed by the ANP at an illegal VCP [vehicle checkpoint] so he sent in the militia and for whatever reason a firefight broke out that resulted in five of the militia being injured and their leader arrested: Comment, the ANP training programme paying off here – no casualties but despite the ISAF presence tribal culture still obtains – feudal and dominated by narcotics smugglers and warlords who control the future.[36]

This was very much learning on the job, a role his great-great grandfather would easily have understood from the days of the North-West Frontier:

10th April 2009: A routine patrol today revealed some good intelligence from the first check point visited. The chief of police, Colonel Sherzad, a man of questionable allegiances who is rumoured to have significant interests in poppy production was involved in a firefight with Taliban at Bolan CP which left 5 ANP dead and a number injured. However, the interest lies in the fact that the Colonel omitted to disclose his presence in the report, suggesting he might have had an ulterior motive, perhaps concerning narcotics. Finally, at another police CP we came across two vehicles involved in a previous IED incident that had holes from ball bearings which had pierced the car and continued out of the other side showing the force of the explosion.[37]

Meanwhile there was an uneasy truce as the Taliban had condescended not to attack ISAF during the all-important poppy harvest; this was purely on economic grounds and hostilities would instantly be resumed once the indispensable crop was safely gathered in. In the stillness of the night, the quiet of the dark has been the soldier's constant companion since Trojans watched Greek campfires burning beyond their walls:

12th April 2009: It is now about 00.30 and I've noticed how quiet it is in the location, there is no traffic at night, just a few crickets and the occasional vocal Afghan fighting dog, so quiet that the strong desert breeze can be heard whistling around the compound and the Afghan national flag ripples with the prevailing wind. The almost full moon casts an incredible amount of light, enhanced by night vision goggles – the night is our friend and the enemy's foe.[38]

Afghanistan is crowded with its own history, a saga of conquests, of rise and fall, rugged crests and sweeping valleys, high desert and fertile alluvial plains, ospreys swirling in the eddying currents. Old mud-brick forts seek to dominate timeless settlements, crowd hilltops and look over the teeming maze of compounds. But this is the enemy's country, and he really knows no other. He is at home here and his fathers fought the Russians over the same ground and ultimately beat them. The Gurkhas' only casualty during this phase was a severe injury caused by 'blue on blue' – one soldier inadvertently shot another at close range with a 9mm pistol, one of those daft accidents that so dent morale.[39]

Operation Pishet Sataal took place from 23–25 April 2009, as Meadows details:

> We were tasked to escort the Shar Karez Militia, a group of essentially bandits and mercenaries to a desert laager south of Musa Quala. This militia had been formed with President Karzai's permission by Mullah Salamand, loyal to Mohammed Nabi, a small man with a fantastic beard and gentle manner who had been a senior mujahedeen commander against the Russians.

The militia was being deployed to protect the provincial governor, an ex-Taliban with a big price on his head.[40] The journey covered 62 miles (100km) of tarmac and 125 miles (200km) more over desert terrain. Meadows had to check out over a hundred culverts for IEDs.

As soon at the convoy got as far as Gereshk the Afghan mercenaries began pillaging as the vehicles moved off tarmac onto sand; one broke down and had to be secured by a defensive cordon, wagon-laager style. No enemy fighters were seen but everyone knew they were watching. 'That night in the desert was amazing, the stars more clear than I'd ever seen and the threat from the enemy made it all very exciting.' On the way back, as they passed a jumble of local traffic: 'one man aged 25–35 stared me down and at that moment, I knew he was the enemy. I was staring into his eyes and there was nothing I could do …'.[41]

* * *

Day one of Operation Zarfar, 27 April 2009: this was a joint ANA, ANP and ISAF bid to clear an area along the west bank of the Helmand River, north-west of Lashkar Gar. Needless to add, it came as no surprise to the Taliban whose well-tended antennae had already detected the drift. Just to show they had got the message they had sown IEDs along the approaches. Meadows was in the second vehicle riding behind the ANP, and everyone was nervous. Rightly so, as the enemy had left an RPG round jammed into the surface, a real 'no entry' sign. Crude but effective and it had to be detonated, like a very loud doorbell.

Soon they were taking fire from a dug-in enemy some 1,300yd (1,200m) off. Their vehicle top-cover let loose with a GPMG, the shocking racket deafening the occupants, brass cartridges sprinkling like martial confetti. Afghan National Army (ANA) forces moved through to contact, calling down fire from 105mm howitzers and a deluge of 500–2,000lb bombs from ISAF planes overhead. As an officer Meadows found himself everybody's favourite target, rounds pinging from the armour and kicking up spouts of dust: 'the whizzing sounds of bullets whistling past your ear, especially from a sniper is an extremely frightening experience for any man'.[42]

The firefight raged. It was now clear where the shooting was coming from so the enemy was pounded by heavy and light machine guns, mortars dropping a nice cocktail of smoke and high explosive. The ground was cleared, and the advance resumed. As the column paused for a mess break there was 'a large explosion with a great plume of black smoke rising'. It turned out an RPG had sliced past a Snatch Land Rover, just missing the vehicle but causing one serious casualty – an Afghan soldier who had sustained shrapnel wounds to his chest, arms and head and was then an urgent casevac case.[43]

The Taliban were not done. Less than 300ft (100m) away another huge bang resounded, and it was raining fragments of Scimitar CVR(T) (Combat Vehicle Reconnaissance (Tracked)), the fighting vehicle having hit either a mine or an IED; a chunk of track thumped perilously close to a Gurkha rifleman. Another ANA trooper hadn't been as lucky. American Black Hawk helicopters swooped in to airlift the injured to base hospitals. As the enemy withdrew, the Gurkhas dug in, hunkering down in a captured compound.

There was no firing, so the men stripped off body armour and helmets to take a breather. Too soon: the Taliban was back, infiltrating along ditches and by low walls, ground the members knew intimately. Back on went the kit. Meadows recalled: 'I saw some of them [Gurkhas] were laughing and smiling which I found incredible.' The contact blazed for another two hours, the banging rattle of smalls arms and HMGs (Heavy Machine Guns) punctuated by the crash of artillery rounds and the fountain bursts of bombs.[44]

This was in many ways an old-fashioned war of outposts, lazy and seemingly calm, yet one mistake could cost you dear. Meadows witnessed just how: '28th April: At around midday Rifleman Prakash, armed with the L96 Sniper Rifle saw one man run across open ground with an I-Com radio in his hand, roughly 300 metres to his front. He engaged the enemy commander with a single shot, dropping him where he stood.'[45] Later that afternoon, the enemy struck back wounding an ANA soldier: 'he had received a bullet through his right testicle through his inner right thigh and out of his right buttock. He was understandably shaken and in a lot of pain as he had also received small injuries to his penis. Corporal Riley of the RAMC went into action ...' Within 15 minutes the casualty had been stabilised – new medication, Hemcon,[46] was applied to help blood coagulate and the wounded man was soon on board a Black Hawk.[47]

A couple of days later Meadows took a patrol of Gurkhas into Basharan village where he met one of the elders, 'a regal looking man with an aura of wisdom about him'. Locals had been warned off by the Taliban and Meadows saw some of the damage caused by ISAF forces during the preceding contact. This was far less major than he'd expected given the weight of ordnance that had been flying, but 'one particular room had been hit with a fragment of 105 mm artillery round which had come down through the roof and landed on a child's cot', happily not occupied at the time, the inhabitants having fled.[48]

In Afghanistan there is no real 'downtime'; there's no front line and so safe harbour. Even a trip down to a supposedly safe waterway for a relaxing bathe could be rudely interrupted by sniper fire, 'the characteristic crack and thump ... Gurkhas scrambling for helmets and body armour'.[49] This is 'war amongst the people' (see Chapter 12): the Taliban aren't a state in any recognisable form and exists as an element, though a major one, in a shifting kaleidoscope of new and old alliances, where profit can determine politics, where ancient clan feuds easily trump any party affiliation. The maze of Afghan politics shifts like the tide, as convoluted as the maze of avenues through jumbled compounds.

* * *

A Gurkha officer is never off duty; he has to be constantly ready regardless of fatigue, loneliness or horror to make snap decisions and accept responsibility, all emotion held at bay. On 7 May 2009, as Meadows recalls: 'At around 20.50 hours I received at TACSAT message from the OC; Silicon 15 was in contact with a suicide IED[50] and we sustained two kilo india alpha [killed in action], Corporal Kumar and Sergeant Ross of the RMP. The heart in his voice was audible and you could feel it was news he never wanted to deliver ...' This sudden nature of random death is something the soldier on such missions faces every day. 'The boys took it hard and the silence which followed the statement made me feel very alone and the burden of command weighed heavily on my shoulders.'[51]

> 11th May 2009: Fear is a strange thing. Last evening, I was handed a warning order to deploy to Gereshk as a two multiple move the following day to support the ANSF. That day another suicide bomber had targeted Gereshk in a very sophisticated attack. It started with a contact to a central CP that diverted attention away from a single suicide bomber, dressed in ANP uniform, who calmly walked into the ANP CP and detonated himself. The second responders arrived at the scene as reinforcements and were engaged by a second suicide bomber. So, you can imagine when we were tasked to move to Gereshk there was a certain amount of anticipation and a healthy fear of what lay ahead.[52]

Happily, the move itself passed without incident and the Gurkhas established liaison with Afghan forces then threw out a security cordon as precursor to a sweep of the bazaar area. In the circumstances this was pretty nerve shredding; 'genuine fear on the men's faces'. Sam Meadows just hoped his own didn't show. Danish forces with their array of AFVs were also taking part. Feelings among the Gurkhas following the loss of one of their own, and heightened tensions after this most recent attack, were a real test of discipline: 'a testament to the Gurkha spirit'.[53]

This form of asymmetric warfare dictates that there's never a fixed frontier and when ISAF moves its efforts into one sector the enemy withdraws, targeting quite often the very ground the British have just moved from. So, it was as the Gurkhas were putting some stick about in Gereshk, the Taliban switched their own efforts back to Lashkar Gar, launching raids against ANSF posts and blitzing a few. During mid-May of that year Silicon 11 took part in another clearance mission to de-louse an area between the Bolan Bridge and north towards an earlier abandoned checkpoint. Again, it was to be led by Afghan forces with Gurkhas following on one tactical bound behind.[54]

It was as rapid as blitzkrieg, at the start at least, as Meadows recorded: 'just a couple of bursts of fire – the main obstacles were numbers of pressure pad IEDs. Mostly, these contained homemade explosives in yellow plastic containers each of say 15–20 kg'. The first one was placed at a canal crossing, well dug into the middle of the track with a fuse line hidden in vehicle ruts.

Locals had been warned off from using the bridge. Ingeniously, the pressure pad, about 50cm across, had been fashioned from a small saw blade of the sort regularly doled out by NGOs to local farmers and connected with a twin flex wire insulated inside a motorcycle inner tube and plastic bag. The battery pack was set up a short distance off to allow the device to be armed whenever it was needed. 'The ANP were incredibly brave and stupid at the same time but they actually did seem to know what they were doing ...'.[55]

On 21 May 2009 it was Meadows' birthday:

> Certainly, the most surreal birthday that I've ever had today. Silicon 13 conducted a relief in place with Silicon 14. On the route out we stopped at Yellow 14 to pick up the goat we'd bought previously and much to my surprise I received my first real piece of Afghan honesty and trust, the honour system that I'd heard existed, finally came to the fore and the commander of the CP, an elderly Afghan who had shaved off his regal beard clearly trusted and treated me as a real friend. The goat was brought in the back of a Snatch [Land Rover] to the CP where I undertook the proud task of decapitating it with my kukri.[56]

The ISAF role was focused on hearts and minds and keeping ahead of the Taliban's creeping influence. On 3 June, Silicon 13 conducted a patrol around the southern edge of Basharan village. Meadows describes the situation: 'On the route out, I stopped the vehicle patrol to talk to a local elder and gave him permission to grow maize as he'd previously been refused such permission – as there's clearly a greater risk of enemy force's infiltration. However, a trade-off had to be made to pacify the locals and there is no money to compensate them, so a deal was struck ...' The consideration was tactical information. The ritual of tea with locals and welcome confirmation by them that ISAF forces were making a difference was a morale booster: 'that's when I finally realised that we are starting to actually achieve things in this area – which is great'.[57] Just afterwards Meadows had a radio conversation with the officer leading a Welsh Guards detachment – almost straightaway, the same officer lost both legs on patrol from an IED blast and died (this was Major Sean Birchall – Coy commander of No IX Coy Welsh Guards).

Two weeks or so later, on 20 June 2009, Meadows recalled:

> At around 02.00 and American Apache Attack Helicopter Callsign engaged 3 x EF laying an IED on route 66 roughly 7 km east

of Lashkar Gar and successfully killed them all. Following this a number of other enemy were seen were seen in a compound 200 metres north. The Apache engaged the compound and killed another 4 enemy. An American Special Forces Callsign was then helicoptered in and exploited the bodies before having a small firefight and extracting again by helicopter. Silicon 13 was tasked at short notice to deploy to the area as the Special Forces stated there were still some IED materials in one of the compounds. Silicon 13 deployed onto the ground at around 08.00 with 45 police in 5 Ranger trucks. When we arrived at the scene I sent the police to search the surrounding compounds and area for any further intelligence while I provided force protection with my heavy weapons. The police returned having found a human foot, a smashed Icom radio and a few other items. I went to have a look at the scene of the Apache strike to be greeted with a scene of destruction, although the bodies had gone, there was blood everywhere together with scraps of bone and flesh from more than one individual …[58]

'What goes in must come out' – the old maxim applies in war. The Taliban is made up of keen students and meticulous observers; they noted all troop movements and waited for columns to attempt a return journey:

They had attempted to contact us with IEDs and possibly a complex ambush. In the end, the first contact occurred about halfway in an area very rarely transited by ISAF if at all. The characteristic bang on an RPG being fired followed by the rapid radio message 'RPG' before impact. The shot was from a compound approximately 700 metres away and an excellent aim, narrowly missing the vehicle and crashing into the canal bank before small arms fire began to open up, 3 x Enemy Forces were seen and engaged, LMG, GPMG and HMG. I was manning the HMG and watched the fall of shot start to hit the tree-line where the insurgents had gone to ground … after roughly 5 minutes, the contact finished and throughout, the convoy continued to keep moving: roughly 2 km north of this location, the enemy had set up a fairly complex ambush.

They had placed three Coke cans in the ground to give a metal reading on the vulnerable point. They must have known there are TTPs [tactics, techniques and procedures] which would mean we'd stop to confirm it was an IED. That allowed the RPG shooter to shift position from where he'd engaged the convoy. His next RPG exploded above the vehicle in front of me. However Rfn Prakash saw the RPG gunner running away with the RPG on his shoulder and dropped him as he tried to escape, adding another confirmed kill to his already impressive tally. There was a chorus of small arms and responses from our MGs seeking out the enemy; despite some radio intercepts we'd insufficient detail to call down an airstrike.[59]

This type of action, nerve shredding and potentially attritional, certainly echoes the previous experience of Russians, as depicted in the impressive film *9 Company*.[60]

Infidel Hill

Typically, a tour of duty lasts six months. Silicon 13 was next tasked to participate in a major brigade operation: Operation 'Panchai Palang' – Panther's Claw. Their role would be during the 'isolate' phase and the principal area of operations would lie north-east of Lashkar Gar and Gereshk on the south bank of the Helmand River. Here, higher ground rears up above the water opening out onto a wide desert plateau, cut with ravines which give access to crossing points used by both peaceable locals and the Taliban. The river line creates a strategic artery and key connection and has done so for centuries, the bluffs dominated by a series of ancient mud-brick forts which could have come straight from the pages of Kipling or Omar Khayyam. Meadows, as an archaeologist, was struck by the historical resonances:

> During the 'isolate' phase of the operation, the strategists of 19 Brigade had come to the same conclusion as the previous strategists of a bye-gone era of empire. Silicon 13 had been tasked with occupying an incredible old fort situated in a very commanding position, (over 150 metres in height, overlooking the river and now labelled by the insurgents as 'Infidel Hill'). Nothing has changed except modern night-sights which turn night into day, so the darkness is no longer EF's [enemy force's] friend but his foe.[61]

The Taliban did still try to mount a night attack and dislodge ISAF forces from the eminence, but this failed to mature. The Gurkhas were heavily dug in with well-constructed *sangars* and C Squadron of the Light Dragoons in support.[62] The operation kept going, as recorded by Meadows:

> The position we've occupied on top of the fort is extremely strong ... the view from the sangar is incredible and actually very beautiful with the crystal clear waters of the Helmand River and a contrast between the lush green zone to the north and barren desert to the south. The cliffs, however, abound in bird life. One particular bird is dark grey in colour with a distinct white band on the back of the wings and is quite striking.[63]

On 4 July 2009, Silicon 13 joined in the battle of Panther's Claw. The Gurkhas found themselves serving alongside Danes and the combined force dealt with fifty-odd IEDs along its axis of advance, clearly suggesting the Taliban had been well aware of their deployment.

Both Callsigns, Silicon 13 and 14, dismounted to carry out a foot patrol on the rim of the fertile green zone. The ground was tricky and the threat of more IEDs loomed. Silicon 14 led with Danish soldiers, supported by Silicon 13 and more Danes. Moving along a narrow track, the Gurkhas crossed over a dank canal; marking their line of intended advance, a line of compounds straggled away to the right; enemy presumed to be towards the east, friendlies in the west. Once in position the British and Danish OCs conferred while Meadows, accompanied by Corporal Hughes pressed forward humping a GPMG, intending to secure their exposed flank and establish an observation post. A radio crackled, advising contact was imminent, and 5 minutes later, as though on cue, the Taliban obliged with rolling small-arms fire kicking dust and shredding vegetation.

'Boss, I've been hit,' the Corporal gasped.

'Where?'

'In the stomach from the right ...'

'Medic, medic, medic; man down ...'[64]

Within seconds the medic was there with a rifleman to provide cover. They couldn't discern where the enemy fire was coming from but brassed up the tree-line and a handy-looking ditch about a hundred metres in front, the GPMG banging away. Now the whole unit took up the refrain, a deluge of fire. Horribly, this was 'blue on blue' – Gurkhas were shooting at Danes. Mercifully there were no more casualties, and the wounded man was casevaced within 5 minutes and quarter of an hour later was on his way to Camp Bastion. Happily, he survived his wound.[65]

Mongoose 53

By March 2011 the Gurkhas had entered a new phase of the same war. Sam Meadows was back in action:

> The Callsign was conducting a ground domination patrol in the vicinity of Shin Kalay – a follow-up patrol on an IED attack directed the previous day against a vehicle convoy. The patrol formed a cordon and a 'rummage' search area of several compounds. At approximately 16.45 hours, a vehicle with 4 x fighting age males in civvies – a white Toyota Corolla – was observed coming at speed towards the cordon. We tried to stop the vehicle at 80–100 metres using hand signals, with a warning shot at 50–60 metres. When this failed, shots were fired, and it was stopped. Our corporal went forward to investigate and found one man wounded and three uninjured. First aid was administered to the casualty including attempts made to apply a chest seal, but a main artery had been severed and the casualty died very quickly.

As it turned out these had not been Taliban but members of a new government-led, ISAF-supported scheme which aimed to encourage, Malaya style, local Home Guard militias, defined as:

> A UK-US sponsored local law enforcement agency, defence force and militia in Afghanistan as part of the Ministry of Interior Affairs. Formed primarily as a local defence force against Taliban insurgents its members have no power of arrest and are only authorised to investigate crime if requested to do so by the Afghan National Police (ANP). It was established at the request of ISAF in Summer 2010 and is paid for by the United States.

These were new recruits. Why they attempted to rush the cordon is unclear but the one who died had been the son of a prominent tribal elder: the fog of war creates waves.[66]

As Kipling or G.A. Henty might have said, echoing Colonel Worthington, quoted above,[67] the Gurkha Officer, NCO and Soldier, while every inch the modern soldier, is still a breed apart. Furthermore, much of the combat in Afghanistan experienced by Gurkhas during this recent conflict is tellingly reminiscent of their ancestors' experiences in the Second and Third Afghan

Wars. Sergeant Dipprasad Pun from 1 RGR, grandson of a VC recipient, certainly maintained the family tradition in 2010 (Herrick 12) when he fought off a platoon-sized group of insurgents, as described in a BBC news feature:

> A Gurkha who single-handedly fought off an attack by at least a dozen Taliban insurgents has been awarded Britain's second highest medal for bravery: Acting Sergeant Dipprasad Pun used up all of his ammunition and resorted to using his machine gun tripod to repel the attack in Afghanistan in September. The Gurkha, 31, of Ashford, Kent, said he was a 'lucky guy' and very proud to get the Conspicuous Gallantry Cross.
>
> Acting Sgt Pun was on sentry duty at a checkpoint near Babaji, in Afghanistan's Helmand province, on 17th September last year when he spotted insurgents trying to plant a bomb beside the front gate. Moments later, militants opened fire on the compound from all sides. For more than a quarter of an hour, alone on the roof, Acting Sgt Pun fought off an onslaught from rocket-propelled grenades and AK-47s.
>
> In total, he fired more than 400 rounds, launched 17 grenades and detonated a mine. At one point, when an insurgent tried to climb up to his position, his rifle failed and he resorted to throwing his machine gun tripod to knock him down. Acting Sgt Pun, who is originally from the Nepalese village of Bima, believed at the time that there were more than thirty attackers; local villagers later told him the figure was more likely to have been twelve to fifteen.
>
> Recalling the incident, he said: 'As soon as it was confirmed [they were] Taliban, I was really scared, but as soon as I opened fire that was gone – [I thought] "Before they kill me I have to kill some." I thought they were going to kill me after a couple of minutes, definitely.' The citation on his medal – which is only one level below the Victoria Cross – states that he saved the lives of three comrades who were inside the checkpoint at the time. 'I think I am a very lucky guy, a survivor,' he added. 'Now I am getting this award, it is very great and I am very happy.'[68]

Operation Tora Gorga (Herrick 14, April/May 2011) was carried out by soldiers from 2 RGR's B Company along with members of the Afghan National Army (ANA) and Police. Major Jamie Murray and Lieutenant Richard Roberts take up the story:

They searched a series of compounds near the village of Shin Kalay in Nad 'Ali district which had been identified as insurgent 'bed-downs' and used by insurgents to launch ambushes from. The operation began with the ISAF and Afghan forces first searching people on a nearby bridge used as a key crossing point by locals, before moving on to the compounds. Major Jamie Murray, Officer Commanding B Company, said: What we're hoping to do is send a strong message to the Taliban that their presence in this area will not be tolerated. They bring nothing for the people of Nad Ali. We're here to protect the people here and tell them too that if the Taliban were to come, we'd come and support them. The Gurkhas provided the security as the Afghan forces approached and searched the compounds.

Lieutenant Richard Roberts, a platoon commander with B Company, said: They've [the Afghan security forces] got the cultural awareness and they show they have the type of counter-insurgency tactics to keep the local population as on side as possible. Not long ago it would have been ISAF troops searching the compounds while the Afghans stayed outside: during this operation the Afghans insisted on taking the lead.

Lieutenant Mohammad Khalis Sakhidzada, an ANA commander, said: There are a lot of benefits in searching the compounds. If there are any enemy there, when we come and search, it will frighten them, and they'll leave. Lieutenant Roberts added: The main success of this operation was disrupting any insurgent activity there may have been there. We had Afghan National Police as well as Afghan National Army with us who know the local faces so if there had been any insurgents, we'd have been there to detain them.[69]

Out of Afghanistan

A few years ago, in the midst of the Afghan War, the National Army Museum mounted a superb special exhibition which grimly recreated a dusty street in a typical Afghan township. All the visitors had to do was to get from one end to the other without killing themselves when an unseen IED went up in your face: not for real obviously, but nonetheless a very salutary experience.

Outfought and unable to take on the British in the open, the Taliban fell back on the use of IEDs: cheap, easy and utterly deadly. A street becomes a killing ground and any stretch of road an invitation. An IED is generally defined as a form of bomb constructed and deployed in ways other than in conventional military action. Happily, for the Taliban, the plethora of Russian gear left behind in their rout provided an ample supply and IEDs became the weapon of choice. They won't ever win a war but can add up to a telling and nerve-shredding attrition. Such ungentlemanly devices aren't new: the 1940 *Dad's Army Manual* is full of them. Sam Meadows would see many of them:

> The most significant threat ... was the IED. The insurgents were extremely agile, mobile and adaptive in their tactics. The asymmetric nature of the campaign led to the insurgents adopting the IED as their weapon of choice. During Operation *Herrick 9* the IED was responsible for 63% of all casualties, a 39% increase compared to Operation *Herrick 8*.[70]

After thirteen years, eight of them involving bloody fighting in Helmand, Britain's latest war in Afghanistan finally came to an end. In a ceremony at the main British base at Camp Bastion on 27 October 2014, the Union Flag was lowered, and the camp was handed over to the Afghans, who will be left behind to look after their own security in what has been one of the hardest provinces to tame.

Krishna Pun was deployed there first on Herrick 7, primarily in the northern sector of Helmand province, and his section was attached as infantry support often away from the squadron base area: 'This was a wide ranging and fast-moving tour as the incipient threat from IED's was just beginning to emerge and hadn't reached its full terrible potency and he felt this was an exhilarating, fully kinetic tour'.[71]

It was vastly different on Herrick 11 where the sappers were deployed in search times to seek out and neutralise IEDs which by now had proliferated and had become the enemy's main weapon of choice. This time at least Krishna got to see more of the southern region of Helmand and Lashkar Gar:

> The engineers were distributed around the sector in 7-man teams. It was a stressful and difficult job though initially and thankfully serious casualties were avoided. Four teams from my regiment, a total of 28 soldiers who had trained and worked together, forming a close-knit group. During a two-week break period one of my

close friends died as a result of an IED blast, followed soon after by another fatality'.

Inevitably such losses take a toll on morale and the survivors had to rebuild their focus before they went out again. It was hard but the men rose to the challenge, conquering their natural fears and continued with the remainder of their tour without further tragedy.[72]

The Gurkhas weren't done with Afghanistan: their versatility, toughness, ability to live off the land and overall combat effectiveness pretty much guaranteed they would be back. Major Richard Streatfeild (of the Rifles) served at Sangin for six months in 2009. He and his men experienced over 800 contacts, had 10 men killed and 50 injured, as he describes:

> 1RGR personnel were deployed in various locations under different units' command. D (Kandahar) Company deployed to Nad-e-Ali AO in PB Wahid under 1 Mercian command within an Afghan Transition Enabling Company (ATEC) role. We took over from 1 Royal Welsh. PB Wahid is located on the southern side of the Nahr-e-Bughra [NEB] canal [a major feature] which runs east to west. Our AO is huge and most of the area is covered by villages which are dominated by ALP and AUP with the NEB canal protected by ISAF and the ANA: our mission is to support advisory teams, sustain the ANSF in the area and protect the Canal Zone to our south.
>
> We were mainly involved in providing support to advisor teams in terms of manpower, vehicles and taxi-services. Advisory teams are responsible for mentoring the AUP, ALP and ANA in their check-points. This is known as the transition phase and involved responsibility of AOs being handed over to the ANSF at a rapid rate. Every week we conduct joint planning for joint operations by holding security shuras (local operations groups), which will allow us to create joint ISAF/ANSF patrol matrices.
>
> Compared to previous HERRICKs our framework patrols are significantly reduced and our remit for conducting patrols are limited. Therefore, our patrols had to be partnered, or else limited to short range GDA [Ground Defence Area] patrols for force protection purposes. Although we are in an ATEC role we conducted a number of Ops with the ANSF into the Dashte – where the SAF and IED threat was extremely high. On a

number of occasions, we supported the ANA and AUP directly and indirectly. The IED and SAF threat was extremely high throughout the tour; however, there was limited threat of IDF. More sophisticated ISTAR assets are introduced in HERRICK 17 which really help us to observe IED seeding teams during both day and night. However, due to the more restrictive rules of engagement of this tour we found it difficult to engage them. This was really frustrating and created a lot of anger in the ops room.

My experiences throughout my three HERRICK tours have been different, though ultimately the goal has always been the same. It is satisfying that during HERRICK 17 – which is likely to be my final tour, that the ANSF is taking up the reins and are now responsible for security. It demonstrates that the sacrifices and hard work have not been for nothing and that a real difference has been made. Ultimately, the question of whether we have been successful in our mission in Afghanistan will not be answered for many years.

It will be the continued development of a strong Government of the Islamic Republic of Afghanistan (GIRoA) backed by a functioning and confident ANSF delivering a meaningful and prosperous future to a secure population that will serve as evidence of our efforts. We feel proud of our contribution and hope for the best for Afghanistan's future, secure in the knowledge that RGR's reputation is stronger for our endeavours here.[73]

Throughout, the Gurkhas were at the forefront; after all, they had been there before. And indeed, still are. Operation Herrick has been followed, post-2014, by Operation Toral, an ongoing advisory and mentoring mission to support Afghan army and security forces.

Chapter 12

'I Must Not Cry Out – I am a Gurkha'

> No drums they wished, whose thoughts were tied
> To girls and jobs and mother,
> Who rose and drilled and killed and died
> Because they saw no other,
> Who died without the hero's throb,
> And if they trembled, hit it,
> Who did not fancy much their job
> But thought it best and did it.
>
> Michael Thwaites,
> *Epitaph on a New Army* (November 1939)[1]

Tradition – Echoes of the Raj

There is something very Kipling-esque about the Brigade of Gurkhas even today. The officers' mess in Sir John Moore Barracks at Folkestone is hung with oils depicting long-ago battles of empire, festooned with tiger skins and decorated with Snider and Martini–Henry Rifles. It's something the *gauleiters* of political correctness would have nightmares about. At the same time, that crucial and enduring bond between officers and men is very real. Respect isn't given, it has to be earned. Most who you encounter there have seen active service in Afghanistan, in numerous cases several tours (five for my son-in-law). The regiment embodies a unique fusion of imperial tradition rooted in the Raj blended with a contemporary readiness. Gurkhas are still the cutting edge of Britain's sword.

Current Recruitment and Service

Despite political vicissitudes, a sometimes 'open-season' approach to fellow royals in Nepal and the emergence of Maoist political elements, naturally antipathetic to the old imperial order, in-country recruitment remains largely unaffected. Aside from anything else, the economic arguments are too compelling.[2] Britain actually recruits (as previously discussed) only a very small percentage of hopefuls and an even smaller number get to join the Gurkha Contingent Singapore Police Force.[3] India hires in rather more, about 2,000 per annum.[4] The UK official responsible not just for recruitment but for the welfare of ex-Gurkhas is the defence attaché to Nepal and he/she supervises the nineteen welfare centres scattered across the country. These smooth pebbles on a largely chaotic shore look after pensions and health care for former servicemen.[5]

Currently, there are two recruiting stations in Nepal, at Dharan in the east and Pokhara to the west. Those potential recruits who have been born into a Gurkha family or dynasty, and only they, can apply at Kathmandu. One thing which has changed in recent years is that educational standards in Nepal have improved significantly and most lads arrive with the equivalent of five good GCSEs, putting them academically a step ahead of the average green army recruit from the UK.[6]

Rifleman Dal Bahadur Pun (who featured previously recalling his experiences in Malaya) was born in Begkhola village, Magdi District. The family house was very small, and he lived with his parents, three brothers and a sister. There weren't any schools at that time, and he used to camp out in a buffalo shed in the bush, seeing to the buffalos and other animals. They were very poor, but he remembers high points such as festivals: during one the lads from his village would cook a particular pudding with milk collected from cows or buffalos, then go to the next village to visit the girls. They would sing together and then the girls would share roti and robust homemade wine with the young men.

The recruiters used to go round everywhere and one day one came into their village and doled out cash to the lads. If they took it then they had to go off with the recruiter. Bahadur didn't want to enlist, but having taken the Queen's shilling as it were, he appeared to have no choice. He was given a date to muster and philosophically his parents concurred: 'If you want to go then OK.' He was one of half a dozen recruits from his settlement.

They had been told it was a two-week trek to the recruiting centre, but as they had little or no kit and their destination lay downhill, they jogged, covering the ground in just over a week. They arrived at the Paklihawa recruiting depot, where their vital statistics were measured and logged. His weight at only 106lb (48kg) was 4lb (1.8kg) short of the minimum requirement. As he was still only a boy and could argue convincingly he wasn't fully grown, he still got in.[7]

Captain Umesh Kumar Pun achieved his youthful ambition of enlisting in the Gurkhas in 1979 at the age of 17½. He enlisted at Pokhara where competition was fierce as the village boys saw all the benefits service in the Gurkhas could provide. It was Colonel Cross himself who was his recruiting officer. The colonel knew all about the settlement he came from and checked to see the recruit had the trademark calluses on his hands from long hours of agricultural work. The hopefuls weren't called by name but by number for fear someone might think family connection or caste carried any weight. Both Umesh Pun and his friend were called forward.[8]

After years of steadily climbing through the ranks Umesh Pun was commissioned. He served as the Queen's Gurkha Orderly Officer from 2006 to 2007 and retired three years later, after completing three tours in Afghanistan. He became an instructor in the arts of jungle warfare, based in Brunei. As well as warfighting he served with peacekeeping missions in Bosnia and trained Sierra Leone forces in dealing with fissiparous militias such as the dreaded 'West Side Boys'.[9]

Since his retirement Umesh Kumar Pun has lived in Colchester with his family running a local inn and Gurkha restaurant. He is also a co-founder of Abbeygate House, the Gurkha Homes Project, which houses over two-dozen Gurkha veterans in the town. He remains an active member of the current Army Reserve (formerly the Territorial Army or just 'Terriers').

Krishna Pun, another former Gurkha, describes his own experiences:

> [I] joined up in 1995 in Nepal. My grandfather who retired in 1963 had served with the Sirmoor Battalion during WWII and had been a POW in Singapore. I also have an uncle who served with 1 RGR so I was brought up in what was very much a military family, and I can clearly recall the older generation sharing their experiences! This heritage combined with the fact I lived so close to the recruiting depot influenced my resolve to join up and successfully passed selection. I'd hoped I might do my training in Hong Kong but this was diverted to the UK.
>
> At this time there were no social media or internet access and up till then my image of Britain was mainly formed by magazine photos which showed views of London and landmarks such as Tower Bridge! Small wonder then I found Church Crookham a surprise, wide open, dank, cold and frosty. I freely admit I found the initial training tough and demanding, considerable pressure for squad and platoon teams to excel in competitive sports and drill. NCOs added their own additional exercise programmes onto the daily round, and you might find yourself doing an extra

25 laps after evening meal! Despite this demanding regime, my platoon of recruits, 28/29 strong, soon bonded, building fitness, strength and endurance.

Subsequently whilst stationed at Catterick I've been involved in the development of new physical training regimens, far more balanced and well thought out to achieve the same goals but minimising risks of injury or long-term wear. I've now completed 25 years' service with 5 more years remaining. Overall, I feel I made an excellent choice of career and army life has offered an exhilarating range of roles and challenges through a variety of differing postings and as a sapper I'm also part of the close-knit family of the Royal Engineers.

Krishna has five more years of service and has not definitively concluded planning for his eventual retirement. In 2015 and 2016 he was deployed back to Nepal to assist with relief work following the devastating earthquake there. Much of this re-construction was carried out under the auspices of the Gurkha Welfare Trust (GWT) and included constructing houses for dispossessed veterans, and in total the Gurkhas erected twenty-eight new dwellings and then went on to build a new school. Krishna was most impressed with the good work GWT was and is doing. He thinks post-retirement he may return to Nepal and deploy his own formidable skills set in working on infrastructure projects. Of course, he needs a consensus from his wife and son beforehand.[10]

One of the residents at Abbeygate, Dharam Prashad Limbu, who lives there with his wife, Sukmaya, is from a military line. His father served with the Indian Army between the wars and Limbu himself joined the Gurkhas in 1959, battling for three years in the jungles of Malaysia/Brunei. His next posting was more peaceful – Aldershot – and then he went on to become a member of the Gurkha Demonstration Company at RMA Sandhurst in the mid-1970s:

> He was only 16 when he joined up but managed to convince the recruiters he was two years older. He served for 15 years and was still in his early 30s when he left the colours. At only 90 rupees a month his pension was meagre even by Nepal standards and he had numerous children to raise. When he turned up at the recruiting centre there would be 1,600–1,700 other young hopefuls already there. They were subjected to a range of health and fitness checks. Failure meant automatic de-selection.

Recruits had to swear an oath of allegiance on the flag. He and the others took such matters seriously. He wasn't that good at running or indeed at swimming – his village didn't have access to many clear stretches of water! Still he got through and joined 10 Gurkha Rifles, B Company, 4th Platoon. After basic training they were thrown in at the deep end: 'We had a big war.' He was soon learning his trade the hard way in the unforgiving school of jungle warfare, the dangerous uncertain world of patrolling and setting ambushes.

He remembers the constant fear and the realities of death all around: it never left him during the struggle. Once in action the terror was wiped away in the intensity of the moment, 'but after the firing happened, you don't really think about anything. You just shoot them.' He stayed three years on active service and was then re-assigned on training duties to RMA Sandhurst. 'After that I went back for training and later on, I went to Sandhurst to demonstrate how to use guns, so it was really good for me. But there are a lot of stories about war, it's infinite. Good times, good times, you can forget it easily, but bad times; it comes to you a lot, like getting shouted at and going to the war.[11]

Soldiers' Wives

Military wives are an essential component of the army's success. Despite this and throughout history their situation has frequently been dire. Marriage, as in all societies, is an important element in Nepali culture. As recently as 2007, once a Gurkha soldier had served in the army for three years, he was given his 'Nepali leave' of six months to return home for the first time since he joined up. It was his chance to show his village and his family what he had achieved. During this time, the soldier usually chose his wife through a process of arranged marriage. If the couple was fortunate, they could return together to his army base in Brunei, Hong Kong etc., but usually his wife would stay in Nepal for the next three years until he returned once again on a second period of extended leave.[12]

After his second Nepali leave, a Gurkha usually had permission to return with his wife and live in married quarters on base. It has become clear to me after speaking with many Gurkhas, both soldiers and wives, how women are the strong backbone of their family and home life. A Gurkha's wife is relied upon to run the home and the children's lives for years when, as is frequently the case, she is separated from her husband. In fact, it wouldn't be unusual for them to live together for only three to five years out of her husband's fifteen-year career in the army:

> Bhui Maya Rana lived in a place called Manakamana and the nearest town was Gorkha, about a day's walk away. Pokhara was around three times as far. She didn't go to school because there was none. She had to do farm chores and housework, like most women then. She didn't necessarily like the drudgery but there wasn't an alternative.
>
> It was always an early start in the morning: they had to grind corn and wheat and paint the house and plaster walls with mud. She used to look after the cows and had to fetch water from a distant well. This universal job specification didn't include many choices and the work had to be done whether you felt like it or not. She did have several sisters; one died at seven and another at sixteen, two more survived and subsequently married, one in Assam and the other in India. Her childhood memories generally are pretty vague – both her parents are now dead and sorely missed.
>
> There were a few Gurkhas in her village, and it was an exciting time when they came back on their extended leave. Her husband was her first cousin; he lived in the next village, and it was an arranged marriage. She was about 15. Her husband was also a serving Gurkha and, after their simple ceremony she couldn't go with him to Singapore. She remained with his family pretty much as she had done at home. They only wrote intermittently as his English wasn't particularly good – perhaps one letter every six months, no more. He could write in Roman Gurkhali only as that was what the army had taught him, so she had to rely on a translator, usually another Gurkha she could then dictate a reply to. Their exchanges were fairly brief! He would be back, he said, in two or three years.
>
> She was already pregnant when he left but their son died after only three days of life. There was nobody to help her frame a letter and it was only when her husband returned some six months later that he learned of the birth and death of his son. He went back to Singapore for another two years, but their second son happily

survived and both mother and child were able to join him on his subsequent posting to Hong Kong. She had never been on a train before or on a plane: both were nerve-wracking but exciting and Hong Kong was an incredible change, a great experience after growing up in such a small village.

All was new; she had never experienced fresh water on tap or flushing toilets. Just as well she was a quick learner, as her husband was posted to Brunei in the same week, she and her baby son arrived and left her with $180. This was to last a month and there was no shortage of shops. It was a steep learning curve, but she encountered honest grocers who helped her with understanding the cash, and soon got the hang of things.[13]

When visiting many UK military establishments, it is telling how, in many instances, Gurkha wives quietly organise the catering. Whenever I've stayed at RMA Sandhurst or RE Chatham, I'm struck by how quietly, efficiently and seamlessly Gurkha wives pretty much run the show – their curries are without equal.

Meena Kambang met her future husband, a Gurkha, aged only 19. It was an arranged marriage and they wed three months after their initial meeting. At that point she wasn't really ready to marry, but her parents insisted. In Nepal, if women aren't married by 25, families think they're 'on the shelf'. A *Guardian* feature tells one story:

> I wasn't eager to marry a soldier. My dad was in the British army, so he was away all the time and I missed him a lot. I don't remember much of him in my childhood, and I didn't want that for my own children. But my mum was so pleased for me to marry a Gurkha soldier; in Nepal they are believed to be strong and brave. But I was very pleased with their choice of husband. We have been happily married for more than 10 years.[14]

It was in 1997, shortly after she married, that Meena came to live in Britain with her soldier husband. They spent a year in York, one of only two Gurkha families in the area. The local community was very friendly and well-disposed. Then they spent another year in Nuneaton, before going back to Nepal, where she taught in a primary school. This was quite unusual in Nepal as most women stay within the home. It felt good to be back; she was glad to see family and friends. At the same time there were a lot of things about the UK she missed.

After some years her husband was promoted to staff sergeant and they were given family accommodation, which meant they could return to the UK.

> What I love about this country is that women are treated equally. They have access to work, and education opportunities. Since I moved back to the UK, I've got a driving licence, having that independence, being able to drive wherever I want, feels like a huge achievement. We have a son now, who is eight. He likes living in the UK, particularly the food. He loves Yorkshire pudding, cakes and chocolate. I miss Nepalese food, though, the dry meats, chillies and vegetables grown in Nepal. I particularly miss the sweet corn. I'm not sure what the gardeners do here, but the vegetables don't taste as good.[15]

She now works full-time for the Army Welfare Service as a Gurkha welfare support worker, liaising with around ninety-five Gurkha families in Stafford, Cosford and Lichfield. In addition, she helps out in schools and nurseries, interprets for Gurkha families at medical and dental appointments, whilst encouraging them to get more involved in community activities.

Before this, Meena studied English as a second language (ESOL) at college with a number of other Gurkha wives. Her ESOL teacher, Lynn Evans, was brilliant, and the students wanted to show her how grateful they were. Eight of them got together and, during a cultural diversity day, performed a traditional dance they had learnt as children.

> Learners at colleges can audition to perform at the ceremony for the Learning and Skills Improvement Service Star awards, which are held in London every year. We were so pleased when Lynn was nominated for an award; we decided to give it a try. We were very excited when we heard we'd been accepted and would be performing at the awards ceremony. In Nepal, teachers are treated like gold. Students will do anything to thank their teacher. We are delighted to have an opportunity to show our appreciation.[16]

The Future?

What is the British Army's likely future role and what of the Gurkhas themselves? Odds are they will keep their unique place as they are both a key current component and also a link to Britain's imperial past, the last real remaining connection to the Raj. Their relevance to Britain's overall fighting capacity hasn't changed – especially if Britain remains wedded (as may be assumed) to the practice of expeditionary warfare. It is worth reflecting on how and where see future conflicts may arise.

In 1908 Lord Haldane[17] famously asked, 'What is the army for?'[18] This question has been asked continually ever since and the answer is complex and ever-changing. This, however, is my view. In the past, guerrilla armies from David seeking sanctuary in The Cave of Adullam to Patrick Leigh Fermor and Stanley Moss spiriting Axis commander General Kreipe across the Cretan mountains[19] have sought refuge in the high ground. Geronimo led an entire American army a merry dance through the sharp peaks and ravines of Arizona for decades with a mere handful of followers.

With the 'War on Terror', the rise of asymmetric and now hybrid warfare, interstate wars are an increasingly rare phenomenon, at least until 24 February 2022. International rivalries, as illustrated by the long decades of the Cold War, are often fought out vicariously. Conflicting ideologies, control of diminishing resources and the rise of nationalism fuel a proliferation of modern conflicts. Special Forces and elite combat units are now deployed on the front line rather than purely for intelligence gathering and raiding.

In this context it is tempting to include Gurkhas as Special Forces, though, of course, they are very different from the SAS or other commando-style units. Nonetheless, they are an elite and highly adaptable professional fighting force, ideally suited to counterterrorist and counterinsurgency roles in any asymmetric conflict. The clear and high moral plateau offered by the fight against fascism or communism no longer exists. Civilians are very often first in the firing line, the 'enemy' a shifting, faceless chiaroscuro of changing factions and alliances.

Britons woke up to the reality of a continuing and morphing Islamist threat at 5.50 a.m. on 16 January 2013 when terrorists attacked the giant Tigantourine natural gas installation near In Amenas, Algeria. The sudden eruption of the crisis, and the costly ruthlessness of the government's response, threw into stark relief the potential danger to British workers in that region. Such facilities are isolated, sprawling and virtually impossible to defend, apart from a massive military deployment. The terrorist will always have the advantage that only he knows where, when and exactly how he will strike. The incident left many hostages dead and injured including a number from the UK.[20]

On 28 January that year, French and Malian troops drove rebels from the fabled city of Timbuktu which, over a very long history, has seen its fair share of invaders. Islamist fighters, who had opted for a conventional, non-guerrilla response to the French deployment, had been easily routed and driven back from their earlier gains. Despite their major and pivotal role, the French have been keen to stress that their intervention is only part of a coordinated African response.[21] Thus far, however, the hoped for Senegalese, Nigerian and Ivorian reinforcements have yet to arrive and demonstrate their capacity. It seems inevitable that the French will be staying for the foreseeable future. The lessons of Afghanistan clearly show that defeating the enemy in a conventional battle will certainly lead to a sustained asymmetric conflict, rather than to any immediate and conclusive victory.

As discussed above, Britain's most recent and fourth war in Afghanistan began within days of 9/11. At the time the UK was conducting Exercise *Swift-Sword* in and off Oman – deploying 22,000 personnel, 6,500 vehicles, 20 warships and close air support. The United States already possessed a substantial forward base in Uzbekistan. The West had to respond swiftly once the ultimatums to the Taliban expired. Ground operations thus began on 7 October – essential to gain as much ground as possible before the onset of winter.[22] Such tactical flexibility is a vital component of modern operations and Gurkhas are the perfect exponents, they always have been.

At this point the Taliban, as noted, was pitted against the Northern Alliance and both had been conducting sporadic conventional warfare with massed forces on the ground, fortress complexes and extended trench lines. The early phase of the conflict was thus a conventional war for which the Taliban was neither ready nor equipped. As they were attempting to fight a conventional war, they were massively outgunned and quickly routed; overall the Taliban put up a poor showing.[23] The rest, as explored in the previous chapter, was far from easy and the final verdict remains in the balance.

How can the nature of such 'small' wars be predicted and what will be the role of the Gurkhas in these emerging conflicts? In the case of Libya in the wake of Gaddafi's fall, Prime Minister David Cameron was too canny to respond directly to the question of whether British 'boots on the ground' would be needed. He did not rule out the possibility and this is an eventuality which many may view with understandable alarm, given the fate of recent interventions in Iraq and Afghanistan, whose long-term effectiveness is still open to question.[24]

At present there is no encompassing answer to this quandary: in all probability, Western governments are equally undecided but significantly the Malian intermeddling is a European, rather than United States-led, deployment. France is Britain's ally; UK forces now train extensively with their Gallic counterparts and share operational capacities (how this will pan out post-Brexit is impossible to fathom). France has 'form' in the Sub-Saharan region after a long period of colonial involvement and clearly, the established state governments, finding themselves under concerted attack, are more than willing to look to Europe for assistance.

The subsequent terrorist attack on the Westgate Shopping Mall in Nairobi offered a stark reminder of the vulnerability of 'soft' urban targets. Large retail parks present a complex labyrinth with built-in security features which may be used by attackers to thwart security forces. Such scenarios are, if the arguments put forward by a leading expert in the field, David Kilcullen,[25] are accepted, the shape of horrors to come. This murderous spree in Kenya bears similarities to the attack in Mumbai five years earlier.

Now, modern surveillance and satellite tracking systems have largely stripped the hills of comfort. It is estimated that by 2050 some 75 per cent of the world's population, which will by then have increased by another 3 billion, will be crowded into urban centres. In the developing world sprawling cities, an irresistible magnet to the rural poor, will grow exponentially in a riot of slums and shanties, perfect conditions for the rise of extremism. Kilcullen cites four main drivers priming the powder keg:

1. Huge growth in populations.
2. Concentration of people in cities.
3. Movement towards the world's coastlines.
4. A spiralling revolution in technology-driven connectivity.

He foresees in some instances (Syria being a case in point perhaps) doomsday outcomes where states and their governments fail, and cities become a jungle and battleground. The major powers, rather than deploying troops for counterinsurgency across barren plains and rock-strewn deserts, may find themselves fighting in the tangled rookeries of urban hives where all order has gone. The American experience in Mogadishu, vividly recalled in *Black Hawk Down*,[26] illustrates the perils such conflicts hold.

Street fighting is inevitably harder, far costlier and demands infinitely more boots on the ground. Firepower, aerial observation and heavy weapons are far less effective (ask General Paulus). Worse, there is unlikely to be a defined 'enemy' as such, no Saddam or Bin Laden to focus on, no 'Elvis' to pursue. The current, awful civil war in Syria is being fought on the rebel side by a multiplicity of often diverse groups, at best uneasy allies, very often mutually antipathetic, enmeshed in a quicksand of changing allegiances.

Conventional armies like conventional enemies but Western forces could find themselves up against Daesh lookalikes or franchises, drug cartels, or sectarian mercenaries such as Hezbollah, fighting under the instructions and in the pay of a hostile or rogue state; war by proxy. The earlier Nairobi shopping mall attack, Kilcullen argues, like Mumbai, demonstrates how a small gang of well-prepared, murderously ruthless terrorists can bring a whole city to a standstill.[27] Planning a response will demand Special Forces as the remedy in a targeted, hopefully surgical pre-emptive strike.

No one anticipated the Arab Spring, fuelled largely by Internet connectivity; nobody really understands how it may yet finally play out. Libya and Egypt are both balanced on the edge of chaos, the void of failure which provides an open door for extremists. Kilcullen takes a view that while huge areas of urban slum housing are nothing new, the Internet changes everything, alters the dynamic in a way that has never been seen before. Tinder for these conflagrations is provided by the deep wells of inequality, lack of opportunity and 'permanent exclusion and marginalization'. Awareness without hope is a dangerous pairing.[28]

In his most recent work, *The Dragons and the Snakes* (London: Hurst, 2020), Kilcullen warns against creeping infiltration by foreign powers, particularly China, buying up property assets near American/UK bases worldwide to provide handy listening posts. He also cautions that asymmetric warfare is not a constant. Insurgents learn from their mistakes and will adapt their tactics accordingly: beating them the first time around doesn't mean it will be so easy the next. Adaptability is therefore key, and nobody has more experience of adaption than Gurkhas.

Catastrophe

The Brigade of Gurkhas doesn't just wage war. It responds to international emergencies such as the earthquake, centred on Barpak, which laid waste to vast tracts of Nepal on 25 April 2015. Over 9,000 people died; 22,000 were injured; tens of thousands, including many veterans and their families, were left homeless.[29] Individual Gurkhas did outstanding work in the immediate aftermath. Gurkha engineers were deployed to provide emergency supplies and shelter, and the Gurkha Welfare Trust gave significant financial and logistical support. Joanna Lumley led a public appeal which raised large amounts of cash.

Gurkha Captain Buddhi Bahadur Bhandari was born in Nepal. He lives in Kent with his wife and two children. He describes what happened when the 7.8 earthquake hit Mount Everest on 25 April 2015: 'I still remember the first contact was like being hit by rocks, all over my back and legs. Initially it was quite painful but then my body became numb. I was thrown about 10 metres, along with the tent. I don't really remember being thrown but I remember everything else.'[30]

Captain Bhandari had sustained a quite severe gash on the right side of his head but at least the whole party, even though three were injured, had survived. His training kicked in, he was a Gurkha. He didn't feel scared, never thought he'd die. Everything went into slow motion. The party had been scattered and the first job was to find friends, attend to first aid and gather their kit.

Captain Bhandari recalled: 'Everything was flattened. We couldn't find our belongings, but we searched for clothes to keep warm. We walked to the hospital, and they gave us bandages and painkillers, soup and tea. The doctors and paramedics were great. The following day we were rescued by two search and rescue helicopters'. He pretty soon got bored with sitting down and doing nothing so volunteered to help the rescue teams. 'I feel very privileged to be part of it. I decided to do whatever I could –coming out with the boys. I'm supposed to be resting but I'm so happy to be out and doing something. I'm alive.'[31]

In spite of the terrible devastation and loss of life Captain Bhandari remains proud of the speed and effectiveness of the UK response and that he and other Gurkha comrades were a part of the relief effort, doing something, not just being spectators; Gurkhas never are.

In 2020 the Covid-19 pandemic together with potential disruption caused by Brexit came to the fore. Due to French concerns over spread of a second, even more transmissible strain of the virus, the Channel ports were temporarily closed in December, resulting in huge tailbacks of lorries and vast parked up immobile legions of vehicles. When the deadlock was ended it was Gurkhas who, in a matter of hours, managed to clear out and get moving all those stuck on the old RAF Manston site, a significant logistical feat.

Another Two-Hundred Years?

When I began writing, pre-pandemic, the MoD had announced the formation of a 3rd Battalion of RGR, perhaps a response to the growing appreciation of the nature of conflict in the twenty-first century. This would be in recognition of their continuing role and came in the wake of much uncertainty. After the UK general election of 2010 there were fears of swingeing defence cuts and a view the Gurkhas might be victims. Patrick Mercer MP, a former soldier, commented in the press:

> The first people to go will be the Brigade of Gurkhas, probably in their entirety. In the past, the Gurkhas' existence was guaranteed by the fact they are cheaper to run than British troops and that there was a shortage of British troops. Recent changes mean they are now just as expensive, and recruitment is extremely healthy at the moment. I am afraid the writing is on the wall.[32]

Happily, for the brigade, the world has shifted again in the last decade. The UK's involvement in two large-scale, prolonged counterinsurgency and stabilisation operations in Iraq and Afghanistan has seen the British Army evolve to meet the needs of modern warfare and peacekeeping. As Peter Antill and Jeremy Smith noted in 2017: 'Under the plans for Army 2020 (part of Future Force 2020), the British Army would – in an effort to re-orientate itself back to being more flexible and mobile – have three 'forces': the Reaction Force (headquarters – 3 UK Division); the Adaptable Force (headquarters – 1 UK Division); and the Force Troops Command (headquarters located at Upavon).'[33] This is now slightly dated, and the MoD website (https://www.army.mod.uk/what-we-do/) clearly sets out a template for the army's present roles which offers a fairly wide brief:

1. Protecting the UK (anti-terrorism and support to the emergency services).
2. Prevention of conflict; peacekeeping and reacting to dangerous instability wherever, on a global basis, it arises.
3. Responding to natural disasters.
4. Fighting the nation's enemies.

The Gurkhas have proved effective in all of these roles.

In 2023, the plans for this fresh Gurkha battalion have effectively been mothballed and what effect the war in Ukraine will have on UK and NATO defence thinking cannot easily be predicted. At best this heralds the dawn of a new Cold War where NATO nations will be called upon to significantly increase both their fiscal and military involvement. It can only be hoped that is as far as it goes. Whether this will lead to an increase in Gurkha numbers within Britain's armed forces also remains unclear.

'Peace in our time' is a nice idea that has been around for a very long time; it isn't ever going to happen. A Roman military theorist, Vegetius, said it pithily in the fourth century AD: '*Si vis pacem, para bellum*' ('if you wish for peace prepare for war').[34] President Harry Truman, as the Second World War ended and the Cold War got started, provided the updated quote: 'If you're not prepared to pay the price of peace, you better be prepared to pay the price of war.'[35]

There is a realisation in defence circles that Gurkhas represent good value for money and there's never a shortage of good quality recruits, lean, fit, young men coming forward at a time when many 'green army' recruits struggle to hit minimum fitness levels. 'The headline is that the Brigade of Gurkhas will grow by *c.* 75% over the next 4–5 years.'[36] This development, very much in contrast to the earlier pessimism, has been sparked by a failure to recruit sufficient numbers generally. Gurkhas have, since 2007, been able, after five years' service, to transfer into the wider army, offering enhanced prospects for Gurkha soldiers. Also from 2008, new Gurkha recruits joined on the basis of the Versatile Engagement (VEng) (Short) for an initial span of a dozen years and then potentially for a further twelve on a longer contract. This was impacting adversely on the brigade.[37]

In 2016, an opportunity arose within the Allied Rapid Reaction Corps (ARRC) Support Battalion which had lost its Pioneer capability and the Brigade of Gurkhas, Officers and Soldiers took this role on. At the same time the brigade increased its various existing training roles, all of which created 233 new posts.[38] A couple of new signal squadrons were also authorised in 2016, as were several additional logistical units: 'two new squadrons of QGS were authorised; one to support 3 Div Signal regiment which supports 3 (UK) Division HQ, a very high profile role … two additional QOGLR squadrons were endorsed to support the RLC …'.[39] Both 2017 and 2018 witnessed a slew of new opportunities with a further 113 posts being created.[40]

From 2019, there has been a new package:

> QGS; four more QGS Squadrons (of which there will now be six).
> ARRC Support Battalion, to be badged as a Gurkha unit.
> Band of the Brigade of Gurkhas; this will be augmented and 'uplifted'.
> Two new QCE field squadrons.
> The 2015 Defence Review provided for five new specialised infantry battalions, one of which will be 3 RGR (if indeed this now happens); assuming it does take place within the foreseeable future this will play an important role in 'training other armies in a high-threat environment'.
> UK RGR Battalion; this will benefit from an uplift in its role as part of 16 Air Assault brigade – this will be a big step up as it will take its turn with two Para Battalions on the Air Manoeuvre Battle Group roster as the High Readiness Standby Intervention Unit.[41]

'I MUST NOT CRY OUT – I AM A GURKHA'

In total the brigade will expand from about 2,650 to nearer 4,700:[42] a very significant increase. The brigade is here to stay. The Gurkhas are ready. A true testament to their ability is praise for their prowess from friend and foe alike. Indian Army Chief of Staff Field Marshal Sam Manekshaw once stated, 'If a man says he is not afraid of dying, he is either lying or is a Gurkha.' Prince Charles once said, 'In the world there is only one secure place, that's when you are between Gurkhas.' Osama bin Laden once claimed he would 'eat Americans alive' if he had Gurkhas on his side. Adolf Hitler said of them, 'If I had Gurkhas, no armies in the world would defeat me.'[43] At the time of writing, however, this is very far from certain.

In September 2010, an ex-Indian Army Gurkha Bishnu Prasad Shrestha was making his way home after retiring. At about midnight he was onboard the Maurya Express train from Ranchi to Gorakhpur when forty or so armed criminals attacked the train, robbing at will. He didn't resist at first, allowing them to take his gear. That changed when they began molesting an 18-year-old girl as her parents watched helplessly. This was too much, he might not draw his kukri to defend himself but he'd fight to save this young woman.

He took them all on, killing three and wounding another eight, the chastened survivors bolting. When interviewed he explained:

> They started snatching jewellery, cell phones, cash, laptops and other belongings from the passengers. They had carried out their robbery with swords, blades and pistols. The pistols may have been fake as they didn't fire the girl cried for help saying, 'you are a soldier, please save a sister'. I prevented her from being raped, thinking of her as my own sister.

In the melee he received a nasty wound to his left hand and the girl suffered a small cut on the neck. He recovered no fewer than 200 mobiles, 40 laptops, a significant amount of jewellery, and nearly $10,000 in cash. When the girl's family offered him a hefty financial reward, he refused, saying: 'Fighting the enemy in battle is my duty as a soldier, taking on the thugs on the train was my duty as a human being'.[44]

When you arrive at Sir John Moore Barracks in Folkestone – a name with constant resonance for any rifleman – the place does have a kind of Raj Quartet feeling; the barrack piles are named after many famous battles of the past and the trophies of war, French Hotchkiss MGs and Japanese mountain guns, guard entrances like temple dogs. It sums up the Gurkhas – very British and yet somehow not. Now, the Gurkhas qualify as 'us' but quite what that means hasn't always been clear.

Prior to 2004, Gurkha veterans couldn't settle in the UK – they had to return to Nepal. For many this was perfectly fine, even though their service didn't guarantee any jobs in the civil service. Gurkhas I have spoken to are ambivalent; some do want to stay and pursue second careers in other fields; many have become successful restaurateurs. At Albemarle Barracks in Northumberland, the gunners have regular open or family days and as the full complement on site is made up of a variety of soldiers from different backgrounds, there's fierce competition in the culinary stakes as every nationality seeks to woo visitors with regional specialities and they're all damn good. But it's always the Gurkha curries that go down best – and that's against serious competition.

With the extinguishing of the last beacon of empire in Hong Kong in 1997, Tony Blair's government modified the rules but those retired prior to this didn't automatically gain full parity. This kicked off the 'Gurkha Justice campaign' and from 2008 actress Joanna Lumley became the face of the cause. The objective was to secure an automatic right of retirement in the UK for all soldiers who had quit service before 1997. That same year the UK courts ruled that the existing policy was unconstitutional.

During the following year, 2009, the government (Gordon Brown was by now prime minister) set out new rules which pleased nobody. The right to stay had to be earned and one or several boxes would have to be ticked by any applicant: three years' continuous UK residence during or after service; close family in the UK; a gallantry award of level one to three; service of twenty years or more in the Brigade of Gurkhas (in fact most serve no more than fifteen); or a long-term medical condition arising from the years of service.

While this might mean a few, perhaps a hundred or so, could stay, the majority would slip through the net (as many suspected the government intended). Having such a dynamic and high-profile front-of-the-house as Joanna Lumley, who led a well-staged march upon 10 Downing Street with a 250,000-name petition, produced results. The Conservatives and Liberal Democrats favoured a more level playing field and a motion to that effect was passed in April 2009.

Lumley displayed doggedness worthy of any Gurkha, meeting with Gordon Brown and, when that proved less than satisfactory, bearding immigration minister Phil Woodas at the BBC's Westminster studio and hanging onto his ankles like a bulldog. There was no escape. This epic pursuit finally frightened the government into throwing in the towel.[45]

This was a signal victory, though not all agreed it was, of necessity, a good thing as Nepal continues to need the resources which come back with veterans. But now they are at least free to choose. It does seem only right that after two centuries of such magnificent service the soldiers themselves should be granted the right to choose. And they continue to serve; their arm of the service is expanding at a time when a global future is very far from certain and fraught with major challenges.

But it isn't residency rights or even their well-honed sense of etiquette that inspires such terror in Britain's enemies; it is the Gurkhas' extreme toughness, hardiness and their ability to fight effectively across every type of terrain. Their tremendous elan and matchless courage inspire admiration in allies and terror among foes and over two centuries they have encountered and overcome some of the toughest: dacoits, Pathans, Germans and Japanese. They have fought in mountains, jungles, across plains, in urban centres and in the open. They have never been defeated. While they form part of the cutting edge of UK and NATO forces, their own bespoke cutting edge, the kukri, is a remainder of an ancient past and a proud warrior tradition – that's *Kaida* (tradition)! As inheritors of the heraldic and stratified age of chivalry soldiers tend to fixate upon dress and etiquette, even though the distinctive, traditional 'dice-board' mark is no longer worn.

Whatever the crisis, a Gurkha will always be ready and well dressed.[46] The current CGS, General Sir Mark Carleton-Smith, summed up the essence of being a Gurkha superbly when addressing recruits at Pokhara in 2020:

> It is a great honour as Chief of the General Staff to take your attestation parade; to witness your oath of allegiance to Her Majesty Queen Elizabeth the Second; and to welcome you into the British Army. This morning you start a new life; a new life as a soldier in the Brigade of Gurkhas. A new life as a Gurkha in the British Army. Selection has been hard. The competition has been intense. But you have met the very high standards necessary to be a British Gurkha soldier. You have shown yourselves committed, fit and ready for the greatest challenge of your lives. You deserve to feel very proud of your achievement. And I am proud on behalf of all your families to inspect such an impressive contingent of 'Gurkha' recruits. Just being called a 'Gurkha' is an honour in itself. *Tulo sha-bash!* (Big well done!)
>
> Good luck wherever your service to the Crown and your Soldiering takes you.
>
> *Jai Brigade of Gurkhas!* (Forward the Brigade of Gurkhas).

That pretty much says it all.

Appendix 1

The Gurkha Battalions

1st Gurkha Rifles

1815, 1st Nasiri Battalion
1823, 5th, 6th, or 1st Nasiri Local Battalion
1826, 4th, or Nasiri Local Battalion
1843, 4th, or Nasiri (Rifle Battalion)
1850, 66th, or Goorkha Regiment, Bengal Native Infantry
1856, 66th, or Goorkha Light Infantry Regiment of Bengal Native Infantry
1861, 11th Regiment of Bengal Native Infantry
1861, 1st Goorkha Regiment (Light Infantry)
1886, 1st Goorkha Regiment (Light Infantry)
1891, 1st Gurkha (Rifle) Regiment
1901, 1st Gurkha Rifles
1903, 1st Gurkha Rifles (the Malaun Regiment)
1906, 1st Prince of Wales's Own Gurkha Rifles
1910, 1st King George's Own Gurkha Rifles (the Malaun Regiment)
1937, 1st King George V's Own Gurkha Rifles (the Malaun Regiment)
1947, left British service

2nd Gurkha Rifles

1815, Sirmoor Battalion
1823, 8th (or Sirmoor) Local Battalion
1826, 6th (or Sirmoor) Local Battalion
1850, Sirmoor Battalion
1858, Sirmoor Rifle Battalion
1858, Sirmoor Rifle Regiment
1861, 17th Regiment of Bengal Native Infantry

THE GURKHA BATTALIONS

1861, 2nd Goorkha Regiment
1861, 2nd Goorkha (the Sirmoor Rifles) Regiment
1876, 2nd (Prince of Wales's Own) Goorkha Regiment (the Sirmoor Rifles)
1886, 2nd (Prince of Wales's Own) Goorkha Regiment (the Sirmoor Rifles)
1891, 2nd (Prince of Wales's Own) Gurkha Rifles); Regiment (the Sirmoor Rifles)
1901, 2nd (Prince of Wales's Own) Gurkha Rifles (the Sirmoor Rifles)
1906, 2nd King Edward's Own Gurkha Rifles (the Sirmoor Rifles)
1936, 2nd King Edward VII's Own Gurkha Rifles (the Sirmoor Rifles)
1947, stayed in British service

3rd Gurkha Rifles

1815, the Kumaon Battalion
1816, Kumaon Provincial Battalion
1823, 9th (or Kumaon) Battalion
1826, 7th (or Kumaon) Battalion
1860, Kumaon Battalion
1861, 18th Regiment of Bengal Native Infantry
1861, 3rd Goorkha Regiment
1864, 3rd (the Kumaon) Goorkha Regiment
1887, 3rd Gurkha Regiment
1891, 3rd Gurkha (Rifle) Regiment
1901, 3rd Gurkha Rifles
1907, 3rd The Queen's Own Gurkha Rifles
1908, 3rd Queen Alexandra's Own Gurkha Rifles
1947, left British service

4th Gurkha Rifles

1857, extra Goorkha Regiment
1861, 19th regiment of Bengal Native Infantry
1861, 4th Goorkha Regiment
1891, 4th Gurkha (Rifle) Regiment
1901, 4th Gurkha Rifles
1924, 4th Prince of Wales's Own Gurkha Rifles
1947, left British service

5th Gurkha Rifles

1858, 25th Punjab Infantry, or Hazara Goorkha Battalion
1861, 7th Regiment of Infantry (or Hazara Goorkha Battalion), Punjab Irregular Force
1861, 5th Goorkha Regiment or Hazara Goorkha Battalion
1886, 5th Goorkha Regiment or Hazara Goorkha Battalion
1887, 5th Gurkha Regiment
1891, 5th Gurkha (Rifle) Regiment
1901, 5th Gurkha Rifles
1903, 5th Gurkha Rifles (Frontier Force)
1923, 5th Royal Gurkha Rifles (Frontier Force)
1947, left British service

6th Gurkha Rifles

1817, the Cuttack Legion
1823, Rangpur Light Infantry Battalion
1826, 8th (or Rangpur) Local Light Infantry Battalion
1826, 8th (or Assam) Local Light Infantry Battalion
1828, 8th (or Assam) Local Light Infantry Battalion
1844, 1st Assam Light Infantry
1861, 42nd Regiment of Bengal Native Infantry
1864, 42nd (Assam) Regiment of Bengal (Light) Infantry
1885, 42nd (Assam) Regiment of Bengal (Light) Infantry
1886, 42nd Regiment Goorkha Light Infantry
1889, 42nd (Goorkha) Regiment of Bengal (Light) Infantry
1891, 42nd Gurkha (Rifle) Regiment of Bengal Infantry
1901, 42nd Gurkha Rifles
1903, 6th Gurkha Rifles
1947, remained in UK service
1959, 6th Queen Elizabeth's Own Gurkha Rifles

7th Gurkha Rifles

1902, 8th Gurkha Rifles
1903, 2nd Battalion, 10th Gurkha Rifles

1907, 7th Gurkha Rifles
1947, remained in UK service
1959, 7th Duke of Edinburgh's Own Gurkha Rifles

8th Gurkha Rifles

1824, 16th or Sylhet Local Battalion
1826, 11th or Sylhet Local (Light) Infantry Battalion
1861, 44th Regiment of Bengal Native Infantry
1885, 44th (Sylhet) Regiment of Bengal (Light) Infantry
1886, 44th Regiment, Goorkha (Light) Infantry
1889, 44th (Goorkha) Regiment of Bengal (Light) Infantry
1891, 44th Gurkha (Rifle) Regiment of Bengal Infantry
1901, 44th Gurkha Rifles
1903, 8th Gurkha Rifles
1907, became 1st Battalion
1907, 2nd Battalion raised at Gauhati; pedigree:
    1835, Assam Sebundy Corps
    1835, Lower Assam Sebundy Corps
    1839, 1st Assam Sebundy Corps
    1844, 2nd Assam Light Infantry
    1861, 47th Regiment of Bengal Native Infantry
    1861, 43rd Regiment of Bengal Native Infantry
    1865, 43rd (Assam) Regiment of Bengal (Light) Infantry
    1886, 43rd Regiment Goorkha Light Infantry
    1889, 43rd (Goorkha) Regiment of Bengal (Light) Infantry
    1891, 43rd Gurkha (Rifle) Regiment of Bengal Infantry
    1901, 43rd Gurkha Rifles
    1903, 7th Gurkha Rifles,
1907, became 2nd Battalion 8th Gurkhas
1947, left British service

9th Gurkha Rifles

1817, Fatehgarh Levy
1819, Manipuri Levy
1823, 1st Battalion 32nd Regiment of Bengal Native Infantry

1824, 63rd Regiment of Bengal Native Infantry
1861, 9th Regiment of Bengal Native Infantry
1885, 9th Regiment of Bengal Infantry
1894, 9th (Gurkha Rifles) Regiment of Bengal Infantry
1901, 9th Gurkha Rifles
1947, left British service

10th Gurkha Rifles

1890, 1st Regiment of Burma Infantry
1891, 10th Regiment (1st Burma Battalion) of Madras Infantry
1892, 10th Regiment (1st Burma Rifles) Madras Infantry
1895, 10th Regiment (1st Gurkha Rifles) Madras Infantry
1901, 10th Gurkha Rifles
1947, remained in British service
1949, Princess Mary's Own Gurkha Rifles

11th Gurkha Rifles

1918, formed for late service in the First World War
1922, disbanded

The Current UK Brigade of Gurkhas

From 2019 this now comprises: The Royal Gurkha Rifles (1st, 2nd and 3rd Battalions); The Queen's Gurkha Engineers; Queen's Gurkha Signals; The Queen's Own Gurkha Logistic Regiment; Gurkha Staff and Personnel Support Company and Band of the Brigade of Gurkhas. Additional support units are made up with: Training Support Company (Warminster); Sittang Company, Sandhurst, Royal Military Academy Mandalay Wing, Brecon, Infantry Battle School Tavoleto Company, Warminster, Specialist Weapons School Gurkha Company Catterick, School of Infantry.

Appendix 2

Ranks in the Gurkha Battalions

The Old Indian Army

This had a ranking system that was peculiarly its own. After John Company's *Ragnarok* of the Mutiny, all officers in British service held, as they continue to do, a royal commission:

> Elizabeth the Second, by the Grace of God of the United Kingdom of Great Britain and Northern Ireland, and of Her other Realms and Territories Queen, Head of the Commonwealth, Defender of the Faith, Lord High Admiral/To our Trusty and Well Beloved XXX Greeting: We, reposing especial Trust and Confidence in your Loyalty, Courage, and good Conduct, do by these Presents Constitute and Appoint you to be an Officer in Our XXX from the XXX day of XXX You are therefore carefully and diligently to discharge your Duty as such in the Rank of XXX or in such other Rank as We may from time to time hereafter be pleased to promote you to XXX.

Present Day

As per British Rifles Battalions: Rifleman, Lance Corporal, Corporal, Sergeant, Colour Sergeant, Warrant Officer, Second Lieutenant, Lieutenant, Captain, Major, Lieutenant Colonel.

Appendix 3

Castes

The Nepali caste structure is very complex and split into four main groupings:

1. Brahman – upper crust, priests and politicos.
2. Rajput – the military, knightly elite.
3. Vaisiya – yeomen and trades.
4. Sudra – everyone else and pretty much bottom of the heap.

This may appear reasonably straightforward, but each caste is itself split into many sub-categories: there are seven grades of Brahman and really, really bottom of the league, below everyone are the untouchables, *untermenschen*. Both Brahmans and Rajputs look down on the rest and form an aristocracy of caste, not altogether unlike the feudal pyramid where tenants in chief and sub-tenants form the oligarchies.

There are also the primary classes or socio-economic-religious levels, eleven of them:

1. Brahmans.
2. Thakurs.
3. Chetris or Khas.
4. Gurungs.
5. Magars.
6. Newars.
7. Limbus.
8. Rais.
9. Sunwars.
10. Muranis.
11. Tharus.

These are subtly different to the main groupings above and are frequently dictated by profession: a man may have a relatively lowly trade but still be of high caste. Military rank is by no means the only measure of status.

Appendix 4

Badges of Courage

The Brigade of Gurkhas, quite correctly, is very proud of the large number of bravery awards earned by its soldiers, including their Victoria Crosses. Prior to 21 October 1911, 'other ranks' in the Indian Army were not eligible for the Victoria Cross. The Order of British India was, until that point, the highest award Gurkha soldiers could aspire to. This was for 'native officers', instituted in April 1837. It had two classes: the first permitted the winner to take the title 'Sirdar Bahadur' and a modest cash pension (this was tricky if the Gurkha's name was Bahadur!). If you were given the second-class award you took the title 'Bahadur' with a smaller gratuity.

It was John Company, also in 1837, which created the Indian Order of Merit (IOM). This was for Indian soldiers only and came in three classes. A first-time recipient was awarded third class, then second class for another act of bravery, and finally first class. Each came with a pension entitlement. Kishenbir Nagarkoti of 1/5th Gurkhas worked his way up in an impressively short time through all three classes. When he again displayed conspicuous gallantry during the Black Mountain Expedition of 1888[1] he couldn't be awarded a further decoration so he was given a larger gratuity.[2]

Over the years many more medals would be awarded to the Gurkhas. All recipients of the Victoria Cross are listed below:

1. John Tytler; 66th Bengal Native Infantry later 1st King George V's Own Gurkha Rifles; 1858, Choorpoorah, India.
2. Donald Macintyre; Bengal Staff Corps attached to 2nd King Edward VII's Own Gurkha Rifles; 1872, Lalgnoora, India.
3. George Channer; Bengal Staff Corps attached to 1st King George V's Own Gurkha Rifles; 1875, Perak, Malaya. The Perak War (1875–6) was fought between British and local forces in Perak, a state in north-western Malaysia. The Sultan of Upper Perak and other local leaders attempted to end foreign influence in the region and remove the British administrator James W.W. Birch. Following the murder of Birch in 1875, British forces were sent in to end local resistance.

4. John Cook; Bengal Staff Corps attached to 5th Royal Gurkha Rifles; 1878, 2nd Afghan War, Peiwar Kotal.
5. Richard Ridgeway; Bengal Staff Corps attached to 8th Gurkha Rifles; 1879, Konoma, India.
6. Charles Grant; Indian Staff Corps attached to 8th Gurkha Rifles; 1891, Manipur Expedition, Thobal, Burma.
7. Guy Boisragon; Indian Staff Corps attached to 5th Royal Gurkha Rifles; 1891, Hunza–Naga Campaign, Nilt Fort, India. This campaign was fought against the princely states of Hunza and Naga in the Gilgit Agency, now part of the Gilgit-Baltistan area of Pakistan. It is known in Pakistan as the 'Anglo-Brusho War'.
8. John Manners Smith; Indian Staff Corps attached to 5th Royal Gurkha Rifles; 1891, Hunza–Naga Campaign, Nilt Fort, India.
9. William Walker; 4th Prince of Wales's Own Gurkha Rifles; 1903, 3rd Somaliland Expedition, Daratoleh, Somaliland. Also called the Anglo-Somali War or the Dervish War, this comprised a series of expeditions between 1900 and 1920 in the Horn of Africa, pitting the Dervishes led by Mohammed Abdullah Hassan (nicknamed the 'Mad Mullah') against the British who were assisted in their offensives by both Ethiopians and Italians.
10. John Grant; 8th Gurkha Rifles; 1904, Tibetan Expedition, Gyantse Jong.
11. Kubir Thapa; 3rd Queen Alexandra's Own Gurkha Rifles; 1915, First World War, Mauquissart, France.
12. George Wheeler; 9th Gurkha Rifles; 1917, First World War, Shumran, Mesopotamia.
13. Karanbahadur Rana; 3rd Queen Alexandra's Own Gurkha Rifles; 1918, First World War, El Kefr, Egypt.
14. Lalbahadur Thapa; 2nd King Edward VII's Own Gurkha Rifles; 1943, Second World War, Rass-es-Zouai, Tunisia.
15. Gaje Ghale; 5th Royal Gurkha Rifles; 1943, Second World War, Chin Hills, Burma.
16. Michael Allmand; Indian Armoured Corps attached to 6th Gurkha Rifles; 1944, Second World War, Pin Hmi Road Bridge, Burma.
17. Tulbahadur Pun; 6th Gurkha Rifles; 1944, Second World War, Mogaung, Burma.
18. Netrabahadur Thapa; 5th Royal Gurkha Rifles; 1944, Second World War, Bishenpur, Burma.

19. Sher Bahadur Thapa; 9th Gurkha Rifles; 1944, Second World War, San Marino, Italy.
20. Agansing Rai; 5th Royal Gurkha Rifles; 1944, Second World War, Bishenpur, Burma.
21. Thaman Gurung; 5th Royal Gurkha Rifles; 1944, Second World War, Italy, Monte san Bertolo, Italy.
22. Frank Blaker; Highland Light Infantry attached to 9th Gurkha Rifles; 1944, Second World War, Taunggi, Burma.
23. Ganju Lama; 7th Gurkha Rifles; 1944, Second World War, Ningthoukhong, Burma.
24. Lacchhiman Gurung; 8th Gurkha Rifles; 1945, Second World War, Taungdaw, Burma.
25. Bhanbhagta Gurung; 2nd King Edward VII's Own Gurkha Rifles; 1945, Second World War, Snowdon East Tamandu, Burma.
26. Rambahadur Limbu; 10th Princess Mary's Own Gurkha Rifles; 1965, Indonesia-Malaysia Confrontation, Sarawak, Borneo.

Appendix 5

Indian Army Gurkhas

When India gained independence, after the murderous chaos of Partition, along with the UK and Nepal it entered into the Britain–India–Nepal Tripartite Agreement. Six regiments of Gurkhas, Gorkhas in the Indian Army (see below), remained to serve the new nation and have formed a vital element of the Indian Army ever since. A seventh formation was raised post-independence to take in those Gurkhas from 7th and 10th GR who preferred to transfer rather than remain as part of the UK defence establishment.

The original six comprised:

1. 1st King George V's Own Gurkha Rifles (The Malaun Regiment).
2. 3rd Queen Alexandra's Own Gurkha Rifles.
3. 4th Prince of Wales's Own Gurkha Rifles.
4. 5th Royal Gurkha Rifles (Frontier Force).
5. 8th Gurkha Rifles.
6. 9th Gurkha Rifles.

In 1949 the Indian Army reverted to the traditional spelling of Gorkha and two years after that, having become a republic, all 'royal' designations were dropped.

As ever, the Gorkhas have been in the thick of the action on the Indian subcontinent since independence. They have won many medals including the Param Vir Chakra (PVC)[1] and Maha Vir Chakra (MVC);[2] one of only two full field marshals in the Indian Army, Sam Manekshaw, served with 5th Gorkha Rifles. During the Hyderabad Police Action on 15 September 1948,[3] Naik Nar Bahadur Thapa of 5/5th GR won the first awarded Ashok Chakra 1st Class. In 1971, during the Indo-Pakistan War[4] 1/5th fought a famous fight capturing the Sehjra Salient from the Pakistani Army.[5] During the Battle of Sylhet 4/5th GR launched the first ever helicopter assault undertaken by Indian forces. Indian Army Gorkhas have served their country in Bangladesh, Sri Lanka and Siachen, taking part in various UN peacekeeping missions in Lebanon, Sudan and Sierra Leone.

During the savage Sino-Indian War of 1962,[6] Major Dhan Singh Thapa of 1/8th GR was awarded the coveted Param Vir Chakra. More recently, in 1999 and the Kargil War,[7] Lieutenant Manoj Kumar Pandey earned another. Currently, there are thirty-nine battalions forming seven Gorkha regiments in the Indian Army:

> 1 Gorkha Rifles – six battalions (previously 1st King George V's Own Gurkha Rifles – the Malaun Regiment).

> 3 Gorkha Rifles – five battalions (previously 3rd Queen Alexandra's Own Gurkha Rifles).

> 4 Gorkha Rifles – five battalions (previously 4th Prince of Wales's Own Gurkha Rifles).

> 5 Gorkha Rifles (Frontier Force) – six battalions (previously 5th Royal Gurkha Rifles (Frontier Force).

> 8 Gorkha Rifles – six battalions.

> 9 Gorkha Rifles – five battalions.

> 11 Gorkha Rifles – seven battalions and one TA battalion (107 Inf. Bn. 11GR; raised after the independence of India).

Appendix 6

Gurkha Weaponry and Equipment

The Kukri (Properly the Khukuri)

The origins of the famous fighting blade, so commonly and universally associated with the Gurkhas that it is generally referred to as a Gurkha knife, are obscure. It may have developed from early domestic/agricultural tools such as the sickle, for it is both weapon and utility knife. Possibly the design was influenced by the cavalry blades, *falcatta*, carried by Alexander's horsemen during his great swathe of conquest across Asia; the similarities are certainly marked.

Examples survive from as far back as the seventeeth century and were first encountered by the British in the war of 1814–16. By the time of the Second World War other elite units, such as the Chindits and Merrill's Marauders, were carrying them. Typically, a blade will be 11in (28cm) in length and light, about 1 or 2lb (450–900g) in weight. It is essentially a slashing weapon, designed for a straight cut, and the configuration of the blade creates a 'wedge' effect adding greater power and penetration to the blow. Its angled shape imparts a level of force disproportionate to its length and there's no need, as with a sabre, to angle the wrist as you slash. It's very much for up close and personal, imposing a deep psychological effect on both attacker and target: even more than the bayonet it screams immediate superiority at close quarters.

There's uncertainty as to the purpose of the notch in the blade just below the tang – it may be ritual or some even say it has sexual connotations. The wood and leather scabbard comes with pockets for two smaller, subsidiary knives: the *karda* – a utility blade – and *chakmal* – a sharpener. The *kukri* has always possessed religious significance and a larger blade is used for ritual sacrifice such as at the Hindu festival of Dashain where the single downward cut, properly delivered, can sever a bull's head; it takes tremendous strength, precision and skill.

Every Gurkha soldier now has two issue weapons: the No. 1 for ceremonial use and No. 2 for exercise. These aren't just for tradition or for decoration;

they're still 'real' and get used. As discussed above, in 2010, Bishnu Shrestha, a retired Indian Army Gurkha, equipped just with his service blade, squared up to a gang of forty bandits and routed the lot, leaving three dead and more wounded. At close quarters it's a terrible weapon still.

Firepower

In addition to their kukris, the Gurkhas were equipped with rifles. The Lee–Metford rifle replaced the Martini–Henry in 1888. This was a bolt-action, box-magazine rifle in .303 (7.7mm) calibre, featuring James Paris Lee's rear locking bolt system and William Ellis Metford's innovative seven-groove barrel. It could hold eight or ten rounds and a rifleman might fire fifteen aimed shots a minute and kill at 800yd (730m).

Infantry firepower was increasing at an undreamed of rate. Sir Hiram Stevens Maxim was an American-born British inventor who patented the first recoil-operated machine gun in 1884. This also fired a .303 (7.7mm) round which came in belts of 250 and offered a cyclic rate of up to 600 rounds a minute over a considerable distance. This was the birth of the modern automatic weapon and vastly increased the killing power of European armies. Its day would fully arrive in 1914.

The conflict of 1914–18 was to be industrial warfare on a scale and intensity never before experienced or even imagined. Technology had vastly increased the killing power of both artillery and small arms. The new quick-firers (see below) would move the guns to the prime slot as arbiters on the field. A British soldier could fire twelve to fifteen aimed rounds per minute from his Short Magazine Lee–Enfield – the legendary 'SMLE' (see below). Steamships could transport him over oceans in a fraction of the time sail would have taken.

Railways could move him, his horses, equipment, rations, fodder and ammunition over great distances on land. Tinned food, that most commonplace of commodities, ensured he could be fed and sustained year-round in trenches. Machine guns could spew out 500–600 rounds per minute and kill at 2,000yd. The war itself would witness exponential development in the role of aircraft and in the introduction of new, even more terrible, weapons. Tanks, poison gas and flamethrowers would add fresh dimensions of horror. It would prove a very unlovely war.

An artillery innovation from the 1890s, 'quick-firers' were distinguished from earlier ordnance in that they were fitted with buffers to limit recoil, the breech was adapted to allow rapid re-loading and shell and propellant were combined in cartridge form. Consequently, in the early twentieth century, the killing power of artillery increased exponentially.

The Royal Artillery (RA) comprised Royal Field Artillery (infantry support), Royal Horse Artillery (cavalry support with the lighter 13-pounder gun) and Royal Garrison Artillery (heavy guns); the RFA was formed in brigades, each brigade having four batteries of six guns, commanded by a major with its ammunition column. The 4th Battery in each brigade was equipped with 4.5in howitzers. The six guns in the battery were arranged in three sections, each of two guns, and commanded by a captain with individual gun crews, commanded by a sergeant (no. 1) and referred to as a sub-section or just sub for short.

The SMLE was the standard British service rifle of the era, called 'short' because of the barrel length being shorter than the earlier 'long' Lee–Enfield which did service in the Boer War and with which many territorial units were still armed in 1914. The SMLE was intended both for cavalry and infantry, firing ten rounds of .303 (7.7.mm) ball cartridge. The weapon reached its final pre-war variant, the Mark III, in 1907 and confounded its critics, doing good service throughout the conflict and, depending on circumstance, for decades afterwards.

The Vickers, manufactured by Vickers-Armstrong on Tyneside, was a .303. calibre (7.7mm) belt-fed, water-cooled weapon with a cyclic rate of about 500 rounds per minute. Famed for its reliability and robustness, it required a crew of eight: one firer, one loader and the rest to carry the weapons, tools and ammunition. The Vickers remained in service with the British Army until after the Second World War and provided British and Commonwealth forces with a manageable and robust medium machine gun.

The machine gun was essentially a 'new' weapon in the trenches, although it had been around for some time. Ideal for defence, it was more limited in attack due to its weight; a lighter gun was needed to support infantry assault. The Lewis Automatic machine gun remained in service from 1914–53. It was a .303 (7.7mm) drum-fed light machine gun which used a 47-round box with a cyclic rate of 500 rounds per minute. At 28lb (13kg) in weight, it was far more portable than the Vickers and had a marked effect on British infantry tactics.

During the desert fighting of the Second World War British and imperial forces started out at a severe disadvantage in terms of equipment. Allied tanks were markedly inferior and the standard 2-pounder anti-tank gun largely ineffective. By the late 1930s, there was a recognised need for a new rifle to replace the trusty SMLE. This replacement, No. 4 Mk I, was officially adopted in 1941. The No. 4 action was similar to the Mk VI, but stronger and, most importantly, easier to mass-produce. Unlike the SMLE, that had a nose cap, the No. 4 Lee–Enfield barrels protruded from the end of the fore-stock. The No. 4 rifle was heavier than the No. 1 Mk. III, largely due to its heavier barrel. A new spike bayonet was designed, basically a steel rod with a sharp point swiftly branded 'the pig-sticker' by its users.

In the Malayan Emergency the Gurkhas said goodbye to their .303 Mark IV Lee–Enfields and adopted, as did the whole of the British Armed Forces, the 7.62mm, L1A1 Self-loading Rifle (SLR), a version of the Belgian FN FAL rifle. It was introduced from 1954 and continues in use with some armies today. The round was the standard NATO calibre for most of the Cold War era. An Allied rifle commission of the 1950s had sought to identify a single rifle and standard cartridge that would serve for all member nations. This didn't work out completely as the Americans opted for their own 7.62mm weapon, the M14. The rifles were manufactured by the Royal Small Arms Factory Enfield, Birmingham Small Arms, Royal Ordnance Factory and ROF Fazakerley. The 9mm Sten Gun, of Second World War vintage and dubious efficacy, was also replaced by the far superior Sterling in the same calibre.

Quite early on during the first days of the Emergency, the Gurkhas had replaced their No. 4 Enfields with the handier, shortened No. 5 or Jungle Carbine; some American MI .30 carbines, really good and easily hefted semi-automatic weapons; and the rather odd-looking, Heath-Robinson-style Australian 9mm Owen sub-machine gun. They even got proper lightweight jungle boots.

Armoured Cars

While the Brigade of Gurkhas hasn't traditionally been equipped with its own armoured cars, these have been an invaluable support. Before 1914, scouting and reconnaissance were traditionally preserves of the light cavalry, themselves descended from the 'hobilers' or 'prickers' who formed the eyes and often the teeth of medieval armies.

The First World War provided the stimulus for the development of the armoured car. In the first instance this, more or less, was and did what it implied: a civilian motor vehicle provided with light armament and some attempts at armour, used for scouting. As the war ground on, attempts were made to produce a more specialised vehicle, still based on civilian models but fitted with armour plate and latterly a turret. Some were specifically adapted to anti-aircraft use. In 1914 the Royal Naval Air Service (RNAS) raised a squadron of armoured cars for airfield protection.

These pioneer vehicles utilised a standard Rolls-Royce Silver Ghost chassis but with twin wheels at the rear and a bespoke steel superstructure including a revolving turret which could accommodate a medium machine gun (Vickers). A six-cylinder Rolls-Royce petrol engine provided sufficient power to keep 4.22 tonnes of weight moving at effective speeds. By 1915 many of these early vehicles were transferred to the Middle East theatre for use against Ottoman forces in Palestine and Mesopotamia.

Freed from the grinding attrition of static warfare in the trenches, the armoured cars came into their own. Performing in the light cavalry role, they coped well with desert conditions despite only being two-wheel drive. One of the most romantic uses of the armoured cars was as a component of 'Dunsterforce' – playing the 'Great Game' during the collapse of tsarist Russian armies in 1917.

Major General Lionel Dunsterville commanded a flying column of about a thousand British and Australian troops. Their role was to seal the gap which had opened after tsarist withdrawal from the Caucasus, a wide frontier stretching over 800 miles to Mesopotamia. It was feared that the Ottomans, backed by their German sponsors, might have designs on India. These proved groundless but Dunsterforce was engaged in the savage and bloody fighting for Baku before withdrawing. The city's predominantly Armenian population suffered the full, ghastly consequences of a Turkish victory.

In Afghanistan armoured vehicles quickly proved their worth, nimble as light cavalry but so much better protected and 'tooled up' with Vickers machine guns and Lewis Light machine guns, combining agility, mobility and firepower. They were ideally suited for guarding vulnerable convoys and for providing infantry support. The Gurkhas would come to value them. Those versatile 'Kangaroos' manned by 14/20 Hussars did inestimable service in Italy during 1945.

Notes

Introduction

1. Quoted in B. Farwell, *The Gurkhas* (London, Allen Lane, 1984), p. 29.
2. I was there as a guest of the brigade having taken Gurkha soldiers on several battlefield tours. My son-in-law was (then) adjutant of 2 RGR.
3. Today the average Gurkha recruit is quite often better educated than his green army contemporary.
4. Farwell, *Gurkhas*, p. 32.
5. Ibid., p. 13.
6. Ibid., p. 15.
7. Ibid.
8. This story first appeared in *The Phantom Rickshaw and other Eerie Tales* (Vol. Five of the Indian Railway Library, published by Wheelers of Allahabad in 1888) and collected in *Wee Willie Winkie and Other Stories* in 1895, and in numerous later editions of that collection: http://www.kiplingsociety.co.uk/poems_youngbrit.htm, retrieved 20 February 2019.
9. Farwell, *Gurkhas*, p. 225.
10. Ibid., p. 229.
11. Tony Gould, *Imperial Warriors* (London, Granta, 1999).
12. https://www.bbc.co.uk/programmes/b05xd44k, retrieved 20 February 2019.
13. Interview, May 2016.

Chapter 1

1. E.D. Smith, *Valour, a History of the Gurkhas* (Staplehurst, Spellmount, 1997), p. 24.
2. Calcutta was the capital from 1773–1912 when Delhi once again became the centre.
3. Smith, *Valour*, p. 26.

4. E. Bishop, *Better to Die* (London, New English Library, 1976), p. 39.
5. Farwell, *Gurkhas*, p. 41.
6. General Sir Charles Reid GCB, *Extracts from Letters and Notes Written During the Siege of Delhi in 1857* (London, Naval & Military Press, 2009), p. 1, and Colonel L.W. Shakespear and Lieutenant Colonel G.R. Stevens, *History of the 2nd King Edward's Own Goorkha Rifles (The Sirmoor Rifles)* (London, Gale & Polden, 1952), p. 35.
7. Reid, *Extracts*, p. 3.
8. Shakespear and Stevens, *History*, p. 37.
9. Reid, *Extracts*, p. 16.
10. Farwell, *Gurkhas*, p. 42.
11. Reid, *Extracts*, p. 16 and Shakespear and Stevens, *History*, p. 37.
12. Reid, *Extracts*, p. 18.
13. G. Fremont-Barnes, *The Indian Mutiny 1857–1858* (Oxford, Osprey 'Essential Histories', 2007), p. 37.
14. Ibid.
15. Caesar's siege of Vercingetorix's stronghold in 52 BC; climatic struggle of the Gallic Wars.
16. Bishop, *Better to Die*, p. 27.
17. Reid, *Extracts*, p. 21.
18. Ibid. and Shakespear and Stevens, *History*, p. 39.
19. Shakespear and Stevens, *History*, p. 31.
20. Bishop, *Better to Die*, p. 27.
21. Reid, *Extracts*, p. 27.
22. Ibid., p. 31.
23. Shakespear and Stevens, *History*, p. 40.
24. Ibid.
25. M. Chappell, *The Gurkhas* (Oxford, Osprey 'Elite' Series No. 49, 1993), pp. 45–6.
26. Reid, *Extracts*, p. 32.
27. Ibid. and Shakespear and Stevens, *History*, p. 46.
28. The Battle of Plassey in 1757 saw a decisive victory for the armies of the East India Company and marked the beginning of British rule in India.
29. Shakespear and Stevens, *History*, p. 36.
30. Ibid., p. 37.
31. Ibid.
32. The Indian Order of Merit was instituted by John Company in 1837, taken over by the Crown in 1858.
33. Reid, *Extracts*, p, 38.
34. Ibid., p. 40.

NOTES

35. Ibid., p. 45 and Shakespear and Stevens, *History*, p. 46.
36. Reid, *Extracts*, p. 50 and Shakespear and Stevens, *History*, p. 46.
37. Shakespear and Stevens, *History*, p. 56.
38. J. Parker, *The Gurkhas* (London, Headline, 1999), p. 47.
39. Reid, *Extracts*, p. 62 and Shakespear and Stevens, *History*, p. 43.
40. Shakespear and Stevens, *History*, p. 55.
41. Ibid., p. 56.
42. Ibid., p. 59.
43. Ibid. and Shakespear and Stevens, *History*, p. 47.
44. Farwell, *Gurkhas*, pp. 45–6.
45. Reid, *Extracts*, p. 66; Brigadier John Nicholson (1821–57) was one of those muscular Victorian figures who carved out his own legend as a political officer under Henry Lawrence in the Punjab and along the North-West Frontier. Born in Dublin, dead by the age of 35, he served in the 1st Afghan and Sikh wars. Dogmatic and authoritarian, he remains controversial, sending shudders down the sensitive spines of imperial apologists.
46. Shakespear and Stevens, *History*, p. 49.
47. Ibid.
48. Reid, *Extracts*, p. 74.
49. Ibid., p. 76.
50. Ibid., p. 61 and Shakespear and Stevens, *History*, p. 48.
51. Reid, *Extracts*, p. 77.
52. Ibid., p. 79 and Shakespear and Stevens, *History*, p. 49.
53. Shakespear and Stevens, *History*, p. 85.
54. Ibid., p. 86.
55. Chappell, *Gurkhas*, p. 47; Reid and his battalion gained glowing tributes from Wilson (see dispatch no. 1428, dated 13 August 1857, reproduced in Shakespear and Stevens, *History*, pp. 51–2).
56. Parker, *Gurkhas*, p. 49.
57. Bishop, *Better to Die*, p. 46.
58. Ibid., p. 48.
59. Reid, *Extracts*, p. 63.

Chapter 2

1. The Sirmoor Battalion was made up of 10 companies, each of which had 1 subadar, 4 jemadars, 8 havildars, 8 naiks, 2 buglers, 120 other ranks, a battalion strength of 1,223; see Shakespear and Stevens, *History*, p. 6.

2. The Maurya Empire was an extensive Iron Age civilisation based in Magadha and founded by Chandragupta Maurya which dominated the subcontinent from 322–187 BC.
3. His brother had been a casualty of one of the failed attempts; in retaliation, despite earlier promises, he had his soldiers cut off the noses and lips of all males over 12. This amounted to a tally of 865 noses, which for those interested was 80lb (36kg) of severed flesh; see Parker, *Gurkhas*, p. 31.
4. Francis Rawdon-Hastings, 2nd Earl of Moira and 1st Marquess of Hastings (1754–1826) was an Irish adventurer who had only come to India in his late 50s; sometimes soldier, often gambler and rake. He had nonetheless fulfilled a useful function as the Prince-Regent's resident pimp and procurer. While, bizarrely, he was an opponent of empire he urgently needed the handsome remuneration that went with the job.
5. Bishop, *Better to Die*, p. 12.
6. Ibid., p. 13.
7. Farwell, *Gurkhas*, p. 29.
8. See Evelyn Waugh's *Sword of Honour* trilogy, *Men at Arms* (1952), *Officers & Gentlemen* (1955) and *Unconditional Surrender* (1961) all published in London by Chapman & Hall.
9. John Ship, an ensign in the 87th Foot, quoted in Farwell, *Gurkhas*, p. 30.
10. Both sides erected battlefield memorials and even by 1815 a number of Gurkhas had 'defected' to the British. Alongside POWs these were formed into four Nepalese Irregular Corps, later 1st and 2nd Battalions of the Nassira Regiment (1st Gurkha Rifles) and the Sirmoors (2nd Gurkhas) and the Kumaon Levy (3rd Gurkhas), see Shakespear and Stevens, *History*, p. 1.
11. Sir David Ochterlony, 1st Baronet of Pitforthy, 1st Baronet of Ochterlony GCB (1758–1825) was a Massachusetts-born general who served with the East India Company. Among many successful appointments he held the powerful post of British Resident to the Moghul court at Delhi. He was a classic imperial soldier, born of Scottish gentry stock. At the age of 18, he served in and was captured during the Second Anglo-Mysore War. By 1803, in recognition of his capabilities he had risen to the rank of lieutenant general and saw extensive fighting during the Anglo-Maratha conflict. As resident in Delhi he 'went native' with a baker's dozen of Indian wives (or concubines as Europeans might describe them), who he promenaded around the Red Fort each evening. He was a nabob in the eighteenth-century sense, an era of rather more relaxed attitudes than the prim morality of the nineteenth century could endorse. As such, despite his success

in the Nepalese War, he was rather sidelined in his later years. Imperial swashbucklers in the vein of Clive and Eyre Coote were out of fashion.
12. Farwell, *Gurkhas*, p. 32.
13. The Kot Massacre, 14 September 1846, was a real Jacobean flourish with a final body count of between thirty and forty.
14. https://www.nytimes.com/2001/06/08/world/a-witness-to-massacre-in-nepal-tells-gory-details.html, retrieved 23 April 2019.
15. James Hilton, author of *Lost Horizon* (1933).
16. R. Kipling, *The Man who would be King* (Stansted, Wordsworth Editions, 1994).
17. https://www.bbc.co.uk/news/world-asia-32461019, retrieved 23 April 2019.
18. Farwell, *Gurkhas*, p. 22.
19. Ibid., p. 300.
20. Ibid.
21. Ibid., p. 301.
22. Ibid., p. 302.
23. Ibid., p. 23.
24. Ibid.
25. Smith, *Valour*, pp. 15–16.
26. Parker, *Gurkhas*, p. 29.
27. Nepal-based recruiting agents.
28. The exact origin of this aphorism is unclear but may be attributable to an American military chaplain present during the Battle of Bataan in 1942.
29. This has many spellings, sometimes called *Durga-puja*; see Farwell, *Gurkhas*, p. 136.
30. Thugs – organised gangs of robbers and ritualistic killers, suppressed by the Raj.
31. Farwell, *Gurkhas*, p. 137.
32. Ibid., p. 139.
33. Ibid., p. 49.
34. Ibid.
35. Ibid., p. 51. This may in fact be apocryphal and arises from the fact the officer involved didn't speak Gurkhali.
36. Ibid., p. 52.
37. Ibid., p. 54.
38. http://gurkhastories.com/veteran-stories/dharam-prashad-limbu/, retrieved 29 April 2019.
39. A. Schlacher, *Arc of the Gurkha* (London, Elliott & Thompson, 2014), p. 18.
40. Ibid.

Chapter 3

1. Frederick Young (1786–1874), an Irishman from Donegal, joined the EIC at 15 and rose to general rank; perhaps if anyone he was the founder of the Gurkhas.
2. Garhwal is the western region and administrative division of the northern Indian state of Uttarakhand, home to the Garhwali people. Lying in the Himalayas, it is bounded on the north by Tibet, on the east by Kumaon region.
3. Kumaon (or Kumaun), the other administrative district of Uttarakhand.
4. Bishop, *Better to Die*, p. 13.
5. Farwell, *Gurkhas*, p. 34.
6. He committed suicide in gaol using, appropriately enough, his kukri.
7. 'Dacoit' is a general term used for any bandit in Bengali, Odia, Hindi, Kannada and Urdu; see Shakespear and Stevens, *History*, p. 5.
8. Saharanpur is both a city and Municipal Corporation in the state of Uttar Pradesh in Northern India, the administrative headquarters of Saharanpur District and Division, see Shakespear and Stevens, *History*, p. 5.
9. Forbes (1799–1858) was born in India and became a distinguished botanist, latterly professor of Materia Medica at King's College London.
10. Shore was a Daniel Dravot-like figure, something of a mystic with a tendency to 'go native' at times; Farwell, *Gurkhas*, p. 37.
11. Shakespear and Stevens, *History*, p. 6.
12. Ibid.
13. Ibid.
14. Ibid.
15. The First Sikh War (1845–6) resulted in a partial subjugation of the Sikh state and cession of Jammu and Kashmir as a separate entity under British domination.
16. Farwell, *Gurkhas*, p. 39.
17. Fought on 10 February 1846.
18. Farwell, *Gurkhas*, p. 39.

Chapter 4

1. R.L. Turner, *A Comparative and Etymological Dictionary of the Nepali Language* (London, K. Paul, Trench, Trubner, 1931), Foreword.
2. John Masters (1914–83) was a successful British author who had served in the Indian Army during the pre-war and wartime years. His novels focused

NOTES

on aspects of Anglo-Indian history and perhaps the most successful, *Bhowani Junction* (1954), was filmed in 1956 starring Stewart Granger.
3. J. Masters, *Bugles and a Tiger* (London, Weidenfeld & Nicolson, 2002 edn), pp. 15–16.
4. Kipling, *Man who would be King*, p. 126.
5. Masters, *Bugles*, p. 17.
6. Ibid. The tsar's vast armies were much feared though they performed poorly in the Crimea; badly trained peasant conscripts were even more badly equipped and even worse led. The Bear began, for a while, to resemble a paper Tiger.
7. Ibid.
8. http://www.kiplingsociety.co.uk/poems_youngbrit.htm, retrieved 24 April 2019.
9. Parker, *Gurkhas*, p. 57.
10. Bishop, *Better to Die*, p. 47.
11. Farwell, *Gurkhas*, p. 57.
12. Masters, *Bugles*, p. 16.
13. A Karlani Pushtun tribe from southern Waziristan.
14. Bishop, *Better to Die*, p. 48.
15. A remote Buddhist kingdom clinging to the eastern rim of the Himalayas.
16. Bishop, *Better to Die*, p. 49.
17. Ibid., p. 50.
18. Field Marshal Frederick Sleigh Roberts, 1st Earl Roberts, VC, KG, KP, GCB, OM, GCSI, GCIE, KStJ, VD, PC, FRSGS (1832–1914) was one of the most successful British military commanders of his time.
19. Bishop, *Better to Die*, pp. 50–1.
20. Ibid., p. 51.
21. Directed by Cy Endfield for Diamond Films, the script written by John Prebble.
22. https://www.shorehamfort.co.uk/past/the-martini-henry-rifle/, retrieved 24 April 2019.
23. *London Gazette,* 18 March 1879.
24. Bishop, *Better to Die*, p. 52.
25. Ibid.
26. Ibid.
27. Quoted in Farwell, *Gurkhas*, p. 57.
28. Bishop, *Better to Die*, p. 53.
29. His dates are 1859–1916.
30. Bishop, *Better to Die*, p. 56.
31. Ibid.

32. Ibid., p. 61.
33. Ibid.
34. Farwell, *Gurkhas*, p. 61.
35. Bishop, *Better to Die*, p. 63.
36. Ibid., p. 64.
37. Ibid.
38. These were Major Boileau and Captain Butcher, both of whom were subsequently dishonourably discharged.
39. Farwell, *Gurkhas*, p. 65.
40. Ibid., pp. 65–6.
41. Masters, *Bugles*, pp. 96–7.
42. George Nathaniel Curzon, 1st Marquess Curzon of Kedleston, KG, GCSI, GCIE, PC, FBA (1859–1925) who was styled as Lord Curzon of Kedleston between 1898 and 1911, and as Earl Curzon of Kedleston between 1911 and 1921, Viceroy of India 1899–1905.
43. Lieutenant Colonel Sir Francis Edward Younghusband, KCSI KCIE (1863–1942) was a British Army officer, explorer and spiritual writer. He is remembered for his travels in the Far East and Central Asia; especially the 1904 British expedition to Tibet, led by him, and for his writings on Asia and foreign policy.
44. P. Fleming, *Bayonets to Lhasa* (|Oxford, Oxford University Press, 1961), p. 104.
45. A *sangar* is a temporary defensive enclosure built up from surface rocks and stone.
46. Fleming, *Bayonets to Lhasa*, pp. 147–8.
47. This feature derived its name from coloured etchings of Buddha incised into the rocks.
48. Fleming, *Bayonets to Lhasa*, p. 159.
49. Ibid., p. 157.
50. Ibid.
51. Ibid., pp. 166–7.
52. Ibid., p. 167.
53. Ibid., p. 208.
54. Ibid.
55. *London Gazette*, 24 January 1905.

Chapter 5

1. S. Doherty and T. Donovan, *The Indian Army Corps on the Western Front* (Brighton, Tom Donovan Editions, 2014), p. 56.

NOTES

2. Ibid., p. 10.
3. The original trench system was made up of three parallel lines, interconnected by communications trenches. These were incredibly important and well fortified. The front trench was lightly manned and usually only fully occupied at 'stand to' at dawn and dusk. Behind the front trench was the support trench, where the soldiers would retreat when the front trench was bombarded. Behind the support trench was the reserve trench. It was here that reserve troops could ready themselves for a counterattack if the front trench was captured. This system was made redundant by powerful artillery, but along some of the front line the support trench was maintained as a decoy to direct enemy bombardment away from the front or reserve lines.

   Fighting trenches tended to be about 12ft (3.7m) deep. To stop bomb or shell damage travelling too far down the line, trenches were dug in zigzag patterns. This could also prevent the enemy from firing in a straight line down the trench if they gained access to it. The sides of the trench were made of sandbags, wooden frames and wire mesh; a fire step was included so men could fire or see over the parapet. Loopholes were built into parapets so soldiers could see out of the trenches without exposing their heads.

   The back of the trench could also be built up and was known as the parados; this helped protect the soldiers' backs from fire behind. The floor of the trench was usually covered by wooden duckboards. In later trenches the floor was raised by a wooden frame to provide drainage beneath. Heavy shelling destroyed the water channels which helped to drain the Flanders soil and so any trench dug into the ground would flood quickly. The barbed wire placed in front of trenches was different on either side. The German wire was heavier and thicker, and the British wire cutters, designed for their own thinner product, were unable to cut it.

   The Germans perfected the art of designing and constructing defensive works. They used reinforced concrete to construct deep, shell-proof, ventilated dugouts, as well as strategic strongpoints. They also typically had electricity. German dugouts were much deeper than British ones and sometimes dug three stories down, with concrete stairs leading to the upper levels. By being the first to dig in, the Germans were able to seize the high ground, giving them the tactical advantage and drier trenches. They also built strong redoubts along vulnerable sectors of the front line. Although seemingly isolated, each redoubt could provide supporting fire to other redoubts and trenches.
4. D.J. Sadler and R.B. Serdiville, *Tommy at War 1914–1918* (London, JR Books, 2013), p. 55.

5. Ibid.
6. Ibid., p. 56.
7. Doherty and Donovan, *Indian Army Corps*, p. 146.
8. Extract from the Regimental History, quoted by Doherty and Donovan, *Indian Army Corps*, pp. 50, 75–7.
9. Ibid., p. 40.
10. Ibid., p. 146.
11. Ibid., pp. 75–7.
12. Ibid.
13. Ibid.
14. Ibid.
15. Ibid.
16. Ibid.
17. The 'Race to the Sea' refers to a serious of flanking moves attempted by both sides in late 1914 where each attempted to outflank the solidifying trench line; the last days for any war of manoeuvre until 1918.
18. Doherty and Donovan, *Indian Army Corps*, p. 93.
19. Ibid., pp. 97–9.
20. Ibid.
21. Ibid., p. 102.
22. Ibid., p. 118.
23. If the battlefield visitor moves half a kilometre north from the cemetery to the vicinity of the present industrial estate you will have a grandstand view of the action, though there has been much modern building the nature of the ground and topography has not changed.
24. Doherty and Donovan, *Indian Army Corps*, pp. 119–21.
25. Ibid., pp. 134–5.
26. Ibid., p. 137.
27. Ibid., pp. 138–9.
28. Ibid.
29. General Sir Ian Standish Menteith Hamilton was twice recommended for a VC and had, prior to the Dardanelles, had a glittering career, serving in Afghanistan and both Boer Wars. Gallipoli finished him militarily, though he was later very active in the British Legion; less creditably he became a great admirer of Hitler even after 1933.
30. C. Bullock, *Britain's Gurkhas* (London, Third Millennium, 1999), p. 67.
31. Ibid.
32. In the opening two months of 1915, German-led Turkish forces launched attacks from southern Palestine directed at the vital British-held waterway

of the Suez Canal. Two Gurkha battalions, 2/7th and 2/10th, were deployed as part of the defending forces and several probes were seen off. The 2/7th also led an amphibious raid against a large force of Arabs, dispersing them and killing 194 for the loss of 1 Gurkha who was given a massive send-off; Bullock, *Britain's Gurkhas*, p. 73.

33. Ibid., p. 68.
34. Ibid.
35. Ibid.
36. Jam-tin grenades did what it said on the tin; they were packed with explosives and shrapnel and detonated by a fuse inserted through the lid, very crude but nonetheless far from ineffective.
37. 'Bombing up the traverses' – this was the standard means of taking an enemy trench which was constructed from a line of fire-bays and traverses. The attacking squad was divided into two sections: 'bomb' men with grenades and 'bayonet' men. Once the grenades were thrown, the bayonet section surged through to mop up survivors.
38. Bullock, *Britain's Gurkhas*, p. 69.
39. Ibid.
40. 6th Queen Elizabeth's Own Gurkha Rifles Newsletter, December 2018. https://www.6thgurkhas.org/the-regiment/gallipoli-campaign/, retrieved 29 March 2019.
41. Bullock, *Britain's Gurkhas*, p. 71.
42. Ibid., p. 72.
43. Ibid.
44. Ibid.
45. Ibid.
46. C. Catherwood, *The Battles of World War One* (London, Allison & Busby, 2014); p. 38; note that while the core point is well made, the original text is flawed in that it gives the dates for the siege as being from 1914–15, which is of course incorrect.
47. Bullock, *Britain's Gurkhas*, p. 73.
48. His own apologia *My Campaign in Mesopotamia* was published in 1920 – much good it did him. See also N.S. Nash, *Chitral Charlie: The Rise and Fall of Major-General Charles Townshend* (Barnsley, Pen & Sword, 2010).
49. C.R.M.F. Cruttwell, *A History of the Great War 1914–1918* (USA, Chicago Academy Publishers, 1991), p. 343.
50. Ibid., p. 344.
51. Bullock, *Britain's Gurkhas*, p. 74.
52. Cruttwell, *History of the Great War*, p. 345.

53. Ibid., p. 346.
54. Bullock, *Britain's Gurkhas*, p. 75.
55. Ibid.
56. Cruttwell, *History of the Great War*, p. 347.
57. Ibid., p. 348.
58. Bullock, *Britain's Gurkhas*, p. 77.
59. From the unpublished war diary of Lieutenant Leonard William Henry Mathias DSO.
60. Cruttwell, *History of the Great War*, pp. 352–3.
61. The Armenian Genocide or Armenian Holocaust, 1915–17, was the Turkish slaughter of Armenians, resulting in an estimated 1.5 million deaths.
62. Cruttwell, *History of the Great War*, p. 357.
63. Bullock, *Britain's Gurkhas*, p. 77.
64. Ibid.
65. For his gallantry, Wheeler was awarded a VC.
66. Bishop, *Better to Die*, p. 78.
67. Cruttwell, *History of the Great War*, p. 607.
68. 'Dunsterforce' was raised in late 1917 and named after its CO, General Lionel Dunsterville. The column, only 350 strong, raced across Northern Iran and southern Caucasus in Ford vans and armoured cars attempting to drum up local irregulars to make up for the loss of the tsar's armies. They fought in the Battle of Baku during September 1918 and were disbanded immediately after.
69. Bishop, *Better to Die*, p. 80.
70. Cruttwell, *History of the Great War*, p. 611.
71. Bishop, *Better to Die*, p. 80.
72. Cruttwell, *History of the Great War*, pp. 616–17.
73. Ibid., p. 618.
74. Ibid., p. 619.
75. Bishop, *Better to Die*, p. 82.
76. Cruttwell, *History of the Great War*, p. 621.
77. Ibid.
78. Bishop, *Better to Die*, p. 83.
79. Lieutenant General William Marshall (1865–1939), who had replaced Maude as Commander in Chief Mesopotamia.
80. Colonel B.R. Mullaly, *Bugle & Kukri, the Story of the 10th Princess Mary's Own Gurkha Rifles* (Edinburgh, William Blackwood, 1957), p. 128.
81. Lieutenant William Ross-Stewart, Indian Medical Service, serving with 1/4th Gurkhas Gallipoli 1915 (Gurkha Museum archives).

Chapter 6

1. Reiver – to *be-reave*, theft of livestock and/or goods.
2. *Bastle* – a stone blockhouse, possibly from the French *bastille* – tower.
3. *Threap* – wasteland.
4. *The Third Afghan War 1919 – Official Account* (Calcutta, Government of India Central Publication Branch, 1926), compiled in the General Staff Branch, Army HQ, India, p. 1.
5. From 1917–22.
6. The Triple Entente with Russia of 1907 followed the Dual Entente between Britain and France, three years earlier.
7. The author has, in his collection, a battered German First World War helmet (*Stahlhelm*) recovered from Afghanistan.
8. Son of that Chelmsford, of Zulu War notoriety.
9. The Amritsar (Jallianwala Bagh) Massacre occurred on 13 April 1919 and involved soldiers from 1/9th Gurkhas. Brigadier General R.E.H. Dyer commanded Indian Army troops at Amritsar in the Punjab where a large crowd had gathered in the Bagh, a wide area of public gardens 6 to 7 acres (2.8 ha) in extent, walled all around with five gateways in the circuit. These protesters were all civilians and had come to protest at the proposed deportation of two nationalist leaders. The Raj's grip might still be tight but the stirrings of independence were rising. Heavy losses suffered by Indian troops during the First World War hadn't helped and what was about to happen that Sunday would reverberate across the country.

    Dyer had given an order banning any such gathering but probably few of the huge crowd of Sikhs, Muslims and Hindus who gathered inside the Bagh – perhaps as many as 20,000 – had heard of the order. Dyer's detachment of Gurkhas, Sikhs and Rajputs (less than a full company all told), marched in through the main entrance and took up positions along an elevated embankment. Having blocked off all exits Dyer then gave the order to fire and 10 minutes of orgiastic slaughter followed. Those who escaped bullets were crushed in the press at the exits and shooting only stopped as ammo was exhausted. Dyer later claimed his men had fired 1,650 rounds leaving 379 dead and over 1,000 injured; nationalist sources put both figures much higher.

    This atrocity stunned India and hugely fuelled the swelling independence movement. Initially, Dyer avoided censure but as the tide of acrimony both in India and within Britain began to swell, he was sidelined and finally dropped. Both Churchill as home secretary and former PM Asquith were appalled.

10. *The Third Afghan War 1919*, p. 6 and Smith, *Valour*, pp. 70–1.
11. *The Third Afghan War 1919*, pp. 26–7 and D. Chandler and I. Beckett (eds), *The Oxford Illustrated History of the British Army* (Oxford, Oxford University Press, 1994), pp. 388–9.
12. Located in Baluchistan, second largest settlement after Quetta, just south of the Wesh-Chaman border crossing into Kandahar Province.
13. Mullaly, *Bugle & Kukri*, pp. 152–3.
14. Ibid.
15. Ibid., p. 153.
16. Ibid., p. 154 and *The Third Afghan War 1919*, pp. 98–107.
17. Ibid., and *The Third Afghan War 1919*, p. 106.
18. Ibid.
19. The book was published in 1954 with a film version released two years later starring Stewart Granger, Ava Gardner and Bill Travers.
20. First published in 1951.
21. First published in 1956.
22. His famous Burma memoir is *Quartered Safe Out Here* (London, HarperCollins, 2000).
23. 1897–1960, a steadfast troublemaker to the end.
24. Masters, *Bugles*, p. 190.
25. This Brigade was constituted after 1903 by Kitchener when he was C in C, India. They formed part of the Northern Army deployed along the frontier. The brigade comprised 25th Cavalry (Frontier Force), 33rd Punjabis, 52nd Sikhs (Frontier Force), 55th Coke's Rifles (Frontier Force) and 29 Mountain Battery.
26. A Pashtun tribal confederacy based in both what is now Pakistan and Afghanistan.
27. https://royalsignalsoperationalawards.com/2018/01/04/the-shahur-tangi-ambush-north-west-frontier-1937/, retrieved 16 April 2019.
28. Masters, *Bugles*, p. 199.
29. Ibid.
30. Ibid., p. 200.
31. Ibid., p. 210.
32. Ibid.
33. Ibid., pp. 210–11.
34. Ibid.
35. Ibid., p. 213.
36. Ibid., p. 216.
37. Also called the Gambila River, flowing through Northern Waziristan.

NOTES

38. Masters, *Bugles,* pp. 218–19.
39. Ibid., p. 220.
40. Ibid., p. 221.
41. Ibid., pp. 221–2.
42. Ibid., p. 222.
43. Ibid.
44. Ibid., pp. 223–4.
45. Ibid., pp. 224–5, also the same day on which George VI was crowned.
46. Ibid., p. 225.
47. Ibid.
48. Ibid., p. 226.
49. M. Arthur, *Forgotten Voices of the Second World War* (London, Ebury Press, 2005), p. 5.
50. Ibid.
51. 1897–1945, a fervent Indian nationalist who was prepared to ally with the Axis and Japan to end Britain's Imperial rule. He was killed in a plane crash; the aircraft was Japanese but there is a healthy school of conspiracy theorists who point at targeted assassination.

Chapter 7

1. R. Hillary, *The Last Enemy* (London, Pimlico Edition, 1997), p. 2.
2. Churchill, with his habitual trenchant prose, dubbed El Alamein 'the end of the beginning' – and indeed he was right.
3. P. Warner, *Alamein, Recollections of the Heroes* (Barnsley, Pen & Sword, 1979), p. 39.
4. The war in the Western Desert is often described as a pendulum, swinging one way and then the other; there were a good few swings between the years 1940 and 1943.
5. J. Crawford, *I was an Eighth Army Soldier* (London, Victor Gollancz, 1944), p. 36.
6. Field Marshal the Viscount B.L. Montgomery, *Memoirs* (London, Collins, 1958), p. 90.
7. Bullock, *Britain's Gurkhas*, p. 96.
8. Ibid.
9. J. Strawson, *The Battle for North Africa* (Barnsley, Pen & Sword, 2004), p. 104 and R.R. Parkinson, *War in the Desert* (London, HarperCollins, 1976), p. 105.
10. *The Third Afghan War 1919*, p. 229.

11. Ibid., p. 233.
12. Bullock, *Britain's Gurkhas*, p. 100.
13. Ibid., p. 101.
14. Parkinson, *War in the Desert*, p. 110.
15. Ibid.
16. *The Third Afghan War 1919*, p. 246.
17. Bullock, *Britain's Gurkhas*, pp. 101–2.
18. N. Barr, *Pendulum of War, the Three Battles of El Alamein* (London, Pimlico, 2005), p. 16.
19. Brigadier Eric Dorman-Smith Brigadier (1895–1969). 'Chink' Dorman-Smith was a controversial character who, when he fell out with the military establishment post war, celticised his name to Dorman O'Gowan and became associated with an IRA campaign during the 1950s. Opinions among his contemporaries varied. Sir Basil Liddell Hart regarded him very highly, Montgomery did not.
20. *The Third Afghan War 1919*, p. 332.
21. Barr, *Pendulum of War*, p. 31.
22. Ibid., p. 41.
23. While the desert rat or jerboa was the emblem of 7th Armoured, it became universal throughout the Eighth Army.
24. Bullock, *Britain's Gurkhas*, p. 102.
25. Francis Ivan Simms Tuker (1894–1967) was an Indian Army officer who as a lieutenant colonel commanded 1/2nd Gurkhas in 1937 and served with distinction in Waziristan. At the outset of the war he was given 34th Indian Division and then, from December 1941, 4th Indian Division which he led through the desert campaign and in Italy. His effective war ended when he became quite seriously ill in February 1944, though, once recovered, he went on to hold a number of senior positions prior to his retirement in 1948.
26. Bullock, *Britain's Gurkhas*, p. 103.
27. Ibid.
28. The legendary if not infamous Tiger Tank had entered service early in 1943. Formidably armoured and massively armed, the Tiger still had numerous design faults.
29. P.J. Lewis and I. English, *Into Battle with the Durhams* (London, London Stamp Exchange, 1990), p. 168.
30. Bullock, *Britain's Gurkhas*, p. 104.
31. *London Gazette*, 11 June 1943, p. 2719.
32. Bullock, *Britain's Gurkhas*, p. 110.
33. Ibid., p. 111.

34. Ibid.
35. Ibid.
36. His pistol is still on display in the Gurkha Museum.

Chapter 8

1. Held in French Morocco at the Anfa Hotel, 14–24 January 1943.
2. A memorable Churchillian phrase – Winston was not in favour of a direct assault across the Channel.
3. *Festung Europa* – Hitler's grand, Wagnerian vision of a fortified coastline from Norway to the Bay of Biscay; 'Fortress Europe', it seems, was not one of Churchill's phrases. https://winstonchurchill.hillsdale.edu/soft-underbelly-fortress-europe/, retrieved 13 June 2019.
4. https://www.history.com/topics/world-war-ii/italian-campaign, retrieved 12 June 2019.
5. 1871–1956.
6. 1885–1960.
7. This was a formidable defensive line constructed by the Germans stretching from the Tyrrhenian Sea to the Adriatic. The line ran along the courses of the Garigiliano and Rapido rivers on the west and along the Sangro in the east. It was held by fifteen German divisions well supplied with small arms, artillery, pill boxes, machine-gun emplacements, minefields and plenty of wire. In order to reach Rome, the Allies had to push through. There was no way around.
8. The landings, 22 January–5 June 1944, initially promised much but because of the perceived excessive caution of US General Lucas and Kesselring's swift riposte the potential was dissipated.
9. C. Bellamy, *The Gurkhas – Special Force* (London, John Murray, 2011), p. 249.
10. These were Muslim Moroccan soldiers, part of the French Army in Africa from 1908–56; in the Second World War they formed part of the Free French forces.
11. Monte Cassino lies 80-odd miles (130km) south of Rome; the hill rises some 1,700ft (500m) behind the town and the abbey was founded *c*. AD 520 by St Benedict.
12. Bullock, *Britain's Gurkhas*, p. 115.
13. General Sir Francis Tuker was also an influential author on the Gurkhas; his *Gorkha: The Story of the Gurkhas of Nepal* (London, Constable, 1957) is still a classic.

14. Freyberg (1889–1963) was a tremendous fighting soldier, though as C in C on Crete he was out of his depth. He later became the first New Zealander to be appointed as Governor General there after the war.
15. Bullock, *Britain's Gurkhas*, p. 116.
16. The monastery was rebuilt post-war and reconsecrated in October 1964.
17. Bullock, *Britain's Gurkhas*, p. 116.
18. Ibid., p. 117.
19. Ibid.
20. So named as a broken cable-car pylon resembled a gibbet, an omen if ever there was one; Bullock, *Britain's Gurkhas*, p. 115.
21. Ibid., p. 117.
22. Ibid., p. 118.
23. 1. Fallschirm-Jäger-Division – German paratroopers were very much an elite but actually part of the Luftwaffe and not the Wehrmacht. After the debacle on Crete there were deployed primarily as heavy infantry.
24. C. Ellis, *7th Flieger Division: Students Fallschirmjager Elite* (Shepperton, Ian Allan Publishing, 2002).
25. Bullock, *Britain's Gurkhas*, p. 118.
26. Ibid.
27. Mark Clark (1896–1984) was one of the most despised generals of the war; Tommies I have interviewed universally loathed him.
28. Lorried brigades were intended to work in tandem with armour, acting as conventional infantry to punch gaps for the tanks and also giving protection to tank leaguers at night.
29. Motorised or mechanised infantry.
30. Whose commanders had foolishly failed to batten down in time; see S. Bull, *Encyclopaedia of Military Technology & Innovation* (London, Greenwood, 2004), p. 119.
31. Bullock, *Britain's Gurkhas*, p. 119.
32. *London Gazette*, 28 December 1944.
33. Bellamy, *Gurkhas*, p. 252.
34. Bullock, *Britain's Gurkhas*, p. 122.
35. Personal recollection, 1968.
36. Bullock, *Britain's Gurkhas*.
37. Ibid., pp. 122–3.
38. Ibid., p. 123.
39. *London Gazette*, 20 February 1945.
40. Ibid.

NOTES

41. These were armoured personnel carriers, originally designed by the Canadians based on a tank chassis, a very successful expedient which empowered infantry to advance in tandem with armour.
42. Later, the subject of a dramatic painting by celebrated war artist Terence Cuneo.
43. Bullock, *Britain's Gurkhas*, pp. 124–5.
44. 'The Greek People's Liberation Army'.
45. This reflects an attitude among servicemen that would see Churchill lose the 1945 election, though it's doubtful if the average Gurkha cared much either way.
46. The Civil War was fought between 1946 and 1949 between the government backed by the UK/United States and communist insurgents supported by Yugoslavia, Bulgaria and Albania.

Chapter 9

1. Arthur, *Forgotten Voices*, pp. 391–2.
2. Fortress Europe – *Festung Europa* was Hitler's chain of Atlantic wall defences prepared against Allied invasion – they didn't work.
3. The Burma Road was a road linking Burma with the southwest of China. Its terminals were Kunming, Yunnan, and Lashio, Burma.
4. Chiang Kai-shek (1887–1975) was a Chinese nationalist leader during the Second World War, subsequently defeated in the civil war by the communists under Mao-tse-Tung, he set up a truncated realm on Formosa (now Taiwan).
5. This rag-tag force soon fell apart and surrendered en masse.
6. The fifteenth prime minister of Nepal and effective ruler from 1932–45.
7. King of Nepal.
8. Bellamy, *Gurkhas*, p. 215.
9. 'A day that will live in infamy' – 7 December 1941.
10. 'Burforce' was composed of 17th Indian Division and 1st Burma Division.
11. Bellamy, *Gurkhas*, p. 215.
12. Gurkha Museum, 4GR/406.
13. Ibid.
14. Ibid.
15. Ibid.
16. Ibid.
17. Ibid.
18. Ibid.
19. Bellamy, *Gurkhas*, p. 217.

20. Ibid.
21. Bullock, *Britain's Gurkhas*, p. 141.
22. A 'temporary gentleman' was a war service commission issued to those who had not normally quite made the social grade for a proper gent.
23. W. Murray and A. Millet, *A War to be Won* (Cambridge, Harvard University Press, 2000), pp. 227–8.
24. Fraser, *Quartered Safe Out Here*, p. 37.
25. Field Marshal Sir W. Slim, *Defeat into Victory* (London, Cassell, 1956), p. 188.
26. Bellamy, *Gurkhas*, p. 218.
27. Slim, *Defeat in to Victory*, p. 98.
28. Ibid., p. 104.
29. Ibid., p. 106.
30. *London Gazette*, 30 September 1943.
31. Bellamy, *Gurkhas*, p. 221.
32. Arthur, *Forgotten Voices*, p. 257.
33. F. Spencer Chapman, *The Jungle is Neutral* (England, Marshall Cavendish International (Asia) Pte Ltd, 2nd edn, 2014).
34. Ralph Bagnold was a British officer and pre-war Saharan explorer who created the Long Range Desert Group.
35. Bellamy, *Gurkhas*, p. 221.
36. James Michael Calvert was, in a sense, Wingate's spiritual successor and went on to be highly influential during the Malayan Emergency from 1948–60. Later dismissed on account of a sexual scandal, he ended his life in poverty.
37. An old Tommy phrase, probably Second Boer War in origin: an officer who had failed in any respect or because his face just didn't fit was posted to some nowhere place.
38. Bellamy, *Gurkhas*, p. 222.
39. Ibid.
40. Ibid.
41. Ibid., p. 223.
42. Ibid.
43. Ibid.
44. https://www.chinditslongcloth1943.com/32-gurkha-roll-call.html, retrieved 18 June 2019.
45. https://www.chinditslongcloth1943.com/32-gurkha-roll-call.html, retrieved 18 June 2019.
46. Farwell, *Gurkhas*, p. 258.
47. https://www.chinditslongcloth1943.com/32-gurkha-roll-call.html, retrieved 18 June 2019.

NOTES

48. I. MacHorton, *Safer than a Known Way* (London, HarperCollins, 1975).
49. https://www.chinditslongcloth1943.com/32-gurkha-roll-call.html, retrieved 18 June 2019.
50. Bellamy, *Gurkhas*, p. 225.
51. Fraser, *Quartered Safe Out Here*, p. 38.
52. Bellamy, *Gurkhas*, p. 225.
53. Codenamed *Quadrant,* the conference was held from 17–24 August 1943; present were representatives of the UK, United States and Canada.
54. Bellamy, *Gurkhas*, p. 226.
55. Ibid., pp. 226–7.
56. Ibid., p. 229.
57. At the time Wingate was flying from Imphal to Lalaghat, in a USAAF B-25 Mitchell bomber from the 1st Air Commando Group when the plane crashed into thick jungle. No enemy aircraft was involved.
58. 'Force-multiplier' is a post-war term referring to the tactical boost effect of Special Forces support for a conventional (or irregular) force.
59. *London Gazette*, 26 October 1944: Mogaung Operations, Burma, 11–23 June 1944: Captain Michael Allmand, Indian Armoured Corps, attached 6th Gurkha Rifles. The citation did not go on to say that largely because of Captain Allmand's bravery Mogaung was captured. Michael Allmand is buried in the Taukkyan War Cemetery, Burma.
60. *London Gazette*, 7 November 1944.
61. *London Gazette,* 22 September 1944.
62. Tuker, *Gorkha*, p. 222.
63. Ibid.
64. William Shakespeare, *The Life of King Henry V*, Act IV, sc. iii, l. 24.
65. The division included in 48th Indian Infantry Brigade; 2/5th and 1/7th Gurkhas together with 63rd Indian Infantry Brigade with 1/3rd, 1/4th and 1/10th Gurkhas.
66. R. Lyman, *Bill Slim* (Oxford, Osprey, 2011), p. 15.
67. M. Hastings, *Nemesis* (London, William Collins, 2008), p. 62.
68. Ibid., p. 68.
69. D.J. Sadler, *Dunkirk to Belsen* (London, JR Books, 2010), p. 266.
70. Arthur, *Forgotten Voices*, p. 287.
71. The Naga people are tribes or ethnic groups associated with the north-eastern part of India and north-western Myanmar. They tend to have similar cultures and traditions, and form the majority of population in the Indian state of Nagaland, with significant populations in the areas of Manipur, Arunachal, Pradesh and Assam in India and the Sagaing Division/District of Myanmar.

72. Sadler, *Dunkirk to Belsen*, p. 267.
73. Ibid.
74. Ibid.
75. J.P. Cross, *Jungle Warfare* (Barnsley, Pen & Sword, 2008), p. 93.
76. Ibid., p. 88.
77. Ibid., pp. 88–9.
78. Tuker, *Gorkha*, p. 224.
79. A Bangalore torpedo was an explosive charge placed within one or several connected tubes and deployed by combat engineers to blast obstacles that would otherwise require them to approach directly, possibly under fire; sometimes colloquially referred to as a 'Bangalore mine', 'banger' or simply 'Bangalore'.
80. Tuker, *Gorkha*, p. 224.
81. Ibid., p. 225.
82. Ibid.
83. Ibid. and Bullock, *Britain's Gurkhas*, p. 156.
84. Tuker, *Gorkha*.
85. Ibid.
86. The Far Eastern campaigns and Burma never witnessed the colossal tank battles of north-west Europe or Russia, so Japanese armour tended to be light and fairly backward in comparison.
87. *London Gazette* (Supplement), 5 September 1944; after independence he joined 11 Ghorka Rifles and served until his retirement in 1968 and was subsequently appointed as lifetime ADC (aide-de-camp) to the president. He died aged 75 in 2000.
88. Arthur, *Forgotten Voices*, p. 389.
89. D. Rissik, *The DLI at War 1939–1945* (Durham, 1952), p. 195.
90. Ibid., p. 197.
91. Arthur, *Forgotten Voices*, p. 396.
92. Hastings, *Nemesis*, pp. 75–6.
93. Ibid.
94. Fraser, *Quartered Safe Out Here*, p. 80.
95. Tuker, *Gorkha*, p. 226.
96. Ibid.
97. https://www.scotsman.com/news/obituaries/obituary-lachhiman-gurung-vc-gurkha-rifleman-1-1521738, retrieved 25 June 2019.
98. *London Gazette* (Supplement), 24 July 1945.
99. https://www.thetimes.co.uk/article/havildar-lachhiman-gurung-vc-r5z5n26ddb0, retrieved 25 June 2019.

NOTES

100. Tuker, *Gorkha*, p. 227.
101. https://www.thegazette.co.uk/London/issue/37274/supplement/4680/data.pdf, retrieved 25 June 2019.
102. Tuker, *Gorkha*, p. 227.
103. Hastings, *Nemesis*, p. 67.
104. The First Afghan War hadn't ended well.
105. https://www.collinsdictionary.com/dictionary/english/special-forces, retrieved 3 June 2019.
106. Bellamy, *Gurkhas*, p. 254.
107. Ibid., p. 238.
108. Ibid., p. 239.
109. Ibid.
110. Ibid., p. 240.
111. Ibid.
112. Ibid.
113. Ibid.
114. Ibid., p. 241.
115. Ibid.
116. Ibid.
117. Slim, *Defeat in to Victory*, p. 547.
118. Ibid.

Chapter 10

1. On 1 January 1948 the four battalions kept in the British order of battle were: 2nd King Edward VII's Own Gurkha Rifles, 6th Queen Elizabeth's Own, 7th Duke of Edinburgh's Own and 10th Princess Mary's Own. Since 2006 the brigade has comprised only two, 1 and 2 RGR with a full regiment of logistics, Queen's Own Gurkha Logistic Regiment, Queen's Gurkha Signals and Queen's Gurkha Engineers.
2. Deolali transit camp was a British Army transit camp in Maharashtra, India. Established in 1861, the camp remained in use throughout the time of the British Raj. It served to house soldiers newly arrived in the country and those awaiting ships to take them to Britain. It also housed a military prison and during the two world wars served as a POW camp. Conditions in the camp were said to be poor, especially for those stationed there for long periods, and the term doolally became associated with mental illness. The camp was transferred to the Indian Army following the independence of India.

3. Gurkha Museum, 6GR/549.
4. Ibid.
5. Ibid.
6. Ibid.
7. Ibid.
8. He subsequently became a pacifist.
9. Gurkha Museum, 6GR/549.
10. Ibid.
11. Gurkha Museum, 9GR/1420.
12. Ludhiana: a large industrial city in the Punjab, the largest urban expanse north of Delhi, with a population at the time of over a million.
13. Gurkha Museum, 9GR/1420.
14. Ibid.
15. Gurkha Museum, 10GR/643.
16. Ibid.
17. Ibid.
18. Ibid.
19. Bellamy, *Gurkhas*, p. 292.
20. Farwell, *Gurkhas*, p. 267.
21. Lieutenant Colonel J.P. Cross, *In Gurkha Company* (London, Arms & Armour Press, 1986), p. 25.
22. Bullock, *Britain's Gurkhas*, p. 170.
23. Ibid., p. 171.
24. Ibid., p. 173.
25. Mullaly, *Bugle & Kukri*, p. 407.
26. General Walter Colyear Walker DSO (1912–2001) finished his distinguished career as C in C of Allied Forces, Northern Europe from 1969–72; see also Bellamy, *Gurkhas*, p. 293.
27. http://gurkhastories.com/veteran-stories/dal-bahadur-pun/, retrieved 22 May 2019.
28. http://gurkhastories.com/veteran-stories/dal-prasad/, retrieved 22 May 2019.
29. Farwell, *Gurkhas*, p. 268.
30. Ibid.
31. Bullock, *Britain's Gurkhas*, p. 174.
32. Farwell, *Gurkhas*, p. 269.
33. Ibid.
34. Bullock, *Britain's Gurkhas*, p. 178.
35. Mullaly, *Bugle & Kukri*, p. 419.
36. Bullock, *Britain's Gurkhas*, p. 178.

37. Ibid., p. 176.
38. Ibid.
39. Ibid.
40. Mullaly, *Bugle & Kukri*, p. 423.
41. Ibid., p. 414.
42. Ibid., pp. 414–15.
43. Ibid.
44. Ibid.
45. Ibid.
46. Farwell, *Gurkhas*, p. 269.
47. Ibid., p. 270.
48. Ibid.
49. Bullock, *Britain's Gurkhas*, p. 179.
50. This was the name given by the CTs to the conflict – it refers, contemptuously, to those Malays who remained loyal.
51. C. Tuck, *Confrontation. Strategy and War Termination: Britain's Conflict with Indonesia* (Surrey, Ashgate Publishing Ltd, 2013), p. 2.
52. D. Easter, *Britain and the Confrontation with Indonesia 1960–1966* (New York, I.B. Tauris & Co. Ltd, 2012), p. 1.
53. E. Simpson, *War from the Ground Up: Twenty-First-Century Combat as Politics* (London, Hurst, 2012), p. 158.
54. W. Walker, *Fighting On* (London, New Millennium, 1997), p. 152.
55. Ibid., p. 81.
56. A. Connolly, 'Assess the significance of "Claret" operations during the Borneo Confrontation' (undergraduate War Studies dissertation, King's College London, 2014), p. 17.
57. Walker, *Fighting On*, p. 162.
58. Simpson, *War from the Ground Up*, p. 168.
59. Easter, *Britain and the Confrontation with Indonesia*, p. 86.
60. R. Gregorian, 'Claret Operations and Confrontation 1964–1966', *Conflict Quarterly: Journal for the Centre for Conflict Studies*, No. 1 (1991), p. 54.
61. Ibid.
62. Easter, *Britain and the Confrontation with Indonesia*, p. 124.
63. Ibid., p. 98.
64. Ibid., p. 99.
65. Simpson, *War from the Ground Up*, p. 173.
66. Colonel B.R. Mullaly and R. McAlister, *Bugle and Kukri: the Story of the 10th Princess Mary's Own Gurkha Rifles* (Regimental Trust of the 10th Gurkha Rifles, 1984), Vol. 2, pp. 419–24.

67. Gregorian, 'Claret Operations and Confrontation 1964–1966', p. 59.
68. Easter, *Britain and the Confrontation with Indonesia*, p. 155.
69. P. Dickens, *SAS: Secret War in South-East Asia* (New York, Ivy Books, 1983), p. 323.
70. H. James and D. Sheil-Small, *A Pride of Gurkhas: 2nd King Edward VII's Own Goorkhas (The Sirmoor Rifles) 1948–71* (London, Leo Cooper, 1975), pp. 210–11.
71. Tuck, *Confrontation*, p. 107.
72. Gregorian, 'Claret Operations and Confrontation 1964–1966', p. 62.
73. Connolly, 'Assess the significance of "Claret" operations during the Borneo Confrontation', pp. 24–8.
74. Ibid.
75. Walker, *Fighting On*, pp. 79–87.
76. Connolly, 'Assess the significance of "Claret" operations during the Borneo Confrontation', pp. 24–8.
77. Tuck, *Confrontation*, p. 28.
78. Simpson, *War from the Ground Up*, p. 177.
79. Interview with Captain G.C. Trueman, Cyprus, September 2017.
80. Cross, *In Gurkha Company*, p. 159.
81. Ibid., p. 160.
82. Ibid.
83. Ibid.
84. Ibid., p. 161.
85. Ibid.
86. Ibid.
87. Ibid., p. 162.
88. Ibid., p. 163.
89. Bullock, *Britain's Gurkhas*, p. 213.
90. Ibid., the actual kukri subsequently sold at auction for £1,300.
91. Ibid., p. 217.
92. This withdrawal did not include the Singapore Police Unit and a battalion of Gurkhas remained in Brunei, paid for by the Sultan who would sleep a lot easier for their presence. He still does.
93. Bullock, *Britain's Gurkhas*, p. 204.
94. A. Loyd, *My War Gone by, I miss it So* (London, Atlantic, 1999), pp. 152–3.
95. Chris Bird and Martin Walker in the *Guardian*, 11 June 1999.
96. Nicholas Watt and Richard Norton-Taylor in the *Guardian*, 15 June 1999.
97. Associated Press, 11 October 2019.
98. David Lamb in the *Los Angeles Times*, 17 September 1999.

99. *Guardian* leader, 11 November 2004.
100. https://thegurkhamuseum.co.uk/blog/gurkhas-in-iraq-and-afghanistan/, accessed 11 January 2021.
101. https://www.gurkhabde.com/operation-trenton-from-nepal-to-the-south-sudan/, accessed 11 January 2021.
102. https://www.gurkhabde.com/my-deployment-on-operation-cabrit-estonia/tps://www.gurkhabde.com/my-deployment-on-operation-cabrit-estonia/, accessed 10 January 2021.

Chapter 11

1. S. Meadows, 'Journal' (unpublished memoir).
2. https://www.britannica.com/topic/Taliban, retrieved 8 October 2019.
3. This is not the case.
4. https://www.popularmechanics.com/military/research/g2173/10-amazing-gurkha-stories/, retrieved 15 October 2019 and https://thegurkhamuseum.co.uk/gurkhastoday/, retrieved 15 October 2019.
5. https://www.bbc.co.uk/news/uk-35159951, retrieved 17 March 2017.
6. Directorate Land Warfare Lessons Exploitation Centre, *Operation HERRICK Campaign Study* (Directorate of Land Warfare, 2015).
7. Ibid., p. 34.
8. Ibid. Force multiplier is the effect of boosting local militia with Western Special Forces units, thus achieving overall increased effectiveness, disproportionate to the actual number of commandos on the ground.
9. https://www.channel4.com/news/articles/uk/factcheck%2Ba%2Bshot%2Bin%2Bafghanistan/3266362.html, retrieved 8 October 2019.
10. Directorate Land Warfare Lessons Exploitation Centre, *Operation HERRICK Campaign Study* (Directorate of Land Warfare, 2015), p. xxvii.
11. Ibid., p. xxvii.
12. From Helmand Province in 'Government of Afghanistan and United Nations Development Programme' (Ministry of Rural Rehabilitation and Development, retrieved 7 October 2019).
13. Ibid.
14. Ibid.
15. Directorate Land Warfare Lessons Exploitation Centre, *Operation HERRICK*, p. xxvii.
16. https://www.telegraph.co.uk/news/uknews/defence/11648236/First-Gurkha-autobiography-They-were-trying-to-kill-me-and-my-men.html, retrieved 10 October 2019.

17. K. Limbu, *Gurkha – Better to Die than Live Like a Coward; My Life with the Gurkhas* (London, Little, Brown, 2015), p. 34.
18. https://www.telegraph.co.uk/news/uknews/defence/11648236/First-Gurkha-autobiography-They-were-trying-to-kill-me-and-my-men.html, retrieved 10 October 2019.
19. Ibid.
20. Ibid.
21. Ibid.
22. https://thegurkhamuseum.co.uk/gurkhastoday/, retrieved 15 October 2019.
23. Ibid.
24. A WMiK is a Land Rover variant, the 'Wolf', pronounced 'Wimik' – the acronym stands for Weapons Mount Installation Kit. A Pinzgaur is one of a family of high-mobility, all-terrain 4WD and 6WD military utility vehicles.
25. https://thegurkhamuseum.co.uk/gurkhastoday/, retrieved 15 October 2019.
26. Ibid.
27. Ibid.
28. See, https://www.britannica.com/event/Soviet-invasion-of-Afghanistan, retrieved 14 May 2017.
29. Directorate Land Warfare Lessons Exploitation Centre, *Operation HERRICK*, 1-1_2 – 1-1_3.
30. Ibid., p. xxxi.
31. A Panther Command & Liaison vehicle, British variant of an Iveco original.
32. D. Walsh, 'Sangin troop withdrawal; four years in hell', *Guardian*, 6 July 2010, retrieved 8 October 2019.
33. Meadows, 'Journal'; Sam was then with call-sign Silicon 11 Police Mentoring team, Operation Herrick 10.
34. D. Walsh, 'Sangin troop withdrawal; four years in hell', *Guardian*, 6 July 2010, retrieved 8 October 2019.
35. https://thegurkhamuseum.co.uk/gurkhastoday/, retrieved 15 October 2019.
36. Meadows, 'Journal'.
37. Ibid.
38. Ibid.
39. Ibid.
40. Ibid.
41. Ibid.
42. Ibid.
43. Ibid.
44. Ibid.

NOTES

45. Ibid.
46. Hemcon – a form of bandage that reduces blood loss, a new and vital tool in first-aid treatment for battlefield casualties.
47. Meadows, 'Journal'.
48. Ibid.
49. Ibid.
50. Ibid. Terrorists have become increasingly attracted to suicide attacks because of their unique tactical advantages: devastatingly effective, lethally efficient, with a greater likelihood of success, relatively inexpensive and generally easier to execute than other attack modes, a deliberate instrument of warfare. See also B. Hoffman, *Inside Terrorism* (New York, Columbia University Press, 2006), p. 132.
51. Meadows, 'Journal'.
52. Ibid.
53. Ibid.
54. Ibid.
55. Ibid.
56. Ibid.
57. Ibid.
58. Ibid.
59. Ibid.
60. *9th Company*, directed by Fyodor Bondarchuk (2007).
61. Meadows, 'Journal'.
62. Ibid.
63. Ibid. The bird in question is probably a Bonelli's eagle.
64. Ibid.
65. Ibid.
66. Ibid.
67. Attributed to Lieutenant General Hubert Worthington, Commander in Chief, 5th Royal Indian Mountain Division.
68. https://www.bbc.co.uk/news/uk-12854492 25 March 2011, retrieved 9 October 2019.
69. https://www.gov.uk/government/news/gurkhas-first-helmand-operation-of-the-summer 4 May 2011, retrieved 10 October 2019.
70. Directorate Land Warfare Lessons Exploitation Centre, *Operation HERRICK*, 2-1_6.
71. Meadows, 'Journal'.
72. Telephone interview, December 2020.
73. https://thegurkhamuseum.co.uk/gurkhastoday/, retrieved 15 October 2019.

Chapter 12

1. The quote in the chapter heading is attributed to Rifleman Motilal Thapa, badly wounded at Festubert as he lay out under fire. Though he made it back to the Advance Dressing Station, he succumbed to his wounds. See Parker, *Gurkhas*, p. 15. Thwaites was an Australian who attended New College, Oxford before serving in the North Atlantic, finally commanding a corvette. He had an active post-war career, publishing several volumes of poetry.
2. Bellamy, *Gurkhas*, p. 322.
3. 'The history of the Gurkha Contingent (GC) is intrinsically linked to the formative years of Singapore when it was called upon many times to help restore law and order on the streets. Throughout this period, the unit repeatedly demonstrated its reputation as an effective im-partial force characterised by its total discipline and loyalty. The GC was formed to provide a "strong-arm" within the Police Force capable of quelling civil disturbance and carrying out specialist security tasks. The majority of the unit's police officers are Gurkhas recruited from a small number of hill tribes in Nepal. These Gurkhas possess the qualities best suited to service in the Contingent, specifically: physical and mental robustness, resourcefulness and an uncomplaining dependability. Today, the GC carries out many diverse roles for the Singapore Police Force (SPF). These roles are still very much related to the security tasks for which GC was originally formed.' https://www.police.gov.sg/about-us/organisational-structure/specialist-and-line-units/gurkha-contingent, retrieved 30 April 2019.
4. Bellamy, *Gurkhas*, p. 322.
5. Ibid., p. 323.
6. Ibid.
7. http://gurkhastories.com/veteran-stories/dal-bahadur-pun/, retrieved 30 April 2019.
8. http://gurkhastories.com/veteran-stories/capt-retd-umesh-kumar-pun-mvo/, retrieved 29 April 2019.
9. The West Side Boys were a guerrilla force active in Sierra Leone between 1998 and 2000, heavily influenced by American rap and 'gangsta' culture, who recruited/conscripted many child soldiers; sometimes considered a splinter group of the Armed Forces Revolutionary Council, see https://www.telegraph.co.uk/news/worldnews/africaandindianocean/sierraleone/1353972/Caught-with-their-guard-down.html, retrieved 29 April 2019.

NOTES

10. Interview, December 2020.
11. http://gurkhastories.com/veteran-stories/dharam-prashad-limbu/, retrieved 29 April 2019.
12. http://gurkhastories.com/veteran-stories/bhui-maya-rana/, retrieved 29 April 2019.
13. http://gurkhastories.com/veteran-stories/bhui-maya-rana/, retrieved 29 April 2019.
14. https://www.theguardian.com/education/2008/nov/18/meena-kambang-english-student, retrieved 29 April 2019.
15. Ibid.
16. Ibid.
17. Richard Burdon Haldane, a Scottish Liberal MP, Secretary of State for Defence in Campbell-Bannerman's government, 1st Viscount Haldane (1856–1928).
18. Haldane's Reforms, implemented between the years 1906 and 1912.
19. See W. Stanley-Moss, *Ill Met by Moonlight* (London, Weidenfeld & Nicolson, 2014 edn).
20. https://www.theguardian.com/world/2013/jan/25/in-amenas-timeline-siege-algeria, retrieved, 30 April 2019.
21. https://www.theatlantic.com/photo/2013/01/the-conflict-in-mali/100446/, retrieved 30 April 2019.
22. https://www.bbc.co.uk/newsround/15214375, retrieved 30 April 2019.
23. https://www.bbc.co.uk/newsround/15214375, retrieved 30 April 2019.
24. https://www.bbc.co.uk/newsround/15214375, retrieved 30 April 2019.
25. D. Kilcullen, '*Out of the Mountains, the Coming Age of the Urban Guerrilla*', Talks at Google, retrieved 30 April 2019.
26. See M. Bowden, *Black Hawk Down* (USA, New American Library, 1993).
27. Kilcullen, *Out of the Mountains*.
28. Ibid.
29. https://www.actionaid.org.uk/about-us/what-we-do/emergencies-disasters-humanitarian-response/earthquakes-in-nepal-2015?gclid=EAIaIQobChMI0eaeyPn34QIVNCjTCh03BACREAAYAiAAEgJJ4vD_BwE retrieved 29 April 2019.
30. https://medium.com/nepal-earthquakes/earthquake-on-everest-a-gurkha-s-story-ceba01346b18, retrieved 30 April 2019.
31. Ibid.
32. Writing in *the Observer*, 29 August 2010, quoted in Bellamy, *Gurkhas*, p. 327.

33. Peter Antill and Jeremy Smith, 'The British Army in Transition', *RUSI Journal*, 162:3 (2017), 50–8, DOI: 10.1080/03071847.2017.1353249, p. 51.
34. First published as *Epithoma Rei Militaris* (Utrecht, 1473).
35. https://trumanlibrary.org/publicpapers/index.php?pid=1417, retrieved 30 April 2019.
36. *Brigade of Gurkhas Update*, April 2019.
37. Ibid.
38. Ibid.
39. Ibid.
40. Ibid.
41. Ibid.
42. Ibid.
43. https://www.wearethemighty.com/articles/gurkha-train-robbery, retrieved 3 June 2019.
44. Ibid.
45. Joanna Lumley, 'I'll quit Britain if there is no justice for Gurkhas', *Daily Telegraph*, 19 September 2008, archived from the original on 20 September 2008, retrieved 5 February 2020.
46. 'The 5th Battalion of 8 GR, which until 1948 was 4th Battalion 2 GR has continued to use our dice-board in many ways. The dice-board is as distinctive and distinguished in today's Indian Army as it was in the British Indian Army and later, in the British Army. For many years the dice board has been widely used as a distinctive mark in civilian dress on such things as hats, neckwear and stockings. Indeed, it caused a lot of amusement that one officer was so hugely devoted to the regiment that he wore the dice-board on his green silk pyjamas!', Gurkha Museum, 8GR/515.

    Since the early 1930s, officers have worn round their straw hats and boaters a dice-board strip, two squares deep and some 11mm across, embroidered on rifle-green silk ribbon about 3cm wide. It looks well. A regimental tie was introduced (during the 1930s) for wear by all ranks. There are various types; some woven in silk, others in man-made fibres, from several different makers in the UK, India, Nepal or Hong Kong. Their background colour of rifle green is intersected by diagonal dice-board stripes, two squares thick, running from top right to bottom left as one looks at them. The stripes, approximately 1cm wide, are about 26mm apart. When the regimental association (later re-named the Sirmoor Club) was formed in 1948, its tie was differenced by using narrower dice-board stripes, again two squares thick but only about 5–7mm wide and 32mm apart. Gurkha Museum, 8GR/515.

NOTES

Appendix 4

1. The Black Mountain Expedition 1888 – also described as the Hazara Expedition or the First Hazara Expedition – was a campaign waged against the tribes of Kala Dhaka in the Hazara region of what is now Pakistan.
2. Farwell, *Gurkhas*, p. 68.

Appendix 5

1. The PVC is the highest award for gallantry, equivalent to the VC; only twenty-one have been awarded since 1950.
2. The MVC is an award for conspicuous gallantry – similar to a DSO.
3. Operation *Polo* was the invasion and annexation of the independent state of Hyderbad.
4. The war was fought from 3–16 December and resulted in the loss of East Pakistan which became the independent state of Bangladesh. As short and decisive as it was, the conflict witnessed an avalanche of atrocities against the civilian population perpetrated by Pakistani forces.
5. In the Kasur District of the Punjab.
6. This lasted from 25 October–21 November and was a Chinese victory.
7. Fought between May and July, a successful Indian campaign against Pakistan.

Bibliography

Primary Sources

Interviews
Connolly, Captain S., 2 RGR, various interviews 2016–19
Kelly, Sir David, interview May 2019
Meadows, Major R., RE, various interviews 2017–19
Meadows, Major S.T., 2 RGR, various interviews 2016–19
Trueman, Captain G.C. (formerly 3 LI), various interviews 2017–19
Various Gurkhas officers, NCOs and men from support company 2 RGR, interviews and informal discussion 2016

Diaries, Essays, Articles, Reports and Unpublished Memoirs
21 Engineer Regt RE, *Exercise Cassino Sapper*, 6–10 October 2008
An Analysis of Military Operations in Northern Ireland, prepared under the direction of the Chief of the General Staff, Army Code 71842
Antill, Peter and Jeremy Smith, 'The British Army in Transition', *RUSI Journal*, 162:3 (2017), 50–8, DOI: 10.1080/03071847.2017.1353249
Bingham, J., 'Gearing up: European Armies bolster the lethality and survivability of their AFV fleets', *Jane's Defence Weekly*
Brigade of Gurkhas Update, April 2019, https://www.gurkhabde.com/parbate-april-2019/, accessed 2 June 2019
Carter, General Sir Nicholas KCB CBE DSO ADC Gen, a speech delivered to RUSI, 22 January 2018
Connolly, A., 'Assess the significance of "Claret" operations during the Borneo Confrontation', undergraduate War Studies dissertation, King's College London, 2014
Directorate Land Warfare Lessons Exploitation Centre, *Operation HERRICK Campaign Study*, March 2015

Easter, D., 'British and Malaysian covert support for rebel movements in Indonesia during the Confrontation', *Intelligence and National Security*, 14:4 (1999)

Exercise URBAN BEAR, Urban Operations Staff Ride, 4th–8th June 2018, Staff Reader

London Gazette, 24 January 1905

Gregorian, R., 'Claret Operations and Confrontation 1964–1966', *Conflict Quarterly: Journal for the Centre for Conflict Studies*, No. 1 (1991)

Hall, R. and A. Ross, 'The political and military effectiveness of Commonwealth forces in Confrontation 1963–66', *Small Wars and Insurgencies* 19:2 (2008)

'Helmand Province', in *Government of Afghanistan and United Nations Development Programme*, Ministry of Rural Rehabilitation and Development, 2009, http://www.fak.dk/biblioteket/publikationer/Documents/UK_Afghan_ Lessons_PART_II_Final-enkeltsidet.pdf, accessed 17 May 2019

Mathias, Lieutenant Leonard William Henry DSO, unpublished war diary, Siege of Kut, 1915–16

Meadows, Major R., RE, *A critical evaluation of the key security challenges facing Somalia highlighting potential implications for UK Defence*, Defence Academy of the United Kingdom, Shrivenham, 2018

Meadows, S., 'Journal'

Reid, General Sir Charles G.C.B., *Extracts from Letters and Notes Written During the Siege of Delhi in 1857*, London, Naval & Military Press, 2009

Slater, J., 'The Domino Theory and International Politics: The Case of Vietnam', *Security Studies*, 3:2, (1993)

Defence Academy Shrivenham

TRDC 02954; Notes from Theatres of War, Vol. 1; Cyrenaica, November 1941
—— 05407; The Retreat to El Alamein, 22nd June 1942–30th August 1942
—— 05408; The German Assault on the Alamein Position, 31st August 1942–7th September 1942
—— 05408; The Battle of El Alamein part II – Opr. Lightfoot
—— 05408; Campaign in the Middle East, Part 3, September–November 1942
—— 05889; Defence in the Land Battle
—— 06347; Tactical Deception
—— 07315; Charles Turner Saga
—— 08225; Pace of Operations
—— 09153; The Battle of Snipe
—— 09657; Engr. Aspects of N. Africa, 1940–1943
—— 09787; Battle of El Alamein

—— 09995; Passage Operations, El Alamein 1942
—— 10728; Culminating Points
—— 11964; The Manoeuvrist Approach
—— 12114; Tactical handling of Artillery
—— 12274; AFM, Vol. 4, Part 3, Historical Desert Supplement
—— 12546; El Alamein BFT
—— 12686; Armour in Battle, 1939–1945
—— 13054; The Battle of El Alamein, Part III
—— 13535; Info, Brief on Tactical Deception
—— 13711; Conquest of North Africa
—— 13846; North Africa Extracts
—— 14118; Air Power at El Alamein
—— 14221; Desert Warfare: The German Experience of WWII
—— 14258; Effectiveness of Anti-Tank Weapons in Combat Vols 1, 2 & 3, Parts A & B
—— 14543; Breakthrough and Manoeuvre Ops, Vols 1 and 3, Parts A & B
—— 14903; Exercise Sphinx Ride – JFHQPXR
—— 75123; Air Power at El Alamein

Regimental and Campaign Histories

10th Gurkha Rifles, *One Hundred Years*, England, Regimental Trust 10th Gurkha Rifles, 1990

Bellers, Brigadier E.V.R., *The History of the 1st King George's Own Gurkha Rifles*, Vol. 1, Aldershot, Gale & Polden, 1956

Huxford, Lieutenant Colonel M.J., *History of the 8th Gurkha Rifles*, Aldershot, Gale & Polden, 1952

MacDonnell, R., and M. Macaulay, *History of the 4th Prince of Wales Own Gurkha Rifles (1857–1937)*, London, Blackwood, 1940

——, *Mackay Colonel J.N., 1938–1948*, London, Blackwood, 1952

——, *History of the 7th Duke of Edinburgh's Own Gurkha Rifles*, London, Blackwood, 1962

Mullaly, Colonel, B.R., *Bugle & Kukri, the Story of the 10th Princess Mary's Own Gurkha Rifles*, Edinburgh, William Blackwood, 1957

Mullaly, Colonel B.R. and R. McAlister, *Bugle & Kukri: The Story of the 10th Princess Mary's Own Gurkha Rifles,* Vol. 2, Regimental Trust of the 10th Gurkha Rifles, 1984

Playfair, Major General I.S.O., *Official History, UK Military Series, Campaigns: Mediterranean and Middle East*, Vols 1–4, London, HMSO, 1962–6

Poynder, Lieutenant Colonel F.S., 'The 9th Gurkha Rifles (1817–1936)', *RUSI*, 1937
——, 'Stevens, Lieutenant-Colonel G.R., 1937 – 1947', *RUSI*, 1953
Ryan, Major D.G.J., Major G.C. Strahan and Captain J.K. Jones, *The Historical Record of the 6th Gurkha Rifles (1817–1919)*, Aldershot, Gale & Polden, 1925
——, *Gibbs, Lieutenant-Colonel H.R.V. Gibbs, 1919–1948*, Aldershot, Gale & Polden, 1955
Shakespear, Colonel L.W. and Lieutenant Colonel G.R. Stevens, *History of the 2nd King Edward's Own Goorka Rifles (The Sirmoor Rifles)*, London, Gale & Polden, 1952
The Third Afghan War 1919 – Official Account, Calcutta, Government of India Central Publication Branch, 1926
Woodyat, Major General N.G., *The Regimental History of the 3rd Queen Alexandra's Own Gurkha Rifles (1815–1927)*, London, Clowes, 1929
——, *Barclay, Brigadier C.N., 1929–1953*, London, Philip Allan, 1953

Secondary Sources

Books and Articles

Adair, R., *British Eighth Army, North Africa 1940–1943*, London, Arms & Armour Press, 1974
Agar-Hamilton, J.A.I. and L.C.F. Turner, *Crisis in the Desert May – July 1942*, Oxford, Geoffrey Cumberledge, 1952
Alexander, Field Marshal the Earl, *The Alexander Memoirs 1940–1945*, London, Cassell, 1962
Allen, C., *The Savage Wars of Peace*, London, Michael Joseph, 1990
Arthur, M., *Forgotten Voices of the Second World War*, London, Ebury Press, 2005
Bailey, Brigadier J.B.A., 'Deep Battle 1914–1941: The Birth of the Modern Style of Warfare', *British Army Review* (2006), No. 120
——, 'The Century of Firepower', *British Army Review* (2006), No. 120
Barr, N., *Pendulum of War, the Three Battles of El Alamein*, London, Pimlico, 2004
Bellamy, C., *The Gurkhas – Special Force*, London, John Murray, 2011
Bidwell, S. and D. Graham, *Firepower, British Army Weapons and Theories of War 1904–1945*, Barnsley, Pen & Sword, 1982

Bierman, J. and C. Smith, *Alamein, War without Hate*, London, Viking, 2002
Bingham, J., K. Wordsworth and W. Haupt, *North African Campaign 1940–1943*, London, MacDonald and Co., 1969
Bishop, C. and I. Drury, *Combat Guns*, London, Book Sales, 1987
Bishop, E., *Better to Die*, London, New English Library, 1976
Bolt, D., *Gurkhas*, London, Weidenfeld & Nicolson, 1967
Bowden, M., *Black Hawk Down*, USA, New American Library, 1993
Braithwaite, R., *Afgansty*, London, Profile, 2012
Bruce, C.J., *War on the Ground 1939–1945*, London, BCA, 1995
Bryant, Sir Arthur, *The Turn of the Tide*, Vols I and II, London, Collins, 1957–9
Bull, S., *Encyclopaedia of Military Technology & Innovation*, London, Greenwood, 2004
Bullock, C., *Britain's Gurkhas*, London, Third Millennium, 1999
Calman, W.Y., *Indian Army Uniforms; Infantry*, London, Morgan-Grampian, 1969
Calvert, M., *Prisoners of Hope*, London, Jonathan Cape, 1952
——, *Chindits – Long Range Penetration*, London, Pan, 1973
Carver, M., *El Alamein*, London, Batsford, 1962
——, *Tobruk*, London, Batsford, 1964
——, *Dilemmas of the Desert War*, London, Greenhill, 1986
Catherwood, C., *The Battles of World War One*, London, Allison & Busby, 1986
Chandler, D. and I. Beckett (eds), *The Oxford Illustrated History of the British Army*, Oxford, Oxford University Press, 1994
Spencer Chapman, F., *The Jungle is Neutral*, England, Marshall Cavendish International (Asia) Pte Ltd, 2nd edn, 2014
Chappell, M., *The Gurkhas*, Oxford, Osprey 'Elite' Series No. 49, 1993
Chapple, J., *The Lineages and Composition of Gurkha Regiments in British Service*, London, Firestep, 2015 (Gurkha Museum, 1984)
Clarke, A., *The Donkeys*, London, Pimlico, 1991
Cloake, J., *Templer – Tiger of Malaya*, London, Harrap, 1985
Clayton, A., *The British Officer*, Harlow, Pearson Longman, 2007
Collett, N., *The Butcher of Amritsar: General Reginald Dyer*, England, A&C Black, 2006
Collier, R., *The Sound of Fury*, London, Collins, 1963
Crawford, J., *I was an Eighth Army Soldier*, London, Victor Gollancz, 1944
Cross, Lieutenant Colonel J.P., *In Gurkha Company*, London, Arms & Armour Press, 1986
——, *Jungle Warfare*, London, New Millennium, 1989

BIBLIOGRAPHY

——, *The Call of Nepal*, London, New Millennium, 1996

Cruickshank, C., *Deception in World War Two*, Oxford, Oxford University Press, 1979

Cruttwell, C.R.M.F., *A History of the Great War 1914–1918*, USA, Chicago Academy Publishers, 1991

Deary, T., *Dirty Little Imps – Stories from the DLI*, Durham, Durham County Record Office, 2004

Dickens, P., *SAS: Secret War in South-East Asia*, New York, Ivy Books, 1983

Doherty, S. and T. Donovan, *The Indian Army Corps on the Western Front*, Brighton, Tom Donovan Editions, 2014

Easter, D., *Britain and the Confrontation with Indonesia 1960–1966*, New York, I.B. Taurus & Co. Ltd, 2012

——, 'British and Malaysian covert support for rebel movements in Indonesia during the Confrontation', *Intelligence and National Security*, 14:4 (1999)

Ellis, C., *7th Flieger Division: Students Fallschirmjager Elite*, Shepperton, Ian Allan Publishing, 2002

Ellis, J., *Eye Deep in Hell*, Crook Helm, London, 1976

——, *Brute Force: Allied Strategy and Tactics in the Second World War*, London, Crook Helm, 1980

——, *The Sharp End of War: The Fighting Man in World War Two*, London, Crook Helm, 1980

Farwell, B., *The Gurkhas*, London, Allen Lane, 1984

Fergusson, Sir Bernard, *Wavell, Portrait of a Soldier*, London, Collins, 1961

Fleming, P., *The Siege of Peking*, London, Hart-Davis, 1959

——, *Bayonets to Lhasa*, Oxford, Oxford University Press, 1961

Fremont-Barnes, G., *The Indian Mutiny 1857–1858*, Oxford, Osprey 'Essential Histories', 2007

Gregorian, R., 'Claret Operations and Confrontation 1964–1966', *Conflict Quarterly: Journal for the Centre for Conflict Studies*, No. 1 (1991)

Gould, T., *Imperial Warriors – Britain & the Gurkhas*, London, Granta, 1999

Gurung, C.B., *British Medals & Gurkhas*, Kathmandu, Gurkha Memorial Trust, 1998

Hall, R. and A. Ross, 'The political and military effectiveness of Commonwealth forces in Confrontation 1963–66', *Small Wars and Insurgencies* 19:2 (2008)

Hastings, M., *Nemesis*, London, William Collins, 2008

Heathcote, T.A., *The India Army: The Garrison of British Imperial India 1822–1922*, Newton Abbot, David & Charles, 1974

Hennessey, P., *The Junior Officer's Reading Club*, London, Allen Lane, 2009

Hillary, R., *The Last Enemy*, London, Pimlico Edition, 1997
Hoffman, B., *Inside Terrorism*, New York, Columbia University Press, 2006
Kipling, R., *The Man who Would be King & Other Stories*, Stansted, Wordsworth Editions, 1994
Jackson, Major Donovan, *India's Army*, New Delhi, Sampson, Low, 1940
James, H. and D. Shiel-Small, *The Gurkhas*, London, Macdonald, 1965
——, *A Pride of Gurkhas: 2nd King Edward VII's Own Goorkhas (The Sirmoor Rifles) 1948–71*, London, Leo Cooper, 1975
Jenkins, L.H., *General Frederick Young*, London, Routledge, 1923
Joslen, Lieutenant Colonel H.F., *Orders of Battle: Second World War*, London, HMSO, 1960
Keegan, Sir J., *The First World War*, London, Bodley Head, 1978
——, *The Face of Battle*, London, Bodley Head, 2004
Leonard, Colonel R.G., *Nepal and the Gurkhas*, London, HMSO, 1965
Lewin, R., *Slim: The Standard Bearer*, London, Leo Cooper, 1976
Lewis, P.J. and I. English, *Into Battle with the Durhams*, London, London Stamp Exchange, 1990
Lewis-Stemple, J., *The Autobiography of the British Soldier*, London, Headline, 2007
Limbu, K., *Gurkha – Better to Die than Live Like a Coward; My Life with the Gurkhas*, London, Little, Brown, 2015
Loyd, A., *My War Gone by, I miss it So*, London, Atlantic, 1999
Lunt, J., *Jai Sixth*, London, Leo Cooper, 1994
Lyman, R., *Bill Slim*, Oxford, Osprey, 2011
MacDonald, J., *Great Battles of World War Two*, London, Smithmark, 1986
MacDonald Fraser, G., *Quartered Safe Out Here*, London, HarperCollins, 2000
McDonough, J.R., *Platoon Leader*, California, Presidio Press, 1985
MacHorton, I., *Safer than a Known Way*, London, HarperCollins, 1975
MacMunn, Lieutenant General Sir George, *The Martial Races of India*, New Delhi, Sampson, Low, 1932
Macksey, K., *Rommel: Battles and Campaigns*, London, BCA, 1979
Majdalany, F., *The Battle of El Alamein*, London, Weidenfeld & Nicolson, 1965
Marrion, R.J. and D.S.V. Potten, *The British Army 1914–1918*, Oxford, Osprey 'Men-At-Arms' No. 81
Martin, M., *An Intimate War: an Oral History of the Helmand Conflict*, England, C. Hurst & Co., 2014
Masters, J., *Bugles and a Tiger*, London, Michael Joseph, 1956
Mayer, S.L. (ed.), *The Japanese War Machine*, London, Bison Books, 1976
Merewether, Lieutenant Colonel J.W.B. and Sir Frederick Smith, *The Indian Corps in France*, London, John Murray, 1919

BIBLIOGRAPHY

Messenger, C., *The Steadfast Gurkha*, London, Leo Cooper, 1985

Montgomery, Field Marshall the Viscount B.L., *Memoirs*, London, Collins, 1958

Moorehead, A., *Mediterranean Front*, London, Hamish Hamilton, 1942

——, *The End in Africa*, London, Hamish Hamilton, 1943

——, *Years of Battle*, London, Hamish Hamilton, 1943

Morris, J., *A Winter in Nepal*, London, Hart-Davis, 1963

Moses, H., *The Gateshead Gurkhas*, England, County Durham Books, 2001

Murray, W. and A. Millet, *A War to be Won*, Cambridge, Harvard University Press, 2000

Nash, N.S., *Chitral Charlie: The Rise and Fall of Major-General Charles Townshend*, Barnsley, Pen & Sword, 2010

Neamatollah, N., *The Rise of the Taliban in Afghanistan*, New York, Palgrave, 2002

North, R., *Ministry of Defeat*, London, Continuum, 2009

Northey, Major W.B. and Captain C.J. Morris, *The Gurkhas, Their Manners, Customs & Country*, London, John Lane & Bodley Head, 1928

Osprey Elite Series 105: *World War II Infantry Tactics: Squad and Platoon*

—— Elite Series 122: *World War Two Infantry Tactics: Company and Battalion*

—— Elite Series 124: *World War Two Infantry Anti-Tank Tactics*

—— Elite Series 162: *World War II Desert Tactics*

—— Battle Orders 20: *Rommel's Afrika Corps – Tobruk to El Alamein*

—— Battle Orders 28: *Desert Rats: British 8th Army in North Africa 1941–1943*

—— New Vanguard 28: *Panzerkampfwagen IV Medium Tank 1936–1945*

—— New Vanguard 33: *M3 and M5 Stuart Light Tank 1940–1945*

—— New Vanguard 46: *88 mm Flak 18/36/37/41 and Pak 43 1936–1945*

—— New Vanguard 98: *British Anti-Tank Artillery 1939–1945*

—— New Vanguard 113: *M3 Lee/Grant Medium Tank 1941–1945*

—— Campaign 158: *El Alamein 1942*

Parker, J., *The Gurkhas*, London, Headline, 1999

Parkinson, R.R., *War in the Desert*, London, HarperCollins, 1976

Pitt, B., *The Crucible of War 1: Wavell's Command*, London, Jonathan Cape, 1986

——, *The Crucible of War 2: Auchinleck's Command*, London, Jonathan Cape, 1986

——, *The Crucible of War 3: Montgomery and Alamein*, London, Jonathan Cape, 1986

Pocock, T., *Fighting General*, London, Collins, 1973

Rissik, D., *The DLI at War 1939–1945*, Durham, 1952

River, C., *The Gurkhas*, Charles River Editors, audiobook, 2018
Roberts, Field-Marshal Lord, *Forty-one Years in India in India: from Subaltern to Commander-in-Chief*, 2 vols, Richard Bentley, 1897
Roy, O., *Jihad and Death – the Global Appeal of Islamic State*, England, C. Hurst & Co., 2017
Ryan, M., *Battlefield Afghanistan*, Staplehurst, Spellmount, 2007
Sadler, D.J., *Dunkirk to Belsen,* London, JR Books, 2010
Sadler, D.J. and R.B. Serdiville, *Tommy at War 1914–1918*, London, JR Books, 2013
Schlacher, A., *Arc of the Gurkha*, London, Elliott & Thompson, 2014
Simpson, E., *War from the Ground Up: Twenty-First-Century Combat as Politics*, London, Hurst, 2012
Slim, Field Marshal Sir William, *Defeat into Victory*, London, Cassell, 1956
Slater, J., 'The Domino Theory and International Politics: The Case of Vietnam', *Security Studies* 3:2 (1993)
Smith, E.D., *Britain's Brigade of Gurkhas*, London, Leo Cooper, 1982
——, *Malaya & Borneo – Counterinsurgency Operations*, London, Ian Allan, 1985
——, *Wars Bring Scars*, Kent, R.J. Leach & Co., 1993
——, *The Autumn Years*, Staplehurst, Spellmount, 1997
——, *Valour: A History of the Gurkhas*, Staplehurst, Spellmount, 1997
Smythies, E.A., *Big Game Shooting in Nepal*, Calcutta, Thacker Spink (1933) Ltd, 1942
Spencer Chapman, F., *The Jungle is Neutral*, England, Marshall Cavendish International (Asia) Pte Ltd, 2nd edn, 2014
Stanley-Moss, W., *Ill Met by Moonlight*, London, Weidenfeld & Nicolson, 2014 edn
Strawson, J., *The Battle for North Africa,* Barnsley, Pen & Sword, 2004
Tuck, C., *Confrontation. Strategy and War Termination: Britain's Conflict with Indonesia*, Surrey, Ashgate Publishing Ltd, 2013
Tuker, General Sir Francis, *Gorkha: The Story of the Gurkhas of Nepal*, London, Constable, 1957
Turner, R.L., *A Comparative and Etymological Dictionary of the Nepali Language*, London, K. Paul, Trench, Trubner, 1931
Van Creveld, M., *Supplying in War: Logistics from Wallenstein to Patton*, New York, Cambridge University Press, 1977
Walker, W., *Fighting On*, London, New Millennium, 1997
Walsh, D., 'Sangin troop withdrawal; four years in hell', the *Guardian*, 6 July 2010
Warner, P., *Alamein, Recollections of the Heroes*, Barnsley, Pen & Sword, 1979

BIBLIOGRAPHY

Useful Websites

https://www.army.mod.uk/who-we-are/corps-regiments-and-units/brigade-of-gurkhas/
http://www.kiplingsociety.co.uk/poems_youngbrit.htm
https://www.bbc.co.uk/programmes/b05xd44k
https://thegurkhamuseum.co.uk/telawrence/
https://www.6thgurkhas.org/the-regiment/gallipoli-campaign/
http://dx.doi.org/10.1080/03071847.2017.1353249
https://www.nytimes.com/interactive/2018/11/25/world/asia/china-economy-strategy.htmlhttps://royalsignalsoperationalawards.com/2018/01/04/the-shahur-tangi-ambush-north-west-frontier-1937/
http://gurkhastories.com/
https://www.police.gov.sg/about-us/organisational-structure/specialist-and-line-units/gurkha-contingent
https://www.telegraph.co.uk/news/worldnews/africaandindianocean/sierraleone/1353972/Caught-with-their-guard-down.html
https://www.theguardian.com/education/2008/nov/18/meena-kambang-english-student
https://www.theguardian.com/world/2013/jan/25/in-amenas-timeline-siege-algeria
https://www.theatlantic.com/photo/2013/01/the-conflict-in-mali/100446/
https://www.bbc.co.uk/newsround/15214375
https://www.bbc.co.uk/newsround/15214375
https://www.bbc.co.uk/newsround/15214375
https://www.independent.co.uk/news/world/americas/mikhail-gorbachev-ussr-last-soviet-premier-russia-world-prepare-war-syria-donald-trump-middle-east-a7548646.html
https://www.independent.co.uk/news/world/americas/mikhail-gorbachev-ussr-last-soviet-premier-russia-world-prepare-war-syria-donald-trump-middle-east-a7548646.html
https://www.independent.co.uk/news/world/americas/mikhail-gorbachev-ussr-last-soviet-premier-russia-world-prepare-war-syria-donald-trump-middle-east-a7548646.html.
https://edition.cnn.com/2015/01/21/europe/2015-paris-terror-attacks-fast-facts/index.html
http://www.telegraph.co.uk/news/uknews/defence/9837238/The-SAS-a-very-special-force.html
https://assets.publishing.service.gov.uk/government/uploads/system/uploads/attachment_data/file/647776/dar_mcdc_hybrid_warfare.pdf

https://www.rferl.org/a/russia-ukraine-crimea/29790037.htmlhttps://www.thebalance.com/cost-of-afghanistan-war-timeline-economic-impact-4122493

https://www.army.mod.uk/who-we-are/formations-divisions-brigades/force-troops-command/77-brigade/

http://www.telegraph.co.uk/news/uknews/defence/9837238/The-SAS-a-very-special-force.html

https://www.e-ir.info/2012/04/06/the-utility-of-force-is-contextual/

https://www.bbc.co.uk/news/world-middle-east-48098528

https://edition.cnn.com/2015/12/08/europe/2015-paris-terror-attacks-fast-facts/index.html

https://www.dailymail.co.uk/news/article-2049987/Gurkha-beheaded-Taliban-soldier-Afghanistan-battle-cleared-return-duty.html

https://www.actionaid.org.uk/about-us/what-we-do/emergencies-disasters-humanitarian-response/earthquakes-in-nepal-2015?gclid=EAIaIQobChMI0eaeyPn34QIVNCjTCh03BACREAAYAiAAEgJJ4vD_BwE

https://medium.com/nepal-earthquakes/earthquake-on-everest-a-gurkha-s-story-ceba01346b18

https://trumanlibrary.org/publicpapers/index.php?pid=1417

https://www.wearethemighty.com/articles/gurkha-train-robbery

https://www.britannica.com/topic/Taliban

https://www.bbc.co.uk/news/uk-35159951

https://www.channel4.com/news/articles/uk/factcheck%2Ba%2Bshot%2Bin%2Bafghanistan/3266362.html

https://www.telegraph.co.uk/news/uknews/defence/11648236/First-Gurkha-autobiography-They-were-trying-to-kill-me-and-my-men.html

https://www.channel4.com/news/articles/uk/factcheck%2Ba%2Bshot%2Bin%2Bafghanistan/3266362.html

https://www.bbc.co.uk/news/uk-12854492

https://www.gov.uk/government/news/gurkhas-first-helmand-operation-of-the-summer

https://www.gov.uk/government/news/army-education-officers-teach-gurkhas-in-helmand

https://www.telegraph.co.uk/news/worldnews/asia/afghanistan/6198444/Major-General-Andrew-Mackay-profile.html

Index

Abbeygate House (the Gurkha Homes Project), 258–9
Abbottabad, 192
Afghanistan, 2–3, 6, 8–9, 42, 50–8, 102, 105, 168, 200, 226–56, 258, 265, 269, 290
   First Afghan War, 186
   Second Afghan War, 57, 102, 104
   Third Afghan War, 6, 102
Afghan National Army ('ANA'), 231, 234, 239–41, 243, 250–2
Afridi Tribe, 58–9
Afrika Korps, 120–1, 177
al-Qaeda, 228–30, 236
Alexander, Field Marshal Sir H., 129, 132, 134, 136, 141, 199
Allanson, Major C.J.L., 89
Allenby, Field Marshal E., 97–9
Allied Forces Headquarters, 136
Allied Rapid Reaction Corps ('ARRC'), 270
Allmand, Captain M., 170–1
Amanullah, 104
Amballa, 11
Amritsar Massacre, 104, 114, 314
Arab Spring, 267
1st Arakan Offensive, 161–2
2nd Arakan Offensive, 169, 174, 177, 202
Archbishop Makarios II, 214–15
Arghandab River, 54, 232
Armstrong Guns, 54, 288

Army Welfare Service, 263
Assam, 60–1, 159, 174, 176, 261
Asymmetric Warfare, 6, 107, 109, 199, 236–7, 245, 253, 264–7
Auchinleck, General Sir C., 118–20, 123–5
Aylmer, Lieutenant-General, 75, 93–4

Badal Sing Thapa, 47
Badoglio, Marshal P., 136
Baghdad, 93, 97
Bahadur Shah II, 11
Baker, S., 55
Baldak Marching, 104–106
Baluchistan, 50, 54, 57
Bangalore Torpedo, 325
Barnes, Major R., 198
Barton, Captain, 79
Battles:
   Aliwal (1846), 20, 47
   Aubers Ridge (1915), 76, 83–4
   Beersheba (1917), 98
   Cassino (1944), 137–9, 141, 147
   Charasiab (1879), 56
   Charasiab (1880), 56
   Ctesiphon (1915), 93
   Dunkirk (1940), 119–20, 159, 187
   1st El Alamein (1942), 115, 125–9
   2nd El Alamein (1942), 129
   Festubert (1915), 75, 83–4

Gallipoli (1915), 2, 71, 85–90, 92, 94, 96, 98, 157, 215
Gazala (1942), 119–121, 124–5
Givenchy (1914), 71, 79–81
Goose Green (1982), 218–19
Imphal (1944), 61, 170, 176, 179–82, 186, 189
Kalunga (1814), 9, 32
Kohima (1944), 2, 170, 176–182, 186, 188–9
Kut (1915/1916), 90–6, 124
Loos (1915), 71, 74, 76
Meggido (1918), 99
Mersa Matruh (1942), 125
Mons (1914), 69
Mount Longdon (1982), 219
Mount Tumbledown (1982), 219
Nankan (1943), 166
Neuve Chapelle (1915), 71, 75–6, 79-81
Plassey (1757), 19
Sobraon (1846), 47
Somme (1916), 72, 77, 106, 181
Verdun (1916), 97
1st Ypres (1914), 69–71
2nd Ypres (1915), 71, 78, 82–3, 86, 118
Becher, Major, 79
Bishnu Prasad Shrestha, 271
Bharnabahadur Rai, 204
Bhimbadur Pun, 200
Bhim Sing Thapa, 81
Bhoora, 44
Bhui Maya Rana, 261
bin Laden, Osama, 228–30, 266, 271
Birbal Nagarkoti, 61
Birenda, King, 33
Bir Shamsher, 57
Black Hawk Down, 266
Blair, A., 228
Blaker, Major F., 172–3
Bogra Reservoir, 105
Bolan Pass, 50, 54

Bombahadur Gharti, 200
Bramall, General Sir E., 218
Brander, Lieutenant-Colonel H., 65
Bren gun, 39, 127–8, 142–3, 146, 154, 171, 173, 179, 195, 202
Briggs Lieutenant-General H., 199, 201–202
British and Imperial forces Army Group:
  'Burforce', 153–60
  Western Desert Force/8th Army, 117-120, 123, 127, 129, 132, 134, 145, 147, 186
  14th Army, 60, 152, 157–8, 175–6, 181
Corps;
  ANZAC, 86–7, 89, 96
  IV Corps, 182
  X Corps, 139
  Punjab Army Corps, 58
  Royal Army Medical Corps, 150
  Royal Engineers, 91, 122, 225, 259
Division;
  1st Canadian Division, 84–5
  3rd Indian Division, 169
  4th Indian Division, 127, 130, 139, 141–2, 149
  5th Indian Division, 157
  7th Indian Division, 161, 169
  8th Indian Division, 145
  10th Indian Division, 157
  14th Indian Division, 161
  17th Indian Division, 153, 160, 174–5
  Lahore Division, 72, 75, 83
  Quetta Division, 105
  6th Poona Division, 90–1
Brigade;
  Brigade of Gurkhas, 1, 3, 7–9, 217, 224–5, 234, 256, 267–72, 278, 281, 289

INDEX

Ferozepore Brigade, 80, 83
Garwhal Brigade, 32, 76
48th Indian Infantry Brigade, 159, 220
50th Indian Parachute Brigade, 188
43rd Lorried Brigade, 61, 141, 143, 146, 194
77th Brigade, 164–5, 169, 188 *see also* Chindits

Regiment;
  Border Regiment, 158
  Connaught Rangers, 79
  Duke of Cornwall's Light Infantry, 106
  Gordon Highlanders, 56, 59, 202
  Highland Light Infantry, 81, 122, 172
  Madras Native Infantry, 161
  Northumberland Fusiliers, 71
  Rajpatana Rifles, 133
  Royal Fusiliers, 66
  Royal Irish Rangers, 224
  60th Rifles, 12, 14–16, 19–25
  95th Rifles, 62

Gurkha Rifles;
  1st Battalion, 145, 198
  2nd Battalion, 188, 203, 234
  3rd Battalion, 78, 188, 268
  4th Battalion, 39
  7th Battalion, 78, 171
  8th Battalion, 57
  9th Battalion, 97
  10th Battalion, 78
  Kumaon Battalion, 22, 43–4, 53
  Malaun Battalion, 52
  Sirmoor Battalion, 17–25, 43–4, 47–8, 258

Battalion;
  11th Bengal Lancers, 57
  Coke's Rifles, 16
  16th DLI, 148
  Hazara Battalion, 53
  14th/20th Hussars, 147, 290
  24th Punjabis, 93
  3rd Sikhs, 59

Special Forces;
  Chindits, 163, 169–70, 174, 177, 190, 202, 286
  Long Range Desert Group, 127, 130, 163–4
  Special Air Service, 127, 187–8, 197, 206, 208, 230, 264
  Special Boat Service, 206, 230

Royal Air Force;
  30th RAF Squadron, (*can't find any*)

Brize Norton, 200
Brown, G., 272
Brunei Revolt, 40, 207, 220
Brunswick Rifle, 18, 62
'Bubble and Squeak', 65
Buddhi Bahadur Bhandari, 267–8
Burma Road, 152

Calvert, 'Mad Mike', 163, 166, 169
Cameron, D., 265
Camp Bastion, 231, 238, 249, 253
Canning, Lord C.J., 26
Cape Helles, 86, 87, 89
Casablanca Conference, 128–9, 135
Cavagnari, Sir L., 56
Chandra Bose, 114, 152
Chandra Pun, 234
Chelmsford, 1st Viscount, 104
Chindwin River, 159–60, 165, 182, 184
Chocolat Menier Corner, 84
'Claret' Operations, 207, 209–12
Curzon, Lord G., 63, 66
Chiang Kai Shek, 152
Chard, Lieutenant J.R., 55
Chin Peng, 197

Cholera, 17, 23, 90, 97
chota bersaht, 181
Churchill, W., 125–7, 134–5, 148–9, 169, 176, 314
Cook, Major J., 55–6
Crawford, Major-General P., 212–13
Cross, Lieutenant-Colonel J., 178, 215–16, 258

Dal Bahadur Pun, 198, 257
Dal Prasad, 199
Damar Singh, 184
Damascus, 99
Damdil, 111
Dargai Heights, 59, 67, 219
Debude, Lieutenant H., 44–5
Delhi, 7, 10, 12–13, 33, 102, 157, 188, 234, 238
Delhi Ridge, 6, 10, 13–22
Deolali, 191
Dera Bugti Desert, 54
Devsur Ale, 165–6
Dhan Gurung, 228
Dharan, 41, 257
Dipprasad Pun, 251
Diwansing Basnet, 133
Dorman-Smith, Brigadier C., 125–6
Dysentery, 17, 90

East India Company, 4–5, 10, 31
Edwardes, Major, 81
Eid Festival, 22
Elephant Point, 189
Elliot, Lieutenant M., 20
Elphinstone, General W.G.K., 52
Enfield Rifle, 287–9
EOKA, 214
Everest, 29, 33, 267

Fallschirmjager (paratroopers), 140, 147, 187
Farwell, B., 7, 32, 38, 60

Ferme du Bois, 84
Ferme Cour d'Averne, 84
Fermor, P.L., 264
Fisher, Colonel J., 47–8
Flanders, 2, 70–2, 75, 141, 310
Fleming P., 64
Foch, Marshal F., 72
Ford, Lieutenant A., 191–3
Fort Bravo, 213–14
Fort Sammy, 24
French, General Sir J., 72, 80, 83

Gaje Ghale, 160–1
Galbraith, Major, 55–6
Gambirsing Pun, 87, 90
Gandamack Treaty, 57, 104
Ganju Lama, 181
Gaza, 95–8
George V, 74
Ghazi Mirzali Khan, 106
Goh Sia, 202–204
Goorkha, 4, 6
Gorey Thapa, 39
Gothic Line, 141–3
Gough, General Sir H., 47–8
Goumiers, 139
Grant, Lieutenant C., 61–62, 67
Great Game, 54–68, 97, 102, 214, 290
Grivas, General G., 214
Greene, G., 201
Grimwood, Ethel, 61–2
Grimwood, Frank St. Clair, 61
Guinness, Sir A., 17
Gurkha Contingent Singapore Police Force, 257
Gurkha Bluff, 87
Gurkha House, 66
Gully Ravine, 87
Gurney Sir H., 201
Gurungs, 35, 192, 280
Gyantse, 62, 65–6
Gyantse Jong, 66–7

INDEX

Haldane, 1st Viscount R., 264
Hamid Karzai, 228
Hamilton, General Sir I., 86–8, 90
Hangman's Hill, 138–141
Hardinge, Sir H., 46
Harkasing Rai, 204
Hastings, Lord F. E. (Earl of Moira), 31–2, 43–4
Hastings, Max, 186
Healey, Dennis, 206
Hearsay, Captain, 5
Helmand Province, 228, 231–9, 251, 253
Helmand River, 231, 243, 248–9
Helmand and Arghandab Valley Authority, 232
Henty G.A., 68, 92, 169, 250
Himalayas, 28, 46
Hindu Rao's House, 2, 6, 10–27, 43, 52
Hitler, A., 115, 117, 120, 129, 135–6, 187, 231, 271
Honey (Stuart) Tank, 179–80
Hybrid Warfare, 264

Improvised Explosive Device ('IED'), 235, 237, 239, 241, 243, 246-248, 250, 252-255
Indian Mutiny, 2, 6, 52, 91
Irrawaddy River, 163, 165, 166–7, 184

James, Lieutenant H., 166
Jerusalem, 97–8
Jindan Rani, 46
Jingal (musket), 64
Jones, Colonel H., 218
Jung Bahadur Rana, 25–7, 33, 44, 53–4

Kabul, 13, 52–7, 102, 104, 228–9, 231
Kailash Limbu, 3, 232–4

Kandahar, 54–7, 105, 168, 228, 234, 236, 254
Kandahar Gun, 6
'Kangaroo', 146–7, 290
Karan Sing Rana, 80
Karanbahadur Rana, 98
Karbir Pun, 67
Karo La, 65, 68
Kashmir Gate, 22–5
Kathmandu, 4, 28–30, 32–3, 37, 44, 119, 218, 257
Kesselring, Marshal A., 129, 136–7, 139, 147
Keys, Captain C., 53
Khalsa, 20, 45–8
Kilcullen, D., 266–7
Kilmarnock, Bonnet, 18
Kipling, R., 6, 10, 34, 51, 60, 102, 113, 178, 184, 233, 248, 250, 256
Kitchener, Field Marshal Lord H., 5, 66, 77, 86, 90
Koonja, 44–5
Krieg ohne hass, 117
Kulbir Thapa, 74, 76

Labis Gang, 199
La Brique Cemetery, 83
Lachhiman Gurung, 7, 184–5
Lachhiman Sarki, 47
Lahore, 13, 46, 72, 75, 80, 194–5
Lahore Treaty, 48
Lalbahadur Thapa, 131–2, 180
Lancaster, M., MP, 9
Lawrence, Captain T.E., 71, 94, 240
Lee Enfield Rifle, 287–9
Lentaingne, Lieutenant-Colonel W.P.A., 153–6, 169
Lethbridge, Brigadier 'Tubby', 183
Lhasa, 63–8
Limbus, 35–6, 280
Lindon-Travers, Major W. ('Bill'), 189
Lloyd George, D., 95, 97–8, 114

Lockhart, General Sir W., 58
'Los barbaros Gurkhas', 217
Lovett, Lieutenant-Colonel O., 128, 140
Luftwaffe, 124, 128, 147
Lumley, J., 1–2, 185, 267, 272
Lushais, 60

Macdonald, Brigadier J., 63–6
Macdonald-Fraser, G., 106, 158, 168
MacHorton, Lieutenant I., 167–8
Magars, 35, 280
Mahendra King, 33
Mahsud-Waziri Campaign, 53
Makwanpur, 30
Manap Jepun, 204
Mandalay, 57, 165, 184
Manju Gurung, 228
Mao Zedong, 220
Mareth Line, 129–30
Makarpal Tamang, 201
Martini-Henry Rifle, 55, 256, 287
Masters, J., 69, 106, 109–12, 192–3
Mastiff AFV, 236
Mathias, Lieutenant, 91
Maude, General Sir S., 96–7
Mauquissart, 74
Mauser Ridge, 83
Maxim Machine Gun, 287
Meadows, Major S.T., 226, 238–53
Meena Kambang, 262–3
Meerut, 11, 31, 75, 79–80, 85
Mercer, P., 268
Mesopotamia, 71, 92–9, 118, 157, 290
Messe, General, 130, 132, 134
Minbahadur Rana, 179
Minie Rifle, 62
Minto, Earl J.G. E-M-K., 20, 31
Mohammad Khalis Sakhidzada Lieutenant, 252
Money, Captain E., 57
Monte Chico, 144

Monte San Barolo, 145
Montgomery, Field Marshal B. L. 1st Viscount of Alamein, 119, 127, 133–4
Moree Bastion Delhi, 14, 24
Moss, S., 264
Mountbatten, Lord L., 175
Murray, Major J., 251–2
Mussolini, B., 120, 132, 136

Nepal, 4–7, 11, 22, 25–50, 53, 57, 63, 74, 95, 117, 119, 143–4, 153, 158, 164, 197, 217–18, 221, 234, 256–60, 262–3, 267, 272, 284
Nicholson, Brigadier J., 17, 22–4
Nixon, General, 93–4
North-West Frontier, 16, 26, 49, 55, 58, 60, 92, 94, 102, 106, 164, 199, 202, 207, 241
North Kalimantan National Army, 205, 207–208

Ochterlony, General D., 32
Omar Khayyam, 248
Operation:
  Attila, 214
  Enduring Freedom, 230
  Fingal, 228, 231
  Herrick, 3, 6, 229, 234–9, 251–5
  High Hurdle, 210
  Husky, 135
  Jacana, 231
  Longcloth, 164–5
  Mountain Thrust, 236
  Panther's Claw/'Panchai Palang', 248
  Pishet Sataal, 242
  Overlord, 141
  Super Shell, 210
  Swift-Sword, 230, 265
  Telic, 224, 231
  Thursday, 169
  Tora Gorga, 251

INDEX

Valiant, 203
Zarfar, 243
Orakzais Tribe, 58

Panzer, 121–2, 128, 142, 179
Panzerarmee, 129
Pathans, 6, 50–1, 53, 102, 105, 108, 110, 112, 190, 273
Pearl Harbor, 153
Peiwar Pass, 54
Pitt, W. (the Elder), 5, 55
Pokhara, 41, 257, 261, 273
Pownall, General H., 173
Prashad Limbu, 259
Prem Chand, General, 216
Premsing Gurung, 167
Princip, G., 69
Prithvi Narayan Shah, 4, 29–30
Projector Infantry Anti-Tank ('PIAT'), 173, 181
Provincial Reconstruction Team ('PRT'), 231

Quebec Conference, 169

Rais, 35–6, 280
Rambahadur Limbu, 205
Rampershad Thapa, 79
Ranjit Singh, 46
Rass-es-Zouai, 130–1
'Razcol', 107
Red Idol Gorge, 64
Reid, Doctor J., 231
Reiwar Kotal, 55
Reid, Major C., 11–27
Reivers, 101
Regiment Etrangere Parachutiste, 42
Reynolds, Lieutenant R.N.P., 193–4
Riley, Corporal, 244
Ripabianca Ridge, 143
Ritchie, General N., 120–4
Ritchie-Hook, Brigadier B., 32
'Road of Bones', 183

Roberts, General Sir F., 54–7
Roberts, Lieutenant R., 251–2
Roberts, Lieutenant S., 194–5
Romanovs, 51
Rommel, General E., 116–29
Ross, Lieutenant, 43
Royal Military Academy Sandhurst, 106, 118, 259–60, 262, 278
Royle, Doctor J.F., 44

Sampagla Pass, 59
Sangar, 111, 249
Sangin ('Sangingrad'), 231–2, 238, 254
San Marino, 142
Sari Bair, 87, 89–90
Satya Bahadur Pun, 39–40
Senio River Line, 146
Senussi, 95
Shahur Tangi Defile, 108, 119
Shakespear, Captain L.W., 60
Sher Ali Khan, 54, 56
Sher Bahadur Thapa, 142–3
Sherman Mark IV Tank, 144, 179
Shore, F., 45
Silicon, 246–9
Sinai, 95
Singapore, 40, 115, 152, 158, 160, 168, 186, 196, 199, 202, 207, 210, 257–8, 261
Sir John Moore Barracks Folkestone, 226, 256, 271
Sittang Railway Bridge, 153–4, 156, 169
Sittang River, 184, 186
Sivalik Hills, 28
Skene, Lieutenant-Colonel C., 61
Smith, Major E. ('Birdie'), 212–13
Smith, Sir H., 47
Snatch Landrover, 236, 243, 246
Snider Conversion Rifle, 55, 60, 256
Snow, D., 1
Special Operations Executive ('SOE'), 189

Spencer-Chapman, F., 162
Spin Baldak fort, 104–106
Springawai Kotal, 55
Steel Bonnets, 102
Strachan, Sir H., 8
Stilwell, General J. ('Vinegar Joe'), 165, 169–70
Student, General K., 187
Sultan of Brunei, 1
Sutlej River, 46–7
Swinton, Lieutenant, 39
Taka Rama, 17
Taliban, 226–65
Taungdaw, 184
Taversham, Brigadier M., 39
Templer, General Sir G., 201, 208
Teschen Monastery, 66
Thaman Gurung, 145–6
Thatcher, Margaret, 218
Thibaw Min King of Burma, 57
Thornton, Captain J., 202
Tigantourine Gas Installation, 264
Tigris River, 91–3, 96, 99
Tillard, Lieutenant A.B., 59
Tirah Campaign, 6, 58–9
Tirah Valley, 59
Tobruk, 120–4, 159
'Tocol', 107
Townshend, Major-General Sir C.V., 92–5
Triple Entente, 102
Truman, President H.S., 191, 269
Tuker, General Sir F., 38, 120, 127, 130, 139, 141, 173, 180, 186, 205
Tytler, Lieutenant G.A., 26

Umesh Kumar Pun Captain, 257–8

Vane, Sir H., 46
Vansittart, E., 35
Vegetius Renatus P.F., 269
Vercingetorix, 94
Vickers Machine Gun, 109–10, 288, 290
Victoria Queen Empress, 25, 49, 53
Von Arnim, General, 129, 130, 134
Von Falkenhayn, General E., 97–8
Von Sanders, General L., 87, 98–9

Wadi Akarit, 130, 133
Walker, Lieutenant-General W., 201, 207–209
'War of Running Dogs', 204
'War on Terror', 264
Wavell, General Sir A., 118, 153, 161, 163–4, 175
Waziristan, 106–107, 110–11
Westgate Shopping Mall Nairobi, 266
Wheeler, General G., 96
Willcocks, General Sir J., 71, 79–81
Wilson, Brigadier A., 12–13, 18, 24
Winchester, Mary, 60
Wingate, Major-General O.C., 5, 163–70, 174
World Trade Center, 228

Yakub Khan, 56
'Year of Living Dangerously', 210
Young, Lieutenant F., 43–5
Young, Brigadier P., 144
Younghusband, Colonel F., 63–6
Ypres, 41, 69–72, 78, 82–3, 86, 118
Yubraj Rai, 228